AF531641

Psychology Applied to Vocational Training

Psychology Applied to Vocational Training

Etash Ranjan

RANDOM PUBLICATIONS

NEW DELHI - 110 002 (INDIA)

Psychology Applied to Vocational Training

ISBN 978-93-51112-98-3
© Reserved

All Rights Reserved. No Part of this book may be reproduced in any manner without written permission.

Published in 2014 in India by

Reprint 2020

RANDOM PUBLICATIONS

4376-A/4B, Gali Murari Lal, Ansari Road
New Delhi-110 002
Phone: +9111-43580356, 23289044
E-mail: randomexports@gmail.com; sales@randompublications.com;
info@randompublications.com

Type Setting by: Friends Media, Delhi-110089
Printed at : Mehra Printers, Delhi-110092

Preface

Counselling psychologists are employed in a variety of settings depending on the services they provide and the client populations they serve. Some are employed in colleges and universities as teachers, supervisors, researchers, and service providers. Others are employed in independent practice providing counselling, psychotherapy; assessment; and consultation services to individuals, couples/families, groups, and organizations. Additional settings in which counselling psychologists practice include community mental health centres, Veterans Administration Medical Centres and other facilities, family services, health maintenance organizations, rehabilitation agencies, business and industrial organizations and consulting within firms. Counselling psychologists are trained in graduate programs. Almost all programs grant a PhD, but a few grant a MCouns, M.Ed, MA, PsyD or EdD. Most doctoral programs take 5–6 years to complete. Graduate work in counselling psychology includes coursework in general psychology and statistics, counselling practice, and research. Students must complete an original dissertation at the end of their graduate training. Students must also complete a one-year full-time internship at an accredited site before earning their doctorate. In order to be licensed to practice, counselling psychologists must gain clinical experience under supervision, and pass a standardized exam. Counselling psychology includes the study and practice of counsellor training and counsellor supervision. As researchers, counselling psychologists may investigate what makes training and supervision effective. As practitioners, counselling psychologists may supervise and train a variety of clinicians. Counsellor training tends to occur in formal classes and training programs. Part of counsellor training may involve counselling clients under the supervision of a licensed clinician. Supervision can also occur between licensed clinicians, as a way to improve clinicians' quality of work and competence with various types of counselling clients.

As the field of counselling psychology formed in the mid-20th century, initial training models included Human Relations Training by Carkuff, Interpersonal Process Recall by Kagan, and Microcounseling Skills by Ivey. Modern training models include Egan's Skilled Helper model, and Hill's three stage (exploration, insight, and action) model. A recent analysis of studies on counsellor training found that modeling, instruction, and feedback are common to most training models, and seem to have medium to large effects on trainees. Like the models of how clients and therapists interact, there are also models of the interactions between therapists and their supervisors. Bordin proposed a model of supervision working alliance similar to his model of therapeutic working alliance. The Integrated Development Model considers the level of a supervisee's motivation/anxiety, autonomy, and self and other awareness. The Systems Approach to Supervision views the relationship between supervisor and supervisee as most important, in addition to characteristics of the supervisee's personal characteristics, counselling clients, training setting, as well as the tasks and functions of supervision. The Critical Events in Supervision model focuses on important moments that occur between the supervisor and supervisee.

This book analyses various aspects of this subject. The book will be highly useful to students and teachers.

I thank all members of my team who have helped in the preparation of the book. My special thanks go to "Random Publications" who have published the book.

—Etash Ranjan

Contents

1.	**Applying Psychology**	**1**
	• Get Motivated	1
	• Clinical Psychology	4
	• Diagnostic Impressions	7
	• Clinical Theories and Interventions	8
	• Four Main Schools	9
	• Comparison with Other Mental Health Professions	14
	• Educational and Child Psychology	17
	• Social, Moral and Cognitive Development	18
	• Developmental Perspective	23
	• Social Cognitive Perspective	24
	• Research Methodology	27
	• Applications in Teaching	30
2.	**Occupational Psychology**	**39**
	• Industrial and Organizational Psychology	39
	• Training and Training Evaluation	42
	• Motivation in the Workplace	44

- Organizational Resources 47
- Productive Behaviour 50
- Organizational Citizenship Behaviour 53
- Innovation 55
- Counterproductive Work Behaviour 58
- Follower-focused Approaches 60
- Organizational Change/development 61
- Learning and Training 62
- Products and Processes of Training 66
- Delivering Training Programmes 72
- Health Psychology 76
- Applications of Health Psychology 84
- Counselling Psychology 87
- Counselling Relationship 90
- Process and Outcome Research Methods 92

3. Psychology in Education 96

- Individual Differences 102
- Measuring Personality 104
- Differential Psychology 107
- Intelligence 108
- Historical Psychometric Theories 112
- Triarchic Theory of Intelligence 116

- Artificial Intelligence 121
- Clinical Psychology 122
- Hong Kong 129
- Psychology in the Diagnosis of Mental Disorders. 130
- Ancient Civilizations 149
- Society and Culture 151
- Media and General Public 156

4. Learning Disorders 158

- Types 159
- Impact on Affected Individuals 166
- Contrast with Other Conditions 169
- Language-based Learning Disability 170
- Personality and its Disorders: Psychopathic Personality. 172
- Classification 175
- Further Considerations 184
- Environmental 193
- Head Injuries 195
- MAO-A 197
- Management 198
- Homesickness 201
- Adjustment, Frustration and Stress 206

- Adjustment Disorder 206
- Frustration 211
- Stress 213

5. Psychology of Mental Hygiene and Mental Health 219

- Significance 220
- Perspectives 221
- Cultural and Religious Considerations 222
- Mental Health Policies in the United States 225
- Therapies 228
- Mental Retardation 229
- Distinction from Other Disabilities 233
- Mental illness : Psychoneurosis and Psychosis 243
- Psychosis 247
- Signs and Symptoms 248
- Cycloid Psychosis 251
- Psychoactive Drugs 253
- Psychotherapy 260
- General Description 269
- Medical and non-medical Models 271
- Modern Conflict Theory 274
- Object Relations Theory 275

6.	**Relational Psychoanalysis**	**279**
	• Interpersonal-relational Psychoanalysis	279
	• Psychopathology (Mental Disturbances)	280
	• Group Therapy and Play Therapy	286
	• Cost and Length of Treatment	287
	• Gestalt Therapy	290
	• Noteworthy Issues	293
	• Influences upon Gestalt Therapy	298
7.	**Positive Psychotherapy**	**301**
	• Main Principles	301
	• Group Psychotherapy	304
	• Therapeutic Principles	305
	• Cognitive Behavioural Therapy	308
	• Specific Applications	309
	• Chronic Fatigue Syndrome	312
	• Methods of Access	313
	• Group Educational Course	315
	• Hypnotherapy	316
	• Behaviour Therapy	317
	• Third Generation	323
	• Treatment Outcomes	326
	• Expressive Therapy	328
	• Human Givens Therapy	330
	Bibliography	333
	Index	335

1

Applying Psychology

Do you think that psychology is just for students, academics and therapists? Then think again. Because psychology is both an applied and a theoretical subject, it can be utilized in a number of ways. While research studies aren't exactly light reading material for the average person, the results of these experiments and studies can have important applications in daily life. The following are some of the top 10 practical uses for psychology in everyday life.

Get Motivated

Whether your goal is to quit smoking, lose weight or learn a new language, some lessons from psychology offer tips for getting motivated. In order to increase your motivational levels when approaching a task, utilize some of the following tips derived from research in cognitive and educational psychology:

- Introduce new or novel elements to keep your interest high.
- Vary the sequence to help stave off boredom.
- Learn new things that build on your existing knowledge.
- Set clear goals that are directly related to the task.
- Reward yourself for a job well done.

Improve Your Leadership Skills

It doesn't matter if you're an office manager or a volunteer at a local youth group, having good leadership skills will probably be essential at some point in your life. Not everyone is a born leader, but a few simple tips gleaned from psychological research can help your improve your leadership skills. One of the most famous studies on this topic looked at three distinct leadership styles. Based on the findings of this study and subsequent research, practice some of the following when you are in a leadership position:

- Offer clear guidance, but allow group members to voice opinions.
- Talk about possible solutions to probelms with members of the group.
- Focus on stimulating ideas and be willing to reward creativity.

Become a Better Communicator

Communication involves much more than how you speak or write. Research suggests that nonverbal signals make up a huge portion of our interpersonal communications. In order to communicate your message effectively, you need to learn how to express yourself nonverbally and to read the nonverbal cues of those around you. A few key strategies include the following:

- Use good eye contact.
- Start noticing nonverbal signals in others.
- Learn to use your tone of voice to reinforce your message.

Learn to Better Understand Others

Much like nonverbal communication, your ability to understand your emotions and the emotions of those around you plays an important role in your relationships and professional life. The term emotional intelligence refers to your ability to understand both your own emotions as well as those of other people. Your emotional intelligence quotient is a measure of this ability. According to psychologist Daniel Goleman, your EQ may actually be more important than your IQ (1995).

What can you do to become more emotionally intelligent? Consider some of the following strategies:

- Carefully assess your own emotional reactions.
- Record your experience and emotions in a journal.
- Try to see situations from the perspective of another person.

Make More Accurate Decisions

Research in cognitive psychology has provided a wealth of information about decision making. By applying these strategies to your own life, you can learn to make wiser choices. The next time you need to make a big decision, try using some of the following techniques:

- Try using the "six thinking hats" approach by looking at the situation from multiple points of view, including rational, emotional, intuitive, creative, positive and negative perspectives.

- Consider the potential costs and benefits of a decision.
- Employ a grid analysis technique that gives a score for how a particular decision will satisfy specific requirements you may have.

Improve Your Memory

Have you ever wondered why you can remember exact details from childhood events yet forget the name of the new client you met yesterday? Research on how we form new memories as well as how and why we forget has led to a number of findings that can be applied directly in your daily life. What are some ways you can increase your memory power?

- Focus on the information.
- Rehearse what you have learned.
- Eliminate distractions.

Make Wiser Financial Decisions

Nobel Prize winning psychologists Daniel Kahneman and Amos Tversky conducted a series of studies that looked at how people manage uncertainty and risk when making decisions. Subsequent research in this area known as behaviour economics has yielded some key findings that you can use to make wiser money management choices. One study (2004) found that workers could more than triple their savings by utilizing some of the following strategies:

- Don't procrastinate! Start investing in savings now.
- Commit in advance to devote portions of your future earnings to your retirement savings.
- Try to be aware of personal biases that may lead to poor money choices.

Get Better Grades

The next time you're tempted to complain about pop quizzes, midterms or final exams, consider this - research has demonstrated that taking tests actually helps you better remember what you've learned, even if it wasn't covered on the test (Chan et al., 2006).

Another study found that repeated test-taking may be a better memory aid than studying (Roediger & Karpicke, 2006). Students who were tested repeatedly were able to recall 61 percent of the material while those in the study group recalled only 40 percent. How can you apply these findings to your own life? When trying to learn new information, self-test frequently in order to cement what you have learned into your memory.

Become More Productive

Sometimes it seems like there are thousands of books, blogs and magazine articles telling us how to get more done in a day, but how much of this advice is founded on actual research? For example, think about the number of times have you heard that multitasking can help you become more productive. In reality, research has found that trying to perform more than one task at the same time seriously impairs speed, accuracy and productivity. So what lessons from psychology can you use to increase your productivity? Consider some of the following:

- Avoid multitasking when working on complex or dangerous tasks.
- Focus on the task at hand.
- Eliminate distractions.

Be Healthier

Psychology can also be a useful tool for improving your overall health. From ways to encourage exercise and better nutrition to new treatments for depression, the field of health psychology offers a wealth of beneficial strategies that can help you to be healthier and happier. Some examples that you can apply directly to your own life:

- Studies have shown that both sunlight and artificial light can reduce the symptoms of seasonal affective disorder.
- Research has demonstrated that exercise can be an effective treatment for depression as well as other mental disorders.
- Studies have found that helping people understand the risks of unhealthy behaviours can lead to healthier choices.

Clinical Psychology

Clinical psychology is the application of abnormal psychology research to the understanding, treatment, and assessment of psychopathology. This primarily includes behavioural and mental health concerns. It has traditionally been associated with psychological treatment and psychotherapy, although modern clinical psychology may take an eclectic approach, including a number of therapeutic approaches. Typically, although working with many of the same clients as psychiatrists, clinical psychologists do not, in general, prescribe psychiatric drugs. Several branches of the armed forces have in the past, and a few graduate schools are presently offering a psychopharmacology speciality for psychologists for them to be able to prescribe mental health medication. Some clinical psychologists may focus on the clinical management of patients with brain injury. This area is known as clinical neuropsychology.

In recent years and particularly in the United States, a major split has been developing between academic research psychologists in universities and some branches of clinical psychology. Many research psychologists believe that many contemporary clinicians use therapies based on discredited theories and unsupported by empirical evidence of their effectiveness. From the other side, these clinicians believe that the research psychologists are ignoring their experience in dealing with actual patients. The disagreement resulted in the formation of the Association for Psychological Science by the research psychologists as a new body distinct from the American Psychological Association.

The work performed by clinical psychologists tends to be done inside various therapy models. A popular model is the Cognitive-Behavioural therapy (CBT) framework. CBT is an umbrella term that refers to a number of therapies which focus on changing cognitions and/or behaviours, rather than changing behaviour exclusively, or discovering the unconscious causes of psychopathology (as in the psychodynamic school). The two most famous CBT therapies are Aaron T. Beck's cognitive therapy and Albert Ellis's rational emotive behaviour therapy, i.e., RET (with cognitive therapy being, by far, the most extensively studied therapy in contemporary clinical psychology).

Counselling

Counselling psychology is a psychology speciality that facilitates personal and interpersonal functioning across the lifespan with a focus on emotional, social, vocational, educational, health-related, developmental, and organizational concerns. Counselling psychology differs from clinical psychology in that it is focused more on normal developmental issues and everyday stress rather than serious mental disorders. Counselling psychologists are employed in a variety of settings, including universities, schools, businesses, private practice, and community mental health centres.

The emerging field of relationship counselling, which characterizes ordinary human relationship successes and failures in concrete terms, has the specific appeal of avoiding psychology's practice of ascribing pathology to individuals who seek assistance. Current health insurance reimbursement for psychological services commonly involves the assignment of mental disease nomenclature(a feature that potential clients may find offensive, and that could potentially be iatrogenic, i.e., when a treatment creates other problems).

Relationship counselling, also referred to as "relationship education", includes psychologists, psychiatrists, and social workers. It is based on decades of university-based research, drawing on knowledge gained through close observation and analysis of both successful and unsuccessful marriages and family units.

Assessment

An important area of expertise for many clinical psychologists is assessment, and there are indications that as many as 91% of psychologists utilize this core clinical practice. Such evaluations are usually conducted in order to gain insight into, and form hypotheses about, psychological or behavioural problems. As such, the results of these assessments are often used to clarify a person's diagnosis and assist in planning treatments or arranging for services. Methods used to gather information include formal tests, clinical interviews, reviews of past records, and behavioural observations.

There exist literally hundreds of various assessment tools, although only a few have been shown to have both high statistical validity (i.e., test actually measures what it claims to measure) and reliability (i.e., consistency). These measures generally fall within one of several categories, including the following:

- Intelligence & achievement tests – These tests are designed to measure certain aspects of cognitive functioning (often referred to as IQ) in comparison to a group of people with similar characteristics (such as age or education). These tests, including the WISC-IV and WAIS-IV, attempt to measure traits such as general knowledge, verbal comprehension, working memory, attention/concentration, logical reasoning, and visual/spatial perception. Several of these tests have been shown to accurately predict scholastic achievement and occupational performance, and help to identify a person's cognitive strengths and weaknesses.
- Personality tests – These tests aim to describe patterns of behaviour, thoughts, and feelings, and generally fall within two categories: objective and projective. Objective measures, such as the MMPI-2 or the MCMI-III, are based on forced-choice responses—such as yes/no, true/false, or a rating scale—and

generate scores that can be compared to a normative group. Projective tests, such as the Rorschach inkblot test, use open-ended responses, often based on ambiguous stimuli, to reveal non-conscious psychological dynamics such as motivations and perceptions of the self and the world.

- Neuropsychological tests - Tests in this category are often used to evaluate a person's cognitive functioning and its relationship to a person's behaviour or psychological functioning. They are used in a variety of settings, for purposes such as clarifying a diagnosis (especially in distinguishing between psychiatric and neurological symptoms), better understanding the impact of a person's neurological condition on their behaviour, treatment planning (especially in rehabilitation settings), and for legal questions, such as determining if a person is faking their symptoms (also referred to as malingering) or if they are capable to stand trial.
- Clinical interviews – Clinical psychologists are also trained to gather data by observing behaviour and collecting detailed histories. The clinical interview is a vital part of assessment, even when using other formalized measures, as it provides a context in which to understand test results. Psychologists can employ a structured format (such as the SCID or the MMSE), a semi-structured format (such as a sequence of questions) or an unstructured format to gather information about a person's symptoms and past and present functioning. Such assessments often include evaluations of general appearance and behaviour, mood and affect, perception, comprehension, orientation, memory, thought process, and/or communication.

Diagnostic Impressions

After assessment, clinical psychologists often provide a diagnostic impression. Many countries use the International Statistical Classification of Diseases and Related Health Problems (ICD-10) while the US most often uses the Diagnostic and Statistical Manual of Mental Disorders (DSM-IV-TR). Both utilize medical concepts and terms, and state that there are categorical disorders that can be diagnosed by set lists of descriptive criteria. Several new models are being discussed, including a "dimensional model" based on empirically validated models of human differences (such as the five factor model of personality and a "psychosocial model," which would place greater emphasis on changing, intersubjective states. In fact, the DSM-5, which is still being edited, will be using a dimensional approach. The proponents of these models claim that they would offer greater diagnostic flexibility and clinical utility without depending on the medical concept of illness. However, they also admit that these models are not yet robust enough to gain widespread use, and should continue to be developed. Some clinical psychologists prefer not to use diagnoses and instead use clinical formulations—an individualized map of the strengths and difficulties that the patient or client faces, with an emphasis on predisposing, precipitating and perpetuating (maintaining) factors.

Clinical Theories and Interventions

Psychotherapy involves a formal relationship between professional and client—usually an individual, couple, family, or small group—that employs a set of procedures intended to form a therapeutic alliance, explore the nature of psychological problems, and encourage new ways of thinking, feeling, or behaving.

Clinicians have a wide range of individual interventions to draw from, often guided by their training—for example, a cognitive behavioural therapy (CBT) clinician might use worksheets to record distressing cognitions, a psychoanalyst might encourage free association, while a psychologist trained in Gestalt techniques might focus on immediate interactions between client and therapist. Clinical psychologists generally seek to base their work on research evidence and outcome studies as well as on trained clinical judgement. Although there are literally dozens of recognized therapeutic orientations, their differences can often be categorized on two dimensions: insight vs. action and in-session vs. out-session.

- Insight – emphasis is on gaining greater understanding of the motivations underlying one's thoughts and feelings (e.g. psychodynamic therapy)
- Action – focus is on making changes in how one thinks and acts (e.g. solution-focused therapy, cognitive behavioural therapy)
- In-session – interventions centre on the here-and-now interaction between client and therapist (e.g. humanistic therapy, Gestalt therapy)
- Out-session – a large portion of therapeutic work is intended to happen outside of session (e.g. bibliotherapy, rational emotive behaviour therapy)

The methods used are also different in regards to the population being served as well as the context and nature of the problem. Therapy will look very different between, say, a traumatized child, a depressed but high-functioning adult, a group of people recovering from substance dependence, and a ward of the state suffering from terrifying delusions. Other elements that play a critical role in the process of psychotherapy include the environment, culture, age, cognitive functioning, motivation, and duration (i.e. brief or long-term therapy).

Four Main Schools

The field is dominated in terms of training and practice by essentially four major schools of practice: psychodynamic, humanistic, behavioural/cognitive behavioural, and systems or family therapy.

Psychodynamic

The psychodynamic perspective developed out of the psychoanalysis of Sigmund Freud. The core object of psychoanalysis is to make the unconscious conscious—to make the client aware of his or her own primal drives (namely those relating to sex and aggression) and the various defences used to keep them in check. The essential tools of the psychoanalytic process are the use of free association and an examination of the client's transference towards the therapist, defined as the tendency to take unconscious thoughts or emotions about a significant person (e.g. a parent) and "transfer" them onto another person. Major variations on Freudian psychoanalysis practiced today include self psychology, ego psychology, and object relations theory. These general orientations now fall under the umbrella term psychodynamic psychology, with common themes including examination of transference and defences, an appreciation of the power of the unconscious, and a focus on how early developments in childhood have shaped the client's current psychological state.

Humanistic

Humanistic psychology was developed in the 1950s in reaction to both behaviourism and psychoanalysis, largely due to the person-centred therapy of Carl Rogers (often referred to as Rogerian Therapy) and existential psychology developed by Viktor Frankl and Rollo May. Rogers believed that a client needed only three things from a clinician to experience therapeutic improvement: congruence, unconditional positive regard, and empathetic understanding. By using phenomenology, intersubjectivity and first-person categories, the humanistic approach seeks to get a glimpse of the whole person and not just the fragmented parts of the personality. This aspect of holism links up with another common aim of humanistic practice in psychotherapy, which is to seek an integration of the whole person, also called self-actualization. According to humanistic thinking, each individual person already has inbuilt potentials and resources that might help them to build a stronger personality and self-concept. The mission of the humanistic psychologist is to help the individual employ these resources via the therapeutic relationship.

Behavioural and Cognitive Behavioural

Cognitive behavioural therapy (CBT) developed from the combination of cognitive therapy and rational emotive behaviour therapy, both of which grew out of cognitive psychology and behaviourism. CBT is based on the theory that how we think (cognition), how we feel (emotion), and how we act (behaviour) are related and interact together in complex ways. In this perspective, certain dysfunctional ways of interpreting and appraising the world (often through schemas or beliefs) can contribute to emotional distress or result in behavioural problems. The object of many cognitive behavioural therapies is to discover and identify the biased, dysfunctional ways of relating or reacting and through different methodologies help clients transcend these in ways that will lead to increased well-being. There are many techniques used, such as systematic desensitization, socratic questioning, and keeping a cognition observation log. Modified approaches that fall into the category of CBT have also developed, including dialectical behaviour therapy and mindfulness-based cognitive therapy.

Behaviour therapy is a rich tradition. It is well-researched with a strong evidence base. Its roots are in behaviourism. In behaviour therapy, environmental events predict the way we think and feel. Our behaviour sets up conditions for the environment to feed back on it. Sometimes the feedback leads the behaviour to increase (reinforcement), and sometimes the behaviour decreases (punishment). Often behaviour therapists are called applied behaviour analysts. They have studied many areas from developmental disabilities to depression and anxiety disorders. In the area of mental health and addictions a recent article looked at APA's list for well-established and promising practices and found a considerable number of them based on the principles of operant and respondent conditioning. Multiple assessment techniques have come from this approach including functional analysis (psychology), which has found a strong focus in the school system. In addition, multiple intervention programmes have come from this tradition including community reinforcement and family training for treating addictions, acceptance and commitment therapy, functional analytic psychotherapy, integrative behavioural couples therapy including dialectical behaviour therapy and behavioural activation. In addition, specific techniques such as contingency management and exposure therapy have come from this tradition.

Systems or Family Therapy

Systems or family therapy works with couples and families, and emphasizes family relationships as an important factor in psychological health. The central focus tends to be on interpersonal dynamics, especially in terms of how change in one person will affect the entire system. Therapy is therefore conducted with as many significant members of the "system" as possible. Goals can include improving communication, establishing healthy roles, creating alternative narratives, and addressing problematic behaviours. Contributors include John Gottman, Jay Haley, Sue Johnson, and Virginia Satir.

Other Major Therapeutic Orientations

There exist dozens of recognized schools or orientations of psychotherapy—the list below represents a few influential orientations not given above. Although they all have some typical set of techniques practitioners employ, they are generally better known for providing a framework of theory and philosophy that guides a therapist in his or her working with a client.

- Existential – Existential psychotherapy postulates that people are largely free to choose who we are and how we interpret and interact with the world. It intends to help the client find deeper meaning in life and to accept responsibility for living. As such, it addresses fundamental issues of life, such as death, aloneness, and freedom. The therapist emphasizes the client's ability to be self-aware, freely make choices in the present, establish personal identity and social relationships, create meaning, and cope with the natural anxiety of living. Important writers in existential therapy include Rollo May, Viktor Frankl, James Bugental, and Irvin Yalom.

One influential therapy that came out of existential therapy is Gestalt therapy, primarily founded by Fritz Perls in the 1950s. It is well known for techniques designed to increase various kinds of self-awareness—the best-known perhaps being the "empty chair technique"—which are generally intended to explore resistance to "authentic contact," resolve internal conflicts, and help the client complete "unfinished business."

- Postmodern – Postmodern psychology says that the experience of reality is a subjective construction built upon language, social context, and history, with no essential truths. Since "mental illness" and "mental health" are not recognized as objective, definable realities, the postmodern psychologist instead sees the goal of therapy strictly as something constructed by the client and therapist. Forms of postmodern psychotherapy include narrative therapy, solution-focused therapy, and coherence therapy.
- Transpersonal – The transpersonal perspective places a stronger focus on the spiritual facet of human experience. It is not a set of techniques so much as a willingness to help a client explore spirituality and/or transcendent states of consciousness. It also is concerned with helping clients achieve their highest potential. Important writers in this area include Ken Wilber, Abraham Maslow, Stanislav Grof, John Welwood, David Brazier and Roberto Assagioli.

Other Perspectives

- Multiculturalism – Although the theoretical foundations of psychology are rooted in European culture, there is a growing recognition that there exist profound differences between various ethnic and social groups and that systems of psychotherapy need to take those differences into greater consideration. Further, the generations following immigrant migration will have some combination of two or more cultures—with aspects coming from the parents and from the surrounding society—and this process of acculturation can play a strong role in therapy (and might itself be the presenting problem). Culture influences ideas about change, help-seeking, locus of control, authority, and the importance of the individual versus the group, all of which can potentially clash with certain givens in mainstream psychotherapeutic theory and practice. As such, there is a growing movement to integrate knowledge of various cultural groups in order to inform therapeutic practice in a more culturally sensitive and effective way.
- Feminism – Feminist therapy is an orientation arising from the disparity between the origin of most psychological theories (which have male authors) and the majority of people seeking counselling being female. It focuses on societal, cultural, and political causes and solutions to issues faced in the counselling

process. It openly encourages the client to participate in the world in a more social and political way.

- Positive psychology – Positive psychology is the scientific study of human happiness and well-being, which started to gain momentum in 1998 due to the call of Martin Seligman, then president of the APA. The history of psychology shows that the field has been primarily dedicated to addressing mental illness rather than mental wellness. Applied positive psychology's main focus, therefore, is to increase one's positive experience of life and ability to flourish by promoting such things as optimism about the future, a sense of flow in the present, and personal traits like courage, perseverance, and altruism. There is now preliminary empirical evidence to show that by promoting Seligman's three components of happiness—positive emotion (the pleasant life), engagement (the engaged life), and meaning (the meaningful life) —positive therapy can decrease clinical depression.

Integration

In the last couple of decades, there has been a growing movement to integrate the various therapeutic approaches, especially with an increased understanding of cultural, gender, spiritual, and sexual-orientation issues. Clinical psychologists are beginning to look at the various strengths and weaknesses of each orientation while also working with related fields, such as neuroscience, genetics, evolutionary biology, and psychopharmacology. The result is a growing practice of eclecticism, with psychologists learning various systems and the most efficacious methods of therapy with the intent to provide the best solution for any given problem.

Professional Ethics

The field of clinical psychology in most countries is strongly regulated by a code of ethics. In the US, professional ethics are largely defined by the APA Code of Conduct, which is often used by states to define licensing requirements. The APA Code generally sets a higher standard than that which is required by law as it is designed to guide responsible behaviour, the protection of clients, and the improvement of individuals, organizations, and society. The Code is applicable to all psychologists in both research and applied fields. The APA Code is based on five principles: Beneficence and Nonmaleficence, Fidelity and Responsibility, Integrity, Justice, and Respect for People's Rights and Dignity. Detailed elements address how to resolve ethical issues, competence, human relations, privacy and confidentiality, advertising, record keeping, fees, training, research, publication, assessment, and therapy.

Comparison with Other Mental Health Professions

Psychiatry:

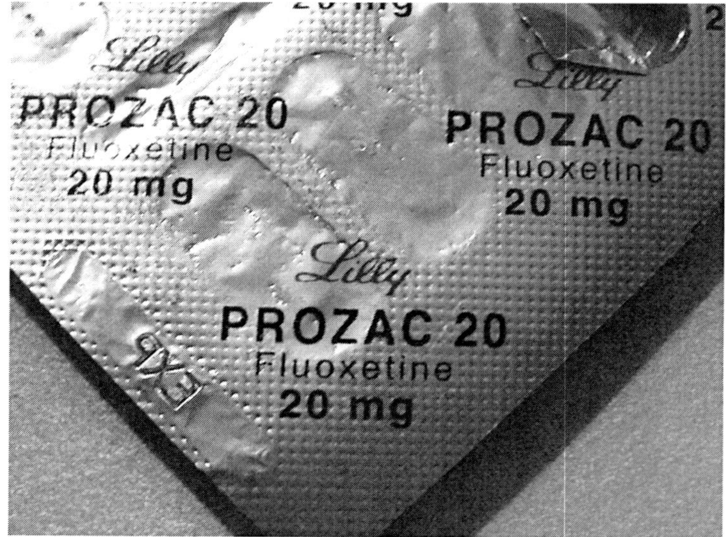

Figure: *Fluoxetine hydrochloride, branded by Lilly as Prozac, is a common antidepressant drug prescribed by psychiatrists. There is a small but growing movement to give prescription privileges to qualified psychologists.*

Although clinical psychologists and psychiatrists can be said to share a same fundamental aim—the treatment of mental disorders—their training, outlook, and methodologies are often quite different. Perhaps the most significant difference is that psychiatrists are licensed physicians. As such, psychiatrists often use the medical model to assess psychological problems (i.e., those they treat are seen as patients with an illness) and rely on psychotropic medications as the chief method of addressing the illness—although many employ psychotherapy as well. Psychiatrists and medical psychologists (who are clinical psychologists that are also licensed to prescribe) are able to conduct physical examinations, order and interpret laboratory tests and EEGs, and may order brain imaging studies such as CT or CAT; MRI; and PET scanning.

Clinical psychologists generally do not prescribe medication, although there is a movement for psychologists to have prescribing privileges. These medical privileges require additional training and education. To date, medical psychologists may prescribe psychotropic medications in Guam, New Mexico, and Louisiana, as well as United States military psychologists. Psychologists usually receive more thorough training in research methods, psychological assessment, and psychotherapeutic treatment, compared with psychiatrists.

Counselling Psychology

Counselling psychologists study and use many of the same interventions and tools as clinical psychologists, including psychotherapy and assessment. Traditionally, counselling psychologists help people with what might be considered normal or moderate psychological problems—such as the feelings of anxiety or sadness resulting from major life changes or events. Many counselling psychologists also receive specialized training in career assessment, group therapy, and relationship counselling, although some counselling psychologists also work with the more serious problems that clinical psychologists are trained for, such as dementia or psychosis.

There are fewer counselling psychology graduate programmes than those for clinical psychology and they are more often housed in departments of education rather than psychology. The two professions can be found working in all the same settings but counselling psychologists are more frequently employed in university counselling centres compared to hospitals and private practice for clinical psychologists.

School Psychology

School psychologists are primarily concerned with the academic, social, and emotional well-being of children and adolescents within a scholastic environment. In the UK, they are known as "educational psychologists." They typically hold a master's degree. Like clinical psychologists, school psychologists with doctoral degrees are eligible for licensure as health service psychologists, and many work in private practice. Unlike clinical psychologists, they receive much more training in education, child development and behaviour, and the psychology of learning. Common degrees include the Educational Specialist Degree (Ed.S.), Doctor of Philosophy (Ph.D.), and Doctor of Education (Ed.D.).

Traditional job roles for school psychologists employed in school settings have focused mainly on assessment of students to determine their eligibility for special education services in schools, and on consultation with teachers and other school professionals to design and carry out interventions on behalf of students. Other major roles also include offering individual and group therapy with children and their families, designing prevention programmes (e.g. for reducing dropout), evaluating school programmes, and working with teachers and administrators to help maximize teaching efficacy, both in the classroom and systemically.

Clinical Social Work

Social workers provide a variety of services, generally concerned with social problems, their causes, and their solutions. With specific training, clinical social workers may also provide psychological counselling (in the US and Canada), in addition to more traditional social work. The Masters in Social Work in the US is a two-year, sixty credit programme that includes a practicum each year, totaling at least 900 hours. The requirements to become a Licensed Clinical Social Worker, which offers similar privileges to that of a psychologist, vary by state. The requirements in NY, for example, include a Master's Degree in Social Work from an accredited graduate school that includes course hours in clinical coursework, 2000 post-graduate, practice hours directly with clients at an approved site providing "diagnosis, psychotherapy and assessment-based treatment planning" under the supervision of a qualified psychiatrit, clinical psychologist, or LCSW; the experience hours must be accumulated over a minimum of 3 years & cannot exceed 6 years, and there is an additional minimum of 60 minutes each week for supervision meeting. After meeting the educational, experience, and supervision requirements, the candidate must pass a written exam demonstrating clinical knowledge and ethical responsibility.

Occupational Therapy

Occupational therapy—often abbreviated OT—is the "use of productive or creative activity in the treatment or rehabilitation of physically, cognitively, or emotionally disabled people." Most commonly, occupational therapists work with people with disabilities to enable them to maximize their skills and abilities. Occupational therapy practitioners are skilled professionals whose education includes the study of human growth and development with specific emphasis on the physical, emotional, psychological, sociocultural, cognitive and environmental components of illness and injury. They commonly work alongside clinical psychologists in settings such as inpatient and outpatient mental health, pain management clinics, eating disorder clinics, and child development services. OT's use support groups, individual counselling sessions, and activity-based approaches to address psychiatric symptoms and maximize functioning in life activities. In chronic pain management, occupational therapists use the common cognitive behavioural therapy approach, often incorporating cognitive behavioural therapy techniques and helping clients generalize or integrate their pain management strategies into their lives. In this way, occupational therapists both support and extend the work that clinical psychologists carry out in a clinical setting.

Criticisms and Controversies

Clinical psychology is a diverse field and there have been recurring tensions over the degree to which clinical practice should be limited to treatments supported by empirical research. Despite some evidence showing that all the major therapeutic orientations are about of equal effectiveness, there remains much debate about the efficacy of various forms treatment in use in clinical psychology.

It has been reported that clinical psychology has rarely allied itself with client groups and tends to individualize problems to the neglect of wider economic, political and social inequality issues that may not be the responsibility of the client. It has been argued that therapeutic practices are inevitably bound up with power inequalities, which can be used for good and bad. A critical psychology movement has argued that clinical psychology, and other professions making up a "psy complex," often fail to consider or address inequalities and power differences and can play a part in the social and moral control of disadvantage, deviance and unrest.

An October 2009 editorial in the journal Nature suggests that a large number of clinical psychology practitioners in the United States consider scientific evidence to be "less important than their personal—that is, subjective—clinical experience."

Educational and Child Psychology

Educational psychology is the study of how humans learn in educational settings, the effectiveness of educational interventions, the psychology of teaching, and the social psychology of schools as organizations. Educational psychology is concerned with how students learn and develop, often focusing on subgroups such as gifted children and those subject to specific disabilities. Researchers and theorists are likely to be identified in the US and Canada as educational psychologists, whereas practitioners in schools or school-related settings are identified as school psychologists. This distinction is, however, not made in the UK, where the generic term for practitioners is "educational psychologist."

Educational psychology can in part be understood through its relationship with other disciplines. It is informed primarily by psychology, bearing a relationship to that discipline analogous to the relationship between medicine and biology. It is also informed by neuroscience. Educational psychology in turn informs a wide range of specialities within educational studies, including instructional design, educational technology, curriculum development, organizational learning, special education and classroom management. Educational psychology both draws from and contributes to cognitive science and the learning sciences. In universities, departments of educational psychology are usually housed within faculties of education, possibly accounting for the lack of representation of educational psychology content in introductory psychology textbooks.

Social, Moral and Cognitive Development

Figure: *An abacus provides concrete experiences for learning abstract concepts.*

To understand the characteristics of learners in childhood, adolescence, adulthood, and old age, educational psychology develops and applies theories of human development. Often represented as stages through which people pass as they mature, developmental theories describe changes in mental abilities (cognition), social roles, moral reasoning, and beliefs about the nature of knowledge.

For example, educational psychologists have conducted research on the instructional applicability of Jean Piaget's theory of development, according to which children mature through four stages of cognitive capability. Piaget hypothesized that children are not capable of abstract logical thought until they are older than about 11 years, and therefore younger children need to be taught using concrete objects and examples. Researchers have found that transitions, such as from concrete to abstract logical thought, do not occur at the same time in all domains. A child may be able to think abstractly about mathematics, but remain limited to concrete thought when reasoning about human relationships. Perhaps Piaget's most enduring contribution is his insight that people actively construct their understanding through a self-regulatory process.

Piaget proposed a developmental theory of moral reasoning in which children progress from a naïve understanding of morality based on behaviour and outcomes to a more advanced understanding based on intentions. Piaget's views of moral development were elaborated by Kohlberg into a stage theory of moral development. There is evidence that the moral reasoning described in stage theories is not sufficient to account for moral behaviour. For example, other factors such as modelling (as described by the social cognitive theory of morality) are required to explain bullying.

Rudolf Steiner's model of child development interrelates physical, emotional, cognitive, and moral development in developmental stages similar to those later described by Piaget.

Developmental theories are sometimes presented not as shifts between qualitatively different stages, but as gradual increments on separate dimensions. Development of epistemological beliefs (beliefs about knowledge) have been described in terms of gradual changes in people's belief in: certainty and permanence of knowledge, fixedness of ability, and credibility of authorities such as teachers and experts. People develop more sophisticated beliefs about knowledge as they gain in education and maturity.

Senses of Seriousness and of Fantasy

A child must learn to develop a sense of seriousness, an ability to distinguish degrees of seriousness as it relates to transgressions and expenditure of time; for example, a child must learn to distinguish between levels of seriousness in admonitions such as between "don't fidget" and "don't forget to look both ways when crossing the street," which have the same linguistic and normative structure, but different levels of seriousness.

Individual Differences and Disabilities

Each person has an individual profile of characteristics, abilities and challenges that result from predisposition, learning and development. These manifest as individual differences in intelligence, creativity, cognitive style, motivation and the capacity to process information, communicate, and relate to others. The most prevalent disabilities found among school age children are attention deficit hyperactivity disorder (ADHD), learning disability, dyslexia, and speech disorder. Less common disabilities include mental retardation, hearing impairment, cerebral palsy, epilepsy, and blindness.

Although theories of intelligence have been discussed by philosophers since Plato, intelligence testing is an invention of educational psychology, and is coincident with the development of that discipline. Continuing debates about the nature of intelligence revolve on whether intelligence can be characterized by a single factor known as general intelligence, multiple factors (e.g., Gardner's theory of multiple intelligences), or whether it can be measured at all. In practice, standardized instruments such as the Stanford-Binet IQ test and the WISC are widely used in economically developed countries to identify children in need of individualized educational treatment. Children classified as gifted are often provided with accelerated or enriched programmes. Children with identified deficits may be provided with enhanced education in specific skills such as phonological awareness. In addition to basic abilities, the individual's personality traits are also important, with people higher in conscientiousness and hope attaining superior academic achievements, even after controlling for intelligence and past performance.

Learning and Cognition

Two fundamental assumptions that underlie formal education systems are that students (a) retain knowledge and skills they acquire in school, and (b) can apply them in situations outside the classroom. But are these assumptions accurate? Research has found that, even when students report not using the knowledge acquired in school, a considerable portion is retained for many years and long-term retention is strongly dependent on the initial level of mastery. One study found that university students who took a child development course and attained high grades showed, when tested ten years later, average retention scores of about 30%, whereas those who obtained moderate or lower grades showed average retention scores of about 20%. There is much less consensus on the crucial question of how much knowledge acquired in school transfers to tasks encountered outside formal educational settings, and how such transfer occurs. Some psychologists claim that research evidence for this type of far transfer is scarce, while others claim there is abundant evidence of far transfer in specific domains. Several perspectives have been established within which the theories of learning used in educational psychology are formed and contested. These include behaviourism, cognitivism, social cognitive theory, and constructivism. This section summarizes how educational psychology has researched and applied theories within each of these perspectives.

Behavioural Perspective

Applied behaviour analysis, a research-based science utilizing behavioural principles of operant conditioning, is effective in a range of educational settings. For example, teachers can alter student behaviour by systematically rewarding students who follow classroom rules with praise, stars, or tokens exchangeable for sundry items. Despite the demonstrated efficacy of awards in changing behaviour, their use in education has been criticized by proponents of self-determination theory, who claim that praise and other rewards undermine intrinsic motivation. There is evidence that tangible rewards decrease intrinsic motivation in specific situations, such as when the student already has a high level of intrinsic motivation to perform the goal behaviour. But the results showing detrimental effects are counterbalanced by evidence that, in other situations, such as when rewards are given for attaining a gradually increasing standard of performance, rewards enhance intrinsic motivation. Many effective therapies have been based on the principles of applied behaviour analysis, including pivotal response therapy which is used to treat autism spectrum disorders.

Cognitive Perspective

Among current educational psychologists, the cognitive perspective is more widely held than the behavioural perspective, perhaps because it admits causally related mental constructs such as traits, beliefs, memories, motivations and emotions. Cognitive theories claim that memory structures determine how information is perceived, processed, stored, retrieved and forgotten. Among the memory structures theorized by cognitive psychologists are separate but linked visual and verbal systems described by Allan Paivio's dual coding theory. Educational psychologists have used dual coding theory and cognitive load theory to explain how people learn from multimedia presentations.

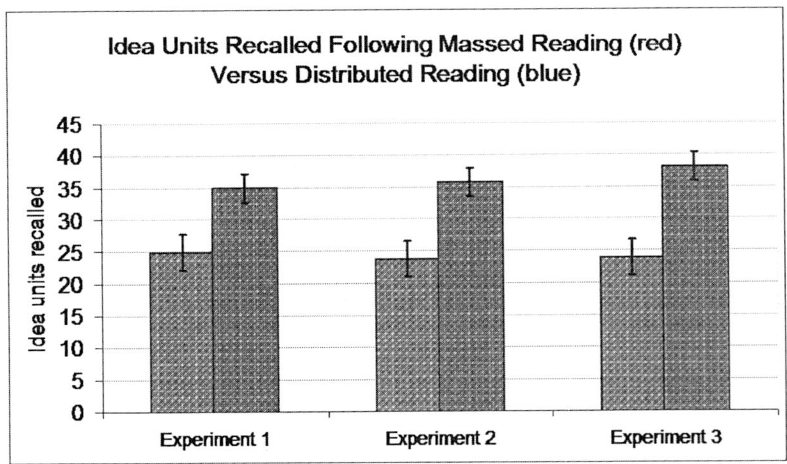

Figure: *Three experiments reported by Krug, Davis and Glover demonstrated the advantage of delaying a 2nd reading of a text passage by one week (distributed) compared with no delay between readings (massed).*

The spaced learning effect, a cognitive phenomenon strongly supported by psychological research, has broad applicability within education. For example, students have been found to perform better on a test of knowledge about a text passage when a second reading of the passage is delayed rather than immediate. Educational psychology research has confirmed the applicability to education of other findings from cognitive psychology, such as the benefits of using mnemonics for immediate and delayed retention of information.

Problem solving, regarded by many cognitive psychologists as fundamental to learning, is an important research topic in educational psychology. A student is thought to interpret a problem by assigning it to a schema retrieved from long-term memory. A problem students run into while reading is called "activation." This is when the student's representations of the text are present during working memory. This causes the student to read through the material without absorbing the information and being able to retain it. When working memory is absent from the readers representations of the working memory they experience something called "deactivation." When deactivation occurs, the student has an understanding of the material and is able to retain information. If deactivation occurs during the first reading, the reader does not need to undergo deactivation in the second reading. The reader will only need to reread to get a "gist" of the text to spark their memory. When the problem is assigned to the wrong schema, the student's attention is subsequently directed away from features of the problem that are inconsistent with the assigned schema. The critical step of finding a mapping between the problem and a pre-existing schema is often cited as supporting the centrality of analogical thinking to problem solving.

Developmental Perspective

Developmental psychology, and especially the psychology of cognitive development, opens a special perspective for educational psychology. This is so because education and the psychology of cognitive development converge on a number of crucial assumptions. First, the psychology of cognitive development defines human cognitive competence at successive phases of development. Education aims to help students acquire knowledge and develop skills which are compatible with their understanding and problem-solving capabilities at different ages. Thus, knowing the students' level on a developmental sequence provides information on the kind and level of knowledge they can assimilate, which, in turn, can be used as a frame for organizing the subject matter to be taught at different school grades. This is the reason why Piaget's theory of cognitive development was so influential for education, especially mathematics and science education. In the same direction, the neo-Piagetian theories of cognitive development suggest that in addition to the concerns above, sequencing of concepts and skills in teaching must take account of the processing and working memory capacities that characterize successive age levels.

Second, the psychology of cognitive development involves understanding how cognitive change takes place and recognizing the factors and processes which enable cognitive competence to develop. Education also capitalizes on cognitive change, because the construction of knowledge presupposes effective teaching methods that would move the student from a lower to a higher level of understanding. Mechanisms such as reflection on actual or mental actions vis-à-vis alternative solutions to problems, tagging new concepts or solutions to symbols that help one recall and mentally manipulate them are just a few examples of how mechanisms of cognitive development may be used to facilitate learning.

Finally, the psychology of cognitive development is concerned with individual differences in the organization of cognitive processes and abilities, in their rate of change, and in their mechanisms of change. The principles underlying intra- and inter-individual differences could be educationally useful, because knowing how students differ in regard to the various dimensions of cognitive development, such as processing and representational capacity, self-understanding and self-regulation, and the various domains of understanding, such as mathematical, scientific, or verbal abilities, would enable the teacher to cater for the needs of the different students so that no one is left behind.

Social Cognitive Perspective

Social cognitive theory is a highly influential fusion of behavioural, cognitive and social elements that was initially developed by educational psychologist Albert Bandura. In its earlier, neo-behavioural incarnation called social learning theory, Bandura emphasized the process of observational learning in which a learner's behaviour changes as a result of observing others' behaviour and its consequences. The theory identified several factors that determine whether observing a model will affect behavioural or cognitive change. These factors include the learner's developmental status, the perceived prestige and competence of the model, the consequences received by the model, the relevance of the model's behaviours and consequences to the learner's goals, and the learner's self-efficacy. The concept of self-efficacy, which played an important role in later developments of the theory, refers to the learner's belief in his or her ability to perform the modelled behaviour.

An experiment by Schunk and Hanson, that studied grade 2 students who had previously experienced difficulty in learning subtraction, illustrates the type of research stimulated by social learning theory. One group of students observed a subtraction demonstration by a teacher and then participated in an instructional programme on subtraction. A second group observed other grade 2 students performing the same subtraction procedures and then participated in the same instructional programme. The students who observed peer models scored higher on a subtraction post-test and also reported greater confidence in their subtraction ability. The results were interpreted as supporting the hypothesis that perceived similarity of the model to the learner increases self-efficacy, leading to more effective learning of modelled behaviours. It is supposed that peer modelling is particularly effective for students who have low self-efficacy.

Over the last decade, much research activity in educational psychology has focused on developing theories of self-regulated learning (SRL) and metacognition. These theories work from the central premise that effective learners are active agents who construct knowledge by setting goals, analyzing tasks, planning strategies and monitoring their understanding. Research has indicated that learners who are better at goal-setting and self-monitoring tend to have greater intrinsic task interest and self-efficacy; and that teaching learning strategies can increase academic achievement.

Constructivist Perspective

Constructivism is a category of learning theory in which emphasis is placed on the agency and prior "knowing" and experience of the learner, and often on the social and cultural determinants of the learning process. Educational psychologists distinguish individual (or psychological) constructivism, identified with Piaget's theory of cognitive development, from social constructivism. A dominant influence on the latter type is Lev Vygotsky's work on sociocultural learning, describing how interactions with adults, more capable peers, and cognitive tools are internalized to form mental constructs. Elaborating on Vygotsky's theory, Jerome Bruner and other educational psychologists developed the important concept of instructional scaffolding, in which the social or information environment offers supports for learning that are gradually withdrawn as they become internalized.

Motivation

Motivation is an internal state that activates, guides and sustains behaviour. Motivation can have several impacting effects on how students learn and how they behave towards subject matter:

- Provide direction towards goals
- Enhance cognitive processing abilities and performance
- Direct behaviour towards particular goals
- Lead to increased effort and energy
- Increase initiation of and persistence in activities

Educational psychology research on motivation is concerned with the volition or will that students bring to a task, their level of interest and intrinsic motivation, the personally held goals that guide their behaviour, and their belief about the causes of their success or failure. As intrinsic motivation deals with activities that act as their own rewards, extrinsic motivation deals with motivations that are brought on by consequences or punishments.

A form of attribution theory developed by Bernard Weiner describes how students' beliefs about the causes of academic success or failure affect their emotions and motivations. For example, when students attribute failure to lack of ability, and ability is perceived as uncontrollable, they experience the emotions of shame and embarrassment and consequently decrease effort and show poorer performance. In contrast, when students attribute failure to lack of effort, and effort is perceived as controllable, they experience the emotion of guilt and consequently increase effort and show improved performance.

The self-determination theory (SDT) was developed by psychologists Edward Deci and Richard Ryan. SDT focuses on the importance of intrinsic and extrinsic motivation in driving human behaviour and posits inherent growth and development tendencies. It emphasizes the degree to which an individual's behaviour is self-motivated and self-determined. When applied to the realm of education, the self-determination theory is concerned primarily with promoting in students an interest in learning, a value of education, and a confidence in their own capacities and attributes.

Motivational theories also explain how learners' goals affect the way they engage with academic tasks. Those who have mastery goals strive to increase their ability and knowledge. Those who have performance approach goals strive for high grades and seek opportunities to demonstrate their abilities. Those who have performance avoidance goals are driven by fear of failure and avoid situations where their abilities are exposed. Research has found that mastery goals are associated with many positive outcomes such as persistence in the face of failure, preference for challenging tasks, creativity and intrinsic motivation. Performance avoidance goals are associated with negative outcomes such as poor concentration while studying, disorganized studying, less self-regulation, shallow information processing and test anxiety. Performance approach goals are associated with positive outcomes, and some negative outcomes such as an unwillingness to seek help and shallow information processing.

Locus of control is a salient factor in the successful academic performance of students. During the 1970s and '80s, Cassandra B. Whyte did significant educational research studying locus of control as related to the academic achievement of students pursuing higher education coursework. Much of her educational research and publications focused upon the theories of Julian B. Rotter in regard to the importance of internal control and successful academic performance. Whyte reported that individuals who perceive and believe that their hard work may lead to more successful academic outcomes, instead of depending on luck or fate, persist and achieve academically at a higher level. Therefore, it is important to provide education and counselling in this regard.

Research Methodology

The research methods used in educational psychology tend to be drawn from psychology and other social sciences. There is also a history of significant methodological innovation by educational psychologists, and psychologists investigating educational problems. Research methods address problems in both research design and data analysis. Research design informs the planning of experiments and observational studies to ensure that their results have internal, external and ecological validity. Data analysis encompasses methods for processing both quantitative (numerical) and qualitative (non-numerical) research data. Although, historically, the use of quantitative methods was often considered an essential mark of scholarship, modern educational psychology research uses both quantitative and qualitative methods.

Quantitative Methods

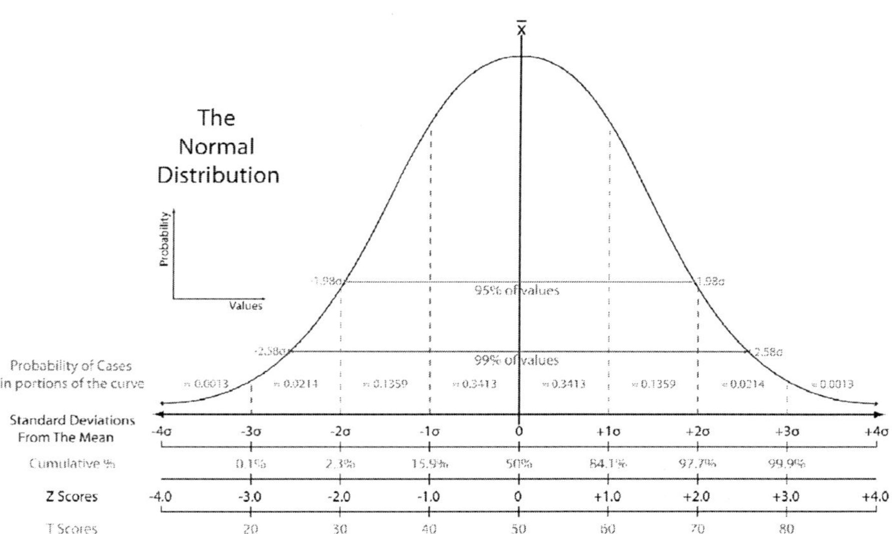

Figure: *Test scores and other educational variables often approximate a normal distribution.*

Perhaps first among the important methodological innovations of educational psychology was the development and application of factor analysis by Charles Spearman. Factor analysis is mentioned here as one example of the many multivariate statistical methods used by educational psychologists. Factor analysis is used to summarize relationships among a large set of variables or test questions, develop theories about mental constructs such as self-efficacy or anxiety, and assess the reliability and validity of test scores. Over 100 years after its introduction by Spearman, factor analysis has become a research staple figuring prominently in educational psychology journals.

Because educational assessment is fundamental to most quantitative research in the field, educational psychologists have made significant contributions to the field of psychometrics. For example, alpha, the widely used measure of test reliability was developed by educational psychologist Lee Cronbach. The reliability of assessments are routinely reported in quantitative educational research. Although, originally, educational measurement methods were built on classical test theory, item response theory and Rasch models are now used extensively in educational measurement worldwide. These models afford advantages over classical test theory, including the capacity to produce standard errors of measurement for each score or pattern of scores on assessments and the capacity to handle missing responses.

Meta-analysis, the combination of individual research results to produce a quantitative literature review, is another methodological innovation with a close association to educational psychology. In a meta-analysis, effect sizes that represent, for example, the differences between treatment groups in a set of similar experiments, are averaged to obtain a single aggregate value representing the best estimate of the effect of treatment. Several decades after Pearson's work with early versions of meta-analysis, Glass published the first application of modern meta-analytic techniques and triggered their broad application across the social and biomedical sciences. Today, meta-analysis is among the most common types of literature review found in educational psychology research.

Other quantitative research issues associated with educational psychology include the use of nested research designs (e.g., a student nested within a classroom, which is nested within a school, which is nested within a district, etc.) and the use of longitudinal statistical models to measure change.

Qualitative Methods

Qualitative methods are used in educational studies whose purpose is to describe events, processes and situations of theoretical significance. The qualitative methods used in educational psychology often derive from anthropology, sociology or sociolinguistics. For example, the anthropological method of ethnography has been used to describe teaching and learning in classrooms. In studies of this type, the researcher may gather detailed field notes as a participant observer or passive observer. Later, the notes and other data may be categorized and interpreted by methods such as grounded theory. Triangulation, the practice of cross-checking findings with multiple data sources, is highly valued in qualitative research.

Case studies are forms of qualitative research focusing on a single person, organization, event, or other entity. In one case study, researchers conducted a 150-minute, semi-structured interview with a 20-year-old woman who had a history of suicidal thinking between the ages of 14 to 18. They analyzed an audio-recording of the interview to understand the roles of cognitive development, identity formation and social attachment in ending her suicidal thinking.

Qualitative analysis is most often applied to verbal data from sources such as conversations, interviews, focus groups, and personal journals. Qualitative methods are thus, typically, approaches to gathering, processing and reporting verbal data. One of the most commonly used methods for qualitative research in educational psychology is protocol analysis. In this method the research participant is asked to think aloud while performing a task, such as solving a math problem. In protocol analysis the verbal data is thought to indicate which information the subject is attending to, but is explicitly not interpreted as an explanation or justification for behaviour. In contrast, the method of verbal analysis does admit learners' explanations as a way to reveal their mental model or misconceptions (e.g., of the laws of motion). The most fundamental operations in both protocol and verbal analysis are segmenting (isolating) and categorizing sections of verbal data. Conversation analysis and discourse analysis, sociolinguistic methods that focus more specifically on the structure of conversational interchange (e.g., between a teacher and student), have been used to assess the process of conceptual change in science learning. Qualitative methods are also used to analyze information in a variety of media, such as students' drawings and concept maps, video-recorded interactions, and computer log records.

Applications in Instructional Design and Technology

Instructional design, the systematic design of materials, activities and interactive environments for learning, is broadly informed by educational psychology theories and research. For example, in defining learning goals or objectives, instructional designers often use a taxonomy of educational objectives created by Benjamin Bloom and colleagues. Bloom also researched mastery learning, an instructional strategy in which learners only advance to a new learning objective after they have mastered its prerequisite objectives. Bloom discovered that a combination of mastery learning with one-to-one tutoring is highly effective, producing learning outcomes far exceeding those normally achieved in classroom instruction. Gagné, another psychologist, had earlier developed an influential method of task analysis in which a terminal learning goal is expanded into a hierarchy of learning objectives connected by prerequisite relations.

- Intelligent tutoring system
- Educational technology
- John R. Anderson
- Cognitive tutor
- Cooperative learning
- Collaborative learning
- Problem-based learning
- Computer-supported collaborative learning
- William Winn
- Constructive alignment

Applications in Teaching

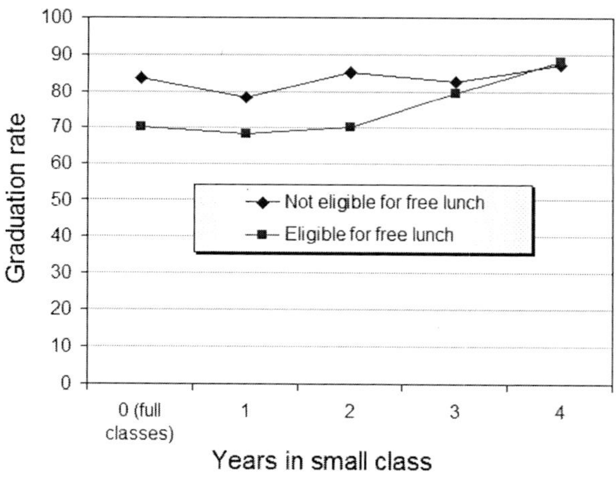

Figure: *A class size experiment in the United States found that attending small classes for 3 or more years in the early grades increased high school graduation of students from low income families.*

Research on classroom management and pedagogy is conducted to guide teaching practice and form a foundation for teacher education programmes. The goals of classroom management are to create an environment conducive to learning and to develop students' self-management skills. More specifically, classroom management strives to create positive teacher–student and peer relationships, manage student groups to sustain on-task behaviour, and use counselling and other psychological methods to aid students who present persistent psychosocial problems.

Introductory educational psychology is a commonly required area of study in most North American teacher education programmes. When taught in that context, its content varies, but it typically emphasizes learning theories (especially cognitively oriented ones), issues about motivation, assessment of students' learning, and classroom management. A developing Wikibook about educational psychology gives more detail about the educational psychology topics that are typically presented in preservice teacher education.

- Special education
- Lesson plan

History

Before 1890: Modern educational psychologists are not the first to analyze educational processes. Philosophers of education such as Juan Vives, Johann Pestalozzi, Friedrich Fröbel, and Johann Herbart had examined, classified and judged the methods of education centuries before the beginnings of psychology in the late 1800s. Juan Vives (1492-1540) proposed induction as the method of study and believed in the direct observation and investigation of the study of nature. He was one of the first to emphasize that the location of the school is important to learning. He suggested that the school should be located away from disturbing noises; the air quality should be good and there should be plenty of food for the students and teachers. Vives emphasized the importance of understanding individual differences of the students and suggested practice as an important tool for learning. He also supported the education of women.

Johann Pestalozzi (1746-1827) emphasized the child rather than the content of the school. He spoke out against the method of rote memorization as the method for learning and suggested direct observation as a better way of learning. He used object teaching, which means when teaching the teacher should proceed gradually from the concrete objects to the abstract and complex material. He believed that the relationship between the teacher and the child was important in providing a basis for the education of the child. He also was interested in the education of poor children. He was the first to establish an elementary school. Friedrich Fröbel (1782-1853) is the founder of the kindergarten movement, which combined work and play to teach children responsibility and cooperation.

Johann Herbart (1776-1841) is considered the father of educational psychology. He believed that learning was influenced by interest in the subject and the teacher. He thought that teachers should consider the students existing mental sets, what they already know, when presenting new information or material. Herbart came up with what is now known as the formal steps. They are 5 steps that teachers should use are:

1. Review material that has already been learned by the teacher
2. Prepare the student for new material by giving them an overview of what they are learning next
3. Present the new material.
4. Relate the new material to the old material that has already been learned.
5. Show how the student can apply the new material and show the material they will learn next.

1890-1920

The period of 1890-1920 is considered the golden era of educational psychology where aspirations of the new discipline rested on the application of the scientific methods of observation and experimentation to educational problems. From 1840 to 1920 37 million people immigrated to the United States. This created an expansion of elementary schools and secondary schools. The increase in immigration also provided educational psychologists the opportunity to use intelligence testing to screen immigrants at Ellis Island. Darwinism influenced the beliefs of the prominent educational psychologists. Even in the earliest years of the discipline, educational psychologists recognized the limitations of this new approach. The pioneering American psychologist William James commented that:

Psychology is a science, and teaching is an art; and sciences never generate arts directly out of themselves. An intermediate inventive mind must make that application, by using its originality".

James is the father of psychology in America but he also made contributions to educational psychology. In his famous series of lectures

Talks to Teachers on Psychology, published in 1899 and now regarded as the first educational psychology textbook, James defines education as “the organization of acquired habits of conduct and tendencies to behaviour”. He states that teachers should “train the pupil to behaviour” so that he fits into the social and physical world. Teachers should also realize the importance of habit and instinct. They should present information that is clear and interesting and relate this new information and material to things the student already knows about. He also addresses important issues such as attention, memory, and association of ideas.

Alfred Binet published Mental Fatigue in 1898, in which he attempted to apply the experimental method to educational psychology. In this experimental method he advocated for two types of experiments, experiments done in the lab and experiments done in the classroom. In 1904 he was appointed the Minister of Public Education. This is when he began to look for a way to distinguish children with developmental disabilities. Binet strongly supported special education programmes because he believed that “abnormality” could be cured. The Binet-Simon test was the first intelligence test and was the first to distinguish between “normal children” and those with developmental disabilities. Binet believed that it was important to study individual differences between age groups and children of the same age. He also believed that it was important for teachers to take into account individual students strengths and also the needs of the classroom as a whole when teaching and creating a good learning environment. He also believed that it was important to train teachers in observation so that they would be able to see individual differences among children and adjust the curriculum to the students. Binet also emphasized that practice of material was important. In 1916 Lewis Terman revised the Binet-Simon so that the average score was always 100. The test became known as the Stanford-Binet and was one of the most widely used tests of intelligence. Terman, unlike Binet, was interested in using intelligence test to identify gifted children who had high intelligence. In his longitudinal study of gifted children, who became known as the Termites, Terman found that gifted children become gifted adults.

Edward Thorndike (1874-1949) supported the scientific movement in education. He based teaching practices on empirical evidence and measurement. Thorndike developed the theory of instrumental conditioning or the law of effect. The law of effect states that associations are strengthened when it is followed by something pleasing and associations are weakened when followed by something not pleasing. He also found that learning is done a little at a time or in increments, learning is an automatic process and all the principles of learning apply to all mammals. Thorndike's research with Robert Woodworth on the theory of transfer found that learning one subject will only influence your ability to learn another subject if the subjects are similar. This discovery led to less emphasis on learning the classics because they found that studying the classics does not contribute to overall general intelligence. Thorndike was one of the first to say that individual differences in cognitive tasks were due to how many stimulus response patterns a person had rather than a general intellectual ability. He contributed word dictionaries that were scientifically based to determine the words and definitions used. The dictionaries were the first to take into consideration the users maturity level. He also integrated pictures and easier pronunciation guide into each of the definitions. Thorndike contributed arithmetic books based on learning theory. He made all the problems more realistic and relevant to what was being studied, not just to improve the general intelligence. He developed test that were standardized to measure performance in school related subjects. His biggest contribution to testing was the CAVD intelligence test which used a mulitdimensional approach to intelligence and the first to use a ratio scale. His later work was on programmed instruction, mastery learning and computer-based learning:

If, by a miracle of mechanical ingenuity, a book could be so arranged that only to him who had done what was directed on page one would page two become visible, and so on, much that now requires personal instruction could be managed by print.

John Dewey (1859-1952) had a major influence on the development of progressive education in the United States. He believed that the classroom should prepare children to be good citizens and facilitate creative intelligence. He pushed for the creation of practical class that could be applied outside of a school setting. He also thought that education should be student-oriented not subject-oriented. For Dewey education was social that helped bring together generations of people. He states that students learn by doing. He believed in an active mind that was able to be educated through observation and problem solving and enquiry. In his 1910 book How We Think he emphasizes that material should be provided in way that is stimulating and interesting to the student and it encourages original thoughts and problem solving. He also stated that material should be relative to the student's own experience.

"The material furnished by way of information should be relevant to a question that is vital in the students own experience"

Jean Piaget (1896-1980) developed the theory of cognitive development. The theory stated that intelligence developed in four different stages. The stages are the sensorimotor stage from birth to 2 years old, the preoperational state from 2 years old to 7 years old, the concrete operational stage from 7 years old to 10 years old, and formal operational stage from 11 years old and up. He also believed that learning was constrained to the child's cognitive development. Piaget influenced educational psychology because he was the first to believe that cognitive development was important and something that should be paid attention to in education. Most of the research on Piagetian theory was mainly tested and done by American educational psychologists

1920-Present

The amount of people receiving a high school and college education increased dramatically from 1920 to 1960. Because of very little jobs available to the teens coming out of eighth grade there was an increase in high school attendance in the 1930s . The progressive movement in the United State took off at this time and led to the idea of progressive education. John Flanagan, an educational psychologist, developed tests for combat trainees and instructions in combat training. In 1954 the work of Kenneth Clark and his wife on the effects of segregation on black and white children was influential in the Supreme Court case Brown v. Board of Education. From the 1960s to present day educational psychology has switched from a behaviourist perspective to a more cognitive based perspective because of the influence and development of cognitive psychology at this time.

Jerome Bruner was the first to apply the cognitive approaches in educational psychology. He was the one who introduced the ideas of Jean Piaget into educational psychology. He advocated for discovery learning where teachers create a problem solving environment that allows the student to question, explore and experiment. In his book The Process of Education Bruner stated that the structure of the material and the cognitive abilities of the person are important in learning. He emphasized the importance of the subject matter. He also believed that how the subject was structured was important for the students understanding of the subject and it is the goal of the teacher to structure the subject in a way that was easy for the student to understand. In the early 1960s Bruner went to Africa to teach math and science to schoolchildren, which influenced his view as schooling as a cultural institution. Bruner was also influential in the development of MACOS, Man a Course of Study, which was an educational programme that combined anthropology and science. The programme explored human evolution and social behaviour. He also helped with the development of the head start programme. He was interested in the influence of culture on education and looked at the impact of poverty on educational development.

Benjamin Bloom (1913-1999) spent over 50 years at the University of Chicago where he worked in the department of education. He believed that all students can learn. He developed taxonomy of educational objectives. The objectives were divided into three domains: cognitive, affective, and psychomotor. The cognitive domain deals with how we think. It is divided into categories that are on a continuum from easiest to more complex. The categories are knowledge or recall, comprehension application, analysis, synthesis and evaluation. The affective domain deals with emotions and has 5 categories. The categories are receiving phenomenon, responding to that phenomenon, valuing, organization, and internalizing values. The psychomotor domain deals with the development of motor skills, movement and coordination and has 7 categories, that also goes from simplest to complex. The 7 categories of the psychomotor domain are perception, set, guided response, mechanism, complex overt response, adaptation, and origination. The taxonomy provided broad educational objectives that could be used to help expand the curriculum to match the ideas in the taxonomy. The taxonomy is considered to have a greater influence internationally than in the United States. Internationally, the taxonomy is used in every aspect of education from training of the teachers to the development of testing material. Bloom believed in communicating clear learning goals and promoting an active student. He thought that teachers should provide feedback to the students on their strengths and weaknesses. Bloom also did research on college students and their problem solving processes. He found that they differ in understanding the basis of the problem and the ideas in the problem. He also found that students differ in process of problem solving in their approach and attitude towards the problem.

Nathaniel Gage is important in educational psychology because he did research to improve teaching and understand the processes involved in teaching. In 1963 he was the editor of the Handbook of Research on Teaching, which became an influential book in educational psychology. The handbook helped set up research on teaching and made research on teaching important to educational psychology. He also was influential in the founding of the Stanford Centre for Research and Development in teaching, which not only contributed important research on teaching but also influenced the teaching of important educational psychologists.

Careers in Educational Psychology

Education and Training: A person may be considered an educational psychologist after completing a graduate degree in educational psychology or a closely related field. Universities establish educational psychology graduate programmes in either psychology departments or, more commonly, faculties of education.

Educational psychologists work in a variety of settings. Some work in university settings where they carry out research on the cognitive and social processes of human development, learning and education. Educational psychologists may also work as consultants in designing and creating educational materials, classroom programmes and online courses.

Educational psychologists who work in k–12 school settings (closely related are school psychologists in the US and Canada) are trained at the master's and doctoral levels. In addition to conducting assessments, school psychologists provide services such as academic and behavioural intervention, counselling, teacher consultation, and crisis intervention. However, school psychologists are generally more individual-oriented towards students.

In the UK, status as a Chartered Educational Psychologist is gained by completing:

- an undergraduate degree in psychology permitting registration with the British Psychological Society
- two or three years experience working with children, young people and their families.
- a three-year professional doctorate in educational psychology.

In New Zealand Registered Educational Psychologist status is gained by completing:

- an undergraduate degree in education and psychology
- completion of a two year masters level training programme in psychology or educational psychology
- completion of a one year post masters internship programme

Internship places are limited and applications exceed places in most years. Since 1999 Massey University delivered the only educational psychology training programme. Victoria University, Wellington started its offering of an educational psychology training programme in 2013.

Professional Organizations

Holding membership among Division 15 of the American Psychological Association and/or multiple divisions of the American Educational Research Association is common among educational psychologists. These organizations each host 1-2 conferences each year and provide peer-reviewed journals of current research in the field.

Employment Outlook

Employment for psychologists in the United States is expected to grow faster than most occupations through the year 2014, with anticipated growth of 18–26%. One in four psychologists are employed in educational settings. In the United States, the median salary for psychologists in primary and secondary schools is US$58,360 as of May 2004.

In recent decades the participation of women as professional researchers in North American educational psychology has risen dramatically. The percentage of female authors of peer-reviewed journal articles doubled from 1976 (24%) to 1995 (51%), and has since remained constant. Female membership on educational psychology journal editorial boards increased from 17% in 1976 to 47% in 2004. Over the same period, the proportion of chief editor positions held by women increased from 22% to 70%.

2

Occupational Psychology

Occupational psychology is the research and study of how well people work and what affects them in their work place, as well as how they interact and behave with others at work. Occupational psychologists collaborate with employees and employers to help improve productivity and efficiency at work, and also help the two understand each other. They also work for large companies in both the public and private sectors, in management training centres and training specialist staff from the industry concerned.

Industrial and Organizational Psychology

Industrial and organizational psychology (also known as I-O psychology or work psychology) is the scientific study of employees, workplaces, and organizations. Industrial and organizational psychologists contribute to an organization's success by improving the performance, satisfaction, safety, health and well-being of its employees. An I-O psychologist conducts research on employee behaviours and attitudes, and how these can be improved through hiring practices, training programmes, feedback, and management systems. I-O psychologists also help organizations transition among periods of change and development. Industrial and organizational psychology is related to organizational behaviour and human capital.

An applied science, I–O psychology is represented by Division 14 of the American Psychological Association, known formally as the Society for Industrial and Organizational Psychology (SIOP). In the UK, industrial and organizational psychologists are referred to as occupational psychologists and this 'protected title' is regulated by the Health and Care Professions Council. In Australia, the title organizational psychologist is also protected and is regulated by the Australian Health Practitioner Regulation Agency (AHPRA).

Personnel Recruitment and Selection

I–O psychologists typically work with HR specialists to design (a) recruitment processes and (b) personnel selection systems. Personnel recruitment is the process of identifying qualified candidates in the workforce and getting them to apply for jobs within an organization. Personnel recruitment processes include developing job announcements, placing ads, defining key qualifications for applicants, and screening out unqualified applicants.

Personnel selection is the systematic process of hiring and promoting personnel. Personnel selection systems employ evidence-based practices to determine the most qualified candidates. Personnel selection involves both the newly hired and individuals who can be promoted from within the organization. Common selection tools include ability tests (e.g., cognitive, physical, or psychomotor), knowledge tests, personality tests, structured interviews, the systematic collection of biographical data, and work samples. I–O psychologists must evaluate evidence regarding the extent to which selection tools predict job performance, evidence that bears on the validity of selection tools.

Personnel selection procedures are usually validated, i.e., shown to be job relevant, using one or more of the following types of validity: content validity, construct validity, and/or criterion-related validity. I–O psychologists adhere to professional standards, such as the Society for Industrial and Organizational Psychology's (SIOP) Principles for Validation and Use of Personnel Selection Procedures and the Standards for Educational and Psychological Testing. The Equal Employment Opportunity Commission's Uniform Guidelines are also influential in guiding personnel selection although they have been criticized as outdated when compared to the current state of knowledge in I–O psychology.

I–O psychologists not only help in the selection and assessment of personnel for jobs, but also assist in the selection of students for admission to colleges, universities, and graduate and professional schools as well as the assessment of student achievement, student aptitude, and the performance of teachers and K–12 schools. Increasingly, I–O psychologists are working for educational assessment and testing organizations and divisions.

A meta-analysis of selection methods in personnel psychology found that general mental ability was the best overall predictor of job performance and training performance.

Performance Appraisal/management

Performance appraisal or performance evaluation is the process of measuring an individual's or a group's work behaviours and outcomes against the expectations of the job. Performance appraisal is frequently used in promotion and compensation decisions, to help design and validate personnel selection procedures, and for performance management. Performance management is the process of providing performance feedback relative to expectations and improvement information (e.g., coaching, mentoring). Performance management may also include documenting and tracking performance information for organization-level evaluation purposes.

An I–O psychologist would typically use information from the job analysis to determine a job's performance dimensions, and then construct a rating scale to describe each level of performance for the job. Often, the I–O psychologist would be responsible for training organizational personnel how to use the performance appraisal instrument, including ways to minimize bias when using the rating scale, and how to provide effective performance feedback. Additionally, the I–O psychologist may consult with the organization on ways to use the performance appraisal information for broader performance management initiatives.

Individual Assessment and Psychometrics

Individual assessment involves the measurement of individual differences. I–O psychologists perform individual assessments in order to evaluate differences among candidates for employment as well as differences among employees. The constructs measured pertain to job performance. With candidates for employment, individual assessment is often part of the personnel selection process. These assessments can include written tests, physical tests, psychomotor tests, personality tests, work samples, and assessment centres.

Psychometrics is the science of measuring psychological variables, such as knowledge, skills, and abilities. I–O psychologists are generally well-trained in psychometric psychology.

Remuneration and Compensation

Compensation includes wages or salary, bonuses, pension/ retirement contributions, and perquisites that can be converted to cash or replace living expenses. I–O psychologists may be asked to conduct a job evaluation for the purpose of determining compensation levels and ranges. I–O psychologists may also serve as expert witnesses in pay discrimination cases when disparities in pay for similar work are alleged.

Training and Training Evaluation

Training is the systematic acquisition of skills, concepts, or attitudes that results in improved performance in another environment. Most people hired for a job are not already versed in all the tasks required to perform the job effectively. Evidence indicates that training is effective and that these training expenditures are paying off in terms of higher net sales and gross proftability per employee. Training can be beneficial for the organization and for employees in terms of increasing their value to their organization as well as their employability in the broader marketplace. Many organizations are using training and development as a way to attract and retain their most successful employees.

Similar to performance management, an I–O psychologist would employ a job analysis in concert with principles of instructional design to create an effective training programme. A training programme is likely to include a summative evaluation at its conclusion in order to ensure that trainees have met the training objectives and can perform the target work tasks at an acceptable level. Training programmes often include formative evaluations to assess the impact of the training as the training proceeds. Formative evaluations can be used to locate problems in training procedures and help I–O psychologists make corrective adjustments while the training is ongoing.

The basic foundation for training programmes is learning. Learning outcomes can be organized into three broad categories: cognitive, skill-based, and affective outcomes. Cognitive is a type of learning outcome that includes declarative knowledge or the knowledge of rules, fasts, and principles. An example is police officers acquire declarative knowledge about laws and court procedures. Skill-based is a learning outcome that concerns procedural knowledge and the development of motor and technical skills. An example is motor skills that involve the coordination of physical movements such as using a special tool or flying a certain aircraft, whereas technical skills might include understanding a certain software programme, or exhibiting effective customer relations behaviours. Affective is a type of learning outcome that includes attitudes or beliefs that predispose a person to behave in a certain way. Attitudes can be developed or changed through training programmes. Examples of these attitudes are organizational commitment and appreciation of diversity.

Before training design issues are considered, a careful needs analysis is required to develop a systematic understanding of where training is needed, what needs to be taught or trained, and who will be trained. Training needs analysis typically involves a three step process that includes organizational analysis, task analysis and person analysis. Organizational analysis examines organizational goals, available resources, and the organizational environment to determine where training should be directed. This analysis identifies the training needs of different departments or subunits and systematically assessing manager, peer, and technological support for transfer of training. Organizational analysis also takes into account the climate of the organization and its subunits. For example, if a climate for safety is emphasized throughout the organization or in particular parts of the organization (e.g., production), then training needs will likely reflect this emphasis. Task analysis uses the results from job analysis on determining what is needed for successful job performance and then determines what the content of training should be. Task analysis can consist of developing task statements, determining homogeneous task clusters, and identifying KSAOs (knowledge, skills, abilities, other characteristics) required for the job. With organizations increasingly trying to identify "core competencies" that are required for all jobs, task analysis can also include an assessment of competencies. Person analysis identifies which individuals within an organization should receive training and what kind of instruction they need. Employee needs can be assessed using a variety of methods that identify weaknesses that training and development can address. The needs analysis makes it possible to identify the training program's objectives, which in turn, represents the information for both the trainer and trainee about what is to be learned for the benefit of the organization.

Therefore with any training programme it is key to establish specify training objectives. Schultz & Schultz (2010) states that need assessment is an analysis of corporate and individual goals undertaken before designing a training programme. Examples of need assessment are based on organizational, task, and work analysis is conducted using job analysis critical incidents, performance appraisal, and self-assessment techniques.

But with any training there are always challenges that one faces. Challenges which I-O psychologists face:

- To identify the abilities required to perform increasingly complex jobs.

- To provide job opportunities for unskilled workers.
- To assist supervisors in the management of an ethnically diverse workforce.
- To retain workers displaced by changing economic, technological, and political forces.
- To help organizations remain competitive in the international marketplace.
- To conduct the necessary research to determine the effectiveness of training programmes.

Motivation in the Workplace

Work motivation "is a set of energetic forces that originate both within as well as beyond an individual's being, to initiate work-related behaviour, and to determine its form, direction, intensity, and duration" Understanding what motivates an organization's employees is central to the study of I–O psychology. Motivation is a person's internal disposition to be concerned with an approach positive incentives and avoid negative incentives. To further this, an incentive is the anticipated reward or aversive event available in the environment. While motivation can often be used as a tool to help predict behaviour, it varies greatly among individuals and must often be combined with ability and environmental factors to actually influence behaviour and performance. Because of motivation's role in influencing workplace behaviour and performance, it is key for organizations to understand and to structure the work environment to encourage productive behaviours and discourage those that are unproductive.

There is general consensus that motivation involves three psychological processes: arousal, direction, and intensity. Arousal is what initiates action. It is fueled by a person's need or desire for something that is missing from their lives at a given moment, either totally or partially. Direction refers to the path employees take in accomplishing the goals they set for themselves. Finally, intensity is the vigor and amount of energy employees put into this goal-directed work performance. The level of intensity is based on the importance and difficulty of the goal. These psychological processes result in four outcomes. First, motivation serves to direct attention, focusing on particular issues, people, tasks, etc. It also serves to stimulate an employee to put forth effort. Next, motivation results in persistence, preventing one from deviating from the goal-seeking behaviour. Finally, motivation results in task strategies, which as defined by Mitchell & Daniels, are "patterns of behaviour produced to reach a particular goal."

Occupational Safety and Health

As specialists in all areas of human behaviour and its relationship to the modern workplace, I/O Psychologists are also involved with the development of organizational stress management programmes within organisations. This involves identification of psychosocial hazards in the workplace using psychometric testing, analysis and reporting. Work safety, particularly psychological health and safety is also an area in which I/O psychologists are increasingly involved.

Organizational Culture

Organizational culture can be described as a set of assumptions shared by the individuals in an organization that directs interpretation and action by defining appropriate behaviour for various situations. There are three levels of organizational culture: artifacts, shared values, and basic beliefs and assumptions. Artifacts comprise the physical components of the organization that relay cultural meaning. Shared values are individuals' preferences regarding certain aspects of the organization's culture (e.g., loyalty, customer service). Basic beliefs and assumptions include individuals' impressions about the trustworthiness and supportiveness of an organization, and are often deeply ingrained within the organization's culture.

In addition to an overall culture, organizations also have subcultures. Examples of subcultures include corporate culture, departmental culture, local culture, and issue-related culture. While there is no single "type" of organizational culture, some researchers have developed models to describe different organizational cultures.

Organizational culture has been shown to have an impact on important organizational outcomes such as performance, attraction, recruitment, retention, employee satisfaction, and employee well-being. Also, organizations with an adaptive culture tend to perform better than organizations with an unadaptive culture.

Group Behaviour

Group behaviour is the interaction between individuals of a collective and the processes such as opinions, attitudes, growth, feedback loops, and adaptations that occur and change as a result of this interaction. The interactions serve to fulfill some need satisfaction of an individual who is part of the collective and helps to provide a basis for his interaction with specific members of the group.

A specific area of research in group behaviour is the dynamics of teams. Team effectiveness refers to the system of getting people in a company or institution to work together effectively. The idea behind team effectiveness is that a group of people working together can achieve much more than if the individuals of the team were working on their own.

Team Effectiveness

Organizations support the use of teams, because teams can accomplish a much greater amount of work in a short period of time than can be accomplished by an individual contributor, and because the collective results of a group of contributors can produce higher quality deliverables. Five elements that are contributors to team effectiveness include: (1) team composition, (2) task design, (3) organizational resources, (4) team rewards, and (5) team goals.

Team Composition

The composition of teams is initially decided during the selection of individual contributors that are to be assigned to specific teams and has a direct bearing on the resulting effectiveness of those teams. Aspects of team composition that should be considered during the team selection process include team member: knowledge, skills and abilities (KSAs), personalities, and attitudes.

As previously stated, one of the reasons organizations support the use of teams is the expectation of the delivery of higher quality results. To achieve these types of results, highly skilled members are more effective than teams built around those with lesser skills, and teams that include a diversity of skills have improved team performance (Guzzo & Shea, 1992). Additionally, increased average cognitive ability of team members has been shown to consistently correlate to increased work group effectiveness (Sundstrom et al., 2000). Therefore, organizations should seek to assign teams with team members that have a mix of KSAs. Teams that are composed of members that have the same KSAs may prove to be ineffective in meeting the team goals, no matter how talented the individual members are.

The personalities and attitudes of the individuals that are selected as team members are other aspects that should be taken into consideration when composing teams, since these individual traits have been found to be good indicators of team effectiveness. For example, a positive relationship between the team-level traits of agreeableness and conscientiousness and the team performance has been shown to exist (Van Vianen & De Dreu, 2001). Differing personalities of individual team members can affect the team climate in a negative way as members may clash and reduce team performance (Barrick, et al., 1998).

Task Design

A fundamental question in team task design is whether or not a task is even appropriate for a team. Those tasks that require predominantly independent work are best left to individuals, and team tasks should include those tasks that consist primarily of interdependent work. When a given task is appropriate for a team, task design can play a key role in team effectiveness (Sundstrom, et al., 2000).

The Job Characteristics Theory of motivation identifies core job dimensions that provide motivation for individuals and include: skill variety, task identity, task significance, autonomy and feedback (Hackman & Oldham, 1980). These dimensions map well to the team environment. Individual contributors that perform team tasks that are challenging, interesting, and engaging are more likely to be motivated to exert greater effort and perform better than those team members that are working on those tasks that do not have these characteristics.

Interrelated to the design of various tasks is the implementation method for the tasks themselves. For example, certain team members may find it challenging to cross train with other team members that have subject matter expertise in areas in which they are not familiar. In utilizing this approach, greater motivation is likely to result for both parties as the expert becomes the mentor and trainer and the cross-training team member finds learning new tasks to be an interesting change of pace. Such expansions of team task assignments can make teams more effective and require teams to spend greater amounts of time discussing and planning strategies and approaches for completing assigned tasks (Hackman, et al., 1976).

Organizational Resources

Organizational support systems impact the effectiveness of teams (Sundstrum, et al., 1990) and provide resources for teams operating in the multi-team environment. In this case, the provided resources include various resource types that teams require to be effective. During the chartering of new teams, organizational enabling resources are first identified. Examples of enabling resources include facilities, equipment, information, training and leadership. Also identified during team chartering are team-specific resources (e.g., budgetary resources, human resources). Team-specific human resources represent the individual contributors that are selected for each team as team members. Intra-team processes (e.g., task design, task assignment) are sufficient for effective utilization of these team-specific resources.

Teams also function in multi-team environments that are dynamic in nature and require teams to respond to shifting organizational contingencies (Salas, et al., 2004). In regards to resources, such contingencies include the constraints imposed by organizational resources that are not specifically earmarked for the exclusive use of certain teams. These types of resources are scarce in nature and must be shared by multiple teams. Examples of these scarce resources include subject matter experts, simulation and testing facilities, and limited amounts of time for the completion of multi-team goals. For these types of shared resources inter-team management processes (e.g.: constraint resource scheduling) must be provided to enable effective multi-team utilization.

Team Rewards

Organizational reward systems are a driver for strengthening and enhancing individual team member efforts that contribute towards reaching collective team goals (Luthans & Kreitner, 1985). In other words, rewards that are given to individual team members should be contingent upon the performance of the entire team (Sundstrom, et al., 1990).

Several design elements of organizational reward systems are needed to meet this objective. The first element for reward systems design is the concept that for a collective assessment to be appropriate for individual team members, the group's tasks must be highly interdependent. If this is not the case, individual assessment is more appropriate than team assessment (Wageman & Baker, 1997). A second design element is the compatibility between individual-level reward systems and team-level reward systems (DeMatteo, Eby, & Sundstrom, 1998). For example, it would be an unfair situation to reward the entire team for a job well done if only one team member did the great majority of the work. That team member would most likely view teams and team work in a negative fashion and not want to participate in a team setting in the future. A final design element is the creation of an organizational culture that supports and rewards employees who believe in the value of teamwork and who maintain a positive mental attitude towards team-based rewards (Haines and Taggar, 2006).

Team Goals

Goals for individual contributors have been shown to be motivating when they contain three elements: (1) difficulty, (2) acceptance, and (3) specificity (Lock & Latham, 1990). In the team setting, goal difficulty is related to group belief that the team can accomplish the tasks required to meet the assigned goal (Whitney, 1994). This belief (collective efficacy) is somewhat counterintuitive, but rests on team member perception that they now view themselves as more competent than others in the organization who were not chosen to complete such difficult goals. This in turn, can lead to higher levels of performance. Goal acceptance and specificity is also applicable to the team setting. When team members individually and collectively commit to team goals, team effectiveness is increased and is a function of increased supportive team behaviours (Aube & Rousseau, 2005).

As related to the team setting, it is also important to be aware of the interplay between the goals of individual contributors that participate on teams and the goals of the teams themselves. The selection of team goals must be done in coordination with the selection of goals for individuals. Individual goals must be in line with team goals (or not exist at all) to be effective (Mitchell & Silver, 1990). For example, a professional ball player that does well in his/her sport is rewarded individually for excellent performance. This individual performance generally contributes to improved team performance which can, in turn, lead to team recognition, such as a league championship.

Job Satisfaction and Commitment

Job satisfaction reflects an employee's overall assessment of their job, particularly their emotions, behaviours, and attitudes about their work experience. It is one of the most heavily researched topics in industrial–organizational psychology with several thousand published studies. Job satisfaction has theoretical and practical utility for the field of psychology and has been linked to important job outcomes including attitudinal variables, absenteeism, employee turnover, and job performance. For instance, job satisfaction is strongly correlated with attitudinal variables such as job involvement, organizational commitment, job tensions, frustration, and feelings of anxiety. Job satisfaction also has a weak correlation with employee's absentee behaviours and turnover from an organization with employees more likely to miss work or find other jobs if they are not satisfied. Finally, research has found that although a positive relationship exists between job satisfaction and performance, it is moderated by the use of rewards at an organization and the strength of employee's attitudes about their job.

Productive Behaviour

Productive behaviour is defined as employee behaviour that contributes positively to the goals and objectives of an organization. When an employee begins a new job, there is a transition period during which he or she is not contributing positively to the organization. To successfully transition from being an outsider to a full-fledged member of an organization, an employee typically needs job-related training as well as more general information about the culture of the organization. In financial terms, productive behaviour represents the point at which an organization begins to achieve some return on the investment it has made in a new employee. Industrial–organizational psychologists are typically more focused on productive behaviour rather than simple job or task performance because of the ability to account for extra-role performance in addition to in-role performance. While in-role performance tells managers or researchers how well the employee performs the required technical aspects of the job, extra-role performance includes behaviours not necessarily required as part of the job but still contribute to organizational effectiveness. By taking both in-role and extra-role performance into account, industrial–organizational psychologists are able to assess employees' effectiveness (how well they do what they were hired to do), efficiency (their relative outputs to relative inputs), and their productivity (how much they help the organization reach its goals). Jex & Britt outline three different forms of productive behaviour that industrial–organizational psychologists frequently evaluate in organizations: job performance; organizational citizenship behaviour; and innovation.

Job Performance

Job performance represents behaviours employees engage in while at work which contribute to organizational goals. These behaviours are formally evaluated by an organization as part of an employee's responsibilities. In order to understand and ultimately predict job performance, it is important to be precise when defining the term. Job performance is about behaviours that are within the control of the employee and not about results (effectiveness), the costs involved in achieving results (productivity), the results that can be achieved in a period of time (efficiency), or the value an organization places on a given level of performance, effectiveness, productivity or efficiency (utility).

To model job performance, researchers have attempted to define a set of dimensions that are common to all jobs. Using a common set of dimensions provides a consistent basis for assessing performance and enables the comparison of performance across jobs. Performance is commonly broken into two major categories: in-role (technical aspects of a job) and extra-role (non-technical abilities such as communication skills and being a good team member). While this distinction in behaviour has been challenged it is commonly made by both employees and management. A model of performance by Campbell breaks performance into in-role and extra-role categories. Campbell labelled job-specific task proficiency and non-job-specific task proficiency as in-role dimensions, while written and oral communication, demonstrating effort, maintaining personal discipline, facilitating peer and team performance, supervision and leadership and management and administration are labelled as extra-role dimensions. Murphy's model of job performance also broke job performance into in-role and extra-role categories. However, task-orientated behaviours composed the in-role category and the extra-role category included interpersonally-oriented behaviours, down-time behaviours and destructive and hazardous behaviours. However, it has been challenged as to whether the measurement of job performance is usually done through pencil/ paper tests, job skills tests, on-site hands-on tests, off-site hands-on tests, high-fidelity simulations, symbolic simulations, task ratings and global ratings. These various tools are often used to evaluate performance on specific tasks and overall job performance. Van Dyne and LePine developed a measurement model in which overall job performance was evaluated using Campbell's in-role and extra-role categories. Here, in-role performance was reflected through how well "employees met their performance expectations and performed well at the tasks that made up the employees' job." Dimensions regarding how well the employee assists others with their work for the benefit of the group, if the employee voices new ideas for projects or changes to procedure and whether the employee attends functions that help the group composed the extra-role category.

To assess job performance, reliable and valid measures must be established. While there are many sources of error with performance ratings, error can be reduced through rater training and through the use of behaviourally-anchored rating scales. Such scales can be used to clearly define the behaviours that constitute poor, average, and superior performance. Additional factors that complicate the measurement of job performance include the instability of job performance over time due to forces such as changing performance criteria, the structure of the job itself and the restriction of variation in individual performance by organizational forces. These factors include errors in job measurement techniques, acceptance and the justification of poor performance and lack of importance of individual performance.

The determinants of job performance consist of factors having to do with the individual worker as well as environmental factors in the workplace. According to Campbell's Model of The Determinants of Job Performance, job performance is a result of the interaction between declarative knowledge (knowledge of facts or things), procedural knowledge (knowledge of what needs to be done and how to do it), and motivation (reflective of an employee's choices regarding whether to expend effort, the level of effort to expend, and whether to persist with the level of effort chosen). The interplay between these factors show that an employee may, for example, have a low level of declarative knowledge, but may still have a high level of performance if the employee has high levels of procedural knowledge and motivation.

Regardless of the job, three determinants stand out as predictors of performance: (1) general mental ability (especially for jobs higher in complexity); (2) job experience (although there is a law of diminishing returns); and (3) the personality trait of conscientiousness (people who are dependable and achievement-oriented, who plan well). These determinants appear to influence performance largely through the acquisition and usage of job knowledge and the motivation to do well. Further, an expanding area of research in job performance determinants includes emotional intelligence.

Occupational Stress

I/O psychology has contributed significantly to the study of occupational stress and its effect on occupational health, since early research in the area began. Occupational stress is concerned with physical and psychosocial working conditions that can elicit negative responses from employees. Stressful working conditions are referred to as stressors that can lead to three types of strains: Behavioural (e.g., absenteeism or poor performance), physical (e.g., headaches or coronary heart disease), and psychological (e.g., anxiety or depressed mood). Hart and Cooper point out that occupational stress can have implications for organizational performance because employee well-being relates to employee performance on the job. A number of models have been developed to explain how job stressors might affect employee health and organizational performance.

Organizational Citizenship Behaviour

Organizational citizenship behaviours ("OCBs") are another form of productive behaviour, having been shown to be beneficial to both organization and team effectiveness. Dennis Organ is often thought of as the father of OCB research and defines OCBs as "individual behaviour that is discretionary, not directly or explicitly recognized by the formal reward system, and that in the aggregate promotes the effective functioning of the organization." Behaviours that qualify as OCBs can fall into one of the following five categories: altruism, courtesy, sportsmanship, conscientiousness, and civic virtue.

Researchers have adapted, elaborated, or otherwise changed Organ's (1988) five OCB categories, but they remain popular today. The categories and their descriptions are as follows:

Altruism

Sometimes referred to as "prosocial behaviour" altruistic OCBs include helping behaviours in the workplace such as volunteering to assist a coworker on a project.

Courtesy

These behaviours can be seen when an employee exhibits basic consideration for others. Examples of courteous OCBs include "checking up" on coworkers to see how they are doing and notifying coworkers of commitments that may cause you to be absent from work.

Sportsmanship

Unlike other forms of OCBs, sportsmanship involves not engaging in certain behaviours, such as whining and complaining about minor issues or tough work assignments.

Conscientiousness

Conscientiousness is basically defined as self-discipline and performing tasks beyond the minimum requirements. Conscientious OCBs involve planning ahead, cleanliness, not "slacking off," adhering to the rules, punctuality, and being an overall good citizen in the workplace.

Civic virtue

Civic virtue differs from other OCBs because the target of the behaviour is the group or organization as a whole, rather than an individual coworker. Civic virtue OCBs include being a good representative of the organization and supporting the organization, especially in its efforts outside of its major business objectives. Examples of civic virtue OCBs are participating in charitable functions held by the organization and defending or otherwise speaking well of the organization.

OCBs are also categorized using other methods. For example, Williams and Anderson categorize OCBs by their intended target, separating them into those targeted at individuals ("OCBIs"), supervisors ("OCBSs"), and those targeted at the organization as a whole ("OCBOs"). Additionally, Vigoda-Gadot uses a sub-category of OCBs called CCBs, or "compulsory OCBs" which is used to describe OCBs that are done under the influence of coercive persuasion or peer pressure rather than out of good will. This theory stems from debates concerning the reasons for conducting OCBs and whether or not they are truly voluntary in nature.

Jex & Britt offer three explanations as to why employees engage in organizational citizenship behaviour. One relates to positive affect; for example, an overall positive mood tends to change the frequency of helping behaviour to a higher rate. This theory stems from a history of numerous studies indicating that positive mood increases the frequency of helping and prosocial behaviours.

A second explanation, which stems from equity theory, is that employees reciprocate fair treatment that they received from the organization. Equity theory researchers found that certain forms of fairness or justice predict OCB better than others. For example, Jex & Britt mention research that indicates that interactional justice is a better predictor than procedural justice, which is in turn a better predictor than distributive justice.

A third explanation Jex & Britt offer is that, on the one hand, some employees hold personal values that tend to skew their behaviour positively to participate in organizational citizenship activities. On the other hand, Jex & Britt's interpretation of research results suggest that other employees will tend to perform organizational citizenship behaviour merely to influence how they are viewed within the organization, not because it reflects their personally held values. While these behaviours are not formally part of the job description, performing them can certainly influence performance appraisals. In contrast to this view, some I–O psychologists believe that employees engage in OCBs as a form of "impression management," a term coined by Erving Goffman in his 1959 book The Presentation of Self in Everyday Life. Goffman defines impression management as "the way in which the individual ... presents himself and his activity to others, the ways in which he guides and controls the impression they form of him, and the kinds of things he may and may not do while sustaining his performance before them." Researchers such as Bolino have hypothesized that the act of performing OCBs is not done out of goodwill, positive affect, etc., but instead as a way of being noticed by superiors and looking good in the eyes of others. The key difference between this view and those mentioned by Jex & Britt is that the intended beneficiary of the behaviour is the individual who engages in it, rather than another individual, the organization, or the supervisor.

With this research on why employees engage in OCBs comes the debate among I–O psychologists about the voluntary or involuntary nature of engaging in OCBs. Many researchers, including the "father of OCB research," Dennis Organ have consistently portrayed OCBs as voluntary behaviours done at the discretion of the individual. However, more recently researchers have brought attention to potential underlying causes of OCBs, including social pressure, coercion, and other external forces. For example, Eran Vigoda-Gadot suggests that some, but not all, OCBs may be performed voluntarily out of goodwill, but many may be more involuntary in nature and "may arise from coercive managerial strategies or coercive social pressure by powerful peers." As mentioned previously, Vigoda-Gadot categorizes these behaviours in a separate category of OCBs as "compulsory OCBs" or CCBs, which he suggests are a form of "abusive supervision" and will result in poorer organizational performance, similar to what has been seen in other research on abusive supervision and coercive persuasion.

Innovation

Industrial and Organizational Psychologists consider Innovation, more often than not, a variable of less importance and often a counter-productive one to include in conducting job performance appraisals when irrelevant to the major job functions for which a given job exists. Nonetheless, Industrial and Organizational Psychologists see the value of that variable where its consideration would, were its reliability and validity questioned, achieve a statisticly significant probability that its results are not due to chance, and that it can be replicated reliably with a statisticly significant ratio of reliability, and that was a court to raise a question on its reliability and validity testing, the Industrial and Organizational Psychologist behind its use would be able to defend it before a court of justice with the belief that it will stand before such a court as reliable, and valid.

With the above in mind, Innovation is often considered a form of productive behaviour that employees exhibit when they come up with novel ideas that further the goals of the organization. Innovation is a form of productive behaviour that employees exhibit when they come up with novel ideas that further the goals of the organization. This section will discuss three topics of interest: research on innovation; characteristics of an individual that may predict innovation; and how organizations may be structured to promote innovation. According to Jex & Britt, individual and organization research can be divided into four unique research focuses.

- Focus One: The examination of the process by which an employee develops innovations and the unique characteristics of an individuals which enables them to be highly innovative. This stream of thought focuses primarily on the employee or the individual contributor.
- Focus Two: The macro perspective which focuses upon the process that innovation is diffused within a specific organization. In short, this is the process of communicating an innovation to members of an organization.
- Focus Three: The process by which an organization adopts an innovation.
- Focus Four: A shared perspective of the role of the individual and the organization's culture which contribute to innovation.

As indicated above, the first focus looks specifically to find certain attributes of an individual that may lead to innovation, therefore, one must ask, "Are there quantifiable predictors that an individual will be innovative?" Research indicates if various skills, knowledge, and abilities are present then an individual will be more apt to innovation. These qualities are generally linked to creativity. A brief overview of these characteristics are listed below.

- Task-relevant skills (general mental ability and job specific knowledge). Task specific and subject specific knowledge is most often gained through higher education; however, it may also be gained by mentoring and experience in a given field.

- Creativity-relevant skills (ability to concentrate on a problem for long periods of time, to abandon unproductive searches, and to temporarily put aside stubborn problems). The ability to put aside stubborn problems is referred to by Jex & Britt as productive forgetting. Creativity-relevant skills also require the individual contributor to evaluate a problem from multiple vantage points. One must be able to take on the perspective of various users. For example, an Operation Manager analyzing a reporting issue and developing an innovative solution would consider the perspective of a sales person, assistant, finance, compensation, and compliance officer.
- Task motivation (internal desire to perform task and level of enjoyment).

In addition to the role and characteristics of the individual, one must consider what it is that may be done on an organizational level to develop and reward innovation. A study by Damanpour identified four specific characteristics that may predict innovation within an organization. They are the following ones:

1. A population with high levels of technical knowledge
2. The organization's level of specialization
3. The level an organization communicates externally
4. Functional Differentiation.

Additionally, organizations could use and institutionalize many participatory system-processes, which could breed innovation in the workplace. Some of these items include providing creativity training, having leaders encourage and model innovation, allowing employees to question current procedures and rules, seeing that the implementation of innovations had real consequences, documenting innovations in a professional manner, allowing employees to have autonomy and freedom in their job roles, reducing the number of obstacles that may be in the way of innovation, and giving employees access to resources (whether these are monetary, informational, or access to key people inside or outside of the organization).

According to the American Productivity & Quality Centre ("APQC") there are basic principles an organization can develop to encourage and reward innovation.

- The creation of a design team.
- Acknowledging those who contribute time, effort, and ideas. This recognition may come from senior leaders or through peer recognition.

- Provide special recognition to innovators while keeping names associated with contributors.
- Disseminate success stories concerning invention.
- Make innovation self-rewarding, such as the perception of being a subject matter expert.
- Linking innovation to the cultural values of the organization.
- Creating a committee of business leaders from various lines of business and human resources focused on developing guidelines and suggestions to encourage

innovation.

In discussing innovation for a Best-Practice report, APQC Knowledge Management expert, Kimberly Lopez, stated, "It requires a blending of creativity within business processes to ensure good ideas become of value to the company ... Supporting a creative environment requires innovation to be recognized, nurtured, and rewarded."

Counterproductive Work Behaviour

Counterproductive work behaviour can be defined as employee behaviour that goes against the goals of an organization. These behaviours can be intentional or unintentional and result from a wide range of underlying causes and motivations. It has been proposed that a person-by-environment interaction can be utilized to explain a variety of counterproductive behaviours (Fox and Spector, 1999). For instance, an employee who steals from the company may do so because of lax supervision (environment) and underlying psychopathology (person) that work in concert to result in the counterproductive behaviour.

The forms of counterproductive behaviour with the most empirical examination are ineffective job performance, absenteeism, job turnover, and accidents. Less common but potentially more detrimental forms of counterproductive behaviour have also been investigated including theft, violence, substance use, and sexual harassment.

Leadership

In I-O psychology, leadership can be defined as a process of influencing others to agree on a shared purpose, and to work towards shared objectives. A distinction should be made between leadership and management. Managers process administrative tasks and organize work environments. Although leaders may be required to undertake managerial duties as well, leaders typically focus on inspiring followers and creating a shared organizational culture and values. Managers deal with complexity, while leaders deal with initiating and adapting to change. Managers undertake the tasks of planning, budgeting, organizing, staffing, controlling and problem solving. In contrast, leaders undertake the tasks of setting a direction or vision, aligning people to shared goals, communicating, and motivating.

Approaches to studying leadership in I-O psychology can be broadly classified into three categories: Leader-focused approaches, Contingency-focused approaches, and Follower-focused approaches.

Leader-focused Approaches

Leader-focused approaches look to organizational leaders to determine the characteristics of effective leadership. According to the trait approach, more effective leaders possess certain traits that less effective leaders lack. More recently, this approach is being used to predict leader emergence. The following traits have been identified as those that predict leader emergence when there is no formal leader: high intelligence, high needs for dominance, high self-motivation, and socially perceptive. Another leader-focused approached is the behavioural approach which focuses on the behaviours that distinguish effective from ineffective leaders. There are two categories of leadership behaviours: (1) consideration; and (2) initiating structure. Behaviours associated with the category of consideration include showing subordinates they are valued and that the leader cares about them. An example of a consideration behaviour is showing compassion when problems arise in or out of the office. Behaviours associated with the category of initiating structure include facilitating the task performance of groups. One example of an initiating structure behaviour is meeting one-on-one with subordinates to explain expectations and goals. The final leader-focused approach is power and influence. To be most effective a leader should be able to influence others to behave in ways that are in line with the organization's mission and goals. How influential a leader can be depends on their social power or their potential to influence their subordinates. There are six bases of power: coercive power, reward power, legitimate power, expert power, referent power, and informational power. A leader can use several different tactics to influence others within an organization. These common tactics include: rational persuasion, inspirational appeal, consultation, ingratiation, exchange, personal appeal, coalition, legitimating, and pressure.

Contingency-focused Approaches

Of the 3 approaches to leadership, contingency-focused approaches have been the most prevalent over the past 30 years. Contingency-focused theories base a leader's effectiveness on their ability to assess a situation and adapt their behaviour accordingly. These theories assume that an effective leader can accurately "read" a situation and skillfully employ a leadership style that meets the needs of the individuals involved and the task at hand. A brief introduction to the most prominent contingency-focused theories will follow.

Fiedler's Contingency Theory holds that a leader's effectiveness depends on the interaction between their characteristics and the characteristics of the situation. Path–Goal Theory asserts that the role of the leader is to help his or her subordinates achieve their goals. To effectively do this, leaders must skillfully select from four different leadership styles to meet the situational factors. The situational factors are a product of the characteristics of subordinates and the characteristics of the environment. The Leader-Member Exchange (LMX) Model focuses on how leader–subordinate relationships develop. Generally speaking, when a subordinate performs well or when there are positive exchanges between a leader and a subordinate, their relationship is strengthened, performance and job satisfaction are enhanced, and the subordinate will feel more commitment to the leader and the organization as a whole. Vroom-Yetton-Jago Model focuses on decision making with respect to a feasibility set which is composed of the situational attributes.

In addition to the contingency-focused approaches mentioned, there has been a high degree of interest paid to three novel approaches that have recently emerged. The first is transformational leadership, which posits that there are certain leadership traits that inspire subordinates to perform beyond their capabilities. The second is transactional leadership, which is most concerned with keeping subordinates in-line with deadlines and organizational policy. This type of leader fills more of a managerial role and lacks qualities necessary to inspire subordinates and induce meaningful change. And the third is authentic leadership which is centred around empathy and a leader's values or character. If the leader understands their followers, they can inspire subordinates by cultivating a personal connection and leading them to share in the vision and goals of the team. Although there has been a limited amount of research conducted on these theories, they are sure to receive continued attention as the field of I–O psychology matures.

Follower-focused Approaches

Follower-focused approaches look at the processes by which leaders motivate followers, and lead teams to achieve shared goals.

Understandably, the area of leadership motivation draws heavily from the abundant research literature in the domain of motivation in I–O psychology. Because leaders are held responsible for their followers' ability to achieve the organization's goals, their ability to motivate their followers is a critical factor of leadership effectiveness. Similarly, the area of team leadership draws heavily from the research in teams and team effectiveness in I–O psychology. Because organizational employees are frequently structured in the form of teams, leaders need to be aware of the potential benefits and pitfalls of working in teams, how teams develop, how to satisfy team members' needs, and ultimately how to bring about team effectiveness and performance. An emerging area of research in the area of team leadership is in leading virtual teams, where people in the team are geographically-distributed across various distances and sometimes even countries. While technological advances have enabled the leadership process to take place in such virtual contexts, they present new challenges for leaders as well, such as the need to use technology to build relationships with followers, and influencing followers when faced with limited (or no) face-to-face interaction.

Organizational Change/development

Organizational Development

Industrial-organizational psychologists have displayed a great deal of consideration for the problems of total organizational change and systematic ways to bring about planned change. This effort, called organizational development (OD), involves techniques such as:

- sensitivity training
- role playing
- group discussion
- job enrichment
- survey feedback
- team building

Within the survey feedback technique, surveys after being answered by employees periodically, are assessed for their emotions and attitudes which are then communicated to various members within the organization. The team building technique was created due to realization that most tasks within the organization are completed by small groups and/or teams. In order to further enhance a team's or group's morale and problem-solving skills, OD consultants (called change agents) help the groups to build their self-confidence, group cohesiveness, and working effectiveness. A change agent's impartiality, gives the managers within the organization a new outlook of the organization's structure, functions, and culture. A change agent's first task is diagnosis, where questionnaires and interviews are used to assess the problems and needs of the organization. Once analyzed, the strengths and weaknesses of the organization are presented and used to create strategies for solving problems and coping with future changes.

Flexibility and adaptability are some strengths of the OD process, as it possesses the ability to conform to the needs of the situation. Regardless of the specific techniques applied, the OD process helps to free the typical bureaucratic organization from its rigidity and formality, hereby allowing more responsiveness and open participation. Public and private organizations both have employed OD techniques, despite their varied results in research conducted. However, the use of the techniques are justified by the significant increases in productivity that was proven by various studies.

Occupational Health and Wellbeing

The psychology of occupational health involves variables such as work schedules (eg. night shifts), work/family conflict, workplace violence, burnout, and their effect on worker physical and psychological health and the control of conditions such as depression and cardiovascular disease. Increasingly I/O psychology is focusing on improving and maintaining employee health and wellbeing with interventions targeted at both the individual and organisational level.

Relationship to Occupational Health Psychology

A separate but related discipline, occupational health psychology (OHP) is a relatively new field that combines elements of industrial–organizational psychology, health psychology, and occupational health. The primary emphasis in OHP is on the physical and mental health and psychological well-being of the person.

Learning and Training

Learning is a natural process, whereas training is a managed or engineered process. The words 'managed' and 'engineered' emphasize that training is effective to a greater or lesser extent by virtue of what a person in control of that training –who might be called a training officer, an instructor, a supervisor or a manager–does to ensure that the conditions that the learner experiences are suitable to enable learning to occur.

Trainees learn when these conditions are appropriate. Training is concerned with manipulating those conditions. This does not mean that in order to train it is necessary to understand how people learn in any scientific sense. Music teachers, driving instructors and parents are often successful in helping others to learn without possessing knowledge of the psychology of learning.

Psychologists have played a significant role over the years in identifying what needs to be learned by trainees, effective conditions for learning and how learning can be evaluated. Some people dismiss learning theory as too theoretical and as having no relevance to the practicalities of training. However, a theoretical understanding of learning can help in generating training hypotheses in order to deal with less familiar problems. So, it is useful to be acquainted with learning theory even though it would be naive to extrapolate from learning to training without extreme caution.

Hypotheses in Training

Despite this link between learning and training, there is a risk in assuming that learning principles established in one context will apply to another context. Work situations vary enormously. Most settings for occupational tasks are unique and will involve factors that were not taken into account during earlier learning research. Therefore, it is by no means certain that a person would learn to do something novel according to the same principles that applied

in situations that were researched previously. This means that when we apply learning ideas to a training situation, we cannot logically know for certain how things will turn out –so we are dealing with training hypotheses. Careful examination of tasks and behaviour, followed by the application of training principles will get us closer to a useful solution, but we cannot know for certain how things will turn out until they have been tried. This is no different from any other design activity and should not be a cause for concern. This is why evaluation of training methods is an important issue and an application of methods from psychology can play an important role in organisations in this respect.

Development

A word commonly encountered in organisations, especially in conjunction with management, is 'development'. The operational definition of training above applies equally to that of development, although the word development has nuances that need to be appreciated by people applying occupational psychology in practice. Development is used in the occupational setting to imply a longer term and more durable change to the behaviour of the individual. It is often used in preference to the word training in the context of management development or staff development to imply processes that change the individual's capability to deal with events in the future in a more flexible and profound way than merely replicating standard pieces of behaviour.

In a development programme we would aim for a person to be able to deal effectively with circumstances that had not been anticipated. Such capability entails less tangible aspects of performance such as attitudes, perceptions, judgements, diagnosis, insights, discretion and flexibility.

Development may be used to describe programmes to enhance a manager's capability to accommodate wider issues in decision making, such as gender, diversity and racial issues, health and safety, leadership, team dynamics, and the need for better monitoring, quantification of production, human factors, human resource management issues, and so on. Management skills often cannot be judged against a defined 'standard' by any explicit formal measurement and often have to be judged by someone suitably experienced in the tasks themselves. So, a manager responsible for the development of a junior colleague might judge that that the colleague being developed is working appropriately in the given circumstances with respect to providing fair and effective leadership to a team, rather than simply saying that the new colleague knows about diversity issues and how good leadership affects the performance of team members.

Development is generally something that is supervised in the context of the real job where the person being developed is required to confront real issues. The word 'coaching' is often preferred to 'instruction' in these situations.

Despite the fact that the word development is often preferred in specific domains which may favour different training methods and different assessment methods, it is important to recognize that the purpose of development complies with the purpose of training as described above.

Contrasts between 'training' and 'development'Preference in adopting the word training or development is not always consistent. Mastery of specific skills is often labelled training, while the processes of learning to handle less tangible judgements may be labelled development. There are other nuances.

Training, while learning to deal with people is often regarded as development. This might reflect the fact that the functioning of equipment and technology is often reasonably predictable, whereas the behaviour of people is not.

Such distinctions can be misleading. Tasks such as controlling a nuclear power plant are often specified in advance by an engineer and these tasks are certainly concerned with interacting with equipment. Tight specification is necessary because such plant needs to be controlled in a particular way to avoid production and safety problems. Because the actions are prescribed, it is sometimes assumed that this sort of skill is straightforward and so teaching it is often referred to as training. This is misleading, because while much of the task can be prescribed, industrial processes do not necessarily function in a wholly predictable fashion. The characteristics of materials change, equipment may not respond according to design, colleagues may make mistakes that have to be taken into account, other events suddenly take precedence and the standard operation may need to be modified. The task will be carried out under the conditions of stress, including the fear of making serious mistakes. While there might be an initial well-structured set of learning objectives and activities that might be referred to as training, there needs to be a later phase of gaining experience onjob, to adapt the learning gained from initial training to cope with the variety of things that can happen in reality. To include off-job training and neglect development in this situation would be bad training practice.

Equally, while for a manager learning to weigh factors in order to determine how to allocate resources requires a period of development, a new manager may well benefit from training concerning the factors that need to be taken into account. This taught element might include systematic and focused training on maintenance requirements, equipment functionality, equipment reliability, and the importance of human resource management in considering flexible ways of operating. Supervisors and managers of air traffic systems need to understand the dynamics and rules of air traffic management, before they can properly oversee operational teams employed to make air transport safe. To concentrate on development and neglect specific

Training in These Contexts would, Therefore, also be Poor Practice

The distinction between training and development made in this section are really just different stages or methods in the process of helping someone to learn to be competent and effective at their job. To train someone to do a job skillfully, reliably and with confidence, whether manager or operative, invariably entails a range of phases and learning activities. This includes teaching basic skills and knowledge in the classroom; providing opportunity to practise in a safe environment; providing opportunities to work closely under the guidance of an experienced colleague; providing the person being trained with opportunities for independent work where the trainee can call on or review progress with an experienced colleague; or encouraging group working where team members can learn to work together and help one another overcome difficulties and adapt to the norms of the group.

Products and Processes of Training

Behind much of what has been discussed so far is the distinction between the product of training and the processes of training.

The product of training refers to the outcome of a training intervention.

Training will be undertaken to teach new capabilities or to improve performance in order to serve the interests of the organisation –to improve productivity, flexibility, accuracy, trainability, attitude, response, good practices, reliability and so on. It is to ensure or improve whatever aspect of performance the organisation values. The resultant performance in the context of work demands is the product of that training.

The processes of training refer to the things that are done in order to attain this training product. This means the conditions that are specified in order to ensure that a person being trained learns what is required and to the required standard. The processes of training will expose the trainee to a number of different methods before competency can be assumed.

Two Perspectives for Training in Occupational Psychology

There are two important strands to the topic of training and development of which we must be aware. These are the human factors strand and the human resource management strand, although this labelling may not be acknowledged widely.

Strand 1: Human Factors (HF)

The HF strand addresses the conditions within a situation that describe how people learn new material and the processes underpinning learning. If these things are understood, then it becomes easier to provide conditions that will help people master new skills and capabilities. These HF issues had their roots in experimental and social Psychology and where basic studies of learning and social interaction established rudimentary concepts and paradigms that could also provide insights for dealing with more complex material. Later, this area was characterized as cognitive psychology with the aim of helping better to understand the complexities of skills in terms of cognitive structures and processes.

This HF strand is concerned with judgements about how best to present the conditions to the person being trained to lead them to master a task, skill or competency. It would be wrong to imply that experimental and cognitive psychology provide all of the answers to practical training issues, but learning is a psychological issue and identifying conditions for learning is an important part of training design and development with roots in occupational psychology. When people are required to master complex ideas and novel skills, applying principles of applied cognitive psychology often provides a way forward.

Strand 2: Human Resource Management (HRM)

The other main strand to the psychology of training concerns how an organisation manages its processes and resources to ensure that training is appropriate to requirements and is delivered effectively. People within the organisation must support training in different ways and so there is a need to manage training as a key part of personnel management or human resource management. HRM has addressed the requirement to deal with the need to train people, who are short of the skills required to do the jobs and to develop people for their future role in the organisation, in a pragmatic way.

This HRM strand is concerned with how people are allocated responsibilities regarding training and how these responsibilities are enshrined within their job descriptions.

Linking the Strands

It would be fair to say that the human resource management (HRM) perspective dominates how training is managed in organisations. However, in the absence of insights gained through the human factors (HF) perspective, the host organisation may not be able to deal most effectively with some of the more complex challenges it faces. The two strands are linked within occupational psychology. By linking these two strands, training requirements are examined in terms of identifying the conditions best suited to enable learning to take place.

Then the resources necessary to provide these training conditions can be addressed and provided through the processes of HRM.

The predominance of the HRM strand in organisations means that some training is less effective than it otherwise would be, because it under-emphasizes aspects of skilled performance. In many cases, the HF strand is only really in evidence when someone working within an HRM framework or from a managerial perspective acknowledges that present provision in the organisation is not having the required effect. Training may be well managed, but if the conditions for learning are not well thought out, then it will be less effective. There is a role for a specialist who can provide more suitable solutions to training problems. For example, complex cognitive tasks are difficult to master simply through basic instruction and experience, no matter how well the basics are taught and the development managed. A specialist approach might indicate that simulation training is required to provide the practice required to master skills.

These two strands and how they are linked need to be understood in an appropriate application of occupational psychology. An intervention will be less effective should either of these strands be neglected.

Making Training decisions in a systematic way When we consider the conditions in which work is undertaken, it becomes clear that our knowledge about human behaviour in different work situations is limited. We must appreciate that ideas that worked in one context must be applied with caution in other contexts. Logically, we are always left with hypotheses (as discussed earlier) that need to be applied and tested. Working systematically in a principled way is the best that can be achieved with respect to identifying training needs and developing training design solutions. But we must also always evaluate the outcome of training to establish whether it was effective, then modify it accordingly. Evaluation also leads to improving the principles and methods to guide training decisions.

Instigating Training and Development

There are a number of reasons why an organisation might consider training its staff.

These include:

- Preparing new staff for their jobs.
- Dealing with redesign of working practices and other changes to the organisation, including emerging safety and productivity issues.

- Preparing staff for dealing with new product lines and services.
- Adapting to new equipment.
- Responding to incidents.
- Maintaining skill levels and general staff development.
- Developing staff including preparing staff for advancement and promotion.
- Preparing staff for retirement and redundancy.
- Helping to resolve organisational problems.

Identifying Training Needs

When the need for training has been instigated, it is necessary to establish who needs training and the behaviours to be mastered.

Training Needs Analysis

(TNA) examines where and what training is required in an organisation. TNA is often discussed as though it were a commonly accepted technique, so it is ad visable to be cautious about what a client means when they refer simply to 'TNA'. It could refer to what individuals need to learn. Or it could refer to what an organisation requires in terms of manning –i.e. how many people need to learn things.

It could refer to identifying those aspects of jobs that need to be trained as opposed to aspects that entail a redesign of an interface, the job or the team configuration. It could refer to several of these decisions.

If asked to conduct a TNA, it would be necessary to establish what the client actually wants, then follow this with an examination of who needs training and what this training should seek to achieve.

Task analysis methods are important for this. These methods were developed within occupational psychology to ensure that what is trained is what is required. This is one of the most important areas in the psychology of training. If performance requirements are not identified, then training judgements may be inappropriate.

Task analysis is also important because it helps the trainer to engage with the client and the client's agents. Establishing training content entails making technical judgements about the nature of tasks. Left to their own devices, training specialists cannot deal appropriately with these decisions because they do not have direct knowledge or experience of the jobs that they are examining, nor the responsibility for how they are carried out. It is important to master methods that engage with subject matter experts in order to establish what is involved in a job, and with managers who are responsible for specifying training objectives in the form of capabilities, performance standards and priorities.

It is important to be systematic and listen carefully to managers and subject matter experts. Through this process, managers and subject matter experts often come to realise that there are aspects of their system that they do not themselves properly understand. Helping the client realize these things is often a very useful byproduct of a training intervention and helps gain the client's commitment to the present work and credibility for further work.

The purpose of training should be made clear as soon as possible and task analysis helps us to do this. A training objective is a statement of what a person or group should be able to do and the standards they should be able to achieve.

For a more complete training objective, we need to take a step further and specify a standard of performance. For example, we might need to specify

- How quickly a person must carry out their task,
- How much resource is expended in carrying out the task and
- What pattern of errors can be tolerated.

Armed with this information, we have a training objective from which to specify training content, method and media, and establish the basis for assessing the quality of performance deriving from that training.

Designing Instructional Activities

When training content has been identified, we must address how training should be conducted in order to meet the identified training needs. This entails making decisions about what information should be provided to the trainee and how it should be delivered. Training design generally requires four issues to be dealt with.

Designing training processes and designing the training media and resources have to be done in conjunction with one another, because the choices made in one generally affect the choices made in the other. Then it is necessary to decide how to fit the bits of training together within a training programme. Then, the whole programme needs to be evaluated to ensure that it will serve the required purpose.

a. Designing training processes includes making judgements about any basic knowledge and concepts that a trainee would benefit from when acquiring new competencies and the sorts of practice the trainee would benefit from in order to develop practical work related skills.

b. Designing training media and resources entails making decisions concerned with how the training processes in (a) will actually be delivered. There are many forms of media that could, in principle, be used to deliver training, including: classrooms, the real work situation, audio-visual equipment, face-to-face communication, computer-based learning, simulators, work groups. Training also requires that people with sufficient expertise are able to facilitate these processes, including training analysts, training designers, instructors, assessors and mentors.

In judging training media, it is important to think about the psychological issues affecting learning. However, it is also important to recognize that choices made have cost implications. It makes no sense for occupational psychologists to prescribe methods that are not cost-effective in terms of what the organisation is trying to achieve.

On the other hand, it makes no sense for managers to make costs paramount and, thereby, destroy any training benefit. Often the OP must confront the client who is excessively concerned with minimizing costs whilst still expecting to obtain satisfactory training benefit.

c. Prescribing the training programme deals with determining the order in which different training events are scheduled in order to obtain the required training benefits.

Invariably, several things need to be taught and it is likely that these are best done in a sensible order, so that later material can build on earlier material. For example, in hazardous tasks, it makes sense first to train people how to take safety precautions, respond to accidents and evacuate the premises. Then attention can be directed towards learning how to do the job.

d. Evaluating the training programme is concerned whether the plans for providing training actually work as intended. That is, if trainees are exposed to the prescribed set of learning activities, presented using the specified training media will they then be able to do what they are required to do?

A training programme can be defined as any prescription that is imposed on:

- The order in which training is delivered
- The amount of training given at any stage before moving on

- The learning that has to be demonstrated before progressing
- The amount of material that has to be mastered before the training programme can be said to be complete.

Training programmes are generally carefully thought through and written down.

Training programmes can be flexible to take into account the progress the learner is making, the learner's preferences in how to learn, the trainer's judgements and the availability of events that present opportunities for learning.

In addition to assessing aspects of progress of individual trainees, it is important to evaluate an overall training programme to determine whether it fulfils or continues to fulfil its intended purpose and whether the training is cost -effective. It is pointless to persist with training methods that are not effective. There needs to be a means of judging whether investment in training is affecting performance at the job in the required manner and to identify how training should be modified.

When we are discussing training we have to discuss separately, for the purpose of clarity, many things that need to be considered together. This risks losing sight of how these things should be integrated. So, when reading the various units in this module, you must keep in mind the whole picture and remember that many of these issues need to be understood with reference to each other. Also, coursework will require you to address how these things link together. The experience you gain in practice will help you further to understand these interactions.

Delivering Training Programmes

While occupational psychology may have been involved substantially in the analysis and design of training, training delivery is the responsibility of management and may not entail any direct psychological input. Usually, training is delivered and controlled by people with actual work experience and responsibilities, for example, line-managers, supervisors and specialist skills instructors. So, a further constraint on prescribing training methods is the need to anticipate the people who will be responsible for delivering them.

Assessing and Accrediting Trainees

There are several reasons for assessing the achievement of trainees.

First, some instruction programmes are designed to enable the trainee to progress according to how effectively they are mastering material. It means that assessment of some kind will continue informally throughout any instructional programme.

Second, as a training programme or parts of a training programme are completed, it may be necessary to assess what trainees have achieved, with a view to allowing them to progress to a later training module or graduate to a full job within the organisation.

This is generally a more formal stage of assessment.

Third, some assessment is aimed at providing a qualification to attest to a person's competence. This can be to satisfy a regulating authority to demonstrate that a person is qualified to undertake certain forms of work. Qualifications are also useful to the person moving from job to job.

Managing Training

Training management within an organisation entails ensuring that all processes described are properly managed to ensure that resources are available to deliver training –qualified staff, equipment, time, trainees –and that all of the stages in the training system are properly delivered in a safe and orderly manner.

A particular difficulty in understanding training management is that there is a wide range of choices available for how training is organised. Some large organisations employ specialist trainers and full-time instructors in specialist management development and operations training departments. At the other extreme operational staff members may take on these responsibilities. There may be no specialist trainers at all, but training may still be discharged effectively.

Training as a Function

In view of these variations, it is helpful to view training within organisations in functional terms. This emphasizes that training is something that must be delivered, irrespective of whether there is a person or department explicitly responsible for it.

To judge whether training provision is appropriate, one must address how the various training management and delivery functions are fulfilled.

The Systems Approach to Training

The systems approach to training is a long-standing idea that has been very influential in the training world for nearly 50 years.

Using Terminology Appropriately

Earlier we discussed definitions of training and learning. We return to this theme now to emphasize the importance of trying to understand how various terms are used in practice within any organisation in which one is working. If we are outsiders, we cannot be prescriptive about how other people use terminology and labels. We must try to translate local usage into functional descriptions that we can work with, then translate outcomes back to match the language that clients understand. Life can get confusing when visiting different organisations, so the importance of thinking about aspects of training in a functional way cannot be overemphasized.

To illustrate these potential confusions further, consider the following:

- A person receiving training is often called a 'trainee'. But sometimes, this person is called the 'learner'.
- Doing something with the intention of helping another person to learn something is called 'training', but it might also be called 'development' or 'instruction'.
- The word 'instruction' often refers to the processes of someone in direct contact with the person they helping to learn; often instruction involves explaining something, arranging circumstances to enable the person learning to practise something or assessing what the person has learned.
- Often 'training' and 'instruction' are interchangeable.
- A person responsible for delivering training is called a 'trainer'. A person responsible for delivering instruction is called an 'instructor'. And since training and instruction are often the same thing, 'trainers' may be called 'instructors' and vice versa. In other contexts, the word 'coach' is preferred in order to emphasize the nature of the training or development that is taking place.
- Sometimes, the word 'development' is preferred to training. This may be because development is seen as an improvement to the whole person, while training is regarded as a relatively minor adjustment to the skills that a person is required to apply at some part of their job. Often 'development' is applied to managers who must acquire strategic and flexible skills related to dealing with complex situations, while training is seen as applying to operatives who are required to do specific things to

carry out their jobs. The processes of development might appear less tangible than those of training; 'development' is often seen as managing the acquisition of experience over a long period, whereas training might be regarded as something whose content is more prescribed and delivered in a more easily specified time-frame.

Some of this may sound a bit fuzzy –and it is. In fact, rereading it, it sounds more like a comedy routine, than anything more profound. This section has been included deliberately to expose you to the patterns of terminology that you are likely to encounter. When we work in organisations, we are not at liberty to define terms exactly as we would choose to use them, because there is a world that is already populated with people with different experiences and perspectives who have adopted different words to describe similar concepts. We just need to be flexible in relating how other people are using words to various training functions. We must show appropriate courtesy to people with whom we work to use words in a way that they will understand. But we still need to use our own concepts in a consistent way to discuss the disciplines of occupational psychology.

Exploration and Research in Designing Training

The hypothetical nature of training design and development means that training remains a research or exploratory activity. Dealing with novel training issues entails dealing with hypotheses. Every training intervention is an experiment of sorts that has then to be evaluated to determine whether it is appropriate.

The design phase of training entails deciding what to include and how to teach it.

Good task analysis and an understanding of training principles is the best way we know for getting as close as we can to a satisfactory outcome. But it remains our best guess.

Evaluation of training entails measuring what is achieved. This might be judged against a set standard or by comparison with an existing method or another competing training method.

In practice, training is rarely formally measured with rigour within organisations.

Managers are often satisfied for a trainer to make an informed guess at what should be provided –although neither party likes to admit that these decisions are informed guesses. Where possible it is appropriate to evaluate training formally and objectively in terms of what is learned and how it affects subsequent performance on the job. Sometimes, conditions do not allow objective evaluation of training, but it is still important that there are systems to enable some form of judgement to be made regarding the benefits of training and possible modification. This can be accomplished by incorporating the processes of training, from analysis, through design, to evaluation and review, into the routines of managing a department in an organisation.

Health Psychology

Health psychology is the study of psychological and behavioural processes in health, illness and healthcare. It is concerned with understanding how psychological, behavioural and cultural factors are involved in physical health and illness, in addition to the biological causes that are well understood by medical science. Psychological factors can affect health directly (such as stress causing the release of hormones such as cortisol which damage the body over time) and indirectly via a person's own behaviour choices which can harm or protect health (such as smoking or taking exercise). Health psychologists take a biopsychosocial approach - this means that they understand health to be the product not only of biological processes (e.g. a virus, tumour, etc.) but also of psychological processes (e.g. stress, thoughts and beliefs, behaviours such as smoking and exercise) and social processes (e.g. socioeconomic status, culture and ethnicity).

By understanding and harnessing psychological factors, health psychologists can improve health by working directly with individual patients, indirectly in large-scale public health programmes, and by training healthcare professionals (e.g. physicians and nurses) to take advantage of this knowledge when working with their patients. Health psychologists work in a variety of settings: alongside other medical professionals in hospitals and clinics, in public health departments working on large-scale behaviour change and health promotion programmes, and in universities and medical schools where they teach and conduct research.

Although its early beginnings can be traced to the kindred field of clinical psychology, four different divisions within health psychology and one allied field have developed over time. The four divisions include clinical health psychology, public health psychology, community health psychology, and critical health psychology. The allied field is occupational health psychology. Professional organizations for the field of health psychology include Division 38 of the American Psychological Association, the Division of Health Psychology of the British

Psychological Society, and the European Health Psychology Society. Advanced credentialing in the U.S. as a Clinical Health Psychologist is provided through the American Board of Professional Psychology.

Recent advances in psychological, medical, and physiological research have led to a new way of thinking about health and illness. This conceptualization, which has been labelled the biopsychosocial model, views health and illness as the product of a combination of factors including biological characteristics (e.g., genetic predisposition), behavioural factors (e.g., lifestyle, stress, health beliefs), and social conditions (e.g., cultural influences, family relationships, social support).

Psychologists who strive to understand how biological, behavioural, and social factors influence health and illness are called health psychologists.Health Psychologists use their knowledge of psychology and health to promote general well-being and understand physical illness. They are specially trained to help people deal with the psychological and emotional aspects of health and illness. The term "health psychology" is often used synonymously with the terms "behavioural medicine" and "medical psychology". Health psychologists work with many different health care professionals (e.g., physicians, dentists, nurses, physician's assistants, dietitians, social workers, pharmacists, physical and occupational therapists, and chaplains) to conduct research and provide clinical assessments and treatment services. Many health psychologists focus on prevention research and interventions designed to promote healthier lifestyles and try to find ways to encourage people to improve their health. For example, they may help people to lose weight or stop smoking. Health Psychologists also use their skills to try to improve the healthcare system. For example, they may advise doctors about better ways to communicate with their patients Health Psychologists work in many different settings including the NHS, private practice, universities, communities, schools and organisations. While many health psychologists provide clinical services as part of their duties, others function in non-clinical roles, primarily involving teaching and research. Leading journals include Health Psychology, the Journal of Health Psychology, the British Journal of Health Psychology, and Applied Psychology: Health and Well-Being. Health Psychologists can work with people on a one-to-one basis, in groups, as a family, or at a larger population level.

- Clinical health psychology (ClHP) is a term that refers to the application of scientific knowledge, derived from the field of health psychology, to clinical questions that may arise across the spectrum of health care. ClHP is one of many speciality practice area for clinical psychologists. It is also a major contributor to the prevention focused field of behavioural health and the treatment oriented field of behavioural medicine. Clinical practice includes education, the techniques of behaviour change, and psychotherapy. In some countries, a clinical health psychologist, with additional training, can become a medical psychologist and, thereby, obtain prescription privileges.

- Public health psychology (PHP) is population oriented. A major aim of PHP is to investigate potential causal links between psychosocial factors and health at the population level. Public health psychologists present research results to educators, policy makers, and health care providers in order to promote better public health. PHP is allied to other public health disciplines including epidemiology, nutrition, genetics and biostatistics. Some PHP interventions are targeted towards at-risk population groups (e.g., undereducated, single pregnant women who smoke) and not the population as a whole (e.g., all pregnant women).
- Community health psychology (CoHP) investigates community factors that contribute to the health and well-being of individuals who live in communities. CoHP also develops community-level interventions that are designed to combat disease and promote physical and mental health. The community often serves as the level of analysis, and is frequently sought as a partner in health-related interventions.
- Critical health psychology (CrHP) is concerned with the distribution of power and the impact of power differentials on health experience and behaviour, health care systems, and health policy. CrHP prioritizes social justice and the universal right to health for people of all races, genders, ages, and socioeconomic positions. A major concern is health inequalities. The critical health psychologist is an agent of change, not simply an analyst or cataloger. A leading organization in this area is the International Society of Critical Health Psychology.

Health psychology is both a theoretical and applied field. Health psychologists employ diverse research methods. These methods include controlled randomized experiments, quasi-experiments, longitudinal studies, time-series designs, cross-sectional studies, and case-control studies as well as action research. Health psychologists study a broad range of variables including genotype, cardiovascular disease (cardiac psychology), smoking habits, religious beliefs, alcohol use, social support, living conditions, emotional state, social class, and much more. Some health psychologists treat individuals with sleep problems, headaches, alcohol problems, etc. Other health psychologists work to empower community members by helping community members gain control over their health and improve quality of life of entire communities.

Origins and Development

Psychological factors in health had been studied since the early 20th century by disciplines such as psychosomatic medicine and later behavioural medicine, but these were primarily branches of medicine, not psychology. Health psychology began to emerge as a distinct discipline of psychology in the United States in the 1970s. In the mid-20th century there was a growing understanding in medicine of the effect of behaviour on health. For example, the Alameda County Study which began in the 1960s showed that people who ate regular meals (e.g. breakfast), maintained a healthy weight, received adequate sleep, did not smoke, drank little alcohol and exercise regularly were in better health and lived longer. At the same time, there was a growing realization of the importance of good communication skills in medical consultations. In addition, psychologists and other scientists were discovering relationships between psychological processes and physiological ones. These included the impact of stress on the cardiovascular and immune systems of the body, and the early finding that the functioning of the immune system could be altered by learning.

Psychologists had been working in medical settings for some years previously in several countries such as the UK (sometimes termed medical psychology). However it was a small field, primarily working with adjustment to illness, with psychological factors usually as (often emotional) reactions to illness. In 1969, William Schofield prepared a report for the American Psychological Association entitled The Role of Psychology in the Delivery of Health Services. While there were exceptions, he found that the psychological research of the time frequently saw mental health and physical health as entirely separate, and devoted very little attention to psychology's impact upon physical health. Of the psychologists working at the time, few were involved with this area, and he proposed that new forms of education and training for future psychologists would be needed. The APA reacted in 1973 by setting up a task force to consider how psychologists could help people to manage their health behaviours, as well as to better manage physical health problems and train healthcare staff to work most effectively with patients.

This set in train a series of events that led in 1977 to the formation of a division of the APA dedicated to health psychology, led by Joseph Matarazzo. At its first conference, Matarazzo gave a speech often seen as a foundation of health psychology, in which he defined the new field as "Health psychology is the aggregate of the specific educational, scientific and professional contributions of the discipline of psychology to the promotion and maintenance of health, the prevention and treatment of illness, the identification of diagnostic and etiologic correlates of health, illness and related dysfunction, and the analysis and improvement of the healthcare system and health policy formation". In the 1980s, similar organisations were set up in the UK as the British Psychological Society's Division of Health Psychology in 1986, and the European Health Psychology Society that same year. Similar organizations developed in other countries such as Australia and Japan. Training programmes were set up in these countries, usually training health psychologists at graduate level, and in the United States, at postdoctoral level after completing a doctoral degree in clinical psychology such as the PsyD or PhD. In addition, PhDs began to be awarded in health psychology. Today, health psychology is one of the most popular courses in undergraduate psychology degrees, as a choice for Masters degrees such as MSc, and as a career choice in psychology.

In hindsight, the emergence of Health Psychology could have been triggered by many different factors, such as the following:

- Emergence of epidemiological evidence demonstrating the important relationship between health and behaviour.
- Behavioural sciences were added to medical school's curriculum, and were often taught by psychologists.
- Health professionals began to receive training in communication skills, with the initial aim of improving patient satisfaction and adherence to medical treatment.
- Primary care became an emphasis for Clinical Psychology and interventions based on psychological theory were often applied.
- Behaviour modification and therapy based on theoretically based models demonstrated they could change behaviours and be useful in clinical populations.

- An increased understanding of the interaction between psychological and physiological factors led to the emergence of Psychophysiology and Psychoneuroimmunology (PNI).
- The health domain was frequently used by social psychologists for testing theoretical models, such as the links between beliefs, attitudes and behaviour
- In the early 1980s the diagnosis of AIDS/HIV led to and increase in funding for behavioural research and a focus on behaviour change.

In the United Kingdom, the British Psychological Society's reconsideration of the role of the Medical Section, prompted the emergence of Health Psychology as a distinct field. It was argued by Marie Johnston and John Weinman in a letter to the 'BPS Bulletin' that there was a great need for a Health Psychology Section, and in December 1986 the section was established at the BPS London Conference, with Marie Johnston as chair. At the Annual BPS Conference in 1993 a review of 'Current Trends in Health Psychology' was invited, and a definition of Health Psychology as 'the study of psychological and behavioural processes in health, illness and healthcare' was proposed. The Health Psychology Section became a Special Group in 1993 and was awarded Divisional Status within the UK in 1997. This meant that the individual training needs and professional practice of Health Psychologists were recognised, and members were able to obtain chartered status with the BPS. The BPS went on to regulate training and practice in Health Psychology until the regulation of professional standards and qualifications was taken over by statutory registration with the Health Professions Council in 2010.

Relationship to Occupational Health Psychology

Occupational health psychology (OHP), a separate but related discipline, is a relatively new field that emerged out of the confluence of health psychology, industrial/organizational psychology, and occupational health. The field is concerned with identifying psychosocial characteristics of workplaces that affect the health and well-being of people who work. OHP is also concerned with developing strategies to effect change at workplaces in order to improve the health of people who work.

Objectives of Health Psychology

Understanding Behavioural and Contextual Factors: Health psychologists conduct research to identify behaviours and experiences that promote health, give rise to illness, and influence the effectiveness of health care. They also recommend ways to improve health care and health-care policy. Health psychologists have worked on developing ways to reduce smoking and improve daily nutrition in order to promote health and prevent illness. They have also studied the association between illness and individual characteristics. For example, health psychology has found a relation between the personality characteristics of thrill seeking, impulsiveness, hostility/anger, emotional instability, and depression, on one hand, and high-risk driving, on the other.

Health psychology is also concerned with contextual factors, including economic, cultural, community, social, and lifestyle factors that influence health. The biopsychosocial model can help in understanding the relation between contextual factors and biology in affecting health. Physical addiction plays an important role in smoking cessation. Some research suggests that seductive advertising also contributes to psychological dependency on tobacco, although other research has found no relationship between media and smoking in youth. Research in occupational health psychology indicates that people in jobs that combine little decision latitude with a high psychological workload are at increased risk for cardiovascular disease. Other OHP research reveals a relation between unemployment and elevations in blood pressure. OHP research also documents a relation between social class and cardiovascular disease.

Health psychologists also aim to change health behaviours for the dual purpose of helping people stay healthy and helping patients adhere to disease treatment regimens. Health psychologists employ cognitive behaviour therapy and applied behaviour analysis for that purpose.

Preventing Illness

Health psychologists work towards promoting health through behavioural change, as mentioned above; however, they attempt to prevent illness in other ways as well. Health Psychologists try to help people to lead a healthy life by developing and running programmes which can help people to make changes in their lives such as stopping smoking,reducing the amount of alcohol they drink, eating more healthily,and taking regular exercise. Campaigns informed by health psychology have targeted tobacco use. Those least able to afford tobacco products consume them most. Tobacco provides individuals with a way of controlling aversive emotional states accompanying daily experiences of stress that characterize the lives of deprived and vulnerable individuals. Practitioners emphasize education and effective communication as a part of illness prevention because many people do not recognize, or minimize, the risk of illness present in their lives. Moreover, many individuals are often unable to apply their knowledge of health practices owing to everyday pressures and stresses. A common example of population-based attempts to motivate the smoking public to reduce its dependence on cigarettes is anti-smoking campaigns.

Health psychologists help to promote health and well-being by preventing illness. Some illnesses can be treated better if they are caught early.Health Psychologists have worked to understand why some people do not go for screening or immunisations and are finding ways to encourage people to have health checks for illnesses such as cancer or heart disease. Health Psychologists are also finding ways to try to help people to avoid risky behaviours that may affect their health and well-being, such as unprotected sex and can also help to encourage regular teeth brushing or hand washing to prevent future ill health.

Health psychologists also aim at educating health professionals, including physicians and nurses, in communicating effectively with patients in ways that overcome barriers to understanding, remembering, and implementing effective strategies for reducing exposures to risk factors and making health-enhancing behaviour changes.

There is also evidence from occupational health psychology that stress-reduction interventions at the workplace can be effective. For example, Kompier and his colleagues have shown that a number of interventions aimed at reducing stress in bus drivers has had beneficial effects for employees and bus companies.

The Effects of Disease

Health psychologists investigate how disease affects individuals' psychological well-being. An individual who becomes seriously ill or injured faces many different practical stressors. The stressors include problems meeting medical and other bills; problems obtaining proper care when home from the hospital; obstacles to caring for dependents; having one's sense of self-reliance compromised; gaining a new, unwanted identity as a sick person; and so on. These stressors can lead to depression, reduced self-esteem, etc.

Health psychology also concerns itself with bettering the lives of individuals with terminal illness. When there is little hope of recovery, health psychologist therapists can improve the quality of life of the patient by helping the patient recover at least some of his or her psychological well-being. Health psychologists are also concerned with identifying the best ways for providing therapeutic services for the bereaved.

Critical Analysis of Health Policy

Critical health psychologists explore how health policy can influence inequities, inequalities, and social injustice. These avenues of research expand the scope of health psychology beyond the level of individual health to an examination of the social and economic determinants of health both within and between regions and nations. The individualism of mainstream health psychology has been critiqued and deconstructed by critical health psychologists using newer qualitative methods and frameworks for investigating health experience and behaviour.

Conducting Research

Health Psychologists have advanced skills in a variety of research methods, which enables them to conduct research, provide expert advice or collaborate on a study, for example studying the links between stress and health. Health Psychologists carry out research to answer questions such as:

- What influences healthy eating?
- How is stress linked to heart disease?
- What are the emotional effects of genetic testing?
- How can we change people's health behaviour to improve their health?

Teaching and Communication

Health psychologists can also be responsible for training other health professionals, for example on how to deliver an intervention to help promote healthy eating or stopping smoking, or deliver training in communication skills such as how to break bad news, or support behaviour change. This can also enhance practitioner–patient relationships and adherence to treatment.

Applications of Health Psychology

Improving Doctor–patient Communication

Health psychologists attempt to aid the process of communication between physicians and patients during medical consultations. There are many problems in this process, with patients showing a considerable lack of understanding of many medical terms, particularly anatomical terms (e.g., intestines). One main area of research on this topic involves "doctor-centred" or "patient-centred" consultations. Doctor-centred consultations are generally directive, with the patient answering questions and playing less of a role in decision-making. Although this style is preferred by elderly people and others, many people dislike the sense of hierarchy or ignorance that it inspires. They prefer patient-centred consultations, which focus on the patient's needs, involve the doctor listening to the patient completely before making a decision, and involving the patient in the process of choosing treatment and finding a diagnosis.

Improving Adherence to Medical Advice

Getting people to follow medical advice and adhere to their treatment regimens is a difficult task for health psychologists. People often forget to take their pills or consciously opt not to take their prescribed medications because of side effects. Failing to take prescribed medication is costly and wastes millions of usable medicines that could otherwise help other people. Estimated adherence rates are difficult to measure; there is, however, evidence that adherence could be improved by tailoring treatment programmes to individuals' daily lives.

Ways of Measuring Adherence

Health psychologists have identified a number of ways of measuring patients' adherence to medical regimens:

- Counting the number of pills in the medicine bottle—although this has problems with privacy and/or could be deemed patronizing or showing lack of trust in patients
- Using self-reports—although patients may fail to return the self-report or lie about their adherence
- Asking a doctor or health worker—although this presents problems on doctor–patient confidentiality
- Using "Trackcap" bottles, which track the number of times the bottle is opened; however, this either raises problems of informed consent or, if informed consent is obtained, influence through demand characteristics.

Managing Pain

Health psychology attempts to find treatments to reduce and eliminate pain, as well as understand pain anomalies such as episodic analgesia, causalgia, neuralgia, and phantom limb pain. Although the task of measuring and describing pain has been problematic, the development of the McGill Pain Questionnaire has helped make progress in this area. Treatments for pain involve patient-administered analgesia, acupuncture (found by Berman to be effective in reducing pain for osteoarthritis of the knee), biofeedback, and cognitive behaviour therapy.

Health Psychologist Roles

Below are some examples of the types of positions held by Health Psychologists within applied settings such as the NHS and privatepractice.

- Consultant Health Psychologist: A Consultant Health Psychologist will take a lead for health psychology within public health, including managing tobacco control and smoking cessation services and providing professional leadership in the management of Health Trainers.
- Principal Health Psychologist: A Principal Health Psychologist could, for example lead the health psychology service within one of the UK's leading heart and lung hospitals, providing a clinical service to patients and advising all members of the multidisciplinary team.
- Health Psychologist: An example of a Health Psychologist's role would be to provide health psychology input to a centre for weight management. Psychological assessment of treatment,development and delivery of a tailored weight management programme, and advising on approaches to improve adherence tohealth advice and medical treatment.
- Research Psychologist: Research psychologists carry out health psychology research, for example exploring the psychological impact of receiving a diagnosis of dementia, or evaluating ways of providing psychological support for people with burn injuries. Research can also be in the area of health promotion, for example investigating the determinants of healthy eating or physical activity or understanding why people misuse substances.
- Health Psychologist in Training/Assistant Health Psychologist: As an Assistant/in training, a health psychologist will gain experience assessing patients, delivering psychological interventions to change health behaviours and conducting research, whilst being supervised by a qualified Health Psychologist.

Training in Health Psychology

In the United Kingdom, Health Psychologists are registered by the Health Professions Council (HPC) and have trained to a level to be eligible for full membership of the Division of Health Psychology within the British Psychological Society (BPS). Registered Health Psychologists who are chartered with the British Psychological Society (BPS) will have undertaken a minimum of six years of training and will have specialised in health psychology for a minimum of three years. Health Psychologists in training must have completed BPS stage 1 training and be registered with the BPS Stage 2 training route or with a BPS-accredited university doctoral Health Psychology programme. Once qualified, Health Psychologists can work in a range of settings, for example the NHS, universities, schools, private healthcare, research and charitable organisations. A Health Psychologist in training might be working within applied settings whilst working towards registration and chartered status. A Health Psychologist will have demonstrated competencies in all of the following areas:

- professional skills (including implementing ethical and legal standards, communication and team work),
- research skills (including designing, conducting and analysing psychological research in numerous areas),
- consultancy skills (including planning and evaluation),
- teaching and training skills (including knowledge of designing,delivering and evaluating large and small scale training programmes),
- intervention skills (including delivery and evaluation of behaviour change interventions).

All qualified Health Psychologists must also engage in and record their continuing professional development (CPD) for psychology each year throughout their career.

Counselling Psychology

Counselling psychology is a psychological speciality that encompasses research and applied work in several broad domains: counselling process and outcome; supervision and training; career development and counselling; and prevention and health. Some unifying themes among counselling psychologists include a focus on assets and strengths, person–environment interactions, educational and career development, brief interactions, and a focus on intact personalities. In the United States, the premier scholarly journals of the profession are the Journal of Counselling Psychology and The Counselling Psychologist.

In Europe, the scholarly journals of the profession include the European Journal of Counselling Psychology (under the auspices of the European Association of Counselling Psychology) and the Counselling Psychology Review (under the auspices of the British Psychological Society). Counselling Psychology Quarterly is an international interdisciplinary publication of Routledge (part of the Taylor & Francis Group).

In the U.S., counselling psychology programmes are accredited by the American Psychological Association (APA), while counselling programmes are accredited through the Counsel for Accreditation of Counselling and Related Educational Programmes (CACREP). To become licensed as a counselling psychologist, one must meet the criteria for licensure as a psychologist (4-7 year doctoral degree post-bachelors, 1 year full-time internship, including 3,000 hours of supervised experience and exams). Both doctoral level counselling psychologists and doctoral level counsellors can perform both applied work, as well as research and teaching.

Counselling psychology, like many modern psychology specialities, started as a result of World War II. During the war, the U.S. military had a strong need for vocational placement and training. In the 1940s and 1950s the Veterans Administration created a speciality called "counselling psychology," and Division 17 (now known as the Society for Counselling Psychology) of the APA was formed. This fostered interest in counsellor training, and the creation of the first few counselling psychology PhD programmes. The first counselling psychology PhD programmes were at the University of Minnesota; Ohio State University, University of Maryland, College Park; University of Missouri; Teachers College, Columbia University; and University of Texas at Austin.

Employment and Salary

Counselling psychologists are employed in a variety of settings depending on the services they provide and the client populations they serve. Some are employed in colleges and universities as teachers, supervisors, researchers, and service providers. Others are employed in independent practice providing counselling, psychotherapy; assessment; and consultation services to individuals, couples/families, groups, and organizations. Additional settings in which counselling psychologists practice include community mental health centres, Veterans Administration Medical Centres and other facilities, family services, health maintenance organizations, rehabilitation agencies, business and industrial organizations and consulting within firms.

Process and Outcome

Counselling psychologists are interested in answering a variety of research questions about the counselling process and outcome. Counselling process might be thought of as how or why counselling happens and progresses. Counselling outcome addresses whether or not counselling is effective, under what conditions it is effective, and what outcomes are considered effective—such as symptom reduction, behaviour change, or quality of life improvement. Topics commonly explored in the study of counselling process and outcome include therapist variables, client variables, the counselling or therapeutic relationship, cultural variables, process and outcome measurement, mechanisms of change, and process and outcome research methods.

Therapist Variables

Therapist variables include characteristics of a counsellor or psychotherapist, as well as therapist technique, behaviour, theoretical orientation and training. In terms of therapist behaviour, technique and theoretical orientation, research on adherence to therapy models has found that adherence to a particular model of therapy can be helpful, detrimental, or neutral in terms of impact on outcome (Imel & Wampold, 2008).

Research on the impact of training and experience is still somewhat contradictory and even counter-intuitive. For example, a recent study found that age-related training and experience, but not amount or quality of contact with older people, is related to older clients. However, a recent meta-analysis of research on training and experience suggests that experience level is only slightly related to accuracy in clinical judgement. Higher therapist experience has been found to be related to less anxiety, but also less focus. This suggests that there is still work to be done in terms of training clinicians and measuring successful training.

Client Variables

Client characteristics such as help-seeking attitudes and attachment style have been found to be related to client use of counselling, as well as expectations and outcome. Stigma against mental illness can keep people from acknowledging problems and seeking help. Public stigma has been found to be related to self-stigma, attitudes towards counselling, and willingness to seek help.

In terms of attachment style, clients with avoidant styles have been found to perceive greater risks and fewer benefits to counselling, and are less likely to seek professional help, than securely attached clients. Those with anxious attachment styles perceive greater benefits as well as risks to counselling. Educating clients about expectations of counselling can improve client satisfaction, treatment duration and outcomes, and is an efficient and cost-effective intervention.

Counselling Relationship

The relationship between a counsellor and client is the feelings and attitudes that a client and therapist have towards one another, and the manner in which those feelings and attitudes are expressed. The relationship may be thought of in three parts: transference/ countertransference, working alliance, and the real- or personal-relationship.

Transference can be described as the client's distorted perceptions of the therapist. This can have a great affect on the therapeutic relationship. For instance, the therapist may have a facial feature that reminds the client of their parent. Because of this association, if the client has significant negative/positive feelings towards their parent, they may project these feelings onto the therapist. This can affect the therapeutic relationship in a few ways. For example, if the client has a very strong bond with their parent, they may see the therapist as a father/mother figure and have a strong connection with their therapist. This can be problematic because as a therapist, it is not ethical to have a more than "professional" relationship with a client. It can also be a good thing, because the client may open up greatly to the therapist. In another way, if the client has a very negative relationship with their parent, the client may feel negative feelings towards the therapist. This can then affect the therapeutic relationship as well. For example, the client may have trouble opening up to the therapist because he/she lacks trust in their parent (projecting these feelings of distrust onto the therapist).

Another theory about the function of the counselling relationship is known as the secure-base hypothesis, which is related to attachment theory. This hypothesis proposes that the counsellor acts as a secure-base from which clients can explore and then check in with. Secure attachment to one's counsellor and secure attachment in general have been found to be related to client exploration. Insecure attachment styles have been found to be related to less session depth than securely attached clients.

Cultural Variables

Counselling psychologists are interested in how culture relates to help-seeking and counselling process and outcome. Helms' racial identity model can be useful for understanding how the relationship and counselling process might be affected by the client's and counsellor's racial identity. Recent research suggests that clients who are Black are at risk for experiencing racial micro-aggressions from counsellors who are White.

Efficacy for working with clients who are lesbians, gay men, or bisexual might be related to therapist demographics, gender, sexual identity development, sexual orientation, and professional experience. Clients who have multiple oppressed identities might be especially at-risk for experiencing unhelpful situations with counsellors, so counsellors might need help with gaining expertise for working with clients who are transgender, lesbian, gay, bisexual, or transgender people of colour, and other oppressed populations.

Gender role socialization can also present issues for clients and counsellors. Implications for practice include being aware of stereotypes and biases about male and female identity, roles and behaviour such as emotional expression. The APA guidelines for multicultural competence outline expectations for taking culture into account in practice and research.

Counselling Ethics

Perceptions on ethical behaviours vary depending upon geographical location. Although, ethical mandates are similar throughout our global community. The standard ethical behaviours are centred on "doing no harm" and preventing harm. As counsellors, it is standard that a counsellor should take appropriate action to prevent harm.

Ethical standards are similar in that you should shall not share information that is obtained through the counselling process without specific written consent by the client or legal guardian except to prevent clear, imminent danger to the client or others or when required to do so by a court order.

Counsellors are held to a higher standard that most professionals because of the intimacy of their therapeutic delivery. Counsellors are not only to avoid fraternizing with their clients. They should avoid dual relationships, and never engage in sexual relationships.

Counsellors are to avoid receiving gifts, favours, or trade for therapy. In some communities, it may be avoidable given the economic standing of that community. In cases of children, children and the mentally handicap may feel personally rejected "if" an offering is something such as a "cookie." As counsellors, a judgement call must be made, but in a majority of cases, avoiding gifts, favours, and trade can be maintained.

The National Board for Certified Counsellors states that "...important considerations to avoid exploitation before entering into a non-counselling relationship with a former client. Important considerations to be discussed include amount of time since counselling service termination, duration of counselling, nature and circumstances of client's counselling, the likelihood that the client will want to resume counselling at some time in the future; circumstances of service termination and possible negative effects or outcomes."

Ethical standards are created to help practitioners, clients and the community avoid any possible harm or potential for harm. Ethical standards are a guideline, but for specific standards they are mandates. Recognizing the differences is clear in a majority of organizational codes of ethics.

Outcome Measurement

Counselling outcome measures might look at a general overview of symptoms, symptoms of specific disorders, or positive outcomes, such as subjective well-being or quality of life. The Outcome Questionnaire-45 is a 45-item self-report measure of psychological distress. An example of disorder-specific measure is the Beck Depression Inventory. The Quality of Life Inventory is a 17-item self-report life satisfaction measure.

Process and Outcome Research Methods

Research about the counselling process and outcome uses a variety of research methodologies to answer questions about if, how, and why counselling works. Quantitative methods include randomly controlled clinical trials, correlational studies over the course of counselling, or laboratory studies about specific counselling process and outcome variables. Qualitative research methods can involve conducting, transcribing and coding interviews; transcribing and/or coding therapy sessions; or fine-grain analysis of single counselling sessions or counselling cases.

Training and Supervision

Professional Training Process: Counselling psychologists are trained in graduate programmes. Almost all programmes grant a PhD, but a few grant a MCouns, M.Ed, MA, PsyD or EdD. Most doctoral programmes take 5–6 years to complete. Graduate work in counselling psychology includes coursework in general psychology and statistics, counselling practice, and research. Students must complete an original dissertation at the end of their graduate training. Students must also complete a one-year full-time internship at an accredited site before earning their doctorate. In order to be licensed to practice, counselling psychologists must gain clinical experience under supervision, and pass a standardized exam.

Training Models and Research

Counselling psychology includes the study and practice of counsellor training and counsellor supervision. As researchers, counselling psychologists may investigate what makes training and supervision effective. As practitioners, counselling psychologists may supervise and train a variety of clinicians. Counsellor training tends to occur in formal classes and training programmes. Part of counsellor training may involve counselling clients under the supervision of a licensed clinician. Supervision can also occur between licensed clinicians, as a way to improve clinicians' quality of work and competence with various types of counselling clients.

As the field of counselling psychology formed in the mid-20th century, initial training models included Human Relations Training by Carkuff, Interpersonal Process Recall by Kagan, and Microcounseling Skills by Ivey. Modern training models include Egan's Skilled Helper model, and Hill's three stage (exploration, insight, and action) model. A recent analysis of studies on counsellor training found that modelling, instruction, and feedback are common to most training models, and seem to have medium to large effects on trainees.

Supervision Models and Research

Like the models of how clients and therapists interact, there are also models of the interactions between therapists and their supervisors. Bordin proposed a model of supervision working alliance similar to his model of therapeutic working alliance. The Integrated Development Model considers the level of a supervisee's motivation/anxiety, autonomy, and self and other awareness. The Systems Approach to Supervision views the relationship between supervisor and supervisee as most important, in addition to characteristics of the supervisee's personal characteristics, counselling clients, training setting, as well as the tasks and functions of supervision. The Critical Events in Supervision model focuses on important moments that occur between the supervisor and supervisee.

Problems can arise in supervision and training. First, supervisors are liable for malpractice of their supervisee. Also, questions have arisen as far as a supervisor's need for formal training to be a competent supervisor. Recent research suggests that conflicting, multiple relationships can occur between supervisors and supervisees, such as that of evaluator, instructor, and clinical supervisor. The occurrence of racial micro-aggressions against Black supervisees suggests potential problems with racial bias in supervision. In general, conflicts between a counsellor and his or her supervisor can arise when supervisors demonstrate disrespect, lack of support, and blaming (Ladany & Inman, 2008).

Vocational Development and Career Counselling

Vocational Theories: There are several types of theories of vocational choice and development. These types include trait and factor theories, social cognitive theories, and developmental theories. Two examples of trait and factor theories, also known as person–environment fit, are Holland's Theory and Theory of Work Adjustment. Holland hypothesized six vocational personality/interest types and six work environment types: realistic, investigative, artistic, social, enterprising, and conventional. When a person's vocational interests match his or her work environment types, this is considered congruence. Congruence has been found to predict occupation and college major. The Theory of Work Adjustment (TWA), as developed by Dawis and Lofquist, hypothesizes that the correspondence between a worker's needs and the reinforcer systems predicts job satisfaction, and that the correspondence between a worker's skills and a job's skill requirements predicts job satisfactoriness. Job satisfaction and satisfactoriness together should determine how long one remains at a job. When there is a discrepancy between a worker's needs or skills and the job's needs or skills, then change needs to occur either in the worker or the job environment.

Social Cognitive Career Theory (SCCT) has been proposed by Lent, Brown and Hackett. The theory takes Albert Bandura's work on self-efficacy and expands it to interest development, choice making, and performance. Person variables in SCCT include self-efficacy beliefs, outcome expectations and personal goals. The model also includes demographics, ability, values, and environment. Efficacy and outcome expectations are theorized to interrelate and influence interest development, which in turn influences choice of goals, and then actions. Environmental supports and barriers also affect goals and actions. Actions lead to performance and choice stability over time.

Career development theories propose vocational models that include changes throughout the lifespan. Super's model proposes a lifelong five-stage career development process. The stages are growth, exploration, establishment, maintenance, and disengagement. Throughout life, people have many roles that may differ in terms of importance and meaning. Super also theorized that career development is an implementation of self-concept. Gottfredson also proposed a cognitive career decision-making process that develops through the lifespan. The initial stage of career development is hypothesized to be the development of self-image in childhood, as the range of possible roles narrows using criteria such as sex-type, social class, and prestige. During and after adolescence, people take abstract concepts into consideration, such as interests.

Career Counselling

Career counselling may include provision of occupational information, modelling skills, written exercises, and exploration of career goals and plans. Career counselling can also involve the use of personality or career interest assessments, such as the Myers-Briggs Type Indicator, which is based on Carl Jung's theory of psychological type, or the Strong Interest Inventory, which makes use of Holland's theory. Assessments of skills, abilities, and values are also commonly assessed in career counselling.

3

Psychology in Education

Psychology is the science of the intellects, characters and behaviour of animals including man. Human education is concerned with certain changes in the intellects, characters and behaviour of men, its problems being roughly included under these four topics: Aims, materials, means and methods.

Psychology contributes to a better understanding of the aims of education by defining them, making them clearer; by limiting them, showing us what can be done and what can not; and by suggesting new features that should be made parts of them.

Psychology makes ideas of educational aims clearer. When one says that the aim of education is culture, or discipline, or efficiency, or happiness, or utility, or knowledge, or skill, or the perfection of all one's powers, or development, one's statements and probably one's thoughts, need definition. Different people, even amongst the clearest-headed of them, do not agree concerning just what culture is, or just what is useful. Psychology helps here by requiring us to put our notions of the aims of education into terms of the exact changes that education is to make, and by describing for us the changes which do actually occur in human beings.

Psychology helps to measure the probability that an aim is attainable. For example, certain writers about education state or imply that the knowledge and skill and habits of behaviour which are taught to the children of today are of service not only to this generation and to later generations through the work this generation does, but also to later generations forever through the inheritance of increased capacity for knowledge and skill and morals. But if the mental and moral changes made in one generation are not transmitted by heredity to the next generation, the improvement of the race by direct transfer of acquisitions is a foolish, because futile aim.

Psychology enlarges and refines the aim of education. Certain features of human nature may be and have been thought to be unimportant or even quite valueless because of ignorance of psychology. Thus for hundreds of years in the history of certain races even the most gifted thinkers of the race have considered it beneath the dignity of education to make physical health an important aim. Bodily welfare was even thought of as a barrier to spiritual growth, an undesirable interferer with its proper master. Education aimed to teach it its proper place, to treat it as a stupid and brutish slave. It is partly because psychology has shown the world that the mind is the servant and co-worker as well as the master of the body, that the welfare of our minds and morals is intimately bound up with the welfare of our bodies, particularly of our central nervous systems, that today we can all see the eminence of bodily health as an aim of education.

To an understanding of the material of education, psychology is the chief contributor.

Psychology shares with anatomy, physiology, sociology, anthropology, history and the other sciences that concern changes in man's bodily or mental nature the work of providing thinkers and workers in the field of education with knowledge of the material with which they work. Just as the science and art of agriculture depend upon chemistry and botany, so the art of education depends upon physiology and psychology.

A complete science of psychology would tell every fact about every one's intellect and character and behaviour, would tell the cause of every change in human nature, would tell the result which every educational force —every act of every person that changed any other or the agent himself—would have. It would aid us to use human beings for the world's welfare with the same surety of the result that we now have when we use falling bodies or chemical elements. In proportion as we get such a science we shall become masters of our own souls as we now are masters of heat and light. Progress towards such a science is being made.

Psychology contributes to understanding of the means of education, first, because the intellects and characters of any one's parents, teachers and friends are very important means of educating him, and, second, because the influence of any other means, such as books, maps or apparatus, cannot be usefully studied apart from the human nature which they are to act upon.

Psychology contributes to knowledge of methods of teaching in three ways. First, methods may be deduced outright from the laws of human nature. For instance, we may infer from psychology that the difficulty pupils have in learning to divide by a fraction is due in large measure to the habit established by all the thousands of previous divisions which they have done or seen, the habit, that is, of "division — decrease" or "number divided — result smaller than the number." We may then devise or select such a method as will reduce this interference from the old habits to a minimum without weakening the old habits in their proper functioning.

Second, methods may be chosen from actual working experience, regardless of psychology, as a starting point. Thus it is believed that in the elementary school a class of fifteen pupils for one teacher gives better results than either a class of three or a class of thirty. Thus, also, it is believed that family life is better than institutional life in its effects upon character and enterprise. Thus, also, it is believed that in learning a foreign language the reading of simple discussions of simple topics is better than the translation of difficult literary masterpieces that treat subtle and complex topics. Even in such cases psychology may help by explaining why one method does succeed better and so leading the way to new insights regarding other questions not yet settled by experience.

Third, in all cases psychology, by its methods of measuring knowledge and skill, may suggest means to test and verify or refute the claims of any method. For instance, there has been a failure on the part of teachers to decide from their classroom experience whether it is better to teach the spelling of a pair of homonyms together or apart in time. But all that is required to decide the question for any given pair is for enough teachers to use both methods with enough different classes, keeping everything else except the method constant, and to measure the errors in spelling the words thereafter in the two cases. Psychology, which teaches us how to measure changes in human nature, teaches us how to decide just what the results of any method of teaching are.

It will, of course, be understood that directly or indirectly, soon or late, every advance in the sciences of human nature will contribute to our success in controlling human nature and changing it to the advantage of the common weal. If certain lines of work by psychologists are selected for mention here, it is only because they are the more obvious, more direct and, so far as can now be seen, greater aids to correct thinking about education.

The first line of work concerns the discovery and improvement of means of measurement of intellectual functions. (The study of means of measuring moral functions such as prudence, readiness to sacrifice an immediate for a later good, sympathy, and the like, has only barely begun.) Beginning with easy cases such as the discrimination of sensory differences, psychology has progressed to measuring memory and accuracy of movement, fatigue, improvement with practice, power of observing small details, the quantity, rapidity and usefulness of associations, and even to measuring so complex a function as general intelligence and so subtle a one as suggestibility.

The task of students of physical science in discovering the thermometre, galvanometre and spectroscope, and in defining the volt, calorie erg, and ampère, is being attempted by psychologists in the sphere of human nature and behaviour. How important such work is to education should be obvious. At least three-fourths of the problems of educational practice are problems whose solution depends upon the amount of some change in boys and girls. Of two methods, which gives the greater skill? Is the gain in general ability from a "disciplinary" study so great as to outweigh the loss in specially useful habits? Just how much more does a boy learn when thirty dollars a year is spent for his teaching than when only twenty dollars is spent? Units in which to measure the changes wrought by education are essential to an adequate science of education. And, though the students of education may establish these units by their own investigations, they can use and will need all the experience of psychologists in the search for similar units.

The second line of work concerns race, sex, age and individual differences in all the many elements of intellect and character and behaviour.

How do the Igorottes, Ainus, Japanese and Esquimaux differ in their efficiency in learning to operate certain mechanical contrivances? Is the male sex more variable than the female in mental functions? What happens to keenness of sensory discrimination with age? How do individuals of the same race, sex and age differ in efficiency in perceiving small visual details or in accuracy in equaling a given length, or in the rapidity of movement? These are samples of many questions which psychologists have tried to answer by appropriate measurements.

Such knowledge of the differences which exist amongst men for whatever reason is of service to the thinker about the particular differences which education aims to produce between a man and his former self.

These studies of individual differences or variability are being supplemented by studies of correlations. How far does superior vividness and fidelity in imagery from one sense go with inferiority in other sorts of imagery? To what extent is motor ability a symptom of intellectual ability? Does the quick learner soon forget? What are the mental types that result from the individual variations in mental functions and their inter-correlations? Psychology has already determined with more or less surety the answers to a number of such questions instructive in their bearing upon both scientific insight into human nature and practical arrangements for controlling it.

The extent to which the intellectual and moral differences found inhuman beings are consequences of their original nature and determined by the ancestry from which they spring, is a matter of fundamental importance for education. So also is the manner in which ancestral influence operates. Whether such qualities as leadership, the artistic temperament, originality, persistence, mathematical ability, or motor skill are represented in the germs each by one or a few unit characters so that they "Mendelize" in inheritance, or whether they are represented each by the coöperation of so many unit characters that the laws of their inheritance are those of "blending" is a question whose answer will decide in great measure the means to be employed for racial improvement. Obviously both the amount and the mode of operation of ancestral influence upon intellect and character are questions which psychology should and does investigate.

The results and methods of action of the many forces which operate in childhood and throughout life to change a man's original nature are subjects for study equally appropriate to the work of a psychologist, a sociologist or a student of education, but the last two will naturally avail themselves of all that the first achieves. Although as yet the studies of such problems are crude, speculative and often misguided, we may hope that the influence of climate, food, city life, the specialization of industry, the various forms of the family and of the state, the different "studies" of the schools, and the like will come to be studied by as careful psychologists and with as much care as is now the case with colour-vision or the perception of distance.

The foundation upon which education builds is the equipment of instincts and capacity given by nature apart from training. Just as knowledge of the peculiar inheritance characteristic of any individual is necessary to efficient treatment of him, so knowledge of the unlearned tendencies of man as a species is necessary to efficient planning for education in general. Partly in conscious response to this demand and partly as a result of growing interest in comparative and genetic psychology, there have been in the last two decades many studies by psychologists of both the general laws of instinct and their particular natures, dates of appearance and disappearance, and conditions of modifiability. The instincts of attitude— of interest and aversion — are of course to be included here, as well as the tendencies to more obviously effective responses.

It is unfortunately true that the unlearned tendencies to respond of ants and chickens have been studied with more care than those of men, and also that the extreme complexity and intimate mixture with habits in the case of human instincts prevent studies of them, even when made with great care, from giving entirely unambiguous and elegant results. But the educational theorist or practitioner who should conclude that his casual observations of children in homes and schools needs no reinforcement from the researches of psychologists would be making the same sort of, thought [sic] not so great, an error as the pathologist or physician who should neglect the scientific studies of bacteria and protozoa. Also the psychologist who condemns these studies in toto because they lack the precision and surety of his own studies of sensations and perceptual judgements is equally narrow, though from a better motive.

The modifications of instincts and capacities into habits and powers and the development of the latter are the subjects of researches in dynamic psychology which are replacing the vague verbal and trite maxims of what used to be called "applied psychology" by definite insights into reality far in advance of those which common-sense sagacity alone can make. We are finding out when and why "practice makes perfect" and when and why it does not; wherein the reinforcement of a connection between situation and response by resulting satisfaction is better than the inhibition of alternative connections by discomfort and wherein it is not; what the law of diminishing returns from equal amounts of practice is, what it implies, and how it is itself limited; how far the feelings of achievement, of failure and of fatigue are symptomatic of progress, retardation and unfitness for work. Such a list of topics could be much extended even now and is being increased rapidly as more psychologists and more gifted psychologists come to share in the study of the learning process.

Only twenty years ago a student could do little more than add to his own common-sense deductions from the common facts of life the ordered series of similar deductions by the sagacious Bain. Bain utilized all the psychology of his day as well as the common fund of school-room experience, but today his book is hopelessly outgrown. Although it was the source of the minor books on the topic during the eighties and nineties, no one would now think of presenting the facts of the science of education by a revised edition of Bain.

Other lines of psychological work deserve more than mention. Incidental contributions from studies of sensory and perceptual processes, imagery and memory, attention and distraction, facilitation, inhibition and fatigue, imitation and suggestion, the rate and accuracy of movement and other topics— even from studies made with little or no concern about the practical control of human nature — sum up to a body of facts which do extend and economize that control. The special psychology of babies, children and adolescents is obviously important to education. False infant psychology or false child psychology is harmful, not because it is infant psychology, but because it is false.

The science of education can and will itself contribute abundantly to psychology. Not only do the laws derived by psychology from simple, specially arranged experiments help us to interpret and control mental action under the conditions of school-room life. School-room life itself is a vast laboratory in which are made thousands of experiments of the utmost interest to "pure" psychology. Not only does psychology help us to understand the mistakes made by children in arithmetic. These mistakes afford most desirable material for studies of the action of the laws of association, analysis and selective thinking. Experts in education studying the responses to school situations for the sake of practical control will advance knowledge not only of the mind as a learner under school conditions but also of the mind for every point of view.

Individual Differences

Individual differences are the facts that make people different from each and other. We all know that we are different from each other in many ways such as : our physical aspects, our likes, dislikes, interests, values, psychological makeup (and the list goes on) in other words... the whole "Personality".

Individual differences have been most often studied in the area of personality development. Psychologists have collected vast amounts of data on how people vary from one another in terms of their traits. For instance, they have noted that individual differences on the "Big Five" personality traits first strongly appear during the tween years.

All in all, the study of individual differences helps us to understand not only what makes humans similar to one another, but also what makes them different. By considering the variations that can occur from one person to another, we can best understand the full range of human behaviour. We can also come to understand what constitutes normal variation-such as starting puberty at 9 years of age instead of 10.5 years-and which developmental rates may be red flags for intervention, such as in the case of learning disorders.

Personality

Personality is the particular combination of emotional, attitudinal, and behavioural response patterns of an individual. Different personality theorists present their own definitions of the word based on their theoretical positions. Psychologists such as Freud, and Erik Erikson have attempted to come up with personality theories.

Psychology

Some ideas in the psychological and scientific study of personality include:

- Personality changes
- Personality development, the concept that personality is affected by various sources
- Personality disorder
- Personality genetics, a scientific field that examines the relation between personality and genetics
- Personality pathology, characterized by adaptive inflexibility, vicious cycles of maladaptive behaviour, and emotional instability under stress
- Personality psychology, the theory and study of individual differences, traits, and types
- Personality quiz a series of questions (usually multiple-choice, rating scale, or True/False) intended to describe aspects of an individual's character, thoughts, and feelings
- Personality style

- Personality systematics, among subsystems of personality as they are embedded in the entire ecological system
- Personality test, examples would include the Minnesota Multiphasic Personality Inventory (MMPI-2), Rorschach Inkblot Test, and Thematic Apperception Test (TAT)
- Personality type, refers to patterns of relatively enduring characteristics of behaviour that occur with sufficient frequency
- Personality trait, refers to enduring personal characteristics that are revealed in a particular pattern of behaviour in a variety of situation

Measuring Personality

Personality can be determined through a variety of tests. This may be done through the Minnesota Multiphasic Personality Inventory (MMPI-2), Rorschach Inkblot test, or the Thematic Apperception Test (TAT) The most popular technique is the self-report - a series of answers to a questionnaire that asks people to indicate the extent to which sets of statements or adjectives accurately describe their own behaviour or mental state.

Beginning of Personality Study

The study of personality started with Hippocrates' four humours and gave rise to four temperaments. The explanation was further refined by his successor Galen during the second century CE. The "Four Humours" theory held that a person's personality was based on the balance of bodily humours; yellow bile, black bile, phlegm and blood. Choleric people were characterized as having an excess of yellow bile, making them irascible. High levels of black bile was indicative of melancholy and pessimism. Phlegmatic people were thought to have an excess of phlegm, leading to their sluggish, calm temperament. Finally, people thought to have high levels of blood were said to be sanguine and were characterized by their cheerful, passionate dispositions.

Extraversion and Happiness

Personality is usually broken into components called the Big Five, which are openness to experience, conscientiousness, extroversion, agreeableness, and neuroticism (or emotionality). These components are generally stable over time and appear to be attributable to a person's genetics rather than the effects of one's environment.

Some research has investigated whether the relationship between happiness and extraversion seen in adults can also be seen in children.

The implications of these findings can help identify children that are more likely to experience episodes of depression and develop types of treatment that such children are likely to respond to. In both children and adults, research shows that genetics, as opposed to environmental factors, exert a greater influence on happiness levels. Personality is not believed to become stable until the age of thirty but personality constructs in children are referred to as temperament. Temperament is regarded as the precursor to personality. Whereas McCrae and Costa's Big Five Model assesses personality traits in adults, the EAS model is used to assesses temperament in the children. This model measures levels of emotionality, activity, sociability and shyness in children. The EAS model in children is believed to be the equivalent for the Big Five model in adults. Findings show that high degrees of sociability and low degrees of shyness are equivalent to adult extroversion and are also correlated with higher levels of life satisfaction in children.

Another interesting finding has been the link found between acting extroverted and positive affect. Extroverted behaviours include acting talkative, assertive, adventurous and outgoing and for the purposes of this study, positive affect is defined as experiences of happy and enjoyable emotions. This study investigated the effects of acting in a way that is counter to a person's dispositional nature. In other words, the study looked at the benefits and drawbacks of introverts (people who are shy, socially inhibited and non-aggressive) acting extroverted and extroverts acting introverted. After acting extroverted, introverts' experience of positive affect increased whereas extroverts seemed to experience lower levels of positive affect and suffered from the phenomenon of ego depletion. Ego depletion, or cognitive fatigue is the use of one's energy to overtly act in a way that is contrary to one's inner disposition. When a person acts in a contrary fashion, he diverts most, if not all, (cognitive) energy towards regulated this foreign style of behaviour and attitudes. Because all available energy is being used to maintain this contrary behaviour, the result is the inability to use any energy to make important or tough decisions, plan for the future, control or regulate emotions, or perform effectively on other cognitive tasks.

One question that has been posited is why extroverts tend to be happier than introverts. Two types of explanations attempt to account for this difference: the instrumental theories and temperamental theories. The instrumental theory suggests that extraverts end up making choices that place them in more positive situations and they also react more strongly than introverts to positive situations. The temperamental theory suggests that extroverts have a disposition that generally leads them to experience a higher degree of positive affect. In their study of extroversion, Lucas and Baird found no statistically significant support for the instrumental theory but did, however, find that extraverts generally experience a higher level of positive affect.

Research has also been conducted to uncover some of the mediators that are responsible for the correlation between extroversion and happiness. Self-esteem and self-efficacy are two such mediators. Self-efficacy has been found to be related to the personality traits of extroversion and subjective well-being. Self-efficacy is one's belief about abilities to perform up to personal standards, the ability to produced desired results, and the feeling of having some ability to make important life decisions. However, the relationship between extroversion (and neuroticism) and subjective happiness is only partially mediated by self-efficacy. This implies that there are most likely other factors that mediate the relationship between subjective happiness and personality traits. Another such factor may be self-esteem. It seems that individuals with a greater degree of confidence about themselves and their abilities have both a higher degree of subjective well-being and a higher level of extroversion.

Other research has examined the phenomenon of mood maintenance as another possible mediator. Mood maintenance, the ability to maintain one's average level of happiness in the face of an ambiguous situation (meaning a situation that has the potential to engender either positive or negative emotions in different individuals), has been found to be a stronger force in extroverts. This means that the happiness levels of extroverted individuals are less susceptible to the influence of external events. Another implication of this finding is that extroverts' positive moods last longer than those of introverts.

Cross-cultural Studies

There have recently been some arguments over the subject of studying personality in a different culture. Some people think that personality comes entirely from the culture and therefore there can be no meaningful study in cross-culture study. On the other hand, other people believe that some elements are shared by all cultures and an effort is being made to demonstrate the cross-cultural applicability of "the big five".

Historical Development of the Concept of Individual Personality

The modern sense of individual personality is a result of the shifts in culture originating in the Renaissance, an essential element in modernity. In contrast the Medieval European's sense of self was linked to a network of social roles: "the household, the kinship network, the guild, the corporation- these were the building blocks of personhood", Stephen Greenblatt observes, in recounting the recovery (1417) and career of Lucretius' poem De rerum natura: "at the core of the poem lay key principles of a modern understanding of the world." "Dependant on the family, the individual alone was nothing," Jacques Gélis observes.

Biology of Personality

Anatomical structures located in the brain contribute to personality traits. For instance, in human beings, the frontal lobes are responsible for foresight and anticipation. In addition, certain physiological functions such as hormone secretion also affect personality. For example, the hormone testosterone is necessary for sociability, affectivity, aggressiveness, and sexuality.

Differential Psychology

Differential psychology studies the ways in which individuals differ in their behaviour. This is distinguished from other aspects of psychology in that although psychology is ostensibly a study of individuals, modern psychologists often study groups or biological underpinnings of cognition.

For example, in evaluating the effectiveness of a new therapy, the mean performance of the therapy in one treatment group might be compared to the mean effectiveness of a placebo (or a well-known therapy) in a second, control group. In this context, differences between individuals in their reaction to the experimental and control manipulations are actually treated as errors rather than as interesting phenomena to study.

This is because psychological research depends upon statistical controls that are only defined upon groups of people. Individual difference psychologists usually express their interest in individuals while studying groups by seeking dimensions shared by all individuals but upon which individuals differ.

Importance of Individual Differences

Individual differences are essential whenever we wish to explain how individuals differ in their behaviour. In any study, significant variation exists between individuals. Reaction time, preferences, values, and health-linked behaviours are just a few examples. Individual differences in factors such as personality, intelligence, memory, or physical factors such as body size, sex, age, and other factors can be studied and used in understanding this large source of variance. Importantly, individuals can also differ not only in their current state, but in the magnitude or even direction of response to a given stimulus. Such phenomena, often explained in terms of inverted-U response curves, place differential psychology at an important location in such endeavours as personalized medicine, in which diagnoses are customised for an individual's response profile.

Areas of Study

Individual differences research typically includes personality, motivation, intelligence, ability, IQ, interests, values, self-concept, self-efficacy, and self-esteem (to name just a few). There are few remaining "differential psychology" programmes in the United States, although research in this area is very active. Current researchers are found in a variety of applied and experimental programmes, including educational psychology, Industrial and organizational psychology, personality psychology, social psychology, and developmental psychology programmes, in the neo-Piagetian theories of cognitive development in particular.

Intelligence

Intelligence has been defined in many different ways including logic, abstract thought, understanding, self-awareness, communication, learning, having emotional knowledge, retaining, planning, and problem solving.

Intelligence is most widely studied in humans, but has also been observed in other animals and in plants. Artificial intelligence is the simulation of intelligence in machines.

Within the discipline of psychology, various approaches to human intelligence have been adopted. The psychometric approach is especially familiar to the general public, as well as being the most researched and by far the most widely used in practical settings.

History of the Term

Intelligence derives from the Latin verb intelligere. A form of this verb, intellectus, became the medieval technical term for understanding, and a translation for the Greek philosophical term nous. This term was however strongly linked to the metaphysical and cosmological theories of teleological scholasticism, including theories of the immortality of the soul, and the concept of the Active Intellect (also known as the Active Intelligence). This entire approach to the study of nature was strongly rejected by the early modern philosophers such as Francis Bacon, Thomas Hobbes, John Locke, and David Hume, all of whom preferred the word "understanding" in their English philosophical works. Hobbes for example, in his Latin De Corpore, used "intellectus intelligit" (translated in the English version as "the understanding understandeth") as a typical example of a logical absurdity. The term "intelligence" has therefore become less common in English language philosophy, but it has later been taken up (with the scholastic theories which it now implies) in more contemporary psychology.

Definitions

The definition of intelligence is controversial. Some groups of psychologists have suggested the following definitions:

1. From "Mainstream Science on Intelligence" (1994), an editorial statement by fifty-two researchers:

A very general mental capability that, among other things, involves the ability to reason, plan, solve problems, think abstractly, comprehend complex ideas, learn quickly and learn from experience. It is not merely book learning, a narrow academic skill, or test-taking smarts. Rather, it reflects a broader and deeper capability for comprehending our surroundings—"catching on," "making sense" of things, or "figuring out" what to do.

2. From "Intelligence: Knowns and Unknowns" (1995), a report published by the Board of Scientific Affairs of the American Psychological Association:

Individuals differ from one another in their ability to understand complex ideas, to adapt effectively to the environment, to learn from experience, to engage in various forms of reasoning, to overcome obstacles by taking thought. Although these individual differences can be substantial, they are never entirely consistent: a given person's intellectual performance will vary on different occasions, in different domains, as judged by different criteria. Concepts of "intelligence" are attempts to clarify and organize this complex set of phenomena. Although considerable clarity has been achieved in some areas, no such conceptualization has yet answered all the important questions, and none commands universal assent. Indeed, when two dozen prominent theorists were recently asked to define intelligence, they gave two dozen, somewhat different, definitions.

Besides those definitions, psychology and learning researchers also have suggested definitions of intelligence such as:

Researcher	***Quotation***
Alfred Binet	Judgement, otherwise called "good sense," "practical sense," "initiative," the faculty of adapting one's self to circumstances ... auto-critique.David Wechsler The aggregate or global capacity of the individual to act purposefully, to think rationally, and to deal effectively with his environment.
Lloyd Humphreys	"...the resultant of the process of acquiring, storing in memory, retrieving, combining, comparing, and using in new contexts information and conceptual skills."
Cyril Burt	Innate general cognitive ability
Howard Gardner	To my mind, a human intellectual competence must entail a set of skills of problem solving — enabling the individual to resolve genuine problems or difficulties that he or she encounters and, when appropriate, to create an effective product — and must also entail the potential for finding or creating problems — and thereby laying the groundwork for the acquisition of new knowledge.
Linda Gottfredson	The ability to deal with cognitive complexity.
Sternberg & Salter	Goal-directed adaptive behaviour.
Reuven Feuerstein	The theory of Structural Cognitive Modifiability describes intelligence as "the unique propensity of human beings to change or modify the structure of their cognitive functioning to adapt to the changing demands of a life situation."

What is considered intelligent varies with culture. For example, when asked to sort, the Kpelle people take a functional approach. A Kpelle participant stated "the knife goes with the orange because it cuts it." When asked how a fool would sort, they sorted linguistically, putting the knife with other implements and the orange with other foods, which is the style considered intelligent in other cultures.

Human Intelligence

Psychometrics: The approach to understanding intelligence with the most supporters and published research over the longest period of time is based on psychometric testing. It is also by far the most widely used in practical settings. Intelligence quotient (IQ) tests include the Stanford-Binet, Raven's Progressive Matrices, the Wechsler Adult Intelligence Scale and the Kaufman Assessment Battery for Children.

There are also psychometric tests that are not intended to measure intelligence itself but some closely related construct such as scholastic aptitude. In the United States examples include the SSAT, the SAT, the ACT, the GRE, the MCAT, the LSAT, and the GMAT.

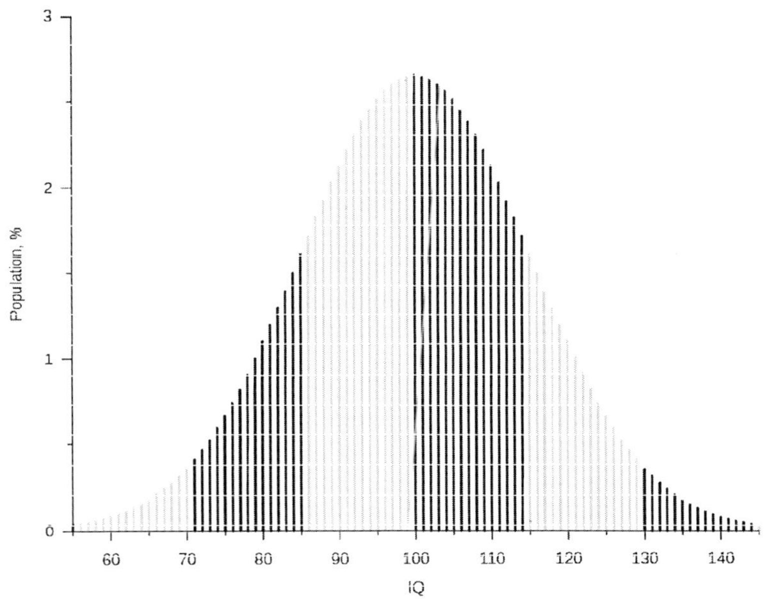

Figure: *The IQs of a large enough population are calculated so that they conform to a normal distribution.*

Intelligence tests are widely used in educational, business, and military settings because of their efficacy in predicting behaviour. IQ and g (discussed in the next section) are correlated with many important social outcomes—individuals with low IQs are more likely to be divorced, have a child out of marriage, be incarcerated, and need long-term welfare support, while individuals with high IQs are associated with more years of education, higher status jobs and higher income. Intelligence is significantly correlated with successful training and performance outcomes, and IQ/g is the single best predictor of successful job performance.

General Intelligence Factor or g

There are many different kinds of IQ tests using a wide variety of test tasks. Some tests consist of a single type of task, others rely on a broad collection of tasks with different contents (visual-spatial, verbal, numerical) and asking for different cognitive processes (e.g., reasoning, memory, rapid decisions, visual comparisons, spatial imagery, reading, and retrieval of general knowledge). The psychologist Charles Spearman early in the 20th century carried out the first formal factor analysis of correlations between various test tasks. He found a trend for all such tests to correlate positively with each other, which is called a positive manifold. Spearman found that a single common factor explained the positive correlations among tests. Spearman named it g for "general intelligence factor". He interpreted it as the core of human intelligence that, to a larger or smaller degree, influences success in all cognitive tasks and thereby creates the positive manifold. This interpretation of g as a common cause of test performance is still dominant in psychometrics. An alternative interpretation was recently advanced by van der Maas and colleagues. Their mutualism model assumes that intelligence depends on several independent mechanisms, none of which influences performance on all cognitive tests. These mechanisms support each other so that efficient operation of one of them makes efficient operation of the others more likely, thereby creating the positive manifold.

IQ tasks and tests can be ranked by how highly they load on the g factor. Tests with high g-loadings are those that correlate highly with most other tests. One comprehensive study investigating the correlations between a large collection of tests and tasks has found that the Raven's Progressive Matrices have a particularly high correlation with most other tests and tasks. The Raven's is a test of inductive reasoning with abstract visual material. It consists of a series of problems, sorted approximately by increasing difficulty. Each problem presents a 3 x 3 matrix of abstract designs with one empty cell; the matrix is constructed according to a rule, and the person must find out the rule to determine which of 8 alternatives fits into the empty cell. Because of its high correlation with other tests, the Raven's Progressive Matrices are generally acknowledged as a good indicator of general intelligence. This is problematic, however, because there are substantial gender differences on the Raven's, which are not found when g is measured directly by computing the general factor from a broad collection of tests.

Historical Psychometric Theories

Several different theories of intelligence have historically been important. Often they emphasized more factors than a single one like in g factor.

Cattell-Horn-Carroll Theory

Many of the broad, recent IQ tests have been greatly influenced by the Cattell-Horn-Carroll theory. It is argued to reflect much of what is known about intelligence from research. A hierarchy of factors is used. g is at the top. Under it there are 10 broad abilities that in turn are subdivided into 70 narrow abilities. The broad abilities are:

- Fluid Intelligence (Gf): includes the broad ability to reason, form concepts, and solve problems using unfamiliar information or novel procedures.
- Crystallized Intelligence (Gc): includes the breadth and depth of a person's acquired knowledge, the ability to communicate one's knowledge, and the ability to reason using previously learned experiences or procedures.
- Quantitative Reasoning (Gq): the ability to comprehend quantitative concepts and relationships and to manipulate numerical symbols.
- Reading & Writing Ability (Grw): includes basic reading and writing skills.
- Short-Term Memory (Gsm): is the ability to apprehend and hold information in immediate awareness and then use it within a few seconds.
- Long-Term Storage and Retrieval (Glr): is the ability to store information and fluently retrieve it later in the process of thinking.
- Visual Processing (Gv): is the ability to perceive, analyze, synthesize, and think with visual patterns, including the ability to store and recall visual representations.
- Auditory Processing (Ga): is the ability to analyze, synthesize, and discriminate auditory stimuli, including the ability to process and discriminate speech sounds that may be presented under distorted conditions.
- Processing Speed (Gs): is the ability to perform automatic cognitive tasks, particularly when measured under pressure to maintain focused attention.
- Decision/Reaction Time/Speed (Gt): reflect the immediacy with which an individual can react to stimuli or a task (typically measured in seconds or fractions of seconds; not to be confused with Gs, which typically is measured in intervals of 2–3 minutes).

Modern tests do not necessarily measure of all of these broad abilities. For example, Gq and Grw may be seen as measures of school achievement and not IQ. Gt may be difficult to measure without special equipment.

g was earlier often subdivided into only Gf and Gc which were thought to correspond to the Nonverbal or Performance subtests and Verbal subtests in earlier versions of the popular Wechsler IQ test. More recent research has shown the situation to be more complex.

Controversies

While not necessarily a dispute about the psychometric approach itself, there are several controversies regarding the results from psychometric research. Examples are the role of genetics vs. environment, the causes of average group differences, or the Flynn effect.

One criticism has been against the early research such as craniometry. A reply has been that drawing conclusions from early intelligence research is like condemning the auto industry by criticizing the performance of the Model T.

Several critics, such as Stephen Jay Gould, have been critical of g, seeing it as a statistical artifact, and that IQ tests instead measure a number of unrelated abilities. The American Psychological Association's report "Intelligence: Knowns and Unknowns" stated that IQ tests do correlate and that the view that g is a statistical artifact is a minority one.

Other Theories

There are critics of IQ, who do not dispute the stability of IQ test scores or the fact that they predict certain forms of achievement rather effectively. They do argue, however, that to base a concept of intelligence on IQ test scores alone is to ignore many important aspects of mental ability.

On the other hand, Linda S. Gottfredson (2006) has argued that the results of thousands of studies support the importance of IQ for school and job performance. IQ also predicts or correlates with numerous other life outcomes. In contrast, empirical support for non-g intelligences is lacking or very poor. She argued that despite this the ideas of multiple non-g intelligences are very attractive to many because they suggest that everyone can be intelligent in some way.

Multiple Intelligences

Howard Gardner's theory of multiple intelligences is based on studies not only of normal children and adults but also by studies of gifted individuals (including so-called "savants"), of persons who have suffered brain damage, of experts and virtuosos, and of individuals from diverse cultures. This led Gardner to break intelligence down into at least a number of different components. In the first edition of his book "Frames of Mind" (1983), he described seven distinct types of intelligence - logical-mathematical, linguistic, spatial, musical, kinesthetic, interpersonal, and intrapersonal. In a second edition of this book, he added two more types of intelligence - naturalist and existential intelligences. He argues that psychometric tests address only linguistic and logical plus some aspects of spatial intelligence. A major criticism of Gardner's theory is that it has never been tested, or subjected to peer review, by Gardner or anyone else, and indeed that it is unfalsifiable. Others (e.g. Locke, 2005) have suggested that recognizing many specific forms of intelligence (specific aptitude theory) implies a political—rather than scientific—agenda, intended to appreciate the uniqueness in all individuals, rather than recognizing potentially true and meaningful differences in individual capacities. Schmidt and Hunter (2004) suggest that the predictive validity of specific aptitudes over and above that of general mental ability, or "g", has not received empirical support.

Howard Gardner mentions in his Multiple Intelligences The Theory in Practice book, briefly about his main seven intelligences he introduced. In his book, he starts off describing Linguistic and Logical Intelligence because he believed that in society, we have put these two intelligences on a pedestal. However, Gardner believes all of the intelligences he found are equal. Note: At the time of the publication of Gardner's book Multiple Intelligences The Theory in Practice, naturalist and existential intelligences were not mentioned.

Linguistic Intelligence: People high in linguistic Intelligence have an affinity for words, both spoken and written.

Logical-Mathematics Intelligence: Is logical and mathematical ability, as well as scientific ability. Howard Gardner believed Jean Piaget may have thought he was studying all intelligence, but in truth, Piaget was really only focusing on the logical mathematical intelligence.

Spatial Intelligence: The ability to form a mental model of a spatial world and to be able to maneuver and operate using that model.

Musical Intelligence: Those with musical Intelligence have excellent pitch, and may even be absolute pitch.

Bodily-kinesthetic Intelligence: The ability to solve problems or to fashion products using one's whole body, or parts of the body. For example, dancers, athletes, surgeons, craftspeople, etc.

Interpersonal Intelligence: The ability to see things from the perspective of others, or to understand people in the sense of empathy. Strong interpersonal intelligence would be an asset in those who are teachers, politicians, clinicians, religious leaders, etc.

Intrapersonal Intelligence: A correlative ability, turned inward. It is a capacity to form an accurate, veridical model of oneself and to be able to use that model to operate effectively in life.

Triarchic Theory of Intelligence

Robert Sternberg proposed the triarchic theory of intelligence to provide a more comprehensive description of intellectual competence than traditional differential or cognitive theories of human ability. The triarchic theory describes three fundamental aspects of intelligence. Analytic intelligence comprises the mental processes through which intelligence is expressed. Creative intelligence is necessary when an individual is confronted with a challenge that is nearly, but not entirely, novel or when an individual is engaged in automatizing the performance of a task. Practical intelligence is bound in a sociocultural milieu and involves adaptation to, selection of, and shaping of the environment to maximize fit in the context. The triarchic theory does not argue against the validity of a general intelligence factor; instead, the theory posits that general intelligence is part of analytic intelligence, and only by considering all three aspects of intelligence can the full range of intellectual functioning be fully understood.

More recently, the triarchic theory has been updated and renamed the Theory of Successful Intelligence by Sternberg. Intelligence is defined as an individual's assessment of success in life by the individual's own (idiographic) standards and within the individual's sociocultural context. Success is achieved by using combinations of analytical, creative, and practical intelligence. The three aspects of intelligence are referred to as processing skills. The processing skills are applied to the pursuit of success through what were the three elements of practical intelligence: adapting to, shaping of, and selecting of one's environments. The mechanisms that employ the processing skills to achieve success include utilizing one's strengths and compensating or correcting for one's weaknesses.

Sternberg's theories and research on intelligence remain contentious within the scientific community.

PASS Theory of Intelligence

Based on A. R. Luria's (1966) seminal work on the modularization of brain function, and supported by decades of neuroimaging research, the PASS Theory of Intelligence proposes that cognition is organized in three systems and four processes. The first is the Planning, which involves executive functions responsible for controlling and organizing behaviour, selecting and constructing strategies, and monitoring performance. The second is the Attention process, which is responsible for maintaining arousal levels and alertness, and ensuring focus on relevant stimuli. The next two are called Simultaneous and Successive processing and they involve encoding, transforming, and retaining information. Simultaneous processing is engaged when the relationship between items and their integration into whole units of information is required. Examples of this include recognizing figures, such as a triangle within a circle vs. a circle within a triangle, or the difference between 'he had a shower before breakfast' and 'he had breakfast before a shower.' Successive processing is required for organizing separate items in a sequence such as remembering a sequence of words or actions exactly in the order in which they had just been presented. These four processes are functions of four areas of the brain. Planning is broadly located in the front part of our brains, the frontal lobe. Attention and arousal are combined functions of the frontal lobe and the lower parts of the cortex, although the parietal lobes are also involved in attention as well. Simultaneous processing and Successive processing occur in the posterior region or the back of the brain. Simultaneous processing is broadly associated with the occipital and the parietal lobes while Successive processing is broadly associated with the frontal-temporal lobes. The PASS (Planning/Attention/Simultaneous/Successive) theory is heavily indebted to both Luria (1966, 1973), and studies in cognitive psychology involved in promoting a better look at intelligence.

Piaget's Theory and Neo-Piagetian Theories

In Piaget's theory of cognitive development the focus is not on mental abilities but rather on a child's mental models of the world. As a child develops, increasingly more accurate models of the world are developed which enable the child to interact with the world better. One example being object permanence where the child develops a model where objects continue to exist even when they cannot be seen, heard, or touched.

Piaget's theory described four main stages and many sub-stages in the development. These four main stages are:

- sensory motor stage (birth-2yrs);
- pre-operational stage (2yrs-7rs);

- concrete operational stage (7rs-11yrs); and
- formal operations stage (11yrs-16yrs)

Degree of progress through these stages are correlated, but not identical with psychometric IQ. Piaget conceptualizes intelligence as an activity more than a capacity.

One of Piaget's most famous studies focused purely on the discriminative abilities of children between the ages of two and a half years old, and four and a half years old. He began the study by taking children of different ages and placing two lines of sweets, one with the sweets in a line spread further apart, and one with the same number of sweets in a line placed more closely together. He found that, "Children between 2 years, 6 months old and 3 years, 2 months old correctly discriminate the relative number of objects in two rows; between 3 years, 2 months and 4 years, 6 months they indicate a longer row with fewer objects to have "more"; after 4 years, 6 months they again discriminate correctly". Initially younger children were not studied, because if at four years old a child could not conserve quantity, then a younger child presumably could not either. The results show however that children that are younger than three years and two months have quantity conservation, but as they get older they lose this quality, and do not recover it until four and a half years old. This attribute may be lost temporarily because of an overdependence on perceptual strategies, which correlates more candy with a longer line of candy, or because of the inability for a four-year-old to reverse situations. By the end of this experiment several results were found. First, younger children have a discriminative ability that shows the logical capacity for cognitive operations exists earlier than acknowledged. This study also reveals that young children can be equipped with certain qualities for cognitive operations, depending on how logical the structure of the task is. Research also shows that children develop explicit understanding at age 5 and as a result, the child will count the sweets to decide which has more. Finally the study found that overall quantity conservation is not a basic characteristic of humans' native inheritance.

Piaget's theory has been criticized for the age of appearance of a new model of the world, such as object permanence, being dependent on how the testing is done. More generally, the theory may be very difficult to test empirically because of the difficulty of proving or disproving that a mental model is the explanation for the results of the testing.

Neo-Piagetian theories of cognitive development expand Piaget's theory in various ways such as also considering psychometric-like factors such as processing speed and working memory, "hypercognitive" factors like self-monitoring, more stages, and more consideration on how progress may vary in different domains such as spatial or social.

Latent Inhibition

Latent inhibition has been related to elements of intelligence, namely creativity and genius.

Evolution of Intelligence

The ancestors of modern humans evolved large and complex brains exhibiting an ever-increasing intelligence through a long evolutionary process. Different explanations have been proposed. Despite being at a higher level than any other animal, human cognition is not unique in its development and there is not a single trait of human beings that at least a few other species do not share.

Improving Intelligence

Eugenics is a social philosophy which advocates the improvement of human hereditary traits through various forms of intervention. Conscious efforts to influence intelligence raise ethical issues. Eugenics has variously been regarded as meritorious or deplorable in different periods of history, falling greatly into disrepute after the defeat of Nazi Germany in World War II.

Neuroethics considers the ethical, legal and social implications of neuroscience, and deals with issues such as the difference between treating a human neurological disease and enhancing the human brain, and how wealth impacts access to neurotechnology. Neuroethical issues interact with the ethics of human genetic engineering.

Because intelligence appears to be at least partly dependent on brain structure and the genes shaping brain development, it has been proposed that genetic engineering could be used to enhance the intelligence, a process sometimes called biological uplift in science fiction. Experiments on mice have demonstrated superior ability in learning and memory in various behavioural tasks.

IQ leads to greater success in education, but independently education raises IQ scores. Attempts to raise IQ with brain training have led to increases on the training tasks – for instance working memory – but it is as yet unclear if these generalise to increased intelligence per se.

Transhumanist theorists study the possibilities and consequences of developing and using techniques to enhance human abilities and aptitudes, and individuals ameliorating what they regard as undesirable and unnecessary aspects of the human condition.

Substances which actually or purportedly improve intelligence or other mental functions are called nootropics.

A 2008 research paper claimed that practicing a dual n-back task can increase fluid intelligence (Gf), as measured in several different standard tests. This finding received some attention from popular media, including an article in Wired. However, a subsequent criticism of the paper's methodology questioned the experiment's validity and took issue with the lack of uniformity in the tests used to evaluate the control and test groups. For example, the progressive nature of Raven's Advanced Progressive Matrices (APM) test may have been compromised by modifications of time restrictions (i.e., 10 minutes were allowed to complete a normally 45-minute test).

Correlates

According to Rosemary Hopcroft, a sociologist at the University of North Carolina at Charlotte, intelligence is inversely linked with sexual frequency (people with higher levels of education often report lower numbers of sexual partners). In parallel, self-reported intelligence has been linked to unconventional sexual practices and frequent sexual activity, thoughts and fantasies.

Some studies have shown a direct link between an increased birth weight and an increased intelligence quotient.

Animal and Plant Intelligence

Figure: *The common chimpanzee can use tools. This chimpanzee is using a stick to get food.*

Although humans have been the primary focus of intelligence researchers, scientists have also attempted to investigate animal intelligence, or more broadly, animal cognition, which encompasses all non-human animals. These researchers are interested in studying both mental ability in a particular species, and comparing abilities between species. They study various measures of problem solving, as well as mathematical and language abilities. Some challenges in this area are defining intelligence so that it means the same thing across species (e.g. comparing intelligence between literate humans and illiterate animals), and then operationalizing a measure that accurately compares mental ability across different species and contexts.

Wolfgang Köhler's pioneering research on the intelligence of apes is a classic example of research in this area. Stanley Coren's book, The Intelligence of Dogs is a notable popular book on the topic. Nonhuman animals particularly noted and studied for their intelligence include chimpanzees, bonobos (notably the language-using Kanzi) and other great apes, dolphins, elephants and to some extent parrots, rats and ravens.

Cephalopod intelligence also provides important comparative study. Cephalopods appear to exhibit characteristics of significant intelligence, yet their nervous systems differ radically from those of backboned animals. Vertebrates such as mammals, birds, reptiles and fish have shown a fairly high degree of intellect that varies according to each species. The same is true with arthropods.

It has been argued that plants should also be classified as being in some sense intelligent based on their ability to sense the environment and adjust their morphology, physiology and phenotype accordingly.

Artificial Intelligence

Artificial intelligence (or AI) is both the intelligence of machines and the branch of computer science which aims to create it, through "the study and design of intelligent agents" or "rational agents", where an intelligent agent is a system that perceives its environment and takes actions which maximize its chances of success. Achievements in artificial intelligence include constrained and well-defined problems such as games, crossword-solving and optical character recognition. General intelligence or strong AI has not yet been achieved and is a long-term goal of AI research.

Among the traits that researchers hope machines will exhibit are reasoning, knowledge, planning, learning, communication, perception, and the ability to move and manipulate objects. In the field of artificial intelligence there is no consensus on how closely the brain should be simulated.

Clinical Psychology

Clinical Psychology is an integration of science, theory and clinical knowledge for the purpose of understanding, preventing, and relieving psychologically-based distress or dysfunction and to promote subjective well-being and personal development. Central to its practice are psychological assessment and psychotherapy, although clinical psychologists also engage in research, teaching, consultation, forensic testimony, and programme development and administration. In many countries, clinical psychology is regulated as a health care profession.

The field is often considered to have begun in 1896 with the opening of the first psychological clinic at the University of Pennsylvania by Lightner Witmer. In the first half of the 20th century, clinical psychology was focused on psychological assessment, with little attention given to treatment. This changed after the 1940s when World War II resulted in the need for a large increase in the number of trained clinicians. Since that time, two main educational models have developed—the Ph.D. scientist–practitioner model (requiring a doctoral dissertation and therefore research as well as clinical expertise) and, in the U.S. the Psy.D. practitioner–scholar model.

Clinical psychologists provide psychotherapy, psychological testing, and diagnosis of mental illness. They generally train within four primary theoretical orientations—psychodynamic, humanistic, behaviour therapy/cognitive-behavioural, and systems or family therapy. Many continue clinical training in post-doctoral programmes in which they might specialize in disciplines such as psychoanalytic approaches or child and adolescent treatment modalities.

History

Although research in psychology is often dated to the opening of the first psychological laboratory by Wilhelm Wundt in 1879, attempts to create methods for assessing and treating mental distress existed long before. The earliest recorded approaches were a combination of religious, magical, and/or medical perspectives. Early examples of such physicians included Patañjali, Padmasambhava, Rhazes, Avicenna, and Rumi.

In the early 19th century, one could have his or her head examined, literally, using phrenology, the study of personality by the shape of the skull. Other popular treatments included physiognomy—the study of the shape of the face—and mesmerism, Mesmer's treatment by the use of magnets. Spiritualism and Phineas Quimby's "mental healing" were also popular.

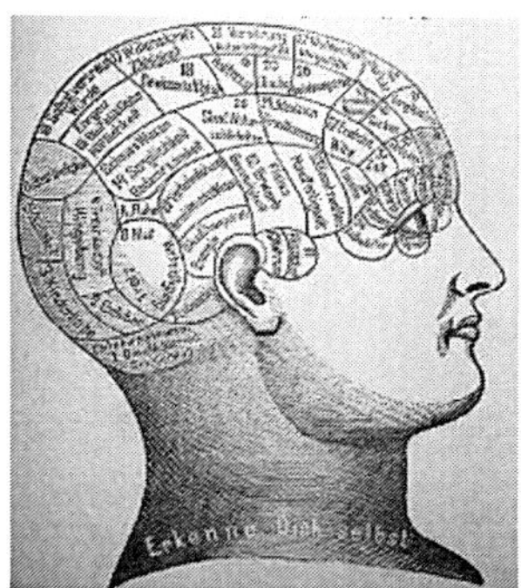

Figure: *Many 18th-century treatments for psychological distress were based on pseudo-scientific ideas, such as phrenology.*

While the scientific community eventually rejected these methods, academic psychologists also were not concerned with serious forms of mental illness. That area was already being addressed by the then-developing fields of psychiatry and neurology within the asylum movement. It was not until the end of the 19th century, around the time when Sigmund Freud was first developing the recent idea of a "talking cure" in Vienna, that the first clinical applications of psychology began.

Early Clinical Psychology

By the second half of the 1800s, the scientific study of psychology was becoming well-established in university laboratories. Although there were a few scattered voices calling for an applied psychology, the general field looked down upon this idea and insisted on "pure" science as the only respectable practice. This changed when Lightner Witmer (1867–1956), a past student of Wundt and head of the psychology department at the University of Pennsylvania, agreed to treat a young boy who had trouble with spelling. His successful treatment was soon to lead to Witmer's opening of the first psychological clinic at Penn in 1896, dedicated to helping children with learning disabilities. Ten years later in 1907, Witmer was to found the first journal of this new field, The Psychological Clinic, where he coined the term "clinical psychology," which he defined as "the study of individuals, by observation or experimentation, with the intention of promoting change." The field was slow to follow Witmer's example, but by 1914, there were 26 similar clinics in the US. Even as clinical psychology was growing, working with issues of serious mental distress remained the domain of psychiatrists and neurologists. However, clinical psychologists continued to make inroads into this area due to their increasing skill at psychological assessment. Psychologists' reputation as assessment experts grew during World War I with the development of two intelligence tests, Army Alpha and Army Beta (testing verbal and nonverbal skills, respectively), which could be used to screen large groups of military recruits. Due in large part to the success of these tests, assessment became the core function of clinical psychology for the next quarter century, when another war would propel the field into treatment.

Early Professional Organizations

The field began to organize under the name "clinical psychology" in 1917, when J. E. Wallace Wallin led the founding of the American Association of Clinical Psychology. This only lasted until 1919, after which the American Psychological Association (founded by G. Stanley Hall in 1892) developed a section on Clinical Psychology, which offered certification until 1927. Growth in the field was slow for the next few years when various unconnected psychological organizations came together as the American Association of Applied Psychology in 1930, which would act as the primary forum for psychologists until after World War II when the APA reorganized. In 1945, the APA created what is now called The Society of Clinical Psychology (Division 12), which remains a leading organization in the field. Psychological societies and associations in other English-speaking countries developed similar divisions, including in Britain, Canada, Australia and New Zealand.

World War II and the Integration of Treatment

When World War II broke out, the military once again called upon clinical psychologists. As soldiers began to return from combat, psychologists started to notice symptoms of psychological trauma labelled "shell shock" (eventually to be termed posttraumatic stress disorder) that were best treated as soon as possible. Because physicians (including psychiatrists) were over-extended in treating bodily injuries, psychologists were called to help treat this condition. At the same time, female psychologists (who were excluded from the war effort) formed the National Council of Women Psychologists with the purpose of helping communities deal with the stresses of war and giving young mothers advice on child rearing. After the war, the Veterans

Administration in the US made an enormous investment to set up programmes to train doctoral-level clinical psychologists to help treat the thousands of veterans needing care. As a consequence, the US went from having no formal university programmes in clinical psychology in 1946 to over half of all Ph.D.s in psychology in 1950 being awarded in clinical psychology.

WWII helped bring dramatic changes to clinical psychology, not just in America but internationally as well. Graduate education in psychology began adding psychotherapy to the science and research focus based on the 1947 scientist–practitioner model, known today as the Boulder Model, for Ph.D. programmes in clinical psychology. Clinical psychology in Britain developed much like in the U.S. after WWII, specifically within the context of the National Health Service with qualifications, standards, and salaries managed by the British Psychological Society.

Development of the Doctor of Psychology Degree

By the 1960s, psychotherapy had become imbedded within clinical psychology, but for many the Ph.D. educational model did not offer the necessary training for those interested in practice rather than research. There was a growing argument that said the field of psychology in the US had developed to a degree warranting explicit training in clinical practice. The concept of a practice-oriented degree was debated in 1965 and narrowly gained approval for a pilot programme at the University of Illinois starting in 1968. Several other similar programmes were instituted soon after, and in 1973, at the Vail Conference on Professional Training in Psychology, the Practitioner–Scholar Model of Clinical Psychology—or Vail Model—resulting in the Doctor of Psychology (Psy.D.) degree was recognized. Although training would continue to include research skills and a scientific understanding of psychology, the intent would be to produce highly trained professionals, similar to programmes in medicine, dentistry, and law. The first programme explicitly based on the Psy.D. model was instituted at Rutgers University. Today, about half of all American graduate students in clinical psychology are enrolled in Psy.D. programmes.

A Changing Profession

Since the 1970s, clinical psychology has continued growing into a robust profession and academic field of study. Although the exact number of practicing clinical psychologists is unknown, it is estimated that between 1974 and 1990, the number in the US grew from 20,000 to 63,000. Clinical psychologists continue to be experts in assessment and psychotherapy while expanding their focus to address issues of gerontology, pastoral counselling, sports, and the criminal justice system to name a few. One important field is health psychology, the fastest-growing employment setting for clinical psychologists in the past decade. Other major changes include the impact of managed care on mental health care; an increasing realization of the importance of knowledge relating to multicultural and diverse populations; and emerging privileges to prescribe psychotropic medication. Approximately 20% of clinical health psychologists identify themselves as counselling psychologists as well.

In the UK psychology is now one of the most popular degree subjects, and over 15,000 people graduate in psychology each year, many with the hope of developing this into a career, although only around 600 places for doctoral training in clinical psychology means there is intense competition for these places. There is also fierce competition to get into US Ph.D. programmes in clinical psychology, with an average acceptance rate of 8%.

Professional Practice

Clinical psychologists can offer a range of professional services, including:

- Administer and interpret psychological assessment and testing
- Conduct psychological research
- Consultation (especially for multi-disciplinary teams in mental health settings, such as psychiatric wards and increasingly other healthcare settings, schools and businesses)
- Development of prevention and treatment programmes
- Programme administration
- Provide expert testimony (forensic psychology)
- Provide psychological/ mental treatment (psychotherapy, or/and psychopharmacology “prescribing psychologists”)
- Teach

In practice, clinical psychologists may work with individuals, couples, families, or groups in a variety of settings, including private practices, hospitals, mental health organizations, schools, businesses, and non-profit agencies. Most clinical psychologists who engage in research and teaching do so within a college or university setting. Clinical psychologists may also choose to specialize in a particular field—common areas of specialization, some of which can earn board certification, include:

- Family therapy and relationship counselling
- Forensic psychology
- Health psychology
- Medical psychology
    - o Psychosomatic medicine
    - o Clinical neuropsychology
- Child psychopathology
- Organization and business
- School psychology
- Mental disorders (e.g. psychological trauma, addiction, eating disorders, sleep disorders, sexual dysfunction, clinical depression, anxiety, or phobia, and psychosis
- Sport psychology
- Geropsychology

Salary and Employment of Clinical Psychologists

In 2007, APA estimated that the median full-time salary for licensed doctoral-level clinical psychologists in the United States was $85,000. According to the US Bureau of Labor Statistics the median salary of US clinical psychologists was $64,140 in 2008, with approximately 34% of psychologists being self-employed, mostly in private practices.

The field is projected to grow at an average pace. Doctoral degree holders from a leading university in an applied speciality will face the best prospects. M.A. degree holders will face keen competition for jobs while there will be very limited positions for those with B.A. degrees in the field of psychology. Average doctoral starting and post-doctoral salaries range from $25,000–90,000.

Training and Certification to Practice

Clinical psychologists study a generalist programme in psychology plus postgraduate training and/or clinical placement and supervision. The length of training differs across the world, ranging from four years plus post-Bachelors supervised practice to a doctorate of three to six years which combines clinical placement.

In the US, clinical psychology doctoral programmes typically range from five to seven years post-college and require a one year full-time clinical internship and dissertation. There is currently an "internship crisis" in the field. Graduates must also accrue 1–2 years of supervised training post-Ph.D. before licensure in most states (3,000 hours) and need to pass the EPPP (plus, other state exams). About half of all clinical psychology graduate students are being trained in Ph.D. programmes—a model that emphasizes research—with the other half in Psy.D. programmes, which has more focus on practice (similar to professional degrees for medicine and law). Both models are accredited by the American Psychological Association and many other English-speaking psychological societies. A smaller number of schools offer accredited programmes in clinical psychology resulting in a Masters degree, which usually take two to three years post-Bachelors. In a 2009 survey, median debt related to doctoral education in clinical psychology was $68,000 for clinical Ph.D. recipients and $120,000 for clinical Psy.D. recipients.

Figure: *The University of Pennsylvania was the first to offer formal education in clinical psychology.*

In the UK, clinical psychologists undertake a Doctor of Clinical Psychology (D.Clin.Psych.), which is a practitioner doctorate with both clinical and research components. This is a three-year full-time salaried programme sponsored by the National Health Service (NHS) and based in universities and the NHS. Entry into these programmes is highly competitive, and requires at least a three-year undergraduate degree in psychology plus some form of experience, usually in either the NHS as an Assistant Psychologist or in academia as a Research Assistant. It is not unusual for applicants to apply several times before being accepted onto a training course as only about one-fifth of applicants are accepted each year. These clinical psychology doctoral degrees are accredited by the British Psychological Society and the Health Professions Council (HPC). The HPC is the statutory regulator for practitioner psychologists in the UK. Those who successfully complete clinical psychology doctoral degrees are eligible to apply for registration with the HPC as a clinical psychologist.

The practice of clinical psychology requires a license in the United States, Canada, the United Kingdom, and many other countries. Although each of the US states is somewhat different in terms of requirements and licenses, there are three common elements:

1. Graduation from an accredited school with the appropriate degree
2. Completion of supervised clinical experience or internship
3. Passing a written examination and, in some states, an oral examination

All US state and Canadian province licensing boards are members of the Association of State and Provincial Psychology Boards (ASPPB) which created and maintains the Examination for Professional Practice in Psychology (EPPP). Many states require other examinations in addition to the EPPP, such as a jurisprudence (i.e. mental health law) examination and/or an oral examination. Most states also require a certain number of continuing education credits per year in order to renew a license, which can be obtained though various means, such as taking audited classes and attending approved workshops. Clinical psychologists require the psychologist license to practice, although licenses can be obtained with a masters-level degree, such as Marriage and Family Therapist (MFT), Licensed Professional Counsellor (LPC), and Licensed Psychological Associate (LPA).

In the UK, registration as a clinical psychologist with the Health Professions Council (HPC) is necessary. The HPC is the statutory regulator for practitioner psychologists in the UK. In the UK the following titles are restricted by law: "registered psychologist" and "practitioner psychologist"; in addition, the specialist title "clinical psychologist" is also restricted by law.

Hong Kong

In Hong Kong, there is no statutory regulation of psychologist profession at present. Hong Kong Psychological Society, Division of Clinical Psychology is the only professional body to represent the practicing Clinical Psychologists in Hong Kong.

Internship Crisis in US Clinical Psychology Programmes

In the US, clinical psychology Ph.D. and Psy.D. programmes typically require students to complete a one-year full-time (or two-year part-time) clinical internship in order to graduate. However, there is currently an "internship crisis" as defined by the American Psychological Association, in that approximately 25% of clinical psychology doctoral students are unable to find an internship each year, and only 50% are able to attend an APA-accredited internship. This crisis has led to many students (approximately 1,000 each year) re-applying for internship the following year (thus delaying graduation) or completing an unaccredited internship, both of which can have emotional and financial consequences. This internship crisis stems from an increase in the production of psychology students. A recent study found that ~30% of unmatched students stem from 15 degree programmes, representing only 4% of all programmes participating in the internship match. These programmes enrolled larger cohorts of students than average and 14 of the 15 were PsyD programmes. All but one was APA accredited. The authors argue that it would be futile to simply increase internship slots. Internship slots already have increased over the years and as internship slots have increased, these schools increase production. Students who do not complete an APA-accredited internship are barred from certain employment settings, such as with the VA Hospitals, and may not be able get licensed in some states. Additionally, the majority of post-doctoral fellowships and other employment settings require or prefer the completion of an APA-accredited internship. The median rate of applicants accepted by APA-accredited internship sites is 5.5% and the median internship stipend was $24,218 in 2011.

Psychology in the Diagnosis of Mental Disorders.

A mental disorder or psychiatric disorder is a mental or behavioural pattern or anomaly that causes distress or disability, and which is not developmentally or socially normative. Mental disorders are generally defined by a combination of how a person feels, acts, thinks or perceives. This may be associated with particular regions or functions of the brain or rest of the nervous system, often in a social context. The recognition and understanding of mental health conditions have changed over time and across cultures and there are still variations in definition, assessment and classification, although standard guideline criteria are widely used. In many cases, there appears to be a continuum between mental health and mental illness, making diagnosis complex. According to the World Health Organisation (WHO), over a third of people in most countries report problems at some time in their life which meet criteria for diagnosis of one or more of the common types of mental disorder.

The causes of mental disorders are varied and in some cases unclear, and theories may incorporate findings from a range of fields. Services are based in psychiatric hospitals or in the community, and assessments are carried out by psychiatrists, clinical psychologists and clinical social workers, using various methods but often relying on observation and questioning. Clinical treatments are provided by various mental health professionals. Psychotherapy and psychiatric medication are two major treatment options, as are social interventions, peer support and self-help. In a minority of cases there might be involuntary detention or involuntary treatment, where legislation allows. Stigma and discrimination can add to the suffering and disability associated with mental disorders (or with being diagnosed or judged as having a mental disorder), leading to various social movements attempting to increase understanding and challenge social exclusion. Prevention is now appearing in some mental health strategies.

Classifications

The definition and classification of mental disorders is a key issue for researchers as well as service providers and those who may be diagnosed. Most international clinical documents use the term mental "disorder", while "illness" is also common. It has been noted that using the term "mental" (i.e., of the mind) is not necessarily meant to imply separateness from brain or body.

There are currently two widely established systems that classify mental disorders;

- 'ICD-10 Chapter V: Mental and behavioural disorders, since 1949 part of the International Classification of Diseases produced by the WHO,
- the Diagnostic and Statistical Manual of Mental Disorders (DSM-IV) produced by the American Psychiatric Association (APA) since 1952.

Both these list categories of disorder and provide standardized criteria for diagnosis. They have deliberately converged their codes in recent revisions so that the manuals are often broadly comparable, although significant differences remain. Other classification schemes may be used in non-western cultures, for example the Chinese Classification of Mental Disorders, and other manuals may be used by those of alternative theoretical persuasions, for example the Psychodynamic Diagnostic Manual. In general, mental disorders are classified separately from neurological disorders, learning disabilities or mental retardation.

Unlike the DSM and ICD, some approaches are not based on identifying distinct categories of disorder using dichotomous symptom profiles intended to separate the abnormal from the normal. There is significant scientific debate about the relative merits of categorical versus such non-categorical (or hybrid) schemes, also known as continuum or dimensional models. A spectrum approach may incorporate elements of both.

In the scientific and academic literature on the definition or classification of mental disorder, one extreme argues that it is entirely a matter of value judgements (including of what is normal) while another proposes that it is or could be entirely objective and scientific (including by reference to statistical norms). Common hybrid views argue that the concept of mental disorder is objective even if only a "fuzzy prototype" that can never be precisely defined, or conversely that the concept always involves a mixture of scientific facts and subjective value judgements. Although the diagnostic categories are referred to as 'disorders', they are presented as medical diseases, but are not validated in the same way as most medical diagnoses. Some neurologists argue that classification will only be reliable and valid when based on neurobiological features rather than clinical interview, while others suggest that the differing ideological and practical perspectives need to be better integrated.

The DSM and ICD approach remains under attack both because of the implied causality model and because some researchers believe it better to aim at underlying brain differences which can precede symptoms by many years.

Disorders

There are many different categories of mental disorder, and many different facets of human behaviour and personality that can become disordered. Anxiety or fear that interferes with normal functioning may be classified as an anxiety disorder. Commonly recognized categories include specific phobias, generalized anxiety disorder, social anxiety disorder, panic disorder, agoraphobia, obsessive-compulsive disorder and post-traumatic stress disorder.

Other affective (emotion/mood) processes can also become disordered. Mood disorder involving unusually intense and sustained sadness, melancholia, or despair is known as major depression (also known as unipolar or clinical depression). Milder but still prolonged depression can be diagnosed as dysthymia. Bipolar disorder (also known as manic depression) involves abnormally "high" or pressured mood states, known as mania or hypomania, alternating with normal or depressed mood. The extent to which unipolar and bipolar mood phenomena represent distinct categories of disorder, or mix and merge along a dimension or spectrum of mood, is subject to some scientific debate.

Patterns of belief, language use and perception of reality can become disordered (e.g., delusions, thought disorder, hallucinations). Psychotic disorders in this domain include schizophrenia, and delusional disorder. Schizoaffective disorder is a category used for individuals showing aspects of both schizophrenia and affective disorders. Schizotypy is a category used for individuals showing some of the characteristics associated with schizophrenia but without meeting cutoff criteria.

Personality—the fundamental characteristics of a person that influence thoughts and behaviours across situations and time—may be considered disordered if judged to be abnormally rigid and maladaptive. Although treated separately by some, the commonly used categorical schemes include them as mental disorders, albeit on a separate "axis II" in the case of the DSM-IV. A number of different personality disorders are listed, including those sometimes classed as "eccentric", such as paranoid, schizoid and schizotypal personality disorders; types that have described as "dramatic" or "emotional", such as antisocial, borderline, histrionic or narcissistic personality disorders; and those sometimes classed as fear-related, such as anxious-avoidant, dependent, or obsessive-compulsive personality disorders. The personality disorders in general are defined as emerging in childhood, or at least by adolescence or early adulthood. The ICD also has a category for enduring personality change after a catastrophic experience or psychiatric illness. If an inability to sufficiently adjust to life circumstances begins within three months of a particular event or situation, and ends within six months after the stressor stops or is eliminated, it may instead be classed as an adjustment disorder. There is an emerging consensus that so-called "personality disorders", like personality traits in general, actually incorporate a mixture of acute dysfunctional behaviours that may resolve in short periods, and maladaptive temperamental traits that are more enduring. Furthermore, there are also non-categorical schemes that rate all individuals via a profile of different dimensions of personality without a symptom-based cutoff from normal personality variation, for example through schemes based on dimensional models.

Eating disorders involve disproportionate concern in matters of food and weight. Categories of disorder in this area include anorexia nervosa, bulimia nervosa, exercise bulimia or binge eating disorder.

Sleep disorders such as insomnia involve disruption to normal sleep patterns, or a feeling of tiredness despite sleep appearing normal.

Sexual and gender identity disorders may be diagnosed, including dyspareunia, gender identity disorder and ego-dystonic homosexuality. Various kinds of paraphilia are considered mental disorders (sexual arousal to objects, situations, or individuals that are considered abnormal or harmful to the person or others).

People who are abnormally unable to resist certain urges or impulses that could be harmful to themselves or others, may be classed as having an impulse control disorder, including various kinds of tic disorders such as Tourette's syndrome, and disorders such as kleptomania (stealing) or pyromania (fire-setting). Various behavioural addictions, such as gambling addiction, may be classed as a disorder. Obsessive-compulsive disorder can sometimes involve an inability to resist certain acts but is classed separately as being primarily an anxiety disorder.

The use of drugs (legal or illegal, including alcohol), when it persists despite significant problems related to its use, may be defined as a mental disorder. The DSM incorporates such conditions under the umbrella category of substance use disorders, which includes substance dependence and substance abuse. The DSM does not currently use the common term drug addiction, and the ICD simply refers to "harmful use". Disordered substance use may be due to a pattern of compulsive and repetitive use of the drug that results in tolerance to its effects and withdrawal symptoms when use is reduced or stopped.

People who suffer severe disturbances of their self-identity, memory and general awareness of themselves and their surroundings may be classed as having a dissociative identity disorder, such as depersonalization disorder or Dissociative Identity Disorder itself (which has also been called multiple personality disorder, or "split personality"). Other memory or cognitive disorders include amnesia or various kinds of old age dementia.

A range of developmental disorders that initially occur in childhood may be diagnosed, for example autism spectrum disorders, oppositional defiant disorder and conduct disorder, and attention deficit hyperactivity disorder (ADHD), which may continue into adulthood.

Conduct disorder, if continuing into adulthood, may be diagnosed as antisocial personality disorder (dissocial personality disorder in the ICD). Popularist labels such as psychopath (or sociopath) do not appear in the DSM or ICD but are linked by some to these diagnoses.

Somatoform disorders may be diagnosed when there are problems that appear to originate in the body that are thought to be manifestations of a mental disorder. This includes somatization disorder and conversion disorder. There are also disorders of how a person perceives their body, such as body dysmorphic disorder. Neurasthenia is an old diagnosis involving somatic complaints as well as fatigue and low spirits/depression, which is officially recognized by the ICD-10 but no longer by the DSM-IV.

Factitious disorders, such as Munchausen syndrome, are diagnosed where symptoms are thought to be experienced (deliberately produced) and/or reported (feigned) for personal gain.

There are attempts to introduce a category of relational disorder, where the diagnosis is of a relationship rather than on any one individual in that relationship. The relationship may be between children and their parents, between couples, or others. There already exists, under the category of psychosis, a diagnosis of shared psychotic disorder where two or more individuals share a particular delusion because of their close relationship with each other.

There are a number of uncommon psychiatric syndromes, which are often named after the person who first described them, such as Capgras syndrome, De Clerambault syndrome, Othello syndrome, Ganser syndrome, Cotard delusion, and Ekbom syndrome, and additional disorders such as the Couvade syndrome and Geschwind syndrome.

Various new types of mental disorder diagnosis are occasionally proposed. Among those controversially considered by the official committees of the diagnostic manuals include self-defeating personality disorder, sadistic personality disorder, passive-aggressive personality disorder and premenstrual dysphoric disorder.

Two recent unique unofficial proposals are solastalgia by Glenn Albrecht and hubris syndrome by David Owen. The application of the concept of mental illness to the phenomena described by these authors has in turn been critiqued by Seamus Mac Suibhne.

Signs and Symptoms

Course: The likely course and outcome of mental disorders varies, depends on numerous factors related to the disorder itself, the individual as a whole, and the social environment. Some disorders are transient, while others may be more chronic in nature.

Even those disorders often considered the most serious and intractable have varied courses i.e. schizophrenia, psychotic disorders, and personality disorders. Long-term international studies of schizophrenia have found that over a half of individuals recover in terms of symptoms, and around a fifth to a third in terms of symptoms and functioning, with some requiring no medication. At the same time, many have serious difficulties and support needs for many years, although "late" recovery is still possible. The World Health Organization concluded that the long-term studies' findings converged with others in "relieving patients, carers and clinicians of the chronicity paradigm which dominated thinking throughout much of the 20th century."

Around half of people initially diagnosed with bipolar disorder achieve syndromal recovery (no longer meeting criteria for the diagnosis) within six weeks, and nearly all achieve it within two years, with nearly half regaining their prior occupational and residential status in that period. However, nearly half go on to experience a new episode of mania or major depression within the next two years. Functioning has been found to vary, being poor during periods of major depression or mania but otherwise fair to good, and possibly superior during periods of hypomania in Bipolar II.

Disability

Some disorders may be very limited in their functional effects, while others may involve substantial disability and support needs. The degree of ability or disability may vary over time and across different life domains. Furthermore, continued disability has been linked to institutionalization, discrimination and social exclusion as well as to the inherent effects of disorders. Alternatively, functioning may be affected by the stress of having to hide a condition in work or school etc., by adverse effects of medications or other substances, or by mismatches between illness-related variations and demands for regularity.

It is also the case that, while often being characterized in purely negative terms, some mental traits or states labelled as disorders can also involve above-average creativity, non-conformity, goal-striving, meticulousness, or empathy. In addition, the public perception of the level of disability associated with mental disorders can change.

Nevertheless, internationally, people report equal or greater disability from commonly occurring mental conditions than from commonly occurring physical conditions, particularly in their social roles and personal relationships. The proportion with access to professional help for mental disorders is far lower, however, even among those assessed as having a severely disabling condition. Disability in this context may or may not involve such things as:

- Basic activities of daily living. Including looking after the self (health care, grooming, dressing, shopping, cooking etc.) or looking after accommodation (chores, DIY tasks etc.)
- Interpersonal relationships. Including communication skills, ability to form relationships and sustain them, ability to leave the home or mix in crowds or particular settings
- Occupational functioning. Ability to acquire a job and hold it, cognitive and social skills required for the job, dealing with workplace culture, or studying as a student.

In terms of total Disability-adjusted life years (DALYs), which is an estimate of how many years of life are lost due to premature death or to being in a state of poor health and disability, mental disorders rank amongst the most disabling conditions. Unipolar (also known as Major) depressive disorder is the third leading cause of disability worldwide, of any condition mental or physical, accounting for 65.5 million years lost. The total DALY does not necessarily indicate what is the most individually disabling, because it also depends on how common a condition is; for example, schizophrenia is found to be the most individually disabling mental disorder on average but is less common. Alcohol-use disorders are also high in the overall list, responsible for 23.7 million DALYs globally, while other drug-use disorders accounted for 8.4 million. Schizophrenia causes a total loss of 16.8 million DALY, and bipolar disorder 14.4 million. Panic disorder leads to 7 million years lost, obsessive-compulsive disorder 5.1, primary insomnia 3.6, and post-traumatic stress disorder 3.5 million DALYs.

The first ever systematic description of global disability arising in youth, published in 2011, found that among 10 to 24 year olds nearly half of all disability (current and as estimated to continue) was due to mental and neurological conditions, including substance use disorders and conditions involving self-harm. Second to this were accidental injuries (mainly traffic collisions) accounting for 12 percent of disability, followed by communicable diseases at 10 percent. The disorders associated with most disability in high income countries were unipolar major depression (20%) and alcohol use disorder (11%). In the eastern Mediterranean region it was unipolar major depression (12%) and schizophrenia (7%), and in Africa it was unipolar major depression (7%) and bipolar disorder (5%).

Suicide, which is often attributed to some underlying mental disorder, is a leading cause of death among teenagers and adults under 35. There are an estimated 10 to 20 million non-fatal attempted suicides every year worldwide.

Causes

Mental disorders can arise from multiple sources, and in many cases there is no single accepted or consistent cause currently established. An eclectic or pluralistic mix of models may be used to explain particular disorders. The primary paradigm of contemporary mainstream Western psychiatry is said to be the biopsychosocial model which incorporates biological, psychological and social factors, although this may not always be applied in practice.

Biological psychiatry follows a biomedical model where many mental disorders are conceptualized as disorders of brain circuits likely caused by developmental processes shaped by a complex interplay of genetics and experience. A common assumption is that disorders may have resulted from genetic and developmental vulnerabilities, exposed by stress in life (for example in a diathesis–stress model), although there are various views on what causes differences between individuals. Some types of mental disorder may be viewed as primarily neurodevelopmental disorders.

Evolutionary psychology may be used as an overall explanatory theory, while attachment theory is another kind of evolutionary-psychological approach sometimes applied in the context of mental disorders. Psychoanalytic theories have continued to evolve alongside cognitive-behavioural and systemic-family approaches. A distinction is sometimes made between a "medical model" or a "social model" of disorder and disability.

Studies have indicated that variation in genes can play an important role in the development of mental disorders, although the reliable identification of connections between specific genes and specific categories of disorder has proven more difficult. Environmental events surrounding pregnancy and birth have also been implicated. Traumatic brain injury may increase the risk of developing certain mental disorders. There have been some tentative inconsistent links found to certain viral infections,to substance misuse, and to general physical health.

Social influences have been found to be important, including abuse, neglect, bullying, social stress, and other negative or overwhelming life experiences. The specific risks and pathways to particular disorders are less clear, however. Aspects of the wider community have also been implicated, including employment problems, socioeconomic inequality, lack of social cohesion, problems linked to migration, and features of particular societies and cultures.

Abnormal functioning of neurotransmitter systems has been implicated in several mental disorders, including serotonin, norepinephrine, dopamine and glutamate systems. Differences have also been found in the size or activity of certain brain regions in some cases. Psychological mechanisms have also been implicated, such as cognitive (e.g. reasoning) biases, emotional influences, personality dynamics, temperament and coping style.

Correlations of mental disorders with drug use include cannabis, alcohol and caffeine.

Diagnosis

Psychiatrists seek to provide a medical diagnosis of individuals by an assessment of symptoms and signs associated with particular types of mental disorder. Other mental health professionals, such as clinical psychologists, may or may not apply the same diagnostic categories to their clinical formulation of a client's difficulties and circumstances. The majority of mental health problems are, at least initially, assessed and treated by family physicians (in the UK general practitioners) during consultations, who may refer a patient on for more specialist diagnosis in acute or chronic cases.

Routine diagnostic practice in mental health services typically involves an interview known as a mental status examination, where evaluations are made of appearance and behaviour, self-reported symptoms, mental health history, and current life circumstances. The views of other professionals, relatives or other third parties may be taken into account. A physical examination to check for ill health or the effects of medications or other drugs may be conducted. Psychological testing is sometimes used via paper-and-pen or computerized questionnaires, which may include algorithms based on ticking off standardized diagnostic criteria, and in rare specialist cases neuroimaging tests may be requested, but such methods are more commonly found in research studies than routine clinical practice.

Time and budgetary constraints often limit practicing psychiatrists from conducting more thorough diagnostic evaluations. It has been found that most clinicians evaluate patients using an unstructured, open-ended approach, with limited training in evidence-based assessment methods, and that inaccurate diagnosis may be common in routine practice. In addition, comorbidity is very common in psychiatric diagnosis, where the same person meets the criteria for more than one disorder. On the other hand, a person may have several different difficulties only some of which meet the criteria for being diagnosed. There may be specific problems with accurate diagnosis in developing countries.

More structured approaches are being increasingly used to measure levels of mental illness.

- HoNOS is the most widely used measure in English mental health services, being used by at least 61 trusts. In HoNOS a score of 0-4 is given for each of 12 factors, based on functional living capacity. Research has been supportive of HoNOS, although some questions have been asked about whether it provides adequate coverage of the range and complexity of mental illness problems, and whether the fact that often only 3 of the 12 scales vary over time gives enough subtlety to accurately measure outcomes of treatment. HoNOS is regarded as the best available tool.
- WEMWBS uses a similar approach, giving a score of 1-5 for each of 14 factors. However in this tool the factors are based very largely on feelings.

Since the 1980s, Paula Caplan has been concerned about the subjectivity of psychiatric diagnosis, and people being arbitrarily "slapped with a psychiatric label". Caplan says because psychiatric diagnosis is unregulated, doctors aren't required to spend much time interviewing patients or to seek a second opinion. The Diagnostic and Statistical Manual of Mental Disorders can lead a psychiatrist to focus on narrow checklists of symptoms, with little consideration of what is actually causing the patient's problems. So, according to Caplan, getting a psychiatric diagnosis and label often stands in the way of recovery.

In 2013, psychiatrist Allen Frances wrote a paper entitled "The New Crisis of Confidence in Psychiatric Diagnosis", which said that "psychiatric diagnosis still relies exclusively on fallible subjective judgements rather than objective biological tests". Frances was also concerned about "unpredictable overdiagnosis". For many years, marginalized psychiatrists (such as Peter Breggin, Thomas Szasz) and outside critics (such as Stuart A. Kirk) have "been accusing psychiatry of engaging in the systematic medicalization of normality". More recently these concerns have come from insiders who have worked for and promoted the American Psychiatric Association (e.g., Robert Spitzer, Allen Frances). A 2002 editorial in the British Medical Journal warned of inappropriate medicalization leading to disease mongering, where the boundaries of the definition of illnesses are expanded to include personal problems as medical problems or risks of diseases are emphasized to broaden the market for medications.

Prevention

The 2004 WHO report "Prevention of Mental Disorders" stated that "Prevention of these disorders is obviously one of the most effective ways to reduce the [disease] burden."

Causal Factors

Risk factors for mental illness include genetic inheritance, life experiences and substance intake. Risk factors involving parenting include parental rejection, lack of parental warmth, high hostility, harsh discipline, high maternal negative affect, parental favouritism, anxious childrearing, modelling of dysfunctional and drug-abusing behaviour, and child abuse (emotional, physical and sexual). Other risk factors may include family history (e.g. of anxiety), temperament and attitudes (e.g. pessimism). In schizophrenia and psychosis, risk factors include migration and discrimination, childhood trauma, bereavement or separation in families, and abuse of drugs.

Risk Assessment

Screening questionnaires for assessing the risks of developing a mental disorder face the problem of low specificity, which means that the majority of the people with an increased risk will not develop the disorder. However combining risk factors gives higher estimated risk. For instance risk of depression is higher for a widow who also has an illness and lives alone.

Research

The 2011 European Psychiatric Association (EPA) guidance on prevention of mental disorders states "There is considerable evidence that various psychiatric conditions can be prevented through the implementation of effective evidence-based interventions."

A 2011 UK Department of Health report on the economic case for mental health promotion and mental illness prevention found that "many interventions are outstandingly good value for money, low in cost and often become self-financing over time, saving public expenditure".

Parenting has many mental illness causality effects, and evidence suggests that helping parents to be more effective with their children can address mental health needs.

For depressive disorders, research has shown a reduction in incidence of new cases when people participated in interventions, for instance by 22% and 38% in meta-analyses. In a study of patients with sub-threshold depression, those who received minimal-contact psychotherapy had an incidence of a major depressive disorder one year later a third lower (an incidence rate of 12% rather than 18%) than the control group. Such interventions also save costs. The Netherlands mental health care system provides preventive interventions, such as the Coping with Depression course for people with subthreshold depression. A meta-analysis showed that people who followed this course had a 38% lower incidence of developing a major depressive disorder than the control group. A stepped-care intervention (watchful waiting, CBT and medication if appropriate) achieved a 50% lower incidence rate in a patient group aged 75 or older. One depression study found a neutral effect compared to personal, social, and health education, and usual school provision, and included a comment on potential for increased depression scores from people who have received CBT due to greater self recognition and acknowledgement of existing symptoms of depression and negative thinking styles. Other studies have seen CBT effectiveness equal to other interventions, or neutral.

For anxiety disorders, use of CBT with people at risk has significantly reduced the number of episodes of generalized anxiety disorder and other anxiety symptoms, and also given significant improvements in explanatory style, hopelessness, and dysfunctional attitudes. Other interventions (parental inhibition reduction, behaviourism, parental modelling, problem-solving and communication skills) have also produced significant benefits. In another study 3% of the group receiving the CBT intervention developed GAD by 12 months postintervention compared with 14% in the control group. Subthreshold panic disorder sufferers were found to significantly benefit from use of CBT. Use of CBT was found to significantly reduce social anxiety prevalence.

For psychosis and schizophrenia, usage of a number of drugs has been associated with development of the disorder, including cannabis, cocaine, and amphetamines. Studies have shown reductions in onset through preventative CBT. Another study showed that schizophrenia prevalence in people with a high genetic risk was significantly influenced by the parenting and family environment. A meta-analysis concluded that it may be possible to delay or prevent transition of high risk people to psychosis.

For bipolar, stress (such as childhood adversity or highly conflictual families) is not a diagnostically specific causal agent, but does place genetically and biologically vulnerable individuals at risk for a more pernicious course of illness. There has been considerable debate regarding the causal relationship between usage of cannabis and bipolar disorder.

Further research is needed both on mental health causal factors, and on the effectiveness of prevention programmes. Universal preventions (aimed at a population that has no increased risk for developing a mental disorder, such as school programmes or mass media campaigns) need very high numbers to be statistically valid (sometimes known as the "power" problem). Approaches to overcome this are (1) focus on high-incidence groups (e.g. by targeting groups with high risk factors), (2) use multiple interventions to achieve greater, and thus more statistically valid, effects, (3) use cumulative meta-analyses of many trials, and (4) run very large trials.

Prevention Programmes

The 2009 US National Academies publication on preventing mental, emotional, and behavioural disorders among young people focused on recent research and programme experience and stated that "A number of promotion and prevention programmes are now available that should be considered for broad implementation." A 2011 review of this by the authors said "A scientific base of evidence shows that we can prevent many mental, emotional, and behavioural disorders before they begin" and made recommendations including

- supporting the mental health and parenting skills of parents,
- encouraging the developmental competencies of children and
- using preventive strategies particularly for children at risk (such as children of parents with mental illness, or with family stresses such as divorce or job loss).

The 2012 UK Schizophrenia Commission recommended "a preventative strategy for psychosis including promoting protective factors for mental wellbeing and reducing risks such as cannabis use in early adolescence."

It is already known that home visiting programmes for pregnant women and parents of young children can produce replicable effects on children's general health and development in a variety of community settings. Similarly positive benefits from social and emotional education are well proven. Research has shown that risk assessment and behavioural interventions in pediatric clinics reduced abuse and neglect outcomes for young children. Early childhood home visitation also reduced abuse and neglect, but results were inconsistent.

Assessing parenting capability has been raised in child protection and other contexts. Delaying of potential very young pregnancies could lead to better mental health causal risk factors such as improved parenting skills and more stable homes, and various approaches have been used to encourage such behaviour change. Some countries run conditional cash transfer welfare programmes where payment is conditional on behaviour of the recipients. Compulsory contraception has been used to prevent future mental illness.

Prevention programmes can face issues in (i) ownership, because health systems are typically targeted at current suffering, and (ii) funding, because programme benefits come on longer timescales than the normal political and management cycle. Assembling collaborations of interested bodies appears to be an effective model for achieving sustained commitment and funding.

Mental Health Strategies

Prevention is currently a very small part of the spend of mental health systems. For instance the 2009 UK Department of Health analysis of prevention expenditure does not include any apparent spend on mental health. The situation is the same in research.

However prevention is beginning to appear in mental health strategies:

- In 2012 Mind, the UK mental health NGO, included "Staying well; Support people likely to develop mental health problems, to stay well." as its first goal for 2012-16.
- The 2011 mental health strategy of Manitoba (Canada) included intents to (i) reduce risk factors associated with mental ill-health and (ii) increase mental health promotion for both adults and children.
- The 2011 US National Prevention Strategy included mental and emotional well-being, with recommendations including (i) better parenting and (ii) early intervention.

- Australia's mental health plan for 2009-14 included "Prevention and Early Intervention" as priority 2.
- The 2008 EU "Pact for Mental Health" made recommendations for youth and education including (i) promotion of parenting skills, (ii) integration of socio-emotional learning into education curricular and extracurricular activities, and (iii) early intervention throughout the educational system.

Some companies, such as Unilever, are moving to use cCBT preventively, to reduce staff anxiety.

Management

The former demesme with a manor house from 1912 is today separated into a special education school („Schule am Tornowsee") and a hotel with integrated work/job- and rehabilitation-training for people with mental disorders. Tornow is situated at the northern bank of the Große Tornowsee (lake) (de)

Treatment and support for mental disorders is provided in psychiatric hospitals, clinics or any of a diverse range of community mental health services. A number of professions have developed that specialize in the treatment of mental disorders. This includes the medical speciality of psychiatry (including psychiatric nursing), the field of psychology known as clinical psychology, and the practical application of sociology known as social work. There is also a wide range of psychotherapists (including family therapy), counsellors, and public health professionals. In addition, there are peer support roles where personal experience of similar issues is the primary source of expertise. The different clinical and scientific perspectives draw on diverse fields of research and theory, and different disciplines may favour differing models, explanations and goals.

In some countries services are increasingly based on a recovery approach, intended to support each individual's personal journey to gain the kind of life they want, although there may also be 'therapeutic pessimism' in some areas.

There are a range of different types of treatment and what is most suitable depends on the disorder and on the individual. Many things have been found to help at least some people, and a placebo effect may play a role in any intervention or medication. In a minority of cases, individuals may be treated against their will, which can cause particular difficulties depending on how it is carried out and perceived.

The UK is moving towards paying mental health providers by the outcome results that their services achieve.

Psychotherapy

A major option for many mental disorders is psychotherapy. There are several main types. Cognitive behavioural therapy (CBT) is widely used and is based on modifying the patterns of thought and behaviour associated with a particular disorder. Psychoanalysis, addressing underlying psychic conflicts and defences, has been a dominant school of psychotherapy and is still in use. Systemic therapy or family therapy is sometimes used, addressing a network of significant others as well as an individual.

Some psychotherapies are based on a humanistic approach. There are a number of specific therapies used for particular disorders, which may be offshoots or hybrids of the above types. Mental health professionals often employ an eclectic or integrative approach. Much may depend on the therapeutic relationship, and there may be problems with trust, confidentiality and engagement.

Medication

A major option for many mental disorders is psychiatric medication and there are several main groups. Antidepressants are used for the treatment of clinical depression, as well as often for anxiety and a range of other disorders. Anxiolytics (including sedatives) are used for anxiety disorders and related problems such as insomnia. Mood stabilizers are used primarily in bipolar disorder. Antipsychotics are used for psychotic disorders, notably for positive symptoms in schizophrenia, and also increasingly for a range of other disorders. Stimulants are commonly used, notably for ADHD.

Despite the different conventional names of the drug groups, there may be considerable overlap in the disorders for which they are actually indicated, and there may also be off-label use of medications. There can be problems with adverse effects of medication and adherence to them, and there is also criticism of pharmaceutical marketing and professional conflicts of interest.

Other

Electroconvulsive therapy (ECT) is sometimes used in severe cases when other interventions for severe intractable depression have failed. Psychosurgery is considered experimental but is advocated by certain neurologists in certain rare cases.

Counselling (professional) and co-counselling (between peers) may be used. Psychoeducation programmes may provide people with the information to understand and manage their problems. Creative therapies are sometimes used, including music therapy, art therapy or drama therapy. Lifestyle adjustments and supportive measures are often used, including peer support, self-help groups for mental health and supported housing or supported employment (including social firms). Some advocate dietary supplements.

Reasonable accommodations (adjustments and supports) might be put in place to help an individual cope and succeed in environments despite potential disability related to mental health problems. This could include an emotional support animal or specifically trained psychiatric service dog.

Epidemiology

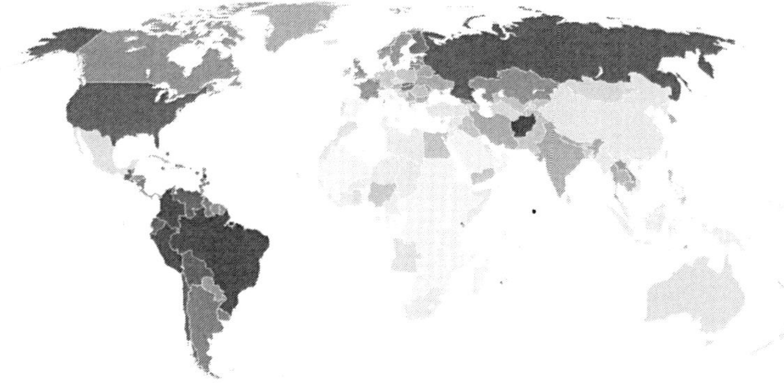

Figure: *Disability-adjusted life year for neuropsychiatric conditions per 100,000 inhabitants in 2004.*

<2200	3200-3400
2200-2400	3400-3600
2400-2600	3600-3800
2600-2800	3800-4000
2800-3000	4000-4200
3000-3200	>4200

Mental disorders are common. World wide more than one in three people in most countries report sufficient criteria for at least one at some point in their life. In the United States 46% qualifies for a mental illness at some point. An ongoing survey indicates that anxiety disorders are the most common in all but one country, followed by mood disorders in all but two countries, while substance disorders and impulse-control disorders were consistently less prevalent. Rates varied by region. A review of anxiety disorder surveys in different countries found average lifetime prevalence estimates of 16.6%, with women having higher rates on average. A review of mood disorder surveys in different countries found lifetime rates of 6.7% for major depressive disorder (higher in some studies, and in women) and 0.8% for Bipolar I disorder.

In the United States the frequency of disorder is: anxiety disorder (28.8%), mood disorder (20.8%), impulse-control disorder (24.8%) or substance use disorder (14.6%).

A 2004 cross-Europe study found that approximately one in four people reported meeting criteria at some point in their life for at least one of the DSM-IV disorders assessed, which included mood disorders (13.9%), anxiety disorders (13.6%) or alcohol disorder (5.2%). Approximately one in ten met criteria within a 12-month period. Women and younger people of either gender showed more cases of disorder. A 2005 review of surveys in 16 European countries found that 27% of adult Europeans are affected by at least one mental disorder in a 12 month period.

An international review of studies on the prevalence of schizophrenia found an average (median) figure of 0.4% for lifetime prevalence; it was consistently lower in poorer countries.

Studies of the prevalence of personality disorders (PDs) have been fewer and smaller-scale, but one broad Norwegian survey found a five-year prevalence of almost 1 in 7 (13.4%). Rates for specific disorders ranged from 0.8% to 2.8%, differing across countries, and by gender, educational level and other factors. A US survey that incidentally screened for personality disorder found a rate of 14.79%.

Approximately 7% of a preschool pediatric sample were given a psychiatric diagnosis in one clinical study, and approximately 10% of 1- and 2-year-olds receiving developmental screening have been assessed as having significant emotional/behavioural problems based on parent and pediatrician reports.

While rates of psychological disorders are often the same for men and women, women tend to have a higher rate of depression. Each year 73 million women are afflicted with major depression, and suicide is ranked 7th as the cause of death for women between the ages of 20-59. Depressive disorders account for close to 41.9% of the disability from neuropsychiatric disorders among women compared to 29.3% among men.

Ancient Civilizations

Ancient civilizations described and treated a number of mental disorders. The Greeks coined terms for melancholy, hysteria and phobia and developed the humorism theory. Mental disorders were described, and treatments developed, in Persia, Arabia and in the medieval Islamic world.

Europe

Middle Ages: Conceptions of madness in the Middle Ages in Christian Europe were a mixture of the divine, diabolical, magical and humoral, as well as more down to earth considerations. In the early modern period, some people with mental disorders may have been victims of the witch-hunts but were increasingly admitted to local workhouses and jails or sometimes to private madhouses. Many terms for mental disorder that found their way into everyday use first became popular in the 16th and 17th centuries.

Eighteenth Century

By the end of the 17th century and into the Enlightenment, madness was increasingly seen as an organic physical phenomenon with no connection to the soul or moral responsibility. Asylum care was often harsh and treated people like wild animals, but towards the end of the 18th century a moral treatment movement gradually developed. Clear descriptions of some syndromes may be rare prior to the 19th century.

Nineteenth Century

Industrialization and population growth led to a massive expansion of the number and size of insane asylums in every Western country in the 19th century. Numerous different classification schemes and diagnostic terms were developed by different authorities, and the term psychiatry was coined, though medical superintendents were still known as alienists.

Twentieth Century

The turn of the 20th century saw the development of psychoanalysis, which would later come to the fore, along with Kraepelin's classification scheme. Asylum "inmates" were increasingly referred to as "patients", and asylums renamed as hospitals.

Europe and the U.S.

Early in the 20th century in the United States, a mental hygiene movement developed, aiming to prevent mental disorders. Clinical psychology and social work developed as professions. World War I saw a massive increase of conditions that came to be termed "shell shock".

World War II saw the development in the U.S. of a new psychiatric manual for categorizing mental disorders, which along with existing systems for collecting census and hospital statistics led to the first Diagnostic and Statistical Manual of Mental Disorders (DSM). The International Classification of Diseases (ICD) also developed a section on mental disorders. The term stress, having emerged from endocrinology work in the 1930s, was increasingly applied to mental disorders.

Electroconvulsive therapy, insulin shock therapy, lobotomies and the "neuroleptic" chlorpromazine came to be used by mid-century. In the 1960s there were many challenges to the concept of mental illness itself. These challenges came from psychiatrists like Thomas Szasz who argued that mental illness was a myth used to disguise moral conflicts; from sociologists such as Erving Goffman who said that mental illness was merely another example of how society labels and controls non-conformists; from behavioural psychologists who challenged psychiatry's fundamental reliance on unobservable phenomena; and from gay rights activists who criticised the APA's listing of homosexuality as a mental disorder. A study published in Science by Rosenhan received much publicity and was viewed as an attack on the efficacy of psychiatric diagnosis.

Deinstitutionalization gradually occurred in the West, with isolated psychiatric hospitals being closed down in favour of community mental health services. A consumer/survivor movement gained momentum. Other kinds of psychiatric medication gradually came into use, such as "psychic energizers" (later antidepressants) and lithium. Benzodiazepines gained widespread use in the 1970s for anxiety and depression, until dependency problems curtailed their popularity.

Advances in neuroscience, genetics and psychology led to new research agendas. Cognitive behavioural therapy and other psychotherapies developed. The DSM and then ICD adopted new criteria-based classifications, and the number of "official" diagnoses saw a large expansion. Through the 1990s, new SSRI-type antidepressants became some of the most widely prescribed drugs in the world, as later did antipsychotics. Also during the 1990s, a recovery approach developed.

Society and Culture

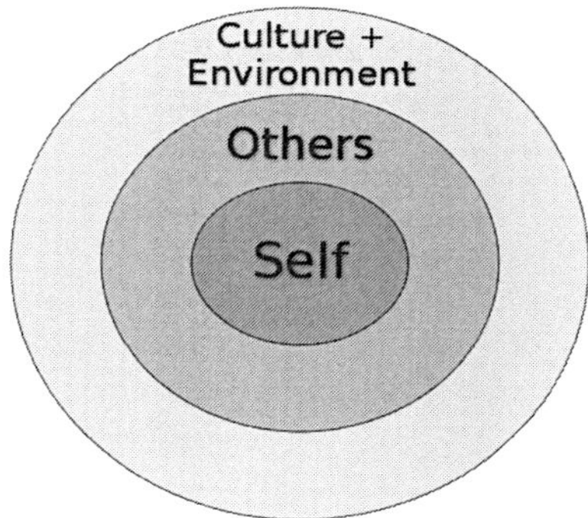

Different societies or cultures, even different individuals in a subculture, can disagree as to what constitutes optimal versus pathological biological and psychological functioning. Research has demonstrated that cultures vary in the relative importance placed on, for example, happiness, autonomy, or social relationships for pleasure. Likewise, the fact that a behaviour pattern is valued, accepted, encouraged, or even statistically normative in a culture does not necessarily mean that it is conducive to optimal psychological functioning.

People in all cultures find some behaviours bizarre or even incomprehensible. But just what they feel is bizarre or incomprehensible is ambiguous and subjective. These differences in determination can become highly contentious. Religious, spiritual, or transpersonal experiences and beliefs are typically not defined as disordered, especially if widely shared, despite meeting many criteria of delusional or psychotic disorders. Even when a belief or experience can be shown to produce distress or disability—the ordinary standard for judging mental disorders—the presence of a strong cultural basis for that belief, experience, or interpretation of experience, generally disqualifies it from counting as evidence of mental disorder.

The process by which conditions and difficulties come to be defined and treated as medical conditions and problems, and thus come under the authority of doctors and other health professionals, is known as medicalization or pathologization.

Movements

Controversy has often surrounded psychiatry, and the term anti-psychiatry was coined by psychiatrist David Cooper in 1967. The anti-psychiatry message is that psychiatric treatments are ultimately more damaging than helpful to patients, and psychiatry's history involves what may now be seen as dangerous treatments. Electroconvulsive therapy was one of these, which was used widely between the 1930s and 1960s. Lobotomy was another practice that was ultimately seen as too invasive and brutal. Valium and other sedatives were sometimes over-prescribed, which led to an epidemic of dependence. There was also concern about the large increase in prescribing psychiatric drugs for children. Two charismatic psychiatrists came to personify the movement against psychiatry. The most influential of these was R.D. Laing who wrote a series of best-selling books, including The Divided Self. Thomas Szasz wrote The Myth of Mental Illness. Some ex-patient groups have become militantly anti-psychiatric, often referring to themselves as "survivors".

The consumer/survivor movement (also known as user/survivor movement) is made up of individuals (and organizations representing them) who are clients of mental health services or who consider themselves survivors of psychiatric interventions. Activists campaign for improved mental health services and for more involvement and empowerment within mental health services, policies and wider society. Patient advocacy organizations have expanded with increasing deinstitutionalization in developed countries, working to challenge the stereotypes, stigma and exclusion associated with psychiatric conditions. There is also a carers rights movement of people who help and support people with mental health conditions, who may be relatives, and who often work in difficult and time-consuming circumstances with little acknowledgement and without pay. An anti-psychiatry movement fundamentally challenges mainstream psychiatric theory and practice, including in some cases asserting that psychiatric concepts and diagnoses of 'mental illness' are neither real nor useful. Alternatively, a movement for global mental health has emerged, defined as 'the area of study, research and practice that places a priority on improving mental health and achieving equity in mental health for all people worldwide'.

Cultural Bias

Current diagnostic guidelines, namely the DSM and to some extent the ICD, have been criticized as having a fundamentally Euro-American outlook. Opponents argue that even when diagnostic criteria are used across different cultures, it does not mean that the underlying constructs have validity within those cultures, as even reliable application can prove only consistency, not legitimacy. Advocating a more culturally sensitive approach, critics such as Carl Bell and Marcello Maviglia contend that the cultural and ethnic diversity of individuals is often discounted by researchers and service providers.

Cross-cultural psychiatrist Arthur Kleinman contends that the Western bias is ironically illustrated in the introduction of cultural factors to the DSM-IV. Disorders or concepts from non-Western or non-mainstream cultures are described as "culture-bound", whereas standard psychiatric diagnoses are given no cultural qualification whatsoever, revealing to Kleinman an underlying assumption that Western cultural phenomena are universal. Kleinman's negative view towards the culture-bound syndrome is largely shared by other cross-cultural critics. Common responses included both disappointment over the large number of documented non-Western mental disorders still left out and frustration that even those included are often misinterpreted or misrepresented.

Many mainstream psychiatrists are dissatisfied with the new culture-bound diagnoses, although for partly different reasons. Robert Spitzer, a lead architect of the DSM-III, has argued that adding cultural formulations was an attempt to appease cultural critics, and has stated that they lack any scientific rationale or support. Spitzer also posits that the new culture-bound diagnoses are rarely used, maintaining that the standard diagnoses apply regardless of the culture involved. In general, mainstream psychiatric opinion remains that if a diagnostic category is valid, cross-cultural factors are either irrelevant or are significant only to specific symptom presentations.

Clinical conceptions of mental illness also overlap with personal and cultural values in the domain of morality, so much so that it is sometimes argued that separating the two is impossible without fundamentally redefining the essence of being a particular person in a society. In clinical psychiatry, persistent distress and disability indicate an internal disorder requiring treatment; but in another context, that same distress and disability can be seen as an indicator of emotional struggle and the need to address social and structural problems. This dichotomy has led some academics and clinicians to advocate a postmodernist conceptualization of mental distress and well-being.

Such approaches, along with cross-cultural and "heretical" psychologies centred on alternative cultural and ethnic and race-based identities and experiences, stand in contrast to the mainstream psychiatric community's alleged avoidance of any explicit involvement with either morality or culture. In many countries there are attempts to challenge perceived prejudice against minority groups, including alleged institutional racism within psychiatric services. There are also ongoing attempts to improve professional cross cultural sensitivity.

Laws and Policies

Three quarters of countries around the world have mental health legislation. Compulsory admission to mental health facilities (also known as involuntary commitment) is a controversial topic. It can impinge on personal liberty and the right to choose, and carry the risk of abuse for political, social and other reasons; yet it can potentially prevent harm to self and others, and assist some people in attaining their right to healthcare when they may be unable to decide in their own interests.

All human rights oriented mental health laws require proof of the presence of a mental disorder as defined by internationally accepted standards, but the type and severity of disorder that counts can vary in different jurisdictions. The two most often utilized grounds for involuntary admission are said to be serious likelihood of immediate or imminent danger to self or others, and the need for treatment. Applications for someone to be involuntarily admitted usually come from a mental health practitioner, a family member, a close relative, or a guardian. Human-rights-oriented laws usually stipulate that independent medical practitioners or other accredited mental health practitioners must examine the patient separately and that there should be regular, time-bound review by an independent review body. The individual should also have personal access to independent advocacy.

In order for involuntary treatment to be administered (by force if necessary), it should be shown that an individual lacks the mental capacity for informed consent (i.e. to understand treatment information and its implications, and therefore be able to make an informed choice to either accept or refuse). Legal challenges in some areas have resulted in supreme court decisions that a person does not have to agree with a psychiatrist's characterization of the issues as constituting an "illness", nor agree with a psychiatrist's conviction in medication, but only recognize the issues and the information about treatment options.

Proxy consent (also known as surrogate or substituted decision-making) may be transferred to a personal representative, a family member or a legally appointed guardian. Moreover, patients may be able to make, when they are considered well, an advance directive stipulating how they wish to be treated should they be deemed to lack mental capacity in future. The right to supported decision-making, where a person is helped to understand and choose treatment options before they can be declared to lack capacity, may also be included in legislation. There should at the very least be shared decision-making as far as possible. Involuntary treatment laws are increasingly extended to those living in the community, for example outpatient commitment laws (known by different names) are used in New Zealand, Australia, the United Kingdom and most of the United States.

The World Health Organization reports that in many instances national mental health legislation takes away the rights of persons with mental disorders rather than protecting rights, and is often outdated. In 1991, the United Nations adopted the Principles for the Protection of Persons with Mental Illness and the Improvement of Mental Health Care, which established minimum human rights standards of practice in the mental health field. In 2006, the UN formally agreed the Convention on the Rights of Persons with Disabilities to protect and enhance the rights and opportunities of disabled people, including those with psychosocial disabilities. The term insanity, sometimes used colloquially as a synonym for mental illness, is often used technically as a legal term. The insanity defense may be used in a legal trial (known as the mental disorder defence in some countries).

Perception and Discrimination

Stigma: The social stigma associated with mental disorders is a widespread problem. The US Surgeon General stated in 1999 that: "Powerful and pervasive, stigma prevents people from acknowledging their own mental health problems, much less disclosing them to others." Employment discrimination is reported to play a significant part in the high rate of unemployment among those with a diagnosis of mental illness. An Australian study found that having a mental illness is a bigger barrier to employment than a physical disability.

Efforts are being undertaken worldwide to eliminate the stigma of mental illness, although the methods and outcomes used have sometimes been criticized.

A 2008 study by Baylor University researchers found that clergy in the US often deny or dismiss the existence of a mental illness. Of 293 Christian church members, more than 32 percent were told by their church pastor that they or their loved one did not really have a mental illness, and that the cause of their problem was solely spiritual in nature, such as a personal sin, lack of faith or demonic involvement. The researchers also found that women were more likely than men to get this response. All participants in both studies were previously diagnosed by a licensed mental health provider as having a serious mental illness. However, there is also research suggesting that people are often helped by extended families and supportive religious leaders who listen with kindness and respect, which can often contrast with usual practice in psychiatric diagnosis and medication.

Media and General Public

Media coverage of mental illness comprises predominantly negative and pejorative depictions, for example, of incompetence, violence or criminality, with far less coverage of positive issues such as accomplishments or human rights issues. Such negative depictions, including in children's cartoons, are thought to contribute to stigma and negative attitudes in the public and in those with mental health problems themselves, although more sensitive or serious cinematic portrayals have increased in prevalence.

In the United States, the Carter Centre has created fellowships for journalists in South Africa, the U.S., and Romania, to enable reporters to research and write stories on mental health topics. Former US First Lady Rosalynn Carter began the fellowships not only to train reporters in how to sensitively and accurately discuss mental health and mental illness, but also to increase the number of stories on these topics in the news media. There is also a World Mental Health Day, which in the US and Canada falls within a Mental Illness Awareness Week.

The general public have been found to hold a strong stereotype of dangerousness and desire for social distance from individuals described as mentally ill. A US national survey found that a higher percentage of people rate individuals described as displaying the characteristics of a mental disorder as "likely to do something violent to others", compared to the percentage of people who are rating individuals described as being "troubled".

Recent depictions in media have included leading characters successfully living with and managing a mental illness, including in Bipolar disorder in Homeland (2011) and Posttraumatic stress disorder in Iron Man 3 (2013).

Violence

Despite public or media opinion, national studies have indicated that severe mental illness does not independently predict future violent behaviour, on average, and is not a leading cause of violence in society.

There is a statistical association with various factors that do relate to violence (in anyone), such as substance abuse and various personal, social and economic factors.

In fact, findings consistently indicate that it is many times more likely that people diagnosed with a serious mental illness living in the community will be the victims rather than the perpetrators of violence. In a study of individuals diagnosed with "severe mental illness" living in a US inner-city area, a quarter were found to have been victims of at least one violent crime over the course of a year, a proportion eleven times higher than the inner-city average, and higher in every category of crime including violent assaults and theft. People with a diagnosis may find it more difficult to secure prosecutions, however, due in part to prejudice and being seen as less credible.

However, there are some specific diagnoses, such as childhood conduct disorder or adult antisocial personality disorder or psychopathy, which are defined by, or are inherently associated with, conduct problems and violence. There are conflicting findings about the extent to which certain specific symptoms, notably some kinds of psychosis (hallucinations or delusions) that can occur in disorders such as schizophrenia, delusional disorder or mood disorder, are linked to an increased risk of serious violence on average. The mediating factors of violent acts, however, are most consistently found to be mainly socio-demographic and socio-economic factors such as being young, male, of lower socioeconomic status and, in particular, substance abuse (including alcoholism) to which some people may be particularly vulnerable.

High-profile cases have led to fears that serious crimes, such as homicide, have increased due to deinstitutionalization, but the evidence does not support this conclusion. Violence that does occur in relation to mental disorder (against the mentally ill or by the mentally ill) typically occurs in the context of complex social interactions, often in a family setting rather than between strangers. It is also an issue in health care settings and the wider community.

4

Learning Disorders

Learning disability or neurobehavioural disorder is a classification including several areas of functioning in which a person has difficulty learning in a typical manner, usually caused by an unknown factor or factors.

While learning disability, learning disorder and learning difficulty are often used interchangeably, they differ in many ways. Learning disability refers to significant learning problems in an academic area. These problems, however, are not enough to warrant an official diagnosis. Learning disorder, on the other hand, is an official clinical diagnosis, whereby the individual meets certain criteria, as determined by a professional (psychologist, pediatrician, etc.) The difference is in degree, frequency, and intensity of reported symptoms and problems, and thus the two should not be confused. When the term "learning disabilities" is used, it describes a group of disorders characterized by inadequate development of specific academic, language, and speech skills. Types of learning disabilities include reading disability (dyslexia), mathematics disability (dyscalculia) and writing disability (dysgraphia).

The unknown factor is the disorder that affects the brain's ability to receive and process information. This disorder can make it problematic for a person to learn as quickly or in the same way as someone who is not affected by a learning disability. People with a learning disability have trouble performing specific types of skills or completing tasks if left to figure things out by themselves or if taught in conventional ways.

Individuals with learning disabilities can face unique challenges that are often pervasive throughout the lifespan. Depending on the type and severity of the disability, interventions and current technologies may be used to help the individual learn strategies that will foster future success. Some interventions can be quite simplistic, while others are intricate and complex. Current technologies may require student training to be effective classroom supports. Teachers, parents and schools can create plans together that tailor intervention and accommodations to aid the individual in successfully becoming independent learners. School psychologists and other qualified professionals quite often help design the intervention and coordinate the execution of the intervention with teachers and parents. Social support may improve the learning for students with learning disabilities.

Types

Learning disabilities can be categorized either by the type of information processing that is affected or by the specific difficulties caused by a processing deficit.

By Stage of Information Processing

Learning disabilities fall into broad categories based on the four stages of information processing used in learning: input, integration, storage, and output.

- Input: This is the information perceived through the senses, such as visual and auditory perception. Difficulties with visual perception can cause problems with recognizing the shape, position and size of items seen. There can be problems with sequencing, which can relate to deficits with processing time intervals or temporal perception. Difficulties with auditory perception can make it difficult to screen out competing sounds in order to focus on one of them, such as the sound of the teacher's voice. Some children appear to be unable to process tactile input. For example, they may seem insensitive to pain or dislike being touched.
- Integration: This is the stage during which perceived input is interpreted, categorized, placed in a sequence, or related to previous learning. Students with problems in these areas may be unable to tell a story in the correct sequence, unable to memorize sequences of information such as the days of the week, able to understand a new concept but be unable to generalize it to other areas of learning, or able to learn facts but be unable to put the facts together to see the "big picture."

A poor vocabulary may contribute to problems with comprehension.

- Storage: Problems with memory can occur with short-term or working memory, or with long-term memory. Most memory difficulties occur in the area of short-term memory, which can make it difficult to learn new material without many more repetitions than is usual. Difficulties with visual memory can impede learning to spell.
- Output: Information comes out of the brain either through words, that is, language output, or through muscle activity, such as gesturing, writing or drawing. Difficulties with language output can create problems with spoken language, for example, answering a question on demand, in which one must retrieve information from storage, organize our thoughts, and put the thoughts into words before we speak. It can also cause trouble with written language for the same reasons. Difficulties with motor abilities can cause problems with gross and fine motor skills. People with gross motor difficulties may be clumsy, that is, they may be prone to stumbling, falling, or bumping into things. They may also have trouble running, climbing, or learning to ride a bicycle. People with fine motor difficulties may have trouble buttoning shirts, tying shoelaces, or with handwriting.

By Function Impaired

Deficits in any area of information processing can manifest in a variety of specific learning disabilities. It is possible for an individual to have more than one of these difficulties. This is referred to as comorbidity or co-occurrence of learning disabilities. In the UK, the term dual diagnosis is often used to refer to co-occurrence of learning difficulties.

Reading Disorder (ICD-10 and DSM-IV codes: F81.0/315.00)

The most common learning disability. Of all students with specific learning disabilities, 70%-80% have deficits in reading. The term "Developmental Dyslexia" is often used as a synonym for reading disability; however, many researchers assert that there are different types of reading disabilities, of which dyslexia is one. A reading disability can affect any part of the reading process, including difficulty with accurate or fluent word recognition, or both, word decoding, reading rate, prosody (oral reading with expression), and reading comprehension. Before the term "dyslexia" came to prominence, this learning disability used to be known as "word blindness."

Common indicators of reading disability include difficulty with phonemic awareness—the ability to break up words into their component sounds, and difficulty with matching letter combinations to specific sounds (sound-symbol correspondence).

Disorder of Written Expression (ICD-10 and DSM-IV-TR codes 315.2)

Speech and language disorders can also be called Dysphasia/ Aphasia (coded F80.0-F80.2/315.31 in ICD-10 and DSM-IV).

The DSM-IV-TR criteria for a Disorder of Written Expression is writing skills (as measured by standardized test or functional assessment) that fall substantially below those expected based on the individual's chronological age, measured intelligence, and age appropriate education, (Criterion A). This difficulty must also cause significant impairment to academic achievement and tasks that require composition of written text (Criterion B), and if a sensory deficit is present, the difficulties with writing skills must exceed those typically associated with the sensory deficit, (Criterion C).

Individuals with a diagnosis of a Disorder of Written Expression typically have a combination of difficulties in their abilities with written expression as evidenced by grammatical and punctuation errors within sentences, poor paragraph organization, multiple spelling errors, and excessively poor handwriting. A disorder in spelling or handwriting without other difficulties of written expression do not generally qualify for this diagnosis. If poor handwriting is due to an impairment in motor coordination, a diagnosis of Developmental coordination disorder should be considered.

By a number of organizations, the term "dysgraphia" has been used as an overarching term for all disorders of written expression. However, the International Dyslexia Association, uses the term "dysgraphia" only to refer to difficulties with handwriting.

Math Disability (ICD-10 and DSM-IV codes F81.2-3/315.1)

Sometimes called dyscalculia, a math disability involves such difficulties as learning math concepts (such as quantity, place value, and time), difficulty memorizing math facts, difficulty organizing numbers, and understanding how problems are organized on the page. Dyscalculics are often referred to as having poor "number sense".

Non ICD-10/DSM

- Nonverbal learning disability: Nonverbal learning disabilities often manifest in motor clumsiness, poor visual-spatial skills, problematic social relationships, difficulty with maths, and poor organizational skills. These individuals often have specific strengths in the verbal domains, including early speech, large vocabulary, early reading and spelling skills, excellent rote-memory and auditory retention, and eloquent self-expression.
- Disorders of speaking and listening: Difficulties that often co-occur with learning disabilities include difficulty with memory, social skills and executive functions (such as organizational skills and time management).

Diagnosis

IQ-Achievement Discrepancy: Learning disabilities are often identified by psychiatrists, school psychologists, clinical psychologists, counselling psychologists and neuropsychologists through a combination of intelligence testing, academic achievement testing, classroom performance, and social interaction and aptitude. Other areas of assessment may include perception, cognition, memory, attention, and language abilities. The resulting information is used to determine whether a child's academic performance is commensurate with his or her cognitive ability. If a child's cognitive ability is much higher than his or her academic performance, the student is often diagnosed with a learning disability. The DSM-IV and many school systems and government programmes diagnose learning disabilities in this way (DSM-IV uses the term "disorder" rather than "disability".)

Although the discrepancy model has dominated the school system for many years, there has been substantial criticism of this approach among researchers. Recent research has provided little evidence that a discrepancy between formally measured IQ and achievement is a clear indicator of LD. Furthermore, diagnosing on the basis of a discrepancy does not predict the effectiveness of treatment. Low academic achievers who do not have a discrepancy with IQ (i.e. their IQ scores are also low) appear to benefit from treatment just as much as low academic achievers who do have a discrepancy with IQ (i.e. their IQ scores are higher than their academic performance would suggest).

Response to Intervention (RTI)

Much current research has focused on a treatment-oriented diagnostic process known as response to intervention (RTI). Researcher recommendations for implementing such a model include early screening for all students, placing those students who are having difficulty into research-based early intervention programmes, rather than waiting until they meet diagnostic criteria. Their performance can be closely monitored to determine whether increasingly intense intervention results in adequate progress. Those who respond will not require further intervention. Those who do not respond adequately to regular classroom instruction (often called "Tier 1 instruction") and a more intensive intervention (often called "Tier 2" intervention) are considered "nonresponders." These students can then be referred for further assistance through special education, in which case they are often identified with a learning disability. Some models of RTI include a third tier of intervention before a child is identified as having a learning disability.

A primary benefit of such a model is that it would not be necessary to wait for a child to be sufficiently far behind to qualify for assistance. This may enable more children to receive assistance before experiencing significant failure, which may in turn result in fewer children who need intensive and expensive special education services. In the United States, the 2004 reauthorization of the Individuals with Disabilities Education Act permitted states and school districts to use RTI as a method of identifying students with learning disabilities. RTI is now the primary means of identification of learning disabilities in Florida.

The process does not take into account children's individual neuropsychological factors such as phonological awareness and memory, that can help design instruction. Second, RTI by design takes considerably longer than established techniques, often many months to find an appropriate tier of intervention. Third, it requires a strong intervention programme before students can be identified with a learning disability. Lastly, RTI is considered a regular education initiative and is not driven by psychologists, reading specialists, or special educators.

Assessment

Many normed assessments can be used in evaluating skills in the primary academic domains: reading, including word recognition, fluency, and comprehension; mathematics, including computation and problem solving; and written expression, including handwriting, spelling and composition.

The most commonly used comprehensive achievement tests include the Woodcock-Johnson III (WJ III), Wechsler Individual Achievement

Test II (WIAT II), the Wide Range Achievement Test III (WRAT III), and the Stanford Achievement Test–10th edition. These tests include measures of many academic domains that are reliable in identifying areas of difficulty.

In the reading domain, there are also specialized tests that can be used to obtain details about specific reading deficits. Assessments that measure multiple domains of reading include Gray's Diagnostic Reading Tests–2nd edition (GDRT II) and the Stanford Diagnostic Reading Assessment. Assessments that measure reading subskills include the Gray Oral Reading Test IV – Fourth Edition (GORT IV), Gray Silent Reading Test, Comprehensive Test of Phonological Processing (CTOPP), Tests of Oral Reading and Comprehension Skills (TORCS), Test of Reading Comprehension 3 (TORC-3), Test of Word Reading Efficiency (TOWRE), and the Test of Reading Fluency. A more comprehensive list of reading assessments may be obtained from the Southwest Educational Development Laboratory.

The purpose of assessment is to determine what is needed for intervention, which also requires consideration of contextual variables and whether there are comorbid disorders that must also be identified and treated, such as behavioural issues or language delays.

Management

Interventions include:

- Mastery model:
    - o Learners work at their own level of mastery.
    - o Practice
    - o Gain fundamental skills before moving onto the next level
        - – Note: this approach is most likely to be used with adult learners or outside the mainstream school system.
- Direct Instruction:
    - o Highly structured, intensive instruction
    - o Emphasizes carefully planned lessons for small learning increments
    - o Scripted lesson plans
    - o Rapid-paced interaction between teacher and students
    - o Correcting mistakes immediately
    - o Achievement-based grouping
    - o Frequent progress assessments

- Classroom adjustments:
  - Special seating assignments
  - Alternative or modified assignments
  - Modified testing procedures
  - Quiet environment
- Special equipment:
  - Word processors with spell checkers and dictionaries
  - Text-to-speech and speech-to-text programmes
  - Talking calculators
  - Books on tape
  - Computer-based activities
- Classroom assistants:
  - Note-takers
  - Readers
  - Proofreaders
  - Scribes
- Special Education:
  - Prescribed hours in a resource room
  - Placement in a resource room
  - Enrollment in a special school for learning disabled students
  - Individual Education Plan (IEP)
  - Educational therapy

Sternberg has argued that early remediation can greatly reduce the number of children meeting diagnostic criteria for learning disabilities. He has also suggested that the focus on learning disabilities and the provision of accommodations in school fails to acknowledge that people have a range of strengths and weaknesses, and places undue emphasis on academic success by insisting that people should receive additional support in this arena but not in music or sports. Other research has pinpointed the use of resource rooms as an important—yet often politicized component of educating students with learning disabilities.

Causes

The causes for learning disabilities are not well understood, and sometimes there is no apparent cause for a learning disability. However, some causes of neurological impairments include:

- Heredity – Learning disabilities often run in the family. Children with learning disabilities are likely to have parents or other relatives with similar difficulties.
- Problems during pregnancy and birth – Learning disabilities can result from anomalies in the developing brain, illness or injury, fetal exposure to alcohol or drugs, low birth weight, oxygen deprivation, or by premature or prolonged labour.
- Accidents after birth – Learning disabilities can also be caused by head injuries, malnutrition, or by toxic exposure (such as heavy metals or pesticides).

Impact on Affected Individuals

Neuropsychological differences can impact the accurate perception of social cues with peers. A diagnosis of a learning disability can be potentially devastating to an individual and their family. Both the individual and their family will need to learn methods of coping with the effects of the disorder; they will also need to learn how to cope with the disorder emotionally. Stress related to the disorder can accumulate, making the coping process difficult. Stigmas that friends/family/peers have about the learning disorder can also contribute to the stress level the individual feels. Learning disabilities are often present throughout the lifespan, so learning appropriate and effective methods of coping are essential to successful management of the disorder.

Social Correlates

Critique of the Medical Model: Learning disability theory is founded in a medical model, in that disability is perceived as an individual deficit that is biological in origin. Researchers working within a social model of disability assert that there are social or structural causes of disability or the assignation of the label of disability, and even that disability is entirely socially constructed. Since the turn of the 19th century, education in the United States has been geared towards producing citizens who can effectively contribute to a capitalistic society, with a cultural premium on efficiency and science. More agrarian cultures, for example, don't even use learning ability as a measure of adult adequacy, whereas learning disabilities are prevalent in Western capitalistic societies because of the high value placed on speed, literacy, and numeracy in both the labour force and school system. The notion of learning disabilities has been described as evidence of America's individualistic obsession with self-reliance. In the bigger picture, these points demonstrate how the label of disability is socially constructed and represents a lack of fit between Western conceptions of educational institutions and proper students.

Culture

By 1980 in the U.S., white children were labelled more often with various learning disabilities, whereas minorities were labelled more often emotionally disturbed or retarded. This is problematic because it may suggest that students who are racially diverse do not have the same opportunities or learning capacities as those who are not. Therefore an underlying racism seems heavily present in the past.

There are three patterns that are well known in regards to mainstream students and minority labels in the US:

- "A higher percentage of minority children than of white children are assigned to special education;"
- "within special education, white children are assigned to less restrictive programmes than are their minority counterparts;"
- "the data — driven by inconsistent methods of diagnosis, treatment, and funding — make the overall system difficult to describe or change".

In present day, it has been reported that white districts have more children from minority backgrounds enrolled in special education than they do majority students. "It was also suggested that districts with a higher percentage of minority faculty had fewer minority students placed in special education suggesting that "minority students are treated differently in predominantly white districts than in predominantly minority districts""

Educators have only recently started to look into the effects of culture on learning disabilities. If a teacher ignores a student's culturally diverse background, the student will suffer in the class. "The cultural repertoires of students from cultural learning disorder backgrounds have an impact on their learning, school progress, and behaviour in the classroom". These students may then act out and not excel in the classroom and will therefore be misdiagnosed: "Overall, the data indicates that there is a persistent concern regarding the misdiagnosis and inappropriate placement of students from diverse backgrounds in special education classes since the 1975". However, if teachers direct their teaching to all students and not just to the mainstream, then students of various cultures and races will be able to relate and therefore excel in school. "Studies show that teachers' culturally shaped ways of delivering instruction have an effect on students' acquisition of meta-cognitive skills. " Students are influenced from various aspect of daily routine, if a child experiences racism and discrimination; this will affect their learning abilities. Artiles et al. (2011) offer that "because of the devaluation and negative identification many have experienced in school contexts coupled with societal stereotypes based on race, gender, language, or social class [it] may influence these learners' academic participation, affect, and performance on assessments". "On average, almost one-fourth of special education teachers' students are from a cultural or linguistic group different from their own, and 7 percent are English language learners". "Cultural, personal, and academic gaps between teachers and students of CLD backgrounds, which is the core relationship of learning, are contributing factors to their underachievement in school".

Social Roots of Learning Disabilities in the U.S.

One of the most clear indications of the social roots of learning disabilities is the disproportionate identification of racial and ethnic minorities and students who have low socioeconomic status (SES). While some attribute the disproportionate identification of racial/ethnic minorities to racist practices or cultural misunderstanding, others have argued that racial/ethnic minorities are overidentified because of their lower status. Similarities were noted between the behaviours of "brain-injured" and lower class students as early as the 1960s. The distinction between race/ethnicity and SES is important to the extent that these considerations contribute to the provision of services to children in need. While many studies have considered only one characteristic of the student at a time, or used district- or school-level data to examine this issue, more recent studies have used large national student-level datasets and sophisticated methodology to find that the disproportionate identification of African American students with learning disabilities can be attributed to their average lower SES, while the disproportionate identification of Latino youth seems to be attributable to difficulties in distinguishing between linguistic proficiency and learning ability. Although the contributing factors are complicated and interrelated, it is possible to discern which factors really drive disproportionate identification by considering a multitude of student characteristics simultaneously. For instance, if high SES minorities have rates of identification that are similar to the rates among high SES whites, and low SES minorities have rates of identification that are similar to the rates among low SES whites, we can know that the seemingly higher rates of identification among minorities result from their greater likelihood to have low SES.

Summarily, because the risk of identification for white students who have low SES is similar to that of black students who have low SES, future research and policy reform should focus on identifying the shared qualities or experiences of low SES youth that lead to their disproportionate identification, rather than focusing exclusively on racial/ethnic minorities. It remains to be determined why lower SES youth are at higher risk of incidence, or possibly just of identification, with learning disabilities.

Contrast with Other Conditions

People with an IQ lower than 70 are usually characterized as having mental retardation and are not included under most definitions of learning disabilities, because their learning difficulties are considered to be related directly to their overall low intelligence.

Attention-deficit hyperactivity disorder (ADHD) is often studied in connection with learning disabilities, but it is not actually included in the standard definitions of learning disabilities. An individual with ADHD may struggle with learning, but he or she can often learn adequately once successfully treated for the ADHD. A person can have ADHD but not learning disabilities or have learning disabilities without having ADHD. The conditions can co-occur.

People diagnosed with ADHD sometimes have impaired learning. Some of the struggles people with ADHD might have include lack of motivation, high levels of anxiety, and the inability to process information. There are studies that suggest people with ADHD generally have a positive attitude towards academics and, with developed study skills, can perform just as well as individuals without learning disabilities. Also, using alternate sources of gathering information, such as websites, study groups, and learning centres, can help a person with ADHD be academically successful.

Some research is beginning to make a case for ADHD being included in the definition of LDs, since it is being shown to have a strong impact on "executive functions" required for learning. This has not as yet affected any official definitions. Scientific research continues to explore the traits, struggles, and learning styles of those with ADHD.

In Different Countries

United States and Canada: In the United States and Canada, the terms learning disability and learning disorder (LD) refer to a group of disorders that affect a broad range of academic and functional skills including the ability to speak, listen, read, write, spell, reason, organize information, and do math. A person's IQ must be average or above to have a learning disability or learning disorder.

USA Legislation

The Section 504 of the Rehabilitation Act 1973 was taken in effect in May 1977, this American legislation guarantees certain rights to people with disabilities, especially in the cases of education and work, such being in schools, colleges and university settings.

The Individuals with Disabilities Education Act, formerly known as the Education for All Handicapped Children Act, is a United States federal law that governs how states and public agencies provide early intervention, special education and related services to children with disabilities. It addresses the educational needs of children with disabilities from birth to the age of 21. Considered as a civil rights law, states are not required to participate.

United Kingdom

In the UK, terms such as specific learning difficulty (SpLD), Developmental Dyslexia, Developmental coordination disorder and dyscalculia are used to cover the range of learning difficulties referred to in the United States as "learning disabilities". In the UK, the term "learning disability" refers to a range of developmental disabilities or conditions that are almost invariably associated with more severe generalized cognitive impairment.

Language-based Learning Disability

Language-based learning disabilities or LBLD are "heterogeneous" disorders associated with young children that affect their academic skills such as listening, reasoning speaking, reading, writing, and maths calculations. It is also associated with movement, coordination, and direct attention. LBLD is not usually identified until the child reaches school age. Most of the children with this disorder find it hard to communicate, to express ideas efficiently and whatever they say can be ambiguous and hard to understand It is caused by brain damage or a structural development of brain usually at birth. It is often hereditary, and is frequently associated to specific language problems.

There are two types of learning disabilities: non-verbal, which includes disabilities from psychomotor difficulties to dyscalculia, and verbal, language based.

Symptoms

LBLD consists of dyslexia which comprises the reading of numbers sequentially, learning the time table, and telling time There are also difficulties associated with written language such as trouble learning new vocabulary, letters and alphabets. Trouble understanding questions and following directions, understanding and remembering the details of a story's plot or a classroom lecture, learning words to songs and rhymes, telling left from right, and having a hard time with reading and writing . Difficulties associated with reading and spoken language involve trouble understanding questions and following directions, understanding and retaining the details of a story's plot or a classroom lecture, nonword repetition, learning words to songs and rhymes, and identifying the sounds that correspond to letters, which makes learning to read difficult Difficulties associated with motor skills include difficulty telling left from right which is part of motor incoordination, visual perceptual problems, and memory problem

Prevalence

15-20% of the children in the United States have a language-based learning disability. Of the students with specific learning disabilities receiving special education services, 70-80% have a discrepancy in reading.

Diagnosis

A speech-language pathologist (SLP), psychologist, social worker, and sometimes neurologist work together or individually to find the proper diagnosis for children with LBLD. Additionally, they evaluate speaking, listening, reading, and written language for children who have LBLD.

- SLPs evaluate the child's comprehension skills, and the child's ability to follow verbal and written directions. Also, they look for responsiveness, and see if the child recognizes familiar signs or holds a book correctly and they look for whether the child knows and/or writes letters, and names.
- Social workers obtain literacy history from the home, and then observe the child during classroom activities, they look for social interactions.
- Psychologists review a child's phonological memory by having him or her repeat series of words, numbers, letters, and sounds. They also look for response from the child to environmental and social factors.

- Neurologists look for motor skills, brain functions which include visual and auditory perception.

Prognosis

LBLD can be an enduring problem. Some people might experience overlapping learning disabilities that make improvement problematic. Others with single disabilities often show more improvement. Most subjects can achieve literacy via coping mechanisms and education.

Treatment

Special education classes are the primary treatment. These classes focus on activities that sustain growth in language skills. The foundation of this treatment is repetition of oral, reading and writing activities. Usually the SLP, psychologist and the teacher work together with the children in small groups in the class room. Another treatment is looking at a child's needs through the Individual Education Plan (IEP). In this programme teachers and parents work together to monitor the progress of the child's comprehensive, verbal, written, social, and motor skills in school and in the home. Then the child goes through different assessments to determine his/her level. The level that the child is placed in will determine the class size, number of teachers, and the need for therapy. There are a number of schools that cater specifically to students with language-based learning disabilities such as Landmark School in Massachusetts and The Kildonan School in Amenia, New York.

Personality and its Disorders: Psychopathic Personality.

Psychopathy is a personality disorder characterised partly by enduring anti-social behaviour, a diminished capacity for empathy or remorse, and poor behavioural controls.

The 4th and 5th editions of the Diagnostic and Statistical Manual of Mental Disorders (DSM) have a diagnosis of Antisocial (Dissocial) Personality Disorder (ASPD), which states: "The essential feature of antisocial personality disorder is a pervasive pattern of disregard for, and violation of, the rights of others that begins in childhood or early adolescence and continues into adulthood. This pattern has also been referred to as psychopathy, sociopathy, or dyssocial personality disorder." While no psychiatric or psychological organization has sanctioned a diagnosis titled "psychopathy", assessments of psychopathy characteristics are widely used in criminal justice settings in some nations, and may have important consequences for individuals. The term is also used by the general public, in popular press, and in fictional portrayals.

Although American psychiatrist Hervey Cleckley's work on psychopathy influenced the initial diagnostic criteria for sociopathic or antisocial personality in the DSM, in 1980 the somewhat different diagnosis of ASPD was introduced. However, Canadian psychologist Robert D. Hare repopularised the construct in criminology with his Psychopathy Checklist.

The word "psychopathy" is a joining of the Greek words psyche—meaning soul—and pathos—meaning suffering or feeling. The first documented use is from 1847 in Germany as psychopatisch, and the noun psychopath has been traced to 1885. In medicine, patho- has a more specific meaning of disease (thus pathology has meant the study of disease since 1610, and psychopathology has meant the study of mental disorder in general since 1847. A sense of "a subject of pathology, morbid, excessive" is attested from 1845, including the phrase pathological liar from 1891 in the medical literature).

The term psychopathy initially had a very general meaning referring to all sorts of mental disorders and social aberrations, popularised from 1891 in Germany by Koch's concept of "psychopathic inferiority" (psychopathische Minderwertigkeiten). Some medical dictionaries still define psychopathy in both a narrow and broad sense, such as MedlinePlus from the U.S. National Library of Medicine. On the other hand, Stedman's Medical Dictionary defines psychopathy only as an outdated term for an antisocial type of personality disorder.

The term psychosis was also used in Germany from 1841, originally in a very general sense. The suffix -osis meant in this case "abnormal condition". This term or its adjective psychotic would come to refer to the more severe mental disturbances and then specifically to mental states or disorders characterized by hallucinations, delusions or in some other sense markedly out of touch with reality.

The slang psycho has been traced to a shortening of the adjective psychopathic from 1936, and from 1942 as a shortening of the noun psychopath, but it is also used as shorthand for psychotic or just mentally crazed in some way.

The label psychopath has been described as strangely nonspecific but probably persisting because it indicates that the source of behaviour lies in the psyche rather than in the situation. The media usually uses the term to designate any criminal whose offenses are particularly abhorrent and unnatural, but that is not its original or general psychiatric meaning. The term sociopathy was introduced from 1909 as an alternative to the term psychopathy, to reflect the belief that the condition is caused more by societal forces or experiences acting on a person than by inborn psychological traits. The element socio has been used in compound words since around 1880.

History

The modern concept of psychopathy has been linked to the early 1800s with the work of Pinel (1801; "mania without delirium") and Pritchard (1835; "moral insanity"), although historians have largely discredited the idea of a direct equivalence. The term "psychopathic" was coined towards the end of the 19th century, by the German psychiatrist Julius Koch (1891). In contrast with current usage, Koch applied the term ""psychopathic inferiority" (psychopathischen Minderwertigkeiten) to various chronic conditions and character disorders.

The term 'psychopathic' came to be used to describe a diverse range of dysfunctional or antisocial behaviour and mental and sexual deviances, including at the time homosexuality. It was often used to imply an underlying constitutional or genetic origin. By contrast, the term "sociopathy," was used by Karl Birnbaum (1909) to imply social origins, later popularised in the US by George E. Partridge. Disparate early descriptions likely set the stage for modern controversies about the definition of psychopathy.

The most influential figure in shaping modern American conceptualizations of psychopathy was American psychiatrist Hervey Cleckley. In his classic monograph, The Mask of Sanity (1976), Cleckley drew on a small series of vivid case studies of psychiatric patients at a Veterans Administration hopsital in Georgia to describe the disorder. Cleckley used the metaphor of the "mask" to refer to the tendency of psychopaths to appear confident, personable, and well-adjusted compared to most psychiatric patients, while revealing underlying pathology through their actions over time. Cleckley formulated sixteen criteria to describe the disorder. The Scottish psychiatrist David Henderson had also been influential in Europe from 1939 in narrowing the diagnosis.

The diagnostic category of sociopathic personality in early editions of the Diagnostic and Statistical Manual (DSM) had some key similarities to Cleckley's ideas, though in 1980 when renamed Antisocial Personality Disorder some of the underlying personality assumptions were removed. In 1980, Canadian psychologist Robert D. Hare introduced an alternative measure, the "Psychopathy Checklist" (PCL) based largely on Cleckley's criteria, which was revised in 1991 (PCL-

R), and is the most widely used measure of psychopathy. There are also several self-report tests, with "The Psychopathic Personality Inventory" (PPI) being the most popular.

Famous individuals have sometimes been diagnosed, albeit at a distance, as psychopaths. In a 1972 version of a report prepared for the Office of Strategic Services in 1943, Walter C. Langer suggested Adolf Hitler was "probably a neurotic psychopath bordering on schizophrenia", although the term had a broader meaning in the 1940s. However, clinical forensic psychologist Glenn Walters argues that Hitler's actions do not warrant a diagnosis of psychopathy as he was not always egocentric, callously disregarding of feelings or lacking impulse control, and that there is no proof he couldn't learn from mistakes—though he did show several characteristics of criminality.

Classification

Sociopathy:

As a Term for the Same Disorder

The word-forming element socio has been common in compound words since around 1880, as in the term sociopathy, introduced in 1909 as an alternative to the term psychopathy. Hare notes that sociopathy and psychopathy are often used interchangeably, but in some cases the term sociopathy is preferred because it is less likely than is psychopathy to be confused with psychosis, whereas in other cases which term is used may "reflect the user's views on the origins and determinates of the disorder," with the term sociopathy preferred by those that see the causes as due to social factors and early environment, and the term psychopathy preferred by those who believe that there are psychological, biological, and genetic factors involved in addition to environmental factors.

Integrating Different Concepts

There has been effort to reconcile seemingly disparate historical conceptions, operationalizations, and research programmes on psychopathy.

Triarchic Model

The triarchic model suggests that different concepts of psychopathy emphasize three observable characteristics to varying degrees:

- Boldness. Low fear including stress-tolerance, toleration of unfamiliarity and danger, and high self-confidence and social assertiveness. PCL-R measures this relatively poorly and mainly through Facet 1 of Factor 1. Similar to PPI Fearless dominance. May correspond to differences in the amygdala and other neurological systems associated with fear.

- Disinhibition. Poor impulse control including problems with planning and foresight, lacking affect and urge control, demand for immediate gratification, and poor behavioural restraints. Similar to PCL-R Factor 2 and PPI Impulsive antisociality. May correspond to impairments in frontal lobe systems that are involved in such control.
- Meanness. Lacking empathy and close attachments with others, disdain of close attachments, use of cruelty to gain empowerment, exploitative tendencies, defiance of authority, and destructive excitement seeking. PCL-R in general is related to this but in particular some elements in Factor 1. Similar to PPI Coldheartedness but also includes elements of subscales in Impulsive antisociality. Meanness may possibly be caused by either high boldness or high disinhibition combined with an adverse environment. Thus, a child with high boldness may respond poorly to punishment but may respond better to rewards and secure attachments which may not be available under adverse conditions. A child with high disinhibition may have increased problems under adverse conditions with meanness developing in response.

Distinct Condition vs. Continuum

A crucial issue regarding the concept of psychopathy is whether it identifies a distinct condition that can be separated from other conditions and "normal" personality types, or whether it is simply a combination of scores on various dimensions of personality found throughout the population in varying combinations.

An early and influential analysis from Harris and colleagues indicated a discrete category may underlie PCL-R psychopathy, but this was only found for the behavioural Factor 2 items, indicating this analysis may be related to ASPD rather than psychopathy. Marcus, John, and Edens more recently performed a series of statistical analysis on PPI scores and concluded psychopathy may best be conceptualized as having a "dimensional latent structure" like depression.

Marcus et al. repeated the study on a larger sample of prisoners, using the PCL-R and seeking to rule out other experimental or statistical issues that may have produced the previously different findings. They again found that the psychopathy measurements do not appear to be identifying a discrete type (a taxon). They suggest that while for legal or other practical purposes an arbitrary cut-off point on trait scores might be used, there is actually no clear scientific evidence for an objective point of difference by which to call some people "psychopaths". The Hare checklist was developed for research not clinical forensic diagnosis, and even for research purposes to improve understanding of the underlying issues, it is necessary to examine dimensions of personality in general rather than only this constellation of traits.

Primary-secondary Distinction

Several researchers have argued that there exist two variants of psychopathy. There is also empirical support for separating persons scoring high on the PCL-R into two groups that do not simply reflect Factor 1 and Factor 2. There is at least preliminary evidence of differences regarding cognition and affect as measured in laboratory tests. Different theories characterize these two variants somewhat differently. Compared to "primary" psychopaths, researchers agree that "secondary" psychopaths have more fear, anxiety, and negative emotions. They are often seen as more impulsive and with more reactive anger and aggression. Some preliminary research have suggested that secondary psychopaths may have had a more abusive childhood according to self-reports (which possibly may be inflated in secondary psychopathy), may have a higher risk of future violence, and may respond better to treatment. Blackburn asserted that secondary psychopaths "may be predominantly borderline personalities." Blackburn found that secondary psychopaths qualify more often for diagnoses of borderline personality disorder than do primary psychopaths, who more often qualify for a diagnoses of either antisocial personality disorder and/or narcissistic personality disorder.

Primary psychopathy has been seen as mainly due to genetic factors while secondary psychopathy has been seen as mainly due to environmental factors which also has implications for treatment possibilities. Such proposed environmental factors include an abusive childhood or a society presenting opportunities for cheating. Other researchers have argued that genetics and environment are important for both variants. David T. Lykken, using Gray's biopsychological theory of personality, have argued that primary psychopaths innately have little fear while secondary psychopaths innately have increased sensitivity to rewards. Proponents of the triarchic model described above see primary psychopaths associated with increased boldness and secondary psychopathy as associated with increased disinhibition.

Subtypes

Atascadero State Hospital (ASH) is a maximum-security forensic hospital that houses male patients with a wide range of psychiatric diagnoses. Psychopaths at this institution appear to be a heterogeneous group of individuals who, while sharing core personality characteristics, manifest substantial variability in their behaviour. Identifying subtypes within this clinical classification can have implications for patient treatment and management, as well as for the safety of the staff who work with them and for the communities to which they will eventually return. Several means of identifying subtypes have been proposed in the literature, and potential subgroups have been identified. Clinical observations at ASH have suggested 4 possible subtypes of psychopathy: narcissistic, borderline, sadistic, and antisocial. Issues related to the conceptualization of psychopathy are addressed, recognizing that additional data are needed to understand the observed variations in cases of psychopathy.

Alternative Personality Dimensions

Some studies have linked psychopathy to other dimensions of personality. Such personality dimensions may be found throughout the general population to varying degrees, and there are different views as to which dimensions are more central in regard to psychopathy. Examples of these personality dimensions include antagonism (high), conscientiousness (low) and anxiousness (low, or sometimes high). Some have also linked psychopathy to high psychoticism—a theorized dimension referring to tough, aggressive or hostile tendencies. Aspects of this that appear associated with psychopathy are lack of socialization and responsibility, impulsivity, sensation-seeking in some cases, and aggression. Otto Kernberg, from a particular psychoanalytic perspective, believes psychopathy should be considered as part of a spectrum of pathological narcissism, that would range from narcissistic personality on the low end, malignant narcissism in the middle, and psychopathy at the high end. However, narcissism is generally seen as only one aspect of psychopathy as generally defined.

Measurement

Hare Psychopathy Checklist: Psychopathy is most commonly assessed with the Psychopathy Checklist, Revised (PCL-R) created by the Canadian researcher Robert D. Hare, based on Cleckley's criteria from the 1940s and on research on criminals and incarcerated offenders in Canada. Each of the 20 items in the PCL-R is scored on a three-point scale, with a rating of 0 if it does not apply at all, 1 if there is a partial match or mixed information, and 2 if there is a reasonably good match to the offender. This is said to be ideally done through a face-to-face interview together with supporting information on lifetime behaviour (e.g. from case files), but is also done based only on file information. It can take up to three hours to collect and review the information.

Psychopathy Checklist-Revised: Factors, Facets, and Items		
Factor 1	***Factor 2***	***Other items***
Facet 1: Interpersonal • Glibness/superficial charm • Grandiose sense of self-worth • Pathological lying • Conning/manipulative *Facet 2: Affective* • Lack of remorse or guilt • Emotionally shallow • Callous/lack of empathy • Failure to accept responsibility for own actions	*Facet 3: Lifestyle* • Need for stimulation/proneness to boredom • Parasitic lifestyle • Lack of realistic, long-term goals • Impulsivity • Irresponsibility *Facet 4: Antisocial* • Poor behavioral controls • Early behavioral problems • Juvenile delinquency • Revocation of conditional release • Criminal versatility	• Many short-term marital relationships • Promiscuous sexual behavior

The PCL-R is referred to by some as the "gold standard" for assessing psychopathy. High PCL-R scores are positively associated with measures of impulsivity and aggression, Machiavellianism, persistent criminal behaviour, and negatively associated with measures of empathy and affiliation. Out of a maximum score of 40, the cut-off for the label of psychopathy is 30 in the United States and 25 in the United Kingdom, although there is little scientific support for these as particular break points. A cut-off score of 25 is also sometimes used for research purposes.

The PCL-R items were designed to be split in two. Factor 1 involves interpersonal or affective (emotion) personality traits and higher values are associated with narcissism and low empathy as well as social dominance and less fear or depression. Factor 2 involves either impulsive-irresponsible behaviours or antisocial behaviours and is associated with a maladaptive lifestyle including criminality. The two factors correlate with each other to some extent. Each factor is sometimes further subdivided in two: interpersonal versus affect items for Factor 1, and impulsive-irresponsible lifestyle versus antisocial behaviour items for Factor 2. "Promiscuous sexual behaviour" and "many short-term marital relationships" have sometimes been left out in such divisions.

Cooke and Michie have argued that a three-factor structure provide a better model than the two-factor structure. Those items from factor 2 strictly relating to antisocial behaviour (criminal versatility, juvenile delinquency, revocation of conditional release, early behavioural problems, and poor behavioural controls) are removed. The remaining items are divided into three factors: Arrogant and Deceitful Interpersonal Style, Deficient Affective Experience, and Impulsive and Irresponsible Behavioural Style. Hare and colleagues have published detailed critiques of the model and argue that there are statistical and conceptual problems.

Because an individual's scores may have important consequences for his or her future, the potential for harm if the test is used or administered incorrectly is considerable. The test can only be considered valid if administered by a suitably qualified and experienced clinician under controlled conditions.

There is also a shorter version of the PCL-R, known as a screening version (PCL-SC), developed for quicker assessments of larger numbers or groups without criminal records. It has only 12 items and a maximum scores of 24 but correlates strongly with the main PCL-R. The corresponding cut-off score is 18.

Hare's concept and checklist have also been criticized. In 2010 there was controversy after it emerged Hare had threatened legal action that stopped publication of a peer-reviewed article on the PCL-R. Hare alleged the article quoted or paraphrased him incorrectly. The article eventually appeared three years later. It alleged that the checklist is wrongly viewed by many as the basic definition of psychopathy, yet it leaves out key factors, while also making criminality too central to the concept. The authors claimed this leads to problems in overdiagnosis and in the use of the checklist to secure convictions. Hare has since stated that he receives less than $35,000 a year from royalties associated with the checklist and its derivatives.

In addition, Hare's concept of psychopathy has been criticised as being only weakly applicable to real-world settings and tending towards tautology. It is also said to be vulnerable to "labelling effects"; to be over-simplistic; reductionistic; to embody the fundamental attribution error; and to not pay enough attention to context and the dynamic nature of human behaviour. Some research suggests that ratings made using this system depend on the personality of the person doing the rating, including how empathic they themselves are. One forensic researcher has suggested that future studies need to examine the class background, race and philosophical beliefs of raters because they may not be aware of enacting biased judgements of people whose section of society or individual lives they have no understanding of or empathy for.

Psychopathic Personality Inventory

Psychopathic Personality Inventory: Factors and Subscales		
PPI–1: Fearless dominance	*PPI–2: Impulsive Antisociality*	*Coldheartedness*
• Social influence • Fearlessness • Stress immunity	• Machiavellian egocentricity • Rebellious nonconformity • Blame externalization • Carefree nonplanfulness	• Coldheartedness

Unlike the PCL, the Psychopathic Personality Inventory (PPI) was developed to comprehensively index personality traits without explicitly referring to anti-social or criminal behaviours themselves. It is a self-report scale that was developed in non-clinical samples (e.g. university students) rather than prisoners, though may be used with the latter. It was revised in 2005 to become the PPI-R (Lilienfeld & Widows) and now comprises 154 items organized into eight subscales. The item scores have been found to group into two overarching and largely separate factors (unlike the PCL-R factors), plus a third factor which is largely independent on scores on the other two:

I: Fearless dominance. From the subscales Social influence, Fearlessness, and Stress immunity. Associated with less anxiety, depression, and empathy as well as higher well-being, assertiveness, narcissism, and thrill-seeking.

II: Impulsive antisociality. From the subscales "Machiavellian" egocentricity, Rebellious nonconformity, Blame externalization, and Carefree lack of planning. Associated with impulsivity, aggressiveness, substance use, antisocial behaviour, negative affect, and suicidal ideation.

III: Coldheartedness. From a subscale with the same name.

A person may score at different levels on the different factors, but the overall score indicates the extent of psychopathic personality. Factor I is associated with social efficacy while factor 2 is associated with maladaptive tendencies.

Cleckley Clinical Profile

In his book The Mask of Sanity, Hervey M. Cleckley described 16 "common qualities" that he thought were characteristic of the individuals he termed psychopaths: The Cleckley checklist formed the basis for Hare's more current PCL-R checklist.

1. Superficial charm and good "intelligence"
2. Absence of delusions and other signs of irrational thinking
3. Absence of "nervousness" or psychoneurotic manifestations
4. Unreliability
5. Untruthfulness and insincerity
6. Lack of remorse and shame
7. Inadequately motivated antisocial behaviour
8. Poor judgement and failure to learn by experience
9. Pathologic egocentricity and incapacity for love
10. General poverty in major affective reactions
11. Specific loss of insight
12. Unresponsiveness in general interpersonal relations
13. Fantastic and uninviting behaviour with drink and sometimes without
14. Suicide threats rarely carried out
15. Sex life impersonal, trivial, and poorly integrated
16. Failure to follow any life plan.

Cleckley stated in the first edition of The Mask of Sanity (p. 257) that those he was calling psychopaths were "frankly and unquestionably psychotic", contrary to later classifications of the condition as a personality disorder. He also did not describe them as particularly hostile or aggressive, contrary to more sinister depictions that others later developed. In addition he proposed the existence of a milder and extremely common form of the condition as he judged it: "If we consider, in addition to these patients (nearly all of whom have records of the utmost folly and misery and idleness over many years and who have had to enter a psychiatric hospital), the vast number of similar people in every community who show the same behaviour pattern in milder form but who are sufficiently protected and supported by relatives to remain at large, the prevalence of this disorder is seen to be appalling."

DSM and ICD

There are currently two widely established systems for classifying mental disorders—the International Classification of Diseases (ICD) produced by the World Health Organization (WHO) and the Diagnostic and Statistical Manual of Mental Disorders (DSM) produced by the

American Psychiatric Association (APA). Both list categories of disorders thought to be distinct types, and have deliberately converged their codes in recent revisions so that the manuals are often broadly comparable, although significant differences remain.

There has never been a diagnosis called "psychopathy" in either the DSM or ICD. The first edition of the DSM in 1952 had a section on sociopathic personality disturbances, then a general term that included such things as homosexuality and alcoholism as well as an "antisocial reaction" and "dyssocial reaction". The latter two eventually became antisocial personality disorder in the DSM and dissocial personality disorder in the ICD. However, traditional and popular conceptions of psychopathy influenced the diagnostic criteria for ASPD, and the DSM states that ASPD is also known as psychopathy. Researchers such as Robert D. Hare and Stephen Hart regard the mainstream psychiatric view as deeply flawed, calling for a return to a traditional model of psychopathy as a distinct disorder.

DSM

Antisocial Personality Disorder: Antisocial personality disorder (ASPD), the criteria of which were based on American psychiatrist Hervey Cleckley's work on psychopathy, is described in the DSM-IV-TR as "... a pervasive pattern of disregard for, and violation of, the rights of others that begins in childhood or early adolescence and continues into adulthood".

A diagnosis of ASPD is based on behavioural patterns, whereas the Hare Psychopathy Checklist also relies on subjective judgements of personality traits. Although Hare wrote that it is possible to obtain reliable and valid measures of the personality traits and behaviours associated with psychopathy, criteria relating to personality traits were excluded from the diagnostic criteria for ASPD in the DSM, in part because it was believed that personality traits were difficult to measure reliably and it was "easier to agree on the behaviours that typify a disorder than on the reasons why they occur". ASPD criteria are thus considered to be strongly associated with Factor 2 items but not as strongly associated with Factor 1 items in the PCL-R. Due to the diagnostic differences, Hare and other critics have argued that psychopathy and ASPD are not synonymous, despite the DSM stating that ASPD is also known as psychopathy.

Although the diagnosis of ASPD covers two to three times as many prisoners as are rated as psychopaths, Hare believes that the PCL-R is better able to predict future criminality, violence, and recidivism than a diagnosis of ASPD. Hare suggests that there are differences between PCL-R-diagnosed psychopaths and non-psychopaths on "processing and use of linguistic and emotional information", while such differences are potentially smaller between those diagnosed with ASPD and without. Hare argued that confusion regarding how to diagnose ASPD, confusion regarding the difference between ASPD and psychopathy, as well as the differing future prognoses regarding recidivism and treatability, may have serious consequences in settings such as court cases where psychopathy is often seen as aggravating the crime.

The DSM-V working party considered a revision of ASPD to be called antisocial/dyssocial personality disorder. There is an 'alternative model' for personality disorders proposed at the end of the DSM-5; this includes 'specifers' which for ASPD could involve: "A distinct variant often termed psychopathy (or "primary" psychopathy) is marked by a lack of anxiety or fear and by a bold interpersonal style that may mask maladaptive behaviours..."

ICD

Dissocial Personality Disorder: The ICD defines a conceptually similar disorder to psychopathy called dissocial personality disorder, "usually coming to attention because of a gross disparity between behaviour and the prevailing social norms, and characterized by" 3 of 6 specific issues.

Other

There are some traditional personality tests that contain subscales relating to psychopathy, though they assess relatively non-specific tendencies towards antisocial or criminal behaviour. These include the Minnesota Multiphasic Personality Inventory (Psychopathic Deviate scale); the California Psychological Inventory (Socialization scale); and the Millon Clinical Multiaxial Inventory (Antisocial Personality Disorder scale). There is also the Levenson Self-Report Psychopathy Scale (LSRP) and the Hare Self-Report Psychopathy Scale (HSRP). However, in terms of self-report tests, the PPI/PPI-R has become the most used in modern psychopathy research on adults.

Further Considerations

Offending:

Criminality

In terms of simple correlations, the PCL-R manual states an average score of 22.1 has been found in North American prisoners samples, and that 20.5% scored 30 or higher. An analysis of prisoner samples from outside North America found a somewhat lower average value of 17.5. A study also found that psychopathy scores correlated with repeated imprisonment, detention in higher security, disciplinary infractions, and substance misuse. Most correlations were similar to those in other studies.

Psychopathy, as measured with the PCL-R in institutional settings, show in meta-analyses small to moderate effect sizes (r = 0.23 to 0.30) with institutional misbehaviour, postrelease crime, or postrelease violent crime with similar effects for the three outcomes. Individual studies give similar results for adult offenders, forensic psychiatric samples, community samples, and youth. The PCL-R is poorer at predicting sexual re-offending. However, this small to moderate effect appears to be due largely to the scale items that assess impulsive behaviours and past criminal history, which are well-established but very general risk factors. The aspects of core personality often held to be distinctively psychopathic, generally show little or no predictive link to crime by themselves. Thus Factor 1 of the PCL-R and Fearless dominance of the PPI-R have smaller or no relationship to crime, including violent crime. In contrast Factor 2 and Impulsive antisociality of the PPI-R are associated more strongly with criminality. Factor 2 has a relationship of similar strength to that of the PCL-R as a whole. The antisocial facet of the PCL-R is still predictive of future violence after controlling for past criminal behaviour which, together with results regarding the PPI-R which by design does not include past criminal behaviour, suggests that impulsive behaviours is an independent risk factor.

Some clinicians suggest that assessment of the construct of psychopathy does not necessarily add value to violence risk assessment. There are several other risk assessment instruments which can predict further crime with an accuracy similar to the PCL-R and some of these are considerably easier, quicker, and less expensive to administrate. This may even be done automatically by a computer simply based on data such as age, gender, number of previous convictions, and age of first conviction. Some of these assessments may also identify treatment change and goals, identify quick changes that may help short-term management, identify more specific kinds of violence that may be at risk, and may have established specific probabilities of offending for specific scores. PCL-R may continue to be popular for risk assessment because of is pioneering role and the large amount of research done using it. Although psychopathy is associated on average with an increased risk of violence, it is difficult to know how to manage the risk. The concept of psychopathy may perform poorly when attempted to be used as a general theory of crime.

Violence

Although high psychopathy scores correlate significantly with violence on average, criminals comprise a heterogeneous group with varying characteristics and high psychopathy scores are not necessarily an underlying trait.

It has been suggested that psychopaths tend to commit more "instrumental" violence than "reactive" violence. One conclusion in this regard was made by a 2002 study of homicide offenders, which reported that the homicides committed by psychopaths were almost always (93.3%) primarily instrumental, while about half (48.4%) of those committed by non-psychopaths were. However, contrary to the equating of this to mean "in cold blood", more than a third of the homicides by psychopaths involved emotional reactivity as well.

In addition, the non-psychopaths still accounted for most of the instrumental homicides, because most of these murderers were not psychopaths. In any case, FBI profilers indicate that serious victim injury is generally an emotional offense, and some research supports this, at least with regard to sexual offending. One study has found more serious offending by non-psychopaths on average than by psychopaths (e.g. more homicides versus more armed robbery and property offenses) and another that the Affective facet of PCL-R predicted reduced offense seriousness.

A large systematic review and meta-regression found that the Hare Psychopathy Checklist performed the poorest out of nine tools for predicting violence. In addition, studies conducted by the authors or translators of violence prediction measures, including the PCL, show on average more positive results than those conducted by more independent investigators.

Sexual Offending

A 2011 study of conditional releases for Canadian male federal offenders found that psychopathy was related to more violent and non-violent offences but not more sexual offences. For child molesters, psychopathy was associated with more offences. Despite "their extensive criminal histories and high recidivism rate", psychopaths showed "a great proficiency in persuading parole boards to release them into the community." It is purported that high-psychopathy offenders (both sexual and non-sexual offenders) are about 2.5 times more likely to be granted conditional release compared to non-psychopathic offenders."

Some studies have found only weak associations between psychopathy and sexual offending overall. The association is more certain for sexual violence. Psychopaths have on average higher sexual arousal to depictions of rape than non-psychopaths. Rapists, especially sadistic rapists, and sexual homicide offenders have a high rate of psychopathy. Some researchers have argued that psychopaths have a preference for violent sexual behaviour.

One study examined the relationship between psychopathy scores and types of aggression expressed in a sample of 38 sexual murderers. 84.2% of the sample had PCL-R scores above 20 and 47.4% above 30. 82.4% of those above 30 had engaged in sadistic violence (defined as enjoyment indicated by self-report or evidence) as compared to 52.6% of those below and total PCL-R and Factor 1 scores correlated significantly with sadistic violence. In considering the challenging issue of possible reunification of some sex offenders into homes with a non-offending parent and children, it has been advised that any sex offender with a significant criminal history should be assessed on the PCL-R, and if they score 18 or higher than they should be excluded from any consideration of being placed in a home with children under any circumstances.

However, there is increasing concern that PCL scores are too inconsistent between different examiners, including in its real world use to evaluate sex offenders, and especially on the evaluation of personality traits.

Other Offending

Terrorists are sometimes called psychopaths, and comparisons can be drawn with traits such as antisocial violence, a selfish worldview that precludes welfare for others, lack of remorse or guilt, and blaming external events. However, such comparisons could also then be drawn more widely, for example to soldiers in wars. In addition, it has been noted that coordinated terrorist activity requires organization, loyalty and ideology; traits such as self-centeredness, unreliability, poor behavioural controls, and unusual behaviours may be disadvantages.

Recently Häkkänen-Nyholm and Nyholm (2012) have discussed the possibility of psychopathy being associated with organised crime, economic crime and war crimes.

It has been speculated that some psychopaths may be socially successful, due to factors such as low disinhibition in the triarchic model in combination with other advantages such as a favourable upbringing and good intelligence. However, there is little research on this, in part because the PCL-R does not include positive adjustment characteristics and most researchers have used the PCL-R on criminals. Some research using the PPI indicate that psychopathic interpersonal and affective traits/boldness and/or meanness in the triarchic model exist in noncriminals and correlate with stress immunity and stability.

Psychologists Fritzon and Board, in their study comparing the incidence of personality disorders in business executives against criminals detained in a mental hospital, found that some personality disorders were more common in the executives. They described the personality-disordered executives as "successful psychopaths" and the personality-disordered criminals as "unsuccessful psychopaths".

Comorbidity

Psychopaths may have various other mental conditions. Comorbidity was found in a study to be strongest with antisocial personality disorder but also with histrionic, narcissistic and borderline disorders. A study designed to examine the association between PCL-R scores and assessments of DSM-IV Axis I disorders and diagnoses of DSM-III-R/DSM-IV Axis II disorders, made on the basis of a semi-structured interview, the preferred method of assessment in personality disorder (PD) research, in a sample of forensic psychiatric patients. Participants were 98 male forensic psychiatric patients admitted to the hospital between January 1, 1996, and December 1, 2001. Valid data were obtained from 94 patients. The results indicated that PCL-R psychopathy was most significantly and positively related with antisocial, borderline, narcissistic, and paranoid personality disorders. The most frequently diagnosed Personality Disorder (PD) in the study was ASPD (n = 45), followed by narcissistic PD (n = 26) and borderline PD (n = 24) and last paranoid PD (n = 18). Another study found that psychopathy scores correlated with ASPD, narcissistic, histrionic, and schizoid personality disorders, but not neurotic disorders or schizophrenia. Additionally, the constellation of traits in psychopathy assessments overlaps considerably with ASPD criteria and also with borderline personality disorder, histrionic personality disorder and narcissistic personality disorder criteria.

Psychopathy is associated with substance use disorders. This appears to be linked more closely to anti-social/criminal lifestyle, as measured by Factor 2 of the PCL-R, than the interpersonal-emotional traits assessed by Factor I of the PCL-R.

Attention deficit hyperactivity disorder (ADHD) is known to be highly comorbid with conduct disorder, and may also co-occur with psychopathic tendencies. This may be explained in part by deficits in executive function.

Anxiety disorders often co-occur with ASPD, and contrary to assumptions psychopathy can sometimes be marked by anxiety; however, this appears to be due to the antisocial aspect (factor 2 of the PCL), and anxiety may be inversely associated with the interpersonal-emotional traits (Factor I of the PCL-R).

Depression appears to be inversely associated with psychopathy. There is little evidence for a link between psychopathy and schizophrenia.

It has been suggested that psychopathy may be comorbid with several other diagnoses than these, but limited work on comorbidity has been carried out. This may be partly due to difficulties in using inpatient groups from certain institutions to assess comorbidity, owing to the likelihood of some bias in sample selection.

Moral Judgement

Psychopaths have been considered notoriously amoral – an absence of, indifference towards, or disregard for moral beliefs. There are few firm data on patterns of moral judgement, however. Studies of developmental level (sophistication) of moral reasoning found all possible results – lower, higher or the same as non-psychopaths. Studies that compared judgements of personal moral transgressions versus judgements of breaking conventional rules or laws, found that psychopaths rated them as equally severe, whereas non-psychopaths rated the rule-breaking as less severe.

A study comparing judgements of whether personal or impersonal harm would be endorsed in order to achieve the rationally maximum (utilitarian) amount of welfare, found no significant differences between psychopaths and non-psychopaths. However, a further study using the same tests found that prisoners scoring high on the psychopathy checklist were more likely to endorse impersonal harm or rule violations than non-psychopaths were. Psychopaths who scored low in anxiety were also more willing to endorse personal harm on average.

Assessing accidents, where one person harmed another unintentionally, psychopaths judged such actions to be more morally permissible. This result is perhaps a reflection of psychopaths' failure to appreciate the emotional aspect of the victim's harmful experience, and furnishes direct evidence of abnormal moral judgement in psychopathy.

Learning Impairment

Dysfunctions in the prefrontal cortex and amygdala regions of the brain are associated with specific learning impairments in psychopathy. Since the 1980s, scientists have linked traumatic brain injury, including damage to these regions, with violent and psychopathic behaviour. Patients with damage in such areas resembled "psychopathic individuals" whose brains were incapable of acquiring social and moral knowledge; those who acquired damage as children may have trouble conceptualizing social or moral reasoning, while those with adult-acquired damage may be aware of proper social and moral conduct but be unable to behave appropriately. Dysfunctions in the amygdala and ventromedial prefrontal cortex may also impair stimulus-reinforced learning in psychopaths, whether punishment-based or reward-based. People scoring ≥25 in the Psychopathy Checklist Revised, with an associated history of violent behaviour, appear to have significantly reduced microstructural integrity in their uncinate fasciculus—white matter connecting the amygdala and orbitofrontal cortex. There is DT-MRI evidence of breakdowns in the white matter connections between these two important areas.

Additionally, studies suggest inverse relationships between psychopathy and intelligence, including with regards to verbal IQ. However, Hare and Neumann (2008) state that a large literature shows that there is at most only a weak association between psychopathy and IQ. They consider that the early pioneer Cleckley included good intelligence in his checklist due to selection bias since many of his patients were "well educated and from middle-class or upper-class backgrounds" and state that "there is no obvious theoretical reason why the disorder described by Cleckley or other clinicians should be related to intelligence; some psychopaths are bright, others less so." Studies indicate that different aspects of the definition of psychopathy (e.g. interpersonal, affective (emotion), behavioural and lifestyle components) can show different links to intelligence, and it can also depend on the type of intelligence assessment (e.g. verbal, creative, practical, analytical).

Sex Differences

Research on psychopathy have largely been done on men and the PCL-R was developed using mainly male criminal samples raising the question how well the results apply to women. There have also been research investigating the sex differences. Men score higher than women on both the PCL-R and the PPI and on both of their main scales. The differences tend to be somewhat larger on the interpersonal-affective scale than on the antisocial scale. Most but not all studies have found broadly similar factor structure for men and women.

Many associations with other personality traits are similar although in one study the antisocial factor was more strongly related with impulsivity in men and more strongly related with openness to experience in women. It has been suggested that psychopathy in men manifest more as an antisocial pattern while it in women manifests more as a histrionic pattern. Studies on this have shown mixed results. PCL-R scores may be somewhat less predictive of violence and recidivism in women. On the other hand, psychopathy may have a stronger relationship with suicide and possibly internalizing symptoms in women. A suggestion is that psychopathy manifests more as externalizing behaviours in men and more as internalizing behaviours in women.

Causes and Pathophysiology

Childhood and Adolescent Precursors: The "Psychopathy Checklist: Youth Version" (PCL:YV) is an adaptation of the PCL-R for 13–18 years old. It is, like the PCL-R, done by a trained rater based on an interview and an examination of criminal and other records. The "Antisocial Process Screening Device" (APSD) is also an adaptation of the PCL-R. It can be administered by parents or teachers for 6–13 year olds or it can be self-administered by 13–18 years olds. High psychopathy scores for both juveniles, as measured with these instruments, and adults, as measured with the PCL-R, have many similar associations with other variables. This include similar predictive ability regarding violence and criminality as well as this mainly being due to the scales measuring impulsive and antisocial behaviours rather than the scales measuring interpersonal and affective features. As for adults, several other measurement tools have similar predictive ability at risk assessment. One difference is that juvenile psychopathy appears to be associated with more negative emotionality such as anger, hostility, anxiety, and, depression. Some recent studies have also found poorer ability at predicting long-term, adult offending such as the predictive ability not being better than unaided clinical judgement in one study.

Conduct disorder is a diagnosis with similarities to ASPD. The DSM-IV allows differentiating between childhood onset before age 10 and adolescent onset at age 10 and later. Childhood onset is argued to be more due to a personality disorder caused by neurological deficits interacting with an adverse environment. For many, but not all, is childhood onset associated with what is in Terrie Moffitt's developmental theory of crime is referred to as "life-course- persistent" antisocial behaviour as well as poorer health and economic status. Adolescent onset is argued to more typically be associated with short-term antisocial behaviour. It has been suggested that the combination of early-onset conduct disorder and ADHD may be associated with life-course-persistent antisocial behaviours as well as psychopathy.

There is evidence that this combination is more aggressive and antisocial than those with conduct disorder alone. However, it is not particularly distinct group since the vast majority of young children with conduct disorder also have ADHD. Some evidence indicates that this group have deficits in behavioural inhibition similar to adult psychopaths. They may not be more likely than those with conduct disorder alone to have the interpersonal/affective features and the deficits in emotional processing characteristic of adult psychopaths. Proponents of different types/dimensions of psychopathy have seen this type as possibly corresponding to adult secondary psychopathy/ disinhibition in the triarchic model.

The DSM-V is proposing the specifier "With Significant Callous-Unemotional Traits" which would require at least two out of four of features for at least a year: lacking of remorse/guilt, lacking empathy (callousness), lacking affect, and lacking concern for performance. It has been suggested that this is a subgroup of early onset conduct disorder distinct from the larger group by having less deficits in inhibition, less fear and anxiety, less emotional reactivity and emotional negativity, more boldness and/or meanness, less intellectual impairment, and less exposure to poor parental practices although parental practices do affect outcomes for this group. It has been argued that this group is at increased risk for future of aggressive, criminal, and other antisocial behaviours but it is unclear how much the callous-unemotinal traits contribute to this since this group also often have higher impulsivity and more prior antisocial behaviour compared to children with conduct disorder without callous-unemotional traits. Proponents of different types/dimensions of psychopathy have seen this type as possibly corresponding to adult primary psychopathy/boldness in the triarchic model.

There are moderate to high correlations between psychopathy rankings from late childhood to early adolescence. The correlations are considerably lower from early- or mid-adolescence to adulthood. In one study most of the similarities were on the Impulsive- and Antisocial-Behaviour scales. Of those adolescents who scored in the top 5% highest psychopathy scores at age 13, less than one third (29%) were classified as psychopathic at age 24.

Three behaviours—bedwetting, cruelty to animals and firestarting, known as the Macdonald triad—were first described by John Macdonald as possible indicators, if occurring together over time during childhood, of future episodic aggressive behaviour. However, subsequent research has found that bedwetting is not a significant factor and the triad as a particular profile has been called an urban legend. Questions remain about a connection between animal cruelty and later violence, though it has been included in the DSM as a possible factor in conduct disorder and later antisocial behaviour.

Environmental

A study by Farrington of a sample of London males followed between age 8 and 48 included studying which factors predicted scoring 10 or more on the PCL: SV at age 48. The strongest factors were "having a convicted father or mother, physical neglect of the boy, low involvement of the father with the boy, low family income, and coming from a disrupted family." Other significant factors included poor supervision, harsh discipline, large family size, delinquent sibling, young mother, depressed mother, low social class, and poor housing.

There has also been association between psychopaths and detrimental treatment by peers. Henry Lee Lucas, a serial killer and diagnosed psychopath, was bullied as a child and later said that his hatred for everyone spawned from mass social rejection.

Proponents of the triarchic model described earlier see psychopathy as due to the interaction of an adverse environment and genetic predispositions. What is adverse may differ depending on the underlying predisposition. Thus, persons having high boldness may respond poorly to punishment but may respond better to rewards and secure attachments.

Neuroscience

Psychopaths have in laboratory research responded differently to aversive stimuli. They have had weak conditioning to painful stimuli and poor learning of avoiding responses that causes punishment. They have had low reactivity in the autonomic nervous system as measured with skin conductance while waiting for a painful stimuli but not when the stimuli occurs. While it has been argued that the reward system functions normally, some studies have also found reduced reactivity to pleasurable stimuli.

Psychopaths have also had difficulty switching from an ongoing action despite environmental cues signaling a need to do so. One possibility is that this explains the difficulty responding to punishment although it is unclear if it can explain findings such as deficient conditioning. There may also be methodological issues regarding the research.

Neuroimaging studies have found structural and functional differences between those scoring high and low on the PCL-R with a 2011 review by Skeem et al. stating that they are "most notably in the amygdala, hippocampus and parahippocampal gyri, anterior and posterior cingulate cortex, striatum, insula, and frontal and temporal cortex". A 2008 review by Weber et al. stated that psychopathy is associated with brain abnormalities in a prefrontal-temporo-limbic regions that are involved in emotional and learning processes, among others. The amygdala and frontal areas has been suggested as particularly important. People scoring e"25 in the Psychopathy Checklist Revised, with an associated history of violent behaviour, appear to have significantly reduced microstructural integrity in their uncinate fasciculus—white matter connecting the amygdala and orbitofrontal cortex. The more extreme the psychopathy, the greater the abnormality. Psychopathic personality traits, called "acquired sociopathy" can develop due to lesions on the orbitofrontal cortex.

In a recent study of how psychopaths respond to emotional words, the right anterior temporal gyrus, whereby, wide spread differences in activation patterns have been shown across the temporal lobe when criminal psychopaths were compared to "normal" volunteers. This is consistent with the view of clinical psychology.

There is DT-MRI evidence of breakdowns in the white matter connections between these two important areas in a small British study of nine criminal psychopaths. This evidence suggests that the degree of abnormality was significantly related to the degree of psychopathy and may explain the offending behaviours.

Some of these findings are consistent with other research and theories, such as psychopaths having low fear being consistent with changes in the amygdala. Detriments in aversive conditioning and instrumental learning are thought to result from amygdala dysfunction, potentially compounded by OFC dysfunction, but the specific reasons are unknown. The amygdala has also been associated also with positive emotions and there have been inconsistent results in the studies regarding particular areas. "Callous-unemotional" traits in children have also been associated with changes in the amygdala but again there may be methodological issues.

Proponents of the primary-secondary psychopathy distinction and triarchic model discussed earlier argue that there are neuroscientific differences between subgroups of psychopaths supporting their views. Thus the boldness factor in the triarchic model is argued to be associated with reduced activity in the amygdala during fearful or aversive stimuli and reduced startle response while the disinhibition factor is argued to be associated with impairment of frontal lobe tasks. There is evidence that boldness and disinhibition are genetically distinguishable.

Head Injuries

Researchers have linked head injuries with psychopathy and violence. Since the 1980s, scientists have correlated traumatic brain injury, including damage to the prefrontal cortex, with psychopathic behaviour and an inability to make morally and socially acceptable decisions. Children with early damage in the prefrontal cortex may never fully develop social or moral reasoning and become "psychopathic individuals ... characterized by high levels of aggression and antisocial behaviour performed without guilt or empathy for their victims." Additionally, damage to the amygdala may impair the ability of the prefrontal cortex to interpret feedback from the limbic system, which could result in uninhibited signals that manifest in violent and aggressive behaviour.

Neurotransmitters and Hormones

High levels of testosterone combined with low levels of cortisol have been theorized as contributing factors. Testosterone is "associated with approach-related behaviour, reward sensitivity, and fear reduction". Cortisol increases "the state of fear, sensitivity to punishment, and withdrawal behaviour". Injecting testosterone "shift[s] the balance from punishment to reward sensitivity", decreases fearfulness, and increases "responding to angry faces". Some studies have found that antisocial and aggressive behaviours are associated with high testosterone levels but it is unclear if psychopaths have high testosterone levels. A few studies have found psychopathy to be linked to low cortisol levels.

High testosterone levels combined with low serotonin levels may increase violent aggression. Some research suggests that testosterone alone does not cause aggression but increases dominance-seeking behaviours. Low serotonin is associated with "impulsive and highly negative reactions" which, if combined with high testosterone, may cause aggression if an individual becomes frustrated.

Psychopathy was also associated in two studies with an increased ratio of HVA (a dopamine metabolite) to 5-HIAA (a serotonin metabolite).

Monoamine oxidase A affected the predictive ability of PCL-R in one study.

Several animal studies note the role of serotonergic functioning in impulsive aggression and antisocial behaviour.

Studies have indicated that individuals with the traits meeting criteria for psychopathy show a greater dopamine response to potential "rewards" such as monetary promises or taking drugs such as amphetamines. This has been theoretically linked to an increased impulsivity.

A 2010 British study found that a large 2D:4D digit ratio, an indication of high prenatal estrogen exposure, was a "positive correlate of psychopathy in females, and a positive correlate of callous affect (psychopathy sub-scale) in males".

Genetics

One approach to studying the role of genetics for crime is to calculate the heritability coefficient. It describes the proportion of the variance that is due to genetic factors for some characteristic that differs between individuals. The non-heritability proportion can be further divided into the "shared environment" which is the non-genetic factors which make siblings similar while the "non-shared environment" is the non-genetic factors which makes siblings different from another. Studies on the personality characteristics typical of psychopathy have found moderate genetic and moderate "non-shared environmental" influences while none from the "shared environment" A study using the PPI found the two factors fearless dominance and impulsive antisociality to be similarly moderately influenced by genetics and uncorrelated with one another which indicated separate genetic influences.

Genetic factors may generally influence the development of psychopathy while environmental factors affect the specific traits that predominate.

A study on a large group of children found more than 60% heritability for "callous-unemotional traits" and that conduct problems among children with these traits had a higher heritability than among children without these traits.

MAO-A

Studies have suggested a connection between a variant of the monoamine oxidase A (MAO-A) gene (dubbed the "warrior gene") and psychopathy. In the variant, the allele associated with behavioural traits consists of 30 bases, and produces comparatively less MAO-A enzyme. Low MAO-A activity was found to result in a significantly increased risk of aggression and antisocial behaviour.

The variant was found to vary widely in demographic prevalence among different ethnic groups. 59% of African-American men, 56% of Maori men and 54% of Chinese men carry the MOA-A 3R genetic variant, compared to 34% of Caucasians, suggesting that the former ethnic groups are more genetically predisposed by the MAO-A gene towards aggression or antisocial tendencies compared to other ethnic groups studied.

Evolutionary explanations

Psychopathy is associated with several adverse life outcomes as well as increased risk of early death due to factors such as homicides, accidents, and suicides. This in combination with the evidence for genetic influences is evolutionarily puzzling and may suggest that there are compensating evolutionary advantages. Researchers within evolutionary psychology have proposed several evolutionary explanations. Some psychopaths may possibly be very socially successful. Another is that some associated traits such as early, promiscuous, adulterous, and coercive sexuality may increase reproductive success. A third is that psychopathy represents a frequency-dependent, socially parasitic strategy. This may work as long as there are few other psychopaths in the community since more psychopaths means increasing the risk of encountering another psychopath as well as non-psychopaths likely adapting more countermeasures against cheaters.

Criticisms include that it may be better to look at the contributing personality factors rather than treat psychopathy as a unitary concept due to poor testability and a lack of empirical evidence regarding reproductive success of psychopaths. Furthermore, if psychopathy is caused by the combined effects of a very large number of adverse mutations then each mutation may have so small an effect that it escapes natural selection.

Management

Clinical Management

Psychopathy has often been considered untreatable. Harris and Rice's Handbook of Psychopathy says that there is little evidence of a cure or effective treatment for psychopathy; no medications can instill empathy, and psychopaths who undergo traditional talk therapy might become more adept at manipulating others and more likely to commit crime. The only study finding increased criminal recidivism after treatment was in a 2011 retrospective study of a treatment programme in the 1960s that had several methodological problems likely not approved today. Some relatively rigorous quasi-experimental studies using more modern treatment methods have found improvements regarding reducing future violent and other criminal behaviour, regardless of PCL-R scores, although none was a randomized controlled trial. Some other studies have found improvements in risk factors for crime such as substance abuse. No study had in a 2011 review examined if the personality traits could be changed by such treatments. It has been shown in some studies that punishment and behaviour modification techniques may not improve the behaviour of psychopaths.

In a study where psychopathic criminals were brain-scanned while they watched videos of a person harming another individual, scientists found that psychopaths' empathic reaction (via the mirror system) initiated the same way it did for controls when they were instructed to empathise with the harmed individual, and that the area of the brain relating to pain was activated when the psychopaths were asked to imagine how the harmed individual felt. The research demonstrated how psychopaths could switch empathy on at will and explained how they could be both callous and charming. Although the team who conducted the study believes that it is still unknown how to transform this willful empathy into the spontaneous empathy most people have, they propose it could be possible to bring psychopaths closer to rehabilitation by helping them to activate their "empathy switch". However, others suggested that despite the results of the study, it remained unclear whether psychopaths' experience of empathy was the same as that of controls, and also questioned whether it was possible to devise therapeutic interventions to make the empathic reactions more automatic.

Legal Response

The PCL-R, the PCL:SV, and the PCL:YV are highly regarded and widely used in criminal justice settings, particularly in North America. They may be used for risk assessment and for assessing treatment potential and be used as part of the decisions regarding bail, sentence, which prison to use, parole, and regarding whether to a youth should be tried as a juvenile or as an adult. There have been several criticisms against this. They include the general criticisms against the PCL-R, the availability of other risk assessment tools which may have advantages, and excessive pessimism regarding prognosis and treatment possibilities.

The interrater reliability of the PCL-R can be high when used carefully in research but tend to be poor in applied settings. In particular Factor 1 items are somewhat subjective. In sexually violent predator cases the PCL-R scores given by prosecution experts were consistently higher than those given by defense experts in one study. The scoring may also be influenced by other differences between raters. In one study it was estimated that of the PCL-R variance, about 45% was due to true offender differences, 20% was due to which side the rater testified for, and 30% was due to other rater differences.

United Kingdom

The PCL-R cut-off for a label of psychopathy is 25 in the United Kingdom, instead of 30 as it is in the United States.

In the United Kingdom, "Psychopathic Disorder" was legally defined in the Mental Health Act (UK), under MHA1983, as, "a persistent disorder or disability of mind (whether or not including significant impairment of intelligence) which results in abnormally aggressive or seriously irresponsible conduct on the part of the person concerned." This term, which did not equate to typical modern concepts of psychopathy, was intended to reflect the presence of a personality disorder, in terms of conditions for detention under the Mental Health Act 1983. With the subsequent amendments to the Mental Health Act 1983 within the Mental Health Act 2007, the term "psychopathic disorder" has been abolished, with all conditions for detention (e.g. mental illness, personality disorder, etc.) now being contained within the generic term of "mental disorder".

In England and Wales, the diagnosis of dissocial personality disorder is grounds for detention in secure psychiatric hospitals under the Mental Health Act if they have committed serious crimes, but since such individuals are disruptive for other patients and not responsive to treatment this alternative to prison is not often used.

United States

"Sexual Psychopath" Laws: Starting in the 1930s, before the modern concept of psychopathy, "sexual psychopath" laws were introduced by some states until by the mid-1960s more than half of the states had such laws. "Sexual psychopaths" were seen as a distinct group of sex offenders who were not seriously mentally ill but had a "psychopathic personality" that could be treated. This was in agreement with the general rehabilitative trends at this time. Courts sent such sex offenders to a mental health facility for community protection and treatment.

Starting in 1970 many of these laws were modified or abolished in favour of more traditional responses such as imprisonment due to criticism of the "sexual psychopath" concept as lacking scientific evidence, the treatment being ineffective, and predictions of future offending being dubious. There were also a series of cases where persons treated and released committed new sex crimes. Starting in the 1990s several states have passed sexually dangerous person laws, not synonymous with the modern concept of psychopathy, which permit confinement after a sentence has been completed. Psychopathy measurements may be used in the confinement decision process.

Epidemiology

A 2008 study using the Psychopathy Checklist: Screening Version (PCL: SV) found that 1.2% of a US sample scored 13 or more which indicates "potential psychopathy". Over half of those studied had scores of 0 or 1 and about two-thirds scored 2 or less. Higher scores were significantly associated with more violence, higher alcohol use, and estimated lower intelligence.

A 2009 British study by Coid et al., also using the PCL: SV, reported a community prevalence of 0.6% scoring 13 or more. The lower prevalence than in the 2008 study may be due to the 2009 sample being more representative of the general population. The scores "correlated with: younger age, male gender; suicide attempts, violent behaviour, imprisonment and homelessness; drug dependence; histrionic, borderline and adult antisocial personality disorders; panic and obsessive–compulsive disorders."

PCL-R creator Robert Hare has stated that many (male) psychopaths have a pattern of mating with, and quickly abandoning women, and as a result, have a high fertility rate. These children may inherit a predisposition to psychopathy. Hare describes the implications as chilling. However, empirical evidence regarding the reproductive success of psychopaths is lacking.

Homesickness

Homesickness is the distress or impairment caused by an actual or anticipated separation from home. Its cognitive hallmark is preoccupying thoughts of home and attachment objects. Sufferers typically report a combination of depressive and anxious symptoms, withdrawn behaviour and difficulty focusing on topics unrelated to home. In its mild form, homesickness prompts the development of coping skills and motivates healthy attachment behaviours, such as renewing contact with loved ones. Indeed, nearly all people miss something about home when they are away, making homesickness a nearly universal experience. However, intense homesickness can be painful and debilitating. Fortunately, prevention and treatment strategies exist for both children and adults. One study showed that this inexpensive intervention can lower the intensity of homesickness of first-year campers by an average 50%.

Diagnosis and Epidemiology

Whereas separation anxiety disorder is characterized by "inappropriate and excessive fear or anxiety concerning separation from those to whom the individual is attached" symptoms of homesickness are most prominent after a separation and include both depression and anxiety. In DSM terms, homesickness may be related to Separation Anxiety Disorder, but it is perhaps best categorized as either an Adjustment Disorder with mixed anxiety and depressed mood (309.28) or, for immigrants and foreign students as a V62.4, Acculturation Difficulty. As noted above, researchers use the following definition: "Homesickness is the distress or impairment caused by an actual or anticipated separation from home. Its cognitive hallmark is preoccupying thoughts of home and attachment objects." Recent pathogenic models support the possibility that homesickness reflects both insecure attachment and a variety of emotional and cognitive vulnerabilities, such as little previous experience away from home and negative attitudes about the novel environment.

The prevalence of homesickness varies greatly, depending on the population studied and the way homesickness is measured. One way to conceptualize homesickness prevalence is as a function of severity. Nearly all people miss something about home when they are away, so the absolute prevalence of homesickness is close to 100%, mostly in a mild form. Roughly 20% of university students and children at summer camp rate themselves at or above the midpoint on numerical rating scales of homesickness severity. And only 5-7% of students and campers report intense homesickness associated with severe symptoms of anxiety and depression. However, in adverse or painful environments, such as the hospital or the battlefield, intense homesickness is far more prevalent. In one study, 50% of children scored themselves at or above the midpoint on a numberical homesickness intensity scale (compared to 20% of children at summer camp). Soldiers report even more intense homesickness, sometimes to the point of suicidal misery. Naturally, aversive environmental elements, such as the trauma associated with war, exacerbate homesickness and other mental health problems.

In sum, homesickness is a normative pathology that can take on clinical relevance in its moderate and severe forms.

Risk and Protective Factors

Risk factors (constructs which increase the likelihood or intensity of homesickness) and protective factors (constructs that decrease the likelihood or intensity of homesickness) vary by population. For example, the environmental stressors associated with a hospital, a battlefield or a foreign country may exacerbate homesickness and complicate treatment. Generally speaking, however, risk and protective factors transcend age and environment.

Risk Factors

The risk factors for homesickness fall into five categories: experience, personality, family, attitude and environment. More is known about some of these factors in adults—especially personality factors—because more homesickness research has been performed with older populations. However, a growing body of research is elucidating the etiology of homesickness in younger populations, including children at summer camp, hospitalized children and students.

- Experience Factors: Young chronological age; little previous experience away from home (for which age can be a proxy); little or no previous experience in the novel environment; little or no previous experience venturing out without primary caregivers.
- Attitude Factors: The belief that homesickness will be strong; negative first impressions and low expectations for the new environment; perceived absence of social support; high perceived

demands (e.g., on academic or vocational functioning); great perceived distance from home

- Personality Factors: Insecure attachment relationship with primary caregivers; low perceived control over the timing and nature of the separation from home; anxious or depressed feelings in the months prior to the separation; low self-directedness; high harm avoidance; rigidity; a wishful-thinking coping style.
- Family Factors: Low decision control (e.g., caregivers forcing a young person to spend time away from home; governments forcing a person to enlist in military service away from home); unsupportive caregiving; caregivers who express anxiety or ambivalence about the separation (e.g., "Have a great time away. I don't know what I'll do without you."
- Environmental Factors: High cultural contrast (e.g., different language, customs, food); threats to physical and emotional safety; dramatic alternations in daily schedule; lack of information about the new place; perceived discrimination

Finally, research has provided no support for a few factors that conventional wisdom had once held to be risk factors. These include: recent separation or divorce of primary caregivers; geographic distance from home; recent geographic move. Most likely, it is not a change in family structure, distance or dwelling that predicts homesickness, but whether these changes have left unanswered (potentially preoccupying) questions in the person's mind.

Protective Factors

Factors which mitigate the prevalence or intensity of homesickness are essentially the inverse of the risk factors cited above. Effective coping (reviewed in the following section) also diminishes the intensity of homesickness over time. Prior to a separation, however, key protective factors can be identified. Positive adjustment to separation from home is generally associated with the following factors:

- Experience Factors: Old chronological age; substantial previous experience away from home (for which age can be a proxy); previous experience in the novel environment; previous experience venturing out without primary caregivers.
- Attitude Factors: The belief that homesickness will be mild; positive first impressions and high expectations for the new environment; perceptions of social support; low perceived

demands (e.g., on academic or vocational functioning); short perceived distance from home

- Personality Factors: Secure attachment relationship with primary caregivers; high perceived control over the timing and nature of the separation from home; good mental health in the months prior to the separation; high self-directedness; adventure-seeking; flexibility; an instrumental coping style.
- Family Factors: High decision control (e.g., caregivers including a young person in the decision to spend time away from home; individuals making their own choice about military service; supportive caregiving; caregivers who express confidence and optimism about the separation (e.g., "Have a great time away. I know you'll do great."
- Environmental Factors: Low cultural contrast (e.g., same language, similar customs, familiar food); physical and emotional safety; few alternations to familiar daily schedule; plenty of information about the new place; feeling welcome and accepted in the new place.

Theories of Coping

How people—especially young people—cope with homesickness deserves careful study for at least three reasons. First, homesickness is experienced by millions of people who spend time away from home including children at boarding schools, residential summer camps and hospitals.

Second, severe homesickness is associated with significant distress and impairment. There is evidence that homesick persons present with non-traumatic physical ailments significantly more than their non-homesick peers. Homesick boys and girls conplain about somatic problems and exhibit more internalizing and externalizing behaviours problems than their nonhomesick peers. First-year college students are three times more likely to drop out of school than their nonhomesick peers. Other data have pointed to concentration and academic problems in homesick students. And maladjustment to separation from home has been documented in hospitalized young people and is generally associated with slower recovery.

Third, learning more about how people cope with homesickness is a helpful guide to designing treatment programmes. By complementing existing theories of depression, anxiety and attachment, a better theoretical understanding of homesickness can shape applied interventions. Among the most relevant theories that could shape interventions are those concerned with Learned Helplessness and Control Beliefs.

Learned helplessness predicts that persons who develop a belief that they cannot influence or adjust to their circumstance of separation from home will become depressed and make fewer attempts to change that circumstance. Control beliefs theory predicts that negative affect is most likely in persons who perceive personal incompetence in the separation environment (e.g., poor social skills at a summer camp or university) and who perceive contingency uncertainty (e.g., uncertainty about whether friendly behaviour will garner friends). Although these are not the only broad etiologic theories that inform homesickness, note that both theories hinge on control, the perception of which "reflects the fundamental human need for competence" (Skinner, 1995, p. 8). This is particularly relevant to coping, because people's choice of how to respond to a stressor hinges partly on their perception of a stressor's controllability.

A equally important coping factor is social connection, which for many people is the antidote to homesickness. As the results of several studies have suggested, social connection is a powerful mediator of homesickness intensity.

Ways of Coping

The most effective way of coping with homesickness is mixed and layered. Mixed coping is that which involves both primary goals (changing circumstances) and secondary goals (adjusting to circumstances). Layered coping is that which involves more than one method. This kind of sophisticated coping is learned through experience, such as brief periods away from home without parents. As an example of mixed and layered coping, one study revealed the following method-goal combinations to be the most frequent and effective ways boys and girls:

- Doing something fun (observable method) to forget about being homesick (secondary goal)
- Thinking positively and feel grateful (unobservable method) to feel better (secondary goal)
- Simply changing feelings and attitudes (unobservable method) to be happy (secondary goal)
- Reframing time (unobservable method) in order to perceive the time away as shorter (secondary goal)

- Renewing a connection with home, through letter writing) (observable method) to feel closer to home (secondary goal)
- Talking with someone (observable method) who could provide support and help me make new friends(primary goal)

Sometimes, people will engage in wishful thinking, attempt to arrange a shorter stay or (rarely) break rules or act violently in order to be sent home. These ways of coping are rarely effective and can produce unintended negative side effects.

Adjustment, Frustration and Stress

Adjustment means regulating, adapting or settling in a variety of contexts:

- Adjustment (law) has several meanings; many relate to insurance, contracts, or the resolution of disputes
- In engineering, mathematics, and geodesy, the optimal parametre estimation of a mathematical model so as to best fit a data set (e.g. least squares adjustment)
- In metrology, the set of operations carried out on an instrument in order that it provides given indications corresponding to given values of the measurand.
- In psychology, the behavioural process of balancing conflicting needs, or needs against obstacles in the environment. Humans and animals regularly do this, for example, when they are stimulated by their physiological state to seek food, they eat (if possible) to reduce their hunger and thus adjust to the hunger stimulus. Adjustment disorder occurs when there is an inability to make a normal adjustment to some need or stress in the environment.

Adjustment Disorder

An adjustment disorder occurs when an individual is unable to adjust to or cope with a particular stressor, like a major life event. Since people with this disorder normally have symptoms that depressed people do, such as general loss of interest, feelings of hopelessness and crying, this disorder is also sometimes known as situational depression. Unlike major depression however, the disorder is caused by an outside stressor and generally resolves once the individual is able to adapt to the situation. One hypothesis for adjustment disorder is that it may represent a sub-threshold clinical syndrome.

The condition is different from anxiety disorder, which lacks the presence of a stressor, or post-traumatic stress disorder and acute stress disorder, which usually are associated with a more intense stressor.

Its common characteristics include mild depressive symptoms, anxiety symptoms, and traumatic stress symptoms or a combination of the three. There are nine different types of adjustment disorders listed in the DSM-III-R. According to the DSM-IV-TR, there are six types of adjustment disorders, which are characterized by the following predominant symptoms: depressed mood, anxiety, mixed depression and anxiety, disturbance of conduct, mixed disturbance of emotions and conduct, and unspecified. However, the criteria for these symptoms are not specified in greater detail. Adjustment disorder may also be acute or chronic, depending on whether it lasts more or less than six months. According to the DSM-IV-TR, if the adjustment disorder lasts less than 6 months, then it may be considered acute. If it lasts more than 6 months, it may be considered chronic. However, the symptoms cannot last longer than six months after the stressor(s), or its consequences, have terminated. Diagnosis of adjustment disorder is quite common; there is an estimated incidence of 5–21% among psychiatric consultation services for adults. Adult women are diagnosed twice as often as are adult men, but among children and adolescents, girls and boys are equally likely to receive this diagnosis. Adjustment disorder was introduced into the psychiatric classification systems almost 30 years ago, but the concept was recognized for many years before that. When considering biopsychosocial disorders, an athlete's overtrained state can be due to an adjustment disorder.

Signs and Symptoms

According to the DSM IV-TR, the development of the emotional or behavioural symptoms of this diagnosis have to occur within three months of the onset of the identifiable stressor(s). Some emotional signs of AD are sadness, hopelessness, lack of enjoyment, crying spells, nervousness, anxiety, worry, desperation, trouble sleeping, difficulty concentrating, feeling overwhelmed and thoughts of suicide. Some behavioural signs of AD are fighting, reckless driving, ignoring important tasks such as bills or homework, avoiding family or friends, performing poorly in school, skipping school, or vandalizing property. However, the stress-related disturbance does not only exacerbation of a pre-existing axis 1 or axis 2 disorder and cannot be diagnostic as axis 1 disorder.

Suicidal behaviour is prominent among people with AD of all ages and up to one fifth of adolescent suicide victims may have an adjustment disorder. Bronish and Hecht (1989) found that 70% of a series of patients with AD attempted suicide immediately before their index admission and they remitted faster than a comparison group with major depression. Asnis et al. (1993) found that AD patients report persistent ideation or suicide attempts less frequently than those diagnosed with major depression. According to a study on 82 AD patients at a clinic, Bolu et al. (2012) found that 22 (26.8%) of these patients were admitted due to suicidal attempt, consistent with previous findings. In addition, it was found that 15 of these 22 patients chose suicidal methods that involved high chances of being saved. Henriksson et al. (2005) states statistically that the stressors are of one half related to parental issues and one third in peer issues.

Risk Factors

Various factors have been found to be more associated with a diagnosis of AD than other Axis I disorders, including:

- younger age
- more identified psychosocial and environmental problems
- increased suicidal behaviour, more likely to be rated as improved by the time of discharge from mental healthcare
- less frequent previous psychiatric history
- shorter length of treatment

Those exposed to repeated trauma are at greater risk, even if that trauma is in the distant past. Age can be a factor due to young children having fewer coping resources; however, children are also less likely to assess the consequences of a potential stressor.

A stressor is generally an event of a serious, unusual nature that an individual or group of individuals experience. The stressors that cause adjustment disorders may be grossly traumatic or relatively minor, like loss of a girlfriend/boyfriend, a poor report card, or moving to a new neighbourhood. It is thought that the more chronic or recurrent the stressor, the more likely it is to produce a disorder. The objective nature of the stressor, however, is of secondary importance. Stressors' most crucial link to their pathogenic potential is their perception by the patient as stressful. The presence of a causal stressor is essential before a diagnosis of adjustment disorder can be made p. 279.

There are certain stressors that are more common in different age groups:

Adulthood:

- Marital conflict
- Financial conflict

Adolescence and childhood:

- Family conflict/parental separation
- School problems/changing schools
- Sexuality issues
- Death/illness in the family

In a study conducted from 1990 till 1994 on 89 psychiatric outpatient adolescent, 25% had attempted suicide in which 37.5% had misused alcohol, 87.5% displayed aggressive behaviour, 12.5% had learning difficulties, and 87.5% had anxiety symptoms.

Diagnosis

The basis of the diagnosis is the presence of a precipitating stressor and a clinical evaluation of the possibility of symptom resolution on removal of the stressor due to the limitations in the criteria for diagnosing AD. In addition, the diagnosis of AD is less clear when patients are exposed to stressors long-term, because this type of exposure is not only associated with AD but also Major Depressive Disorder (MDD) and Generalized Anxiety Disorder (GAD).

Some signs and criteria used to establish a diagnosis are important, however. First, the symptoms must clearly follow a stressor. The symptoms should be more severe than would be expected. There should not appear to be other underlying disorders. The symptoms that are present are not part of a normal grieving for the death of family member or other loved one.

Adjustment disorders have the ability to be self-limiting. Within 5 years of when they are originally diagnosed, approximately 20-50% of the sufferers go on to be diagnosed with psychiatric disorders that are more serious in nature.

Treatment

Often, the recommended treatment for adjustment disorder is psychotherapy. The goal of psychotherapy is symptom relief and behaviour change. Anxiety may be presented as "a signal from the body" that something in the patient's life needs to change. Treatment allows the patient to put his or her distress or rage into words rather than into destructive actions. Individual therapy can help a person gain the support they need, identify these abnormal responses and maximize the use of the individual's strengths. Counselling, psychotherapy, crisis intervention, family therapy, behavioural therapy and self-help group treatment are often used to encourage the verbalization of fears, anxiety, rage, helplessness, and hopelessness. Sometimes small doses of antidepressants and anxiolytics are also used in addition to other forms of treatment. In patients with severe life stresses and a significant anxious component, benzodiazepines are used, although non-addictive alternatives have been recommended for patients with current or past heavy alcohol use, because of the greater risk of dependence. Tianeptine, alprazolam, and mianserin were found to be equally effective in patients with AD with anxiety. Additionally, antidepressants, antipsychotics (rarely) and stimulants (for individuals who became extremely withdrawn) have been used in treatment plans.

There has been little systematic research regarding the best way to manage individuals with an adjustment disorder. Because natural recovery is the norm, it has been argued that there is no need to intervene unless levels of risk or distress are high. However, for some individuals treatment may be beneficial. AD sufferers with depressive and/or anxiety symptoms may benefit from treatments usually used for depressive and/or anxiety disorders. One study found that AD sufferers received similar interventions to those with other psychiatric diagnoses, including psychological therapy and medication. Another study found that AD responded better than major depression to antidepressants. Given the absence of a meaningful evidence base for the treatment of AD per se, watchful waiting should be considered initially, but if symptoms are not improving or causing the sufferer marked distress then treatment should be directed at the predominating symptoms.

In addition to professional help, parents and caregivers can help their children with their difficulty adjusting by:

- offering encouragement to talk about his/her emotions
- offering support and understanding
- reassuring the child that their reactions are normal
- involving the child's teachers to check on their progress in school
- letting the child make simple decisions at home, such as what to eat for dinner or what show to watch on TV
- having the child engage in a hobby or activity they enjoy

ICD 10 Classification

International Statistical Classification of Diseases and Related Health Problems, mostly known as "ICD", is a classification that assigns codes to classify diseases, symptoms, complaints, social behaviours, injuries, and such medical-related findings.

ICD 10 classifies Adjustment disorders under F40-F48 and under Neurotic, stress-related and somatoform disorders.

Criticism

Like many of the items in the DSM, adjustment disorder receives criticism from a minority of the professional community as well as those in semi-related professions outside the health-care field. First, there has been criticism of its classification. It has been criticized for its lack of specificity of symptoms, behavioural parametres, and close links with environmental factors. Relatively little research has been done on this condition.

Adjustment disorder has been classified as being so "vague and all-encompassing...as to be useless," but it has been retained in the DSM-IV because of the belief that it serves a useful clinical purpose for clinicians seeking a temporary, mild, non-stigmatizing label, particularly for patients who need a diagnosis for insurance coverage of therapy.

Frustration

Frustration is a common emotional response to opposition. Related to anger and disappointment, it arises from the perceived resistance to the fulfillment of individual will. The greater the obstruction, and the greater the will, the more the frustration is likely to be. Causes of frustration may be internal or external. In people, internal frustration may arise from challenges in fulfilling personal goals and desires, instinctual drives and needs, or dealing with perceived deficiencies, such as a lack of confidence or fear of social situations. Conflict can also be an internal source of frustration; when one has competing goals that interfere with one another, it can create cognitive dissonance. External causes of frustration involve conditions outside an individual, such as a blocked road or a difficult task. While coping with frustration, some individuals may engage in passive–aggressive behaviour, making it difficult to identify the original cause(s) of their frustration, as the responses are indirect. A more direct, and common response, is a propensity towards aggression.

Causes

To the individual experiencing anger, the emotion is usually attributed to external factors that are beyond his or her control. Although mild frustration due to internal factors (e.g. laziness, lack of effort) is often a positive force (inspiring motivation), it is more often than not a perceived uncontrolled problem that instigates more severe, and perhaps pathological anger. An individual suffering from pathological anger will often feel powerless to change the situation they are in, leading to and, if left uncontrolled, further anger.

It can be a result of blocking motivated behaviour. An individual may react in several different ways. He/she may respond with rational problem-solving methods to overcome the barrier. Failing in this, he/she may become frustrated and behave irrationally. An example of blockage of motivational energy would be the case of a worker who wants time off to go fishing but is denied permission by his/her supervisor. Another example would be the executive who wants a promotion but finds he/she lacks certain qualifications. If, in these cases, an appeal to reason does not succeed in reducing the barrier or in developing some reasonable alternative approach, the frustrated individual may resort to less adaptive methods of trying to reach the goal. He/she may, for example, attack the barrier physically, verbally, or both.

Symptoms

Frustration can be considered a problem–response behaviour, and can have a number of effects, depending on the mental health of the individual. In positive cases, this frustration will build until a level that is too great for the individual to contend with, and thus produce action directed at solving the inherent problem. In negative cases, however, the individual may perceive the source of frustration to be outside of their control, and thus the frustration will continue to build, leading eventually to further problematic behaviour (e.g. violent reaction).

Stubborn refusal to respond to new conditions affecting the goal, such as removal or modification of the barrier, sometimes occurs. As pointed out by J.A.C. Brown, severe punishment may cause individuals to continue nonadaptive behaviour blindly: "Either it may have an effect opposite to that of reward and as such, discourage the repetition of the act, or, by functioning as a frustrating agent, it may lead to fixation and the other symptoms of frustration as well. It follows that punishment is a dangerous tool, since it often has effects which are entirely the opposite of those desired".

Stress

Stress is simply a reaction to a stimulus that disturbs our physical or mental equilibrium. In other words, it's an omnipresent part of life. A stressful event can trigger the "fight-or-flight" response, causing hormones such as adrenaline and cortisol to surge through the body. A little bit of stress, known as "acute stress," can be exciting—it keeps us active and alert. But long-term, or "chronic stress," can have detrimental effects on health. You may not be able to control the stressors in your world, but you can alter your reaction to them.

Some stressors are sudden and severe, some are chronic and serious, some are positive changes that place pressure or demands on you, and still others are expectable life problems. But stress isn't always negative. Positive stress adds anticipation and excitement to life. Insufficient positive stress may leave us feeling bored. On the other hand, too much negative stress can leave us feeling overwhelmed.

The art of stress management is to keep yourself at a level of stimulation that is healthy and enjoyable - to create a balance of positive and negative stress that will motivate but not overwhelm you.

What is Stress?

Stress generally refers to two different things: situations that trigger physical and emotional reactions (stressors) and the reactions themselves (stress response). A stressor could be taking a final exam, going on a date, having a confrontation with your roommate, and interviewing for a job. The stress response for any of these stressors could be that you feel nervous, anxious, tense, sweat profusely, or experience other physical reactions.

The body responds to stress by what is called the General Adaptation Syndrome (GAS). The GAS occurs in three stages - alarm, resistance, and exhaustion. The fight or flight response is the most common type of alarm stage. This is when the sympathetic nervous system releases the chemicals epinephrine and norepinephrine, which prepare the body for action by increasing heart rate, breathing, alertness, and muscle response, and the hormone cortisol, which speeds up the body's metabolism. These actions get the body ready to confront a threat such as an alarming sound (fight) or escape from it (flight). The body usually adapts to a prolonged stressor, such as an upcoming final, by entering the stage of resistance. During resistance, the body's systems return to normal, but remain alert. Following resistance, the body enters exhaustion, at which point it can no longer resist the stressor. Repeated exposure to this response can cause mental and physical damage.

How do I Know When I'm Stressed?

Here's a quick test - place your hand on the back of your neck. If it feels cold against your skin, you're probably stressed out. Blood rushes to your muscles when you're under stress, leaving your hands cold. Other warning signs of stress include:

- Out-of-proportion anxiety
- Excessive moodiness
- Withdrawal from responsibility
- Constant insomnia
- Poor emotional control
- Marked change in appetite or sex drive
- Chronic fatigue

These short-term physical symptoms mainly occur as your body adapts to perceived physical threats, and are caused by the release of epinephrine (adrenaline) during the alarm stage of the GAS. Long-term physical symptoms occur when your body has been exposed to adrenaline over a long period. Adrenaline works by diverting resources from the areas of the body which carry out body maintenance (such as your liver, kidneys and other organs) to the muscles. An example of prolonged stress might be that for the entire semester you and your roommate have not gotten along and you experience feelings of anxiety whenever you go back to your room. This stress may cause your health to deteriorate and it is common to experience frequent colds and infections, sexual disorders, aches and pains, feelings of intense and long-term tiredness, or a change in appetite.

How do Diet and Exercise Relate to Stress?

A healthy lifestyle is an essential companion to any stress-reduction programme. General health and stress resistance can be enhanced by regular exercise, a diet rich in a variety of whole grains, vegetables, and fruits, and by avoiding excessive alcohol, caffeine, and tobacco.

Exercise has been shown in studies to reduce feelings of anxiety, helplessness, hostility and depression, and to decrease muscle tension. Stretching and flexing the muscles of the neck, arms, shoulders, back, thighs, and midsection reduce the chance that these muscles will tighten up and produce common indicators of stress - headache, neckache, and backache.

The chemicals in coffee, drugs, alcohol and cigarettes can contribute to increased stress. Caffeine stimulates the sympathetic nervous system and may promote even more nervousness and tension. Use of alcohol and drugs, a common way to deal with stress, can be addictive and tends to deal only with the symptoms of the problems. They mask the causes of stress without eliminating them. Smokers often report that cigarettes help relieve feelings of stress - however, the stress levels of adult smokers are slightly higher than those of nonsmokers, and smoking cessation leads to reduced stress. The apparent relaxant effect of smoking only reflects the reversal of the tension and irritability that develop during nicotine depletion.

How Can I Cope with Stress?

There are many ways to reduce unwanted stress or manage it productively including:

Managing your physical and psychological well being

- Have a positive attitude! Reversing negative ideas and learning to focus on positive outcomes helps reduce tension and achieve goals. If you catch yourself thinking negative criticisms like — "I'll never get this assignment done! I'm a failure!" — change your inner dialogue. Tell yourself "I'm intelligent and fully capable of getting this assignment done. I will schedule more time tomorrow to work on the assignment and complete it."
- If you've had a serious illness or have had an emergency to respond to, remember that you can get an extension on a paper or other project. Don't be afraid to ask — your professors and advisors are there to support you.
- Tap into your support network. It can be a relief to realize others have had similar experiences - it helps us feel understood, capable, and nurtured. Friends, family, adult mentors (supervisors or professors), and Brown support providers (first-year unit counsellors, faculty advisors or favourite instructors, chaplains, deans from the Dean of the College or the Student Life Office, staff from Psychological Services) are all good sources of emotional support. Sometimes just expressing our feelings, or venting, helps lower our stress.
- If you can't discuss your feelings with your support network, express them some other way - write in a journal, write a poem, or compose a letter that is never mailed.

Monitoring your stress levels.

- A helpful way of monitoring your stress level and identifying sources of stress is to keep a daily stress log. Note activities that put a strain on energy and time, trigger anger or anxiety, or precipitate a negative physical response. Also note your reactions to these stressful events. Review the log and identify 2 or 3 stressful events or activities that you can modify or eliminate.

Avoiding extremely stressful situations

- Stress results when you feel overwhelmed by many things that need to be done at the same time. Plan around the things you find stressful to lessen the effects of stress. Managing your time effectively will even out your workload.
- When working, focus on one thing at a time. Switching from one task to another without fully completing the first task allows for variety, but usually wastes time and causes confusion. Make a list and prioritize the things you need to get done. Start a new homework assignment only after you've completed an earlier assignment.
- Don't be afraid to take a break when you are studying or writing a paper. Schedule it in! A 20-minute power nap can re-energize you for hours.
- Know and accept your limits. Don't over-commit - learn to say no. If you really don't want to go to a performance Friday night with your roommate don't be afraid to say you're not interested this time. It is better to disappoint a person up front than with a last minute cancellation because you find yourself short of time.

What are Some Simple Relaxation Techniques?

Relaxation is the natural unwinding of the stress response. Relaxation lowers blood pressure, respiration, and pulse rates. Combining several techniques, for example deep breathing exercises, muscle relaxation, meditation, and massage therapy can significantly lower stress levels. Yoga or tai chi can be very effective, combining many of the benefits of breathing, muscle relaxation, and meditation while toning and stretching the muscles. They also elevate mood and improve concentration and ability to focus.

Visualization involves the imagining of scenes that are relaxing and peaceful - this can help the body relax. Imagine yourself in a setting that is pleasantly relaxing. Guided relaxation (listening to relaxation tapes or having someone read a relaxation exercise to you) can be a pleasant way to relax. The Canyon Ranch site offers a series of guided meditations that you can try right now as you sit in front of your computer!

What are Warning Signs I Should get Help to Deal with my Stress?

Signals that you are experiencing an overload of stress can range from a general feeling of the "blahs" to serious physical pain. Although most stress can be managed, it is important to obtain professional help before the situation is completely out of control. If you experience the following situations or feelings, you should seek out one of the many professional support resources on campus.

Behavioural symptoms:

- Overreacting to minor problems
- Inappropriate anger or impatience
- Overeating or loss of appetite
- Increased use of alcohol, tobacco or other drugs
- Unable to relax
- Constantly feeling anxious
- Experiencing long periods of boredom
- Disrupted sleeping patterns
- Problems with sexual activity
- Decreased school or work performance
- Diminished ability to set priorities and make decisions
- Prone to make errors or be accident prone

Physical symptoms:

- Increased headaches
- Cold hands and feet
- Indigestion
- Aching neck or back
- Ulcers
- Nausea
- Diarrhea or constipation
- Shortness of breath
- Heart palpitations
- Teeth grinding

- Muscle spasms
- Skin conditions like acne and psoriasis

Stress can be a factor in a variety of physical and emotional illnesses, which should be professionally treated. You should consult your medical provider if you experience physical symptoms in the above list. Brown students can also consult a therapist from Psychological Services for unmanageable acute stress, high levels of anxiety, or depression.

5

Psychology of Mental Hygiene and Mental Health

Mental health describes a level of psychological well-being, or an absence of a mental disorder. From the perspective of 'positive psychology' or 'holism', mental health may include an individual's ability to enjoy life, and create a balance between life activities and efforts to achieve psychological resilience. Mental health can also be defined as an expression of emotions, and as signifying a successful adaptation to a range of demands.

The World Health Organization defines mental health as "a state of well-being in which the individual realizes his or her own abilities, can cope with the normal stresses of life, can work productively and fruitfully, and is able to make a contribution to his or her community". It was previously stated that there was no "official" definition of mental health. Cultural differences, subjective assessments, and competing professional theories all affect how "mental health" is defined. There are different types of mental health problems, some of which are common, such as depression and anxiety disorders, and some not so common, such as schizophrenia and bipolar disorder.

Most recently, the field of global mental health has emerged, which has been defined as 'the area of study, research and practice that places a priority on improving mental health and achieving equity in mental health for all people worldwide'.

In the mid-19th century, William Sweetzer was the first to clearly define the term "mental hygiene", which can be seen as the precursor to contemporary approaches to work on promoting positive mental health. Isaac Ray, one of the thirteen founders of the American

Psychiatric Association, further defined mental hygiene as an art to preserve the mind against incidents and influences which would inhibit or destroy its energy, quality or development.

Dorothea Dix (1802–1887) was an important figure in the development of "mental hygiene" movement. Dix was a school teacher who endeavoured throughout her life to help those suffering from mental illness, and to bring to light the deplorable conditions into which they were put. This was known as the "mental hygiene movement". Before this movement, it was not uncommon that people affected by mental illness in the 19th century would be considerably neglected, often left alone in deplorable conditions, barely even having sufficient clothing. Dix's efforts were so great that there was a rise in the number of patients in mental health facilities, which sadly resulted in these patients receiving less attention and care, as these institutions were largely understaffed.

At the beginning of the 20th century, Clifford Beers founded the National Committee for Mental Hygiene and opened the first outpatient mental health clinic in the United States of America.

The mental hygiene movement, related to the social hygiene movement, had at times been associated with advocating eugenics and sterilisation of those considered too mentally deficient to be assisted into productive work and contented family life.

After 1945, references to mental hygiene were gradually replaced by the term mental health.

Significance

Evidence from the World Health Organization suggests that nearly half the world's population are affected by mental illness with an impact on their self-esteem, relationships and ability to function in everyday life. An individual's emotional health can also impact physical health and poor mental health can lead to problems such as substance abuse.

Maintaining good mental health is crucial to living a long and healthy life. Good mental health can enhance one's life, while poor mental health can prevent someone from living an enriching life. According to Richards, Campania, & Muse-Burke (2010) "There is growing evidence that is showing emotional abilities are associated with prosocial behaviours such as stress management and physical health" (2010). It was also concluded in their research that people who lack emotional expression are inclined to anti-social behaviours. These behaviours are a direct reflection of their mental health. Self-destructive acts may take place to suppress emotions. Some of these acts include drug and alcohol abuse, physical fights or vandalism.

Perspectives

Mental well-being

Mental health can be seen as an unstable continuum, where an individual's mental health may have many different possible values. Mental wellness is generally viewed as a positive attribute, such that a person can reach enhanced levels of mental health, even if the person does not have any diagnosed mental health condition. This definition of mental health highlights emotional well-being, the capacity to live a full and creative life, and the flexibility to deal with life's inevitable challenges. Many therapeutic systems and self-help books offer methods and philosophies espousing strategies and techniques vaunted as effective for further improving the mental wellness of otherwise healthy people. Positive psychology is increasingly prominent in mental health.

A holistic model of mental health generally includes concepts based upon anthropological, educational, psychological, religious and sociological perspectives, as well as theoretical perspectives from personality, social, clinical, health and developmental psychology.

An example of a wellness model includes one developed by Myers, Sweeney and Witmer. It includes five life tasks—essence or spirituality, work and leisure, friendship, love and self-direction—and twelve sub tasks—sense of worth, sense of control, realistic beliefs, emotional awareness and coping, problem solving and creativity, sense of humor, nutrition, exercise, self care, stress management, gender identity, and cultural identity—which are identified as characteristics of healthy functioning and a major component of wellness. The components provide a means of responding to the circumstances of life in a manner that promotes healthy functioning. The population of the USA in its majority is considered to be mostly uneducated on the subjects of mental health . Another model is psychological well-being.

Prevention

Mental health can also be defined as an absence of a mental disorder. Focus is increasing on preventing mental disorders. Prevention is beginning to appear in mental health strategies, including the 2004 WHO report "Prevention of Mental Disorders", the 2008 EU "Pact for Mental Health" and the 2011 US National Prevention Strategy. Prevention of a disorder at a young age may significantly decrease the chances that a child will suffer from a disorder later in life.

Cultural and Religious Considerations

Mental health is a socially constructed and socially defined concept; that is, different societies, groups, cultures, institutions and professions have very different ways of conceptualizing its nature and causes, determining what is mentally healthy, and deciding what interventions, if any, are appropriate. Thus, different professionals will have different cultural, class, political and religious backgrounds, which will impact the methodology applied during treatment.

Research has shown that there is stigma attached to mental illness. In the United Kingdom, the Royal College of Psychiatrists organized the campaign Changing Minds (1998–2003) to help reduce stigma.

Many mental health professionals are beginning to, or already understand, the importance of competency in religious diversity and spirituality. The American Psychological Association explicitly states that religion must be respected. Education in spiritual and religious matters is also required by the American Psychiatric Association.

Emotional Mental Health Issues Around the World

Emotional mental disorders are a leading cause of disabilities worldwide. Investigating the degree and severity of untreated emotional mental disorders throughout the world is a top priority of the World Mental Health (WMH) survey initiative, which was created in 1998 by the World Health Organization (WHO). "Neuropsychiatric disorders are the leading causes of disability worldwide, accounting for 37% of all healthy life years lost through disease.These disorders are most destructive to low and middle-income countries due to their inability to provide their citizens with proper aid. Despite modern treatment and rehabilitation for emotional mental health disorders, "even economically advantaged societies have competing priorities and budgetary constraints".

The World Mental Health survey initiative has suggested a plan for countries to redesign their mental health care systems to best allocate resources. "A first step is documentation of services being used and the extent and nature of unmet needs for treatment. A second step could be to do a cross-national comparison of service use and unmet needs in countries with different mental health care systems. Such comparisons can help to uncover optimum financing, national policies, and delivery systems for mental health care."

Knowledge of how to provide effective emotional mental health care has become imperative worldwide. Unfortunately, most countries have insufficient data to guide decisions, absent or competing visions for resources, and near constant pressures to cut insurance and entitlements. WMH surveys were done in Africa (Nigeria, South Africa), the Americas (Colombia, Mexico, U.S.A), Asia and the Pacific (Japan, New Zealand, Beijing and Shanghai in the Peoples Republic of China), Europe (Belgium, France, Germany, Italy, Netherlands, Spain, Ukraine), and the middle east (Israel, Lebanon). Countries were classified with World Bank criteria as low-income (Nigeria), lower middle-income (China, Columbia, South Africa, Ukraine), higher middle-income (Lebanon, Mexico), and high-income.

The coordinated surveys on emotional mental health disorders, their severity, and treatments were implemented in the aforementioned countries. These surveys assessed the frequency, types, and adequacy of mental health service use in 17 countries in which WMH surveys are complete. The WMH also examined unmet needs for treatment in strata defined by the seriousness of mental disorders. Their research showed that "the number of respondents using any 12-month mental health service was generally lower in developing than in developed countries, and the proportion receiving services tended to correspond to countries' percentages of gross domestic product spent on health care". "High levels of unmet need worldwide are not surprising, since WHO Project ATLAS' findings of much lower mental health expenditures than was suggested by the magnitude of burdens from mental illnesses. Generally, unmet needs in low-income and middle-income countries might be attributable to these nations spending reduced amounts (usually <1%) of already diminished health budgets on mental health care, and they rely heavily on out-of-pocket spending by citizens who are ill equipped for it".

Emotional Mental Health in the United States

According to the World Health Organization in 2004, depression is the leading cause of disability in the United States of America for individuals ages 15 to 44. Absence from work in the U.S. due to depression is estimated to be in excess of $31 billion per year. Depression frequently co-occurs with a variety of medical illnesses such as heart disease, cancer, and chronic pain and is associated with poorer health status and prognosis. Each year, roughly 30,000 Americans take their lives, while hundreds of thousands make suicide attempts (Centres for Disease Control and Prevention). In 2004, suicide was the 11th leading cause of death in the United States of America (Centres for Disease Control and Prevention), third among individuals ages 15–24. Despite the increasingly availability of effectual depression treatment, the level of unmet need for treatment remains high.

There are many factors that influence mental health including:

- Mental illness, disability, and suicide are ultimately the result of a combination of biology, environment, and access to and utilization of mental health treatment.
- Public health policies can influence access and utilization, which subsequently may improve mental health and help to progress the negative consequences of depression and its associated disability.
- Research conducted by Mental Health America found the following factors to be considerably allied with improved depression status and lower suicide rates:
  a) Mental health resources: On average, the higher the number of psychiatrists, psychologists, and social workers per capita in a state, the lower the suicide rate.
  b) Barriers to treatment: The lower the percentage of the population reporting that they could not obtain healthcare because of costs, the lower the suicide rate and the better the state's depression status.
  c) Mental health treatment utilization: The lower the percentage of the population that reported unmet mental healthcare needs, the better the state's depression status. When mental health treatment is utilized more, while holding the baseline level of depression in the state constant, the higher the number of antidepressant prescriptions per capita in the state, and the lower the suicide rate.
  d) Socioeconomic characteristics: The more educated the population and the greater the percentage with health insurance, the lower the suicide rate. The more educated the population, the better the state's depression status.
  e) Mental health policy: The more generous a state's mental health parity coverage, the greater the number of people in the population that receive mental health services.

The Spirit Level: Why More Equal Societies Almost Always Do Better argues about 50% of the reason why Americans have the highest rates of mental illness including depression, anxiety and addiction is due to America having the highest income inequality in the world.

Emotional mental illnesses should be a particular concern in the United States of America since the U.S.A has the highest annual prevalence rates (26 percent) for mental illnesses among a comparison of 14 developing and developed countries. While approximately 80 percent of all people in the United States with a mental disorder eventually receive some form of treatment, on the average persons do not access care until nearly a decade following the development of their illness, and less than one-third of people who seek help receive minimally adequate care.

Mental Health Policies in the United States

The mental health policies in the United States have experienced four major reforms: the American asylum movement led by Dorothea Dix in 1843; the "mental hygiene" movement inspired by Clifford Beers in 1908; the deinstitutionalization started by Action for Mental Health in 1961; and the community support movement called for by The CMCH Act Amendments of 1975.

In 1843, Dorothea Dix submitted a Memorial to the Legislature of Massachusetts, describing the abusive treatment and horrible conditions received by the mentally ill patients in jails, cages, and almshouses. She revealed in her Memorial: "I proceed, gentlemen, briefly to call your attention to the present state of insane persons confined within this Commonwealth, in cages, closets, cellars, stalls, pens! Chained, naked, beaten with rods, and lashed into obedience. . . ." Many asylums were built in that period, with high fences or walls separating the patients from other community members and strict rules regarding the entrance and exit. In those asylums, traditional treatments were well implemented: drugs were not used as a cure for a disease, but a way to reset equilibrium in a person's body, along with other essential elements such as healthy diets, fresh air, middle class culture, and the visits by their neighbouring residents. In 1866, a recommendation came to the New York State Legislature to establish a separate asylum for chronic mentally ill patients. Some hospitals placed the chronic patients into separate wings or wards, or different buildings.

In A Mind That Found Itself (1908) Clifford Whittingham Beers described the humiliating treatment he received and the deplorable conditions in the mental hospital. One year later, the National Committee for Mental Hygiene (NCMH) was founded by a small group of reform-minded scholars and scientists – including Beer himself – which marked the beginning of the "mental hygiene" movement. The movement emphasized the importance of childhood prevention. World War I catalyzed this idea with an additional emphasis on the impact of maladjustment, which convinced the hygienists that prevention was the only practical approach to handle mental health issues. However, prevention was not successful, especially for chronic illness; the condemnable conditions in the hospitals were even more prevalent, especially under the pressure of the increasing number of chronically ill and the influence of the Depression.

In 1961, the Joint Commission on Mental Health published a report called Action for Mental Health, whose goal was for community clinic care to take on the burden of prevention and early intervention of the mental illness, therefore to leave space in the hospitals for severe and chronic patients. The court started to rule in favour of the patients' will on whether they should be forced to treatment. By 1977, 650 community mental health centres were built to cover 43 percent of the population and serve 1.9 million individuals a year, and the lengths of treatment decreased from 6 months to only 23 days. However, issues still existed. Due to inflation, especially in the 1970s, the community nursing homes received less money to support the care and treatment provided. Fewer than half of the planned centres were created, and new methods did not fully replace the old approaches to carry out its full capacity of treating power. Besides, the community helping system was not fully established to support the patients' housing, vocational opportunities, income supports, and other benefits. Many patients returned to welfare and criminal justice institutions, and more became homeless. The movement of deinstitutionalization was facing great challenges.

After realizing that simply changing the location of mental health care from the state hospitals to nursing houses was insufficient to implement the idea of deinstitutionalization, the National Institute of Mental Health in 1975 created the Community Support Programme (CSP) to provide funds for communities to set up a comprehensive mental health service and supports to help the mentally ill patients integrate successfully in the society. The programme stressed the importance of other supports in addition to medical care, including housing, living expenses, employment, transportation, and education; and set up new national priority for people with serious mental disorders. In addition, the Congress enacted the Mental Health Systems Act to prioritize the service to the mentally ill and emphasize the expansion of services beyond just clinical care alone. Later in the 1980s, under the influence from the Congress and the Supreme Court, many programmes started to help the patients regain their benefits. A new Medicaid service was also established to serve people who were suffering from a "chronic mental illness." People who were temporally hospitalized were also provided aid and care and a pre-release programme was created to enable people to apply for reinstatement prior to discharge. Not until 1990, around 35 years after the start of the deinstitutionalization, did the first state hospital begin to close. The number of hospitals dropped from around 300 by over 40 in the 1990s, and finally a Report on Mental Health showed the efficacy of mental health treatment, giving a range of treatments available for patients to choose.

The 2011 National Prevention Strategy included mental and emotional well-being, with recommendations including better parenting and early intervention programmes, which increase the likelihood of prevention programmes being included in future US mental health policies. The NIMH is researching only suicide and HIV/AIDS prevention, but the National Prevention Strategy could lead to it focusing more broadly on longitudinal prevention studies.

Emotional Mental Health Improvement

Being mentally and emotionally healthy does not preclude the experiences of life which we cannot control. As humans we are going to face emotions and events that are a part of life. According to Smith and Segal, "People who are emotionally and mentally healthy have the tools for coping with difficult situations and maintaining a positive outlook in which they also remain focused, flexible, and creative in bad times as well as good" (2011). In order to improve your emotional mental health, the root of the issue has to be resolved. "Prevention emphasizes the avoidance of risk factors; promotion aims to enhance an individual's ability to achieve a positive sense of self-esteem, mastery, well-being, and social inclusion" (Power, 2010). It is very important to improve your emotional mental health by surrounding yourself with positive relationships. We as humans, feed off companionships and interaction with other people. Another way to improve your emotional mental health is participating in activities that can allow you to relax and take time for yourself. Yoga is a great example of an activity that calms your entire body and nerves. According to a study on well-being by Richards, Campania and Muse-Burke, "mindfulness is considered to be a purposeful state, it may be that those who practice it believe in its importance and value being mindful, so that valuing of self-care activities may influence the intentional component of mindfulness" (2010).

Therapies

Activity Therapies: Activity therapies, also called recreation therapy and occupational therapy, promote healing through active engagement. Making crafts can be a part of occupational therapy. Walks can be a part of recreation therapy.

Expressive Therapies

Expressive therapies are a form of psychotherapy that involves the arts or art-making. These therapies include music therapy, art therapy, dance therapy, drama therapy, and poetry therapy.

Alternative Therapies

Alternative therapy is a branch of alternative medicine, which includes a large number of therapies imported from other cultures. It also includes a number of new medicines that have not yet passed through the process of scientific review. Alternative therapies include traditional medicine, prayer, yoga, traditional Chinese medicine, Ayurvedic medicine, homeopathy, hypnotherapy, and more.

Meditation

Increased awareness of mental processes can influence emotional behaviour and mental health. A 2011 study incorporating three types of meditative practice (concentration meditation, mindfulness meditation and compassion towards others) revealed that meditation provides an enhanced ability to recognize emotions in others and their own emotional patterns, so they could better resolve difficult problems in their relationships.

Biofeedback

Biofeedback is a process of gaining control of physical processes and brainwaves. It can be used to decrease anxiety, increase well-being, increase relaxation, and other methods of mind-over-body control.

Group Therapy

Group therapy involves any type of therapy that takes place in a setting involving multiple people. It can include psychodynamic groups, activity groups for expressive therapy, support groups (including the Twelve-step programme), problem-solving and psychoeducation groups.

Pastoral Counselling

Pastoral counselling is the merging of psychological and religious therapies and carried out by religious leaders or others trained in linking the two.

Psychotherapy

Psychotherapy is the general term for scientific based treatment of mental health issues based on modern medicine. It includes a number of schools, such as gestalt therapy, psychoanalysis, cognitive behavioural therapy and dialectical behavioural therapy.

Mental Retardation

Intellectual disability (ID) or general learning disability is a generalized disorder appearing before adulthood, characterized by significantly impaired cognitive functioning and deficits in two or more adaptive behaviours. Intellectual disability is also known as mental retardation (MR), although this older term is becoming less popular. It was historically defined as an intelligence quotient score under 70. Once focused almost entirely on cognition, the definition now includes both a component relating to mental functioning and one relating to individuals' functional skills in their environment. As a result, a person with an unusually low IQ may not be considered intellectually disabled. Intellectual disability is subdivided into syndromic intellectual disability, in which intellectual deficits associated with other medical and behavioural signs and symptoms are present, and non-syndromic intellectual disability, in which intellectual deficits appear without other abnormalities.

The terms used for this condition are subject to a process called the euphemism treadmill. This means that whatever term is chosen for this condition, it eventually becomes perceived as an insult. The terms mental retardation and mentally retarded were invented in the middle of the 20th century to replace the previous set of terms, which were deemed to have become offensive. By the end of the 20th century, these terms themselves have come to be widely seen as disparaging and politically incorrect and in need of replacement. The term intellectual disability is now preferred by most advocates and researchers in most English-speaking countries. As of 2013, the term "mental retardation" is still used by the World Health Organization in the ICD-10 codes, which have a section titled "Mental Retardation" (codes F70–F79). In the next revision, the ICD-11 is expected to replace the term "mental retardation" with "intellectual disability," and the DSM-5 has replaced it with "intellectual disability (intellectual developmental disorder)." Because of its specificity and lack of confusion with other conditions, the term "mental retardation" is still sometimes used in professional medical settings around the world, such as formal scientific research and health insurance paperwork.

Signs and Symptoms

The signs and symptoms of intellectual disability are all behavioural. Most people with intellectual disability do not look like they are afflicted with such, especially if the disability is caused by environmental factors such as malnutrition or lead poisoning. The so-called typical appearance ascribed to people with intellectual disability is only present in a minority of cases, all of which are syndromic.

Children with intellectual disability may learn to sit up, to crawl, or to walk later than other children, or they may learn to talk later. Both adults and children with intellectual disability may also exhibit some or all of the following characteristics:

- Delays in oral language development
- Deficits in memory skills
- Difficulty learning social rules
- Difficulty with problem solving skills
- Delays in the development of adaptive behaviours such as self-help or self-care skills
- Lack of social inhibitors

Children with intellectual disability learn more slowly than a typical child. Children may take longer to learn language, develop social skills, and take care of their personal needs, such as dressing or eating. Learning will take them longer, require more repetition, and skills may need to be adapted to their learning level. Nevertheless, virtually every child is able to learn, develop and become a participating member of the community.

In early childhood, mild intellectual disability (IQ 50–69) may not be obvious, and may not be identified until children begin school. Even when poor academic performance is recognized, it may take expert assessment to distinguish mild intellectual disability from learning disability or emotional/behavioural disorders. People with mild intellectual disability are capable of learning reading and mathematics skills to approximately the level of a typical child aged nine to twelve. They can learn self-care and practical skills, such as cooking or using the local mass transit system. As individuals with intellectual disability reach adulthood, many learn to live independently and maintain gainful employment.

Moderate intellectual disability (IQ 35–49) is nearly always apparent within the first years of life. Speech delays are particularly common signs of moderate MR. People with moderate intellectual disability need considerable supports in school, at home, and in the community in order to participate fully. While their academic potential is limited, they can learn simple health and safety skills and to participate in simple activities. As adults they may live with their parents, in a supportive group home, or even semi-independently with significant supportive services to help them, for example, manage their finances. As adults, they may work in a sheltered workshop.

A person with severe or profound intellectual disability will need more intensive support and supervision his or her entire life. They may learn some activities of daily living. Some will require full-time care by an attendant.

Cause

Among children, the cause is unknown for one-third to one-half of cases. Down syndrome, velocariofacial syndrome, and fetal alcohol syndrome are the three most common inborn causes. However, doctors have found many other causes. The most common are:

- Genetic conditions. Sometimes disability is caused by abnormal genes inherited from parents, errors when genes combine, or other reasons. The most prevalent genetic conditions include Down syndrome, Klinefelter's syndrome, Fragile X syndrome (common among boys), Neurofibromatosis, congenital hypothyroidism, Williams syndrome, Phenylketonuria (PKU), and Prader-Willi syndrome. Other genetic conditions include Phelan-McDermid syndrome (22q13del), Mowat-Wilson syndrome, genetic ciliopathy, and Siderius type X-linked intellectual disability (OMIM 300263) as caused by mutations in the PHF8 gene (OMIM 300560). In the rarest of cases, abnormalities with the X or Y chromosome may also cause disability. 48, XXXX and 49, XXXXX syndrome affect a small number of girls worldwide, while boys may be affected by 47, XYY, 49, XXXXY, or 49, XYYYY.
- Problems during pregnancy. Intellectual disability can result when the fetus does not develop properly. For example, there may be a problem with the way the fetus' cells divide as it grows. A woman who drinks alcohol or gets an infection like rubella during pregnancy may also have a baby with intellectual disability.
- Problems at birth. If a baby has problems during labour and birth, such as not getting enough oxygen, he or she may have developmental disability due to brain damage.

- Exposure to certain types of disease or toxins. Diseases like whooping cough, measles, or meningitis can cause intellectual disability if medical care is delayed or inadequate. Exposure to poisons like lead or mercury may also affect mental ability.
- Iodine deficiency, affecting approximately 2 billion people worldwide, is the leading preventable cause of intellectual disability in areas of the developing world where iodine deficiency is endemic. Iodine deficiency also causes goiter, an enlargement of the thyroid gland. More common than full-fledged cretinism, as intellectual disability caused by severe iodine deficiency is called, is mild impairment of intelligence. Certain areas of the world due to natural deficiency and governmental inaction are severely affected. India is the most outstanding, with 500 million suffering from deficiency, 54 million from goiter, and 2 million from cretinism. Among other nations affected by iodine deficiency, China and Kazakhstan have instituted widespread iodization programmes, whereas, as of 2006, Russia had not.
- Malnutrition is a common cause of reduced intelligence in parts of the world affected by famine, such as Ethiopia.
- Absence of the arcuate fasciculus.

Diagnosis

According to the fourth edition of the Diagnostic and Statistical Manual of Mental Disorders (DSM-IV), three criteria must be met for a diagnosis of intellectual disability: an IQ below 70, significant limitations in two or more areas of adaptive behaviour (as measured by an adaptive behaviour rating scale, i.e. communication, self-help skills, interpersonal skills, and more), and evidence that the limitations became apparent before the age of 18.

It is formally diagnosed by professional assessment of IQ and adaptive behaviour.

IQ below 70

The first English-language IQ test, the Stanford-Binet Intelligence Scales, was adapted from a test battery designed for school placement by Alfred Binet in France. Lewis Terman adapted Binet's test and promoted it as a test measuring "general intelligence." Terman's test was the first widely used mental test to report scores in "intelligence quotient" form ("mental age" divided by chronological age, multiplied by 100). Current tests are scored in "deviation IQ" form, with a performance level by a test-taker two standard deviations below the median score for the test-taker's age group defined as IQ 70. Until the most recent revision of diagnostic standards, an IQ of 70 or below was a primary factor for intellectual disability diagnosis, and IQ scores were used to categorize degrees of intellectual disability.

Since current diagnosis of intellectual disability is not based on IQ scores alone, but must also take into consideration a person's adaptive functioning, the diagnosis is not made rigidly. It encompasses intellectual scores, adaptive functioning scores from an adaptive behaviour rating scale based on descriptions of known abilities provided by someone familiar with the person, and also the observations of the assessment examiner who is able to find out directly from the person what he or she can understand, communicate, and such like. IQ assessment must be based on a current test. This enables diagnosis to avoid the pitfall of the Flynn Effect, which is a consequence of changes in population IQ test performance changing IQ test norms over time.

Distinction from Other Disabilities

Clinically, intellectual disability is a subtype of cognitive deficit or disabilities affecting intellectual abilities, which is a broader concept and includes intellectual deficits that are too mild to properly qualify as intellectual disability, or too specific (as in specific learning disability), or acquired later in life through acquired brain injuries or neurodegenerative diseases like dementia. Cognitive deficits may appear at any age. Developmental disability is any disability that is due to problems with growth and development. This term encompasses many congenital medical conditions that have no mental or intellectual components, although it, too, is sometimes used as a euphemism for intellectual disability.

Significant Limitations in Two or More Areas of Adaptive Behaviour

Adaptive behaviour, or adaptive functioning, refers to the skills needed to live independently (or at the minimally acceptable level for age). To assess adaptive behaviour, professionals compare the functional abilities of a child to those of other children of similar age. To measure adaptive behaviour, professionals use structured interviews, with which they systematically elicit information about persons' functioning in the community from people who know them well. There are many adaptive behaviour scales, and accurate assessment of the quality of someone's adaptive behaviour requires clinical judgement as well. Certain skills are important to adaptive behaviour, such as:

- Daily living skills, such as getting dressed, using the bathroom, and feeding oneself
- Communication skills, such as understanding what is said and being able to answer
- Social skills with peers, family members, spouses, adults, and others

Evidence That the Limitations Became Apparent in Childhood

This third condition is used to distinguish intellectual disability from dementing conditions such as Alzheimer's disease or due to traumatic injuries with attendant brain damage.

Management

By most definitions intellectual disability is more accurately considered a disability rather than a disease. Intellectual disability can be distinguished in many ways from mental illness, such as schizophrenia or depression. Currently, there is no "cure" for an established disability, though with appropriate support and teaching, most individuals can learn to do many things.

There are thousands of agencies around the world that provide assistance for people with developmental disabilities. They include state-run, for-profit, and non-profit, privately run agencies. Within one agency there could be departments that include fully staffed residential homes, day rehabilitation programmes that approximate schools, workshops wherein people with disabilities can obtain jobs, programmes that assist people with developmental disabilities in obtaining jobs in the community, programmes that provide support for people with developmental disabilities who have their own apartments, programmes that assist them with raising their children, and many more. There are also many agencies and programmes for parents of children with developmental disabilities.

Beyond that there are specific programmes that people with developmental disabilities can take part in wherein they learn basic life skills. These "goals" may take a much longer amount of time for them to accomplish, but the ultimate goal is independence. This may be anything from independence in tooth brushing to an independent residence. People with developmental disabilities learn throughout their lives and can obtain many new skills even late in life with the help of their families, caregivers, clinicians and the people who coordinate the efforts of all of these people.

Although there is no specific medication for intellectual disability, many people with developmental disabilities have further medical complications and may be prescribed several medications. For example autistic children with developmental delay may be prescribed antipsychotics or mood stabilizers to help with their behaviour. Use of psychotropic medications such as benzodiazepines in people with intellectual disability requires monitoring and vigilance as side effects occur commonly and are often misdiagnosed as behavioural and psychiatric problems.

Epidemiology

Intellectual disability affects about 2–3 percent of the general population. 75–90% of the affected people have mild intellectual disability .

Non-syndromic or idiopathic ID accounts for 30–50 percent of cases. About a quarter of cases are caused by a genetic disorder.

History

Intellectual disabilities of all kinds have been documented under a variety of names throughout history. Throughout much of human history, society was unkind to those with any type of disability, and people with intellectual disabilities were commonly viewed as burdens on their families.

Greek and Roman philosophers, who valued reasoning abilities, disparaged people with intellectual disabilities as barely human. The oldest physiological view of intellectual disability is in the writings of Hippocrates in the late fifth century BCE, who believed that it was caused by an imbalance in the four humors in the brain.

Until the Enlightenment in Europe, care and asylum was provided by families and the church (in monasteries and other religious communities), focusing on the provision of basic physical needs such as food, shelter and clothing. Negative stereotypes were prominent in social attitudes of the time.

In the 13th century, England declared people with intellectual disabilities to be incapable of making decisions or managing their affairs. Guardianships were created to take over their financial affairs.

In the 17th century, Thomas Willis provided the first description of intellectual disabilities as a disease. He believed that it was caused by structural problems in the brain. According to Willis, the anatomical problems could be either an inborn condition or acquired later in life.

In the 18th and 19th centuries, housing and care moved away from families and towards an asylum model. People were placed by, or removed from, their families (usually in infancy) and housed in large professional institutions, many of which were self-sufficient through the labour of the residents. Some of these institutions provided a very basic level of education (such as differentiation between colours and basic word recognition and numeracy), but most continued to focus solely on the provision of basic needs of food, clothing, and shelter. Conditions in such institutions varied widely, but the support provided was generally non-individualized, with aberrant behaviour and low levels of economic productivity regarded as a burden to society. Individuals of higher wealth were often able to afford higher degrees of care such as home care or private asylums. Heavy tranquilization and assembly line methods of support were the norm, and the medical model of disability prevailed. Services were provided based on the relative ease to the provider, not based on the needs of the individual. A survey taken in 1891 in Cape Town, South Africa shows the distribution between different facilities. Out of 2046 persons surveryed, 1,281 were in private dwellings, 120 in jails, and 645 in asylums, with men representing nearly two thirds of the number surveyed. In situations of scarcity of accommodation, preference was given to white men and black men (whose insanity threatened white society by disrupting employment relations and the tabooed sexual contact with white women).

In the late 19th century, in response to Charles Darwin's On the Origin of Species, Francis Galton proposed selective breeding of humans to reduce intellectual disabilities. Early in the 20th century the eugenics movement became popular throughout the world. This led to forced sterilization and prohibition of marriage in most of the developed world and was later used by Hitler as rationale for the mass murder of intellectually challenged individuals during the holocaust. Eugenics was later abandoned as an evil violation of human rights, and the practice of forced sterilization and prohibition from marriage was discontinued by most of the developed world by the mid-20th century.

In 1905, Alfred Binet produced the first standardized test for measuring intelligence in children.

Although ancient Roman law had declared people with intellectual disability to be incapable of the deliberate intent to harm that was necessary for a person to commit a crime, during the 1920s, Western society believed they were morally degenerate.

Ignoring the prevailing attitude, Civitans adopted service to the developmentally disabled as a major organizational emphasis in 1952. Their earliest efforts included workshops for special education teachers and daycamps for disabled children, all at a time when such training and programmes were almost nonexistent. The segregation of people with developmental disabilities wasn't widely questioned by academics or policy-makers until the 1969 publication of Wolf Wolfensberger's seminal work "The Origin and Nature of Our Institutional Models", drawing on some of the ideas proposed by SG Howe 100 years earlier. This book posited that society characterizes people with disabilities as deviant, sub-human and burdens of charity, resulting in the adoption of that "deviant" role. Wolfensberger argued that this dehumanization, and the segregated institutions that result from it, ignored the potential productive contributions that all people can make to society. He pushed for a shift in policy and practice that recognized the human needs of those with intellectual disability and provided the same basic human rights as for the rest of the population.

The publication of this book may be regarded as the first move towards the widespread adoption of the social model of disability in regard to these types of disabilities, and was the impetus for the development of government strategies for desegregation. Successful lawsuits against governments and an increasing awareness of human rights and self-advocacy also contributed to this process, resulting in the passing in the U.S. of the Civil Rights of Institutionalized Persons Act in 1980.

From the 1960s to the present, most states have moved towards the elimination of segregated institutions. Normalization and deinstitutionalization are dominant. Along with the work of Wolfensberger and others including Gunnar and Rosemary Dybwad, a number of scandalous revelations around the horrific conditions within state institutions created public outrage that led to change to a more community-based method of providing services.

By the mid-1970s, most governments had committed to de-institutionalization, and had started preparing for the wholesale movement of people into the general community, in line with the principles of normalization. In most countries, this was essentially complete by the late 1990s, although the debate over whether or not to close institutions persists in some states, including Massachusetts.

In the past, lead poisoning and infectious diseases were significant causes of intellectual disabilities. Some causes of intellectual disability are decreasing, as medical advances, such as vaccination, increase. Other causes are increasing as a proportion of cases, perhaps due to rising maternal age, which is associated with several syndromic forms of intellectual disability.

Along with the changes in terminology, and the downward drift in acceptability of the old terms, institutions of all kinds have had to repeatedly change their names. This affects the names of schools, hospitals, societies, government departments, and academic journals. For example, the Midlands Institute of Mental Subnormality became the British Institute of Mental Handicap and is now the British Institute of Learning Disability. This phenomenon is shared with mental health and motor disabilities, and seen to a lesser degree in sensory disabilities.

Terminology

Terms that denote mental deficiency have been subjected to the euphemism treadmill. The several traditional terms that long predate psychiatry are simple forms of abuse in common usage today; they are often encountered in such old documents as books, academic papers, and census forms (for example, the British census of 1901 has a column heading including the terms imbecile and feeble-minded).

Negative connotations associated with these numerous terms for intellectual disability reflect society's attitude about the condition. Some elements of society seek neutral medical terms, while others want to use such terms as weapons with which to abuse people.

Today, new words like special or challenged are replacing the term retarded. The term developmental delay is popular among caretakers and parents of individuals with intellectual disability because delay suggests that a person is slowly reaching his or her full potential rather than being disabled.

Usage has changed over the years and differed from country to country. For example, mental retardation in some contexts covers the whole field but previously applied to what is now the mild MR group. Feeble-minded used to mean mild MR in the UK, and once applied in the US to the whole field. "Borderline intellectual functioning" is not currently defined, but the term may be used to apply to people with IQs in the 70s. People with IQs of 70 to 85 used to be eligible for special consideration in the US public education system on grounds of intellectual disability.

- Cretin is the oldest and comes from a dialectal French word for Christian. The implication was that people with significant intellectual or developmental disabilities were "still human" (or "still Christian") and deserved to be treated with basic human dignity. Individuals with the condition were considered to be incapable of sinning, thus "christ-like" in their disposition. This term is not used in scientific endeavours since the middle of the 20th century and is generally considered a term of abuse. Although cretin is no longer in use, the term cretinism is still used to refer to the mental and physical disability resulting from untreated congenital hypothyroidism.

- Amentia has a long history, mostly associated with dementia. The difference between amentia and dementia was originally defined by time of onset. Amentia was the term used to denote an individual who developed deficits in mental functioning early in life, while dementia included individuals who develop mental deficiencies as adults. During the 1890s, amentia meant someone who was born with mental deficiencies. By 1912, ament was a classification lumping "idiots, imbeciles, and feeble minded" individuals in a category separate from a dement classification, in which the onset is later in life.
- Idiot indicated the greatest degree of intellectual disability, where the mental age is two years or less, and the person cannot guard himself or herself against common physical dangers. The term was gradually replaced by the term profound intellectual disability.
- Imbecile indicated an intellectual disability less extreme than idiocy and not necessarily inherited. It is now usually subdivided into two categories, known as severe intellectual disability and moderate intellectual disability.
- Moron was defined by the American Association for the Study of the Feeble-minded in 1910, following work by Henry H. Goddard, as the term for an adult with a mental age between eight and twelve; mild intellectual disability is now the term for this condition. Alternative definitions of these terms based on IQ were also used. This group was known in UK law from 1911 to 1959/60 as feeble-minded.
- Mongolism was a medical term used to identify someone with Down syndrome. The Mongolian People's Republic requested that the medical community cease use of the term as a referent to intellectual disability. Their request was granted in the 1960s, when the World Health Organization agreed that the term should cease being used within the medical community.

- In the field of special education, educable (or "educable intellectual disability ") refers to ID students with IQs of approximately 50–75 who can progress academically to a late elementary level. Trainable (or "trainable intellectual disability") refers to students whose IQs fall below 50 but who are still capable of learning personal hygiene and other living skills in a sheltered setting, such as a group home. In many areas, these terms have been replaced by use of "moderate" and "severe" intellectual disability. While the names change, the meaning stays roughly the same in practice.
- Retarded comes from the Latin retardare, "to make slow, delay, keep back, or hinder," so mental retardation meant the same as mentally delayed. The term was recorded in 1426 as a "fact or action of making slower in movement or time." The first record of retarded in relation to being mentally slow was in 1895. The term retarded was used to replace terms like idiot, moron, and imbecile because retarded was not then a derogatory term. By the 1960s, however, the term had taken on a partially derogatory meaning as well. The noun retard is particularly seen as pejorative; as of 2010, the Special Olympics, Best Buddies and over 100 other organizations are striving to eliminate the use of the "r-word" (analogous to the "n-word") in everyday conversation.

The term mental retardation was a diagnostic term denoting the group of disconnected categories of mental functioning such as idiot, imbecile, and moron derived from early IQ tests, which acquired pejorative connotations in popular discourse. The term mental retardation acquired negative and shameful connotations over the last few decades due to the use of the words retarded and retard as insults. This may have contributed to its replacement with euphemisms such as mentally challenged or intellectually disabled. While developmental disability includes many other disorders, developmental disability and developmental delay (for people under the age of 18), are generally considered more polite terms than mental retardation.

United States

- In North America intellectual disability is subsumed into the broader term developmental disability, which also includes epilepsy, autism, cerebral palsy and other disorders that develop during the developmental period (birth to age 18). Because service provision is tied to the designation 'developmental disability', it is used by many parents, direct support professionals, and physicians. In the United States, however, in school-based settings, the more specific term mental retardation or, more recently (and preferably), intellectual disability, is still typically used, and is one of 13 categories of disability under which children may be identified for special education services under Public Law 108-446.

- The phrase intellectual disability is increasingly being used as a synonym for people with significantly below-average cognitive ability. These terms are sometimes used as a means of separating general intellectual limitations from specific, limited deficits as well as indicating that it is not an emotional or psychological disability. Intellectual disability may also refer to the outcome of traumatic brain injury, lead poisoning, or dementing conditions such as Alzheimer's disease. It is not specific to congenital disorders such as Down syndrome.

The American Association on Mental Retardation continued to use the term mental retardation until 2006. In June 2006 its members voted to change the name of the organization to the "American Association on Intellectual and Developmental Disabilities," rejecting the options to become the AAID or AADD. Part of the rationale for the double name was that many members worked with people with pervasive developmental disorders, most of whom do not have intellectual disability.

United Kingdom

In the UK, mental handicap had become the common medical term, replacing mental subnormality in Scotland and mental deficiency in England and Wales, until Stephen Dorrell, Secretary of State for Health for the United Kingdom from 1995–97, changed the NHS's designation to learning disability. The new term is not yet widely understood, and is often taken to refer to problems affecting schoolwork (the American usage), which are known in the UK as "learning difficulties." British social workers may use "learning difficulty" to refer to both people with MR and those with conditions such as dyslexia. In education, "learning difficulties" is applied to a wide range of conditions: "specific learning difficulty" may refer to dyslexia, dyscalculia or developmental coordination disorder, while "moderate learning difficulties", "severe learning difficulties" and "profound learning difficulties" refer to more significant impairments.

In England and Wales between 1983 and 2008 the Mental Health Act 1983 defined "mental impairment" and "severe mental impairment" as "a state of arrested or incomplete development of mind which includes significant/severe impairment of intelligence and social functioning and is associated with abnormally aggressive or seriously irresponsible conduct on the part of the person concerned." As behaviour was involved, these were not necessarily permanent conditions: they were defined for the purpose of authorizing detention in hospital or guardianship. The term mental impairment was removed from the Act in November 2008, but the grounds for detention remained. However, English statute law uses mental impairment elsewhere in a less well-defined manner—e.g. to allow exemption from taxes—implying that intellectual disability without any behavioural problems is what is meant.

A BBC poll conducted in the United Kingdom came to the conclusion that 'retard' was the most offensive disability-related word. On the reverse side of that, when a contestant on Celebrity Big Brother live used the phrase "walking like a retard", despite complaints from the public and the charity Mencap, the communications regulator Ofcom did not uphold the complaint saying "it was not used in an offensive context and had been used light-heartedly". It was however noted that two previous similar complaints from other shows were upheld.

Australia

In the past, Australia has used British and American terms interchangeably, including "mental retardation" and "mental handicap". Today, "intellectual disability" is the preferred and more commonly used descriptor.

Society and Culture

People with such disabilities are often not seen as full citizens of society. Person-centred planning and approaches are seen as methods of addressing the continued labelling and exclusion of socially devalued people, such as people with disabilities, encouraging a focus on the person as someone with capacities and gifts as well as support needs. The self-advocacy movement promotes the right of self-determination and self-direction by people with intellectual disabilities, which means allowing people with intellectual disabilities to make decisions about their own lives.

Until the middle of the 20th century, people with intellectual disabilities were routinely excluded from public education, or educated away from other typically developing children. Compared to students with intellectual disabilities who were segregated in special schools, students with intellectual disabilities who are mainstreamed or included in regular classrooms report similar levels of stigma and social self-conception, but more ambitious plans for employment.

As adults, people with intellectual disabilities may live independently, with family members, or in different types of institutions organized to support people with intellectual disabilities. About 8% of people with intellectual disability live in an institution or group home.

In the US, the average lifetime cost of intellectual disability amounts to $1,014,000 per person with intellectual disability, in 2003 US dollars. This is slightly more than the costs associated with cerebral palsy, and double that associated with serious vision or hearing impairments. Of that $1,014,000, about 14% is due to increased medical expenses (not including what is normally incurred by the typical person), 10% is due to direct non-medical expenses, such as the excess cost of special education compared to standard schooling, and 76% is indirect costs accounting for reduced productivity and shortened lifespans. Some expenses, such as costs associated with being a family caregiver or living in a group home, were excluded from this calculation.

Abusive terms for intellectual deficits are common insults, and are most commonly applied to non-disabled people. For example, in the 1964 movie Becket, King Henry II calls his son and heir a "cretin." Mental health professionals discourage use of these terms. The abbreviation retard or tard is still used as a generic insult. A BBC survey in 2003 ranked retard as the most offensive disability-related word, ahead of terms such as spastic (or its abbreviation spaz and mong. A campaign led by people with intellectual disabilities and the Special Olympics to eliminate the "R word" has resulted in federal legislation to replace the term mentally retarded with the term intellectual disability in some federal statutes.

Mental illness : Psychoneurosis and Psychosis

Neurosis is a class of functional mental disorders involving distress but neither delusions nor hallucinations, whereby behaviour is not outside socially acceptable norms. It is also known as psychoneurosis or neurotic disorder, and thus those suffering from it are said to be neurotic. The term essentially describes an "invisible injury" and the resulting condition.

The term neurosis was coined by the Scottish doctor William Cullen in 1769 to refer to "disorders of sense and motion" caused by a "general affection of the nervous system". For him, it described various nervous disorders and symptoms that could not be explained physiologically. It derives from the Greek word "íåæñïí" (neuron, "nerve") with the suffix -osis (diseased or abnormal condition). The term was however most influentially defined by Carl Jung and Sigmund Freud over a century later. It has continued to be used in contemporary theoretical writing in psychology and philosophy.

The American Diagnostic and Statistical Manual of Mental Disorders (DSM) has eliminated the category of "neurosis", reflecting a decision by the editors to provide descriptions of behaviour as opposed to hidden psychological mechanisms as diagnostic criteria, and, according to The American Heritage Medical Dictionary, it is "no longer used in psychiatric diagnosis". Instead, the disorders once classified as neuroses are now considered anxiety disorders. These changes to the DSM have been controversial.

Signs and Symptoms

There are many forms of neurosis: obsessive–compulsive disorder, anxiety neurosis, hysteria (in which anxiety may be discharged through a physical symptom), and a nearly endless variety of phobias as well as obsessions such as pyromania. According to C. George Boeree, professor emeritus at Shippensburg University, effects of neurosis can involve:

...anxiety, sadness or depression, anger, irritability, mental confusion, low sense of self-worth, etc., behavioural symptoms such as phobic avoidance, vigilance, impulsive and compulsive acts, lethargy, etc., cognitive problems such as unpleasant or disturbing thoughts, repetition of thoughts and obsession, habitual fantasizing, negativity and cynicism, etc. Interpersonally, neurosis involves dependency, aggressiveness, perfectionism, schizoid isolation, socio-culturally inappropriate behaviours, etc.

Cause

Psychoanalytical Theory: As an illness, neurosis represents a variety of mental disorders in which emotional distress or unconscious conflict is expressed through various physical, physiological, and mental disturbances, which may include physical symptoms (e.g., hysteria). The definitive symptom is anxieties. Neurotic tendencies are common and may manifest themselves as depression, acute or chronic anxiety, obsessive–compulsive tendencies, specific phobias, such as social phobia, arachnophobia or any number of other phobias, and some personality disorders: paranoid, schizotypal, borderline, histrionic, avoidant, dependent and obsessive–compulsive. It has perhaps been most simply defined as a "poor ability to adapt to one's environment, an inability to change one's life patterns, and the inability to develop a richer, more complex, more satisfying personality." Neurosis should not be mistaken for psychosis, which refers to loss of touch with reality, or neuroticism, a fundamental personality trait according to psychological theory.

According to psychoanalytic theory, neuroses may be rooted in ego defense mechanisms, but the two concepts are not synonymous. Defense mechanisms are a normal way of developing and maintaining a consistent sense of self (i.e., an ego), while only those thoughts and behaviour patterns that produce difficulties in living should be termed "neuroses".

Jung's Theory

Carl Jung found his approach particularly fitting for people who are successfully adjusted by normal social standards, but who nevertheless have issues with the meaning of their life.

The majority of my patients consisted not of believers but of those who had lost their faith.

Contemporary man is blind to the fact that, with all his rationality and efficiency, he is possessed by "powers" that are beyond his control. His gods and demons have not disappeared at all; they have merely got new names. They keep him on the run with restlessness, vague apprehensions, psychological complications, an insatiable need for pills, alcohol, tobacco, food – and, above all, a large array of neuroses.

Jung found that the unconscious finds expression primarily through an individual's inferior psychological function, whether it is thinking, feeling, sensing, or intuition. The characteristic effects of a neurosis on the dominant and inferior functions are discussed in Psychological Types.

Horney's Theory

In her final book, Neurosis and Human Growth, Karen Horney laid out a complete theory on the origin and dynamics of neurosis.

In essence, neurosis is a distorted way of looking at the world and at oneself, determined by compulsive needs rather than by a genuine interest in the world as it is.

She proposes that it is transmitted to a child from his or her early environment. She states that there are a large number of ways this can happen, but:

When summarized, they all boil down to the fact that the people in the environment are too wrapped up in their own neuroses to be able to love the child, or even to conceive of him as the particular individual he is; their attitudes towards him are determined by their own neurotic needs and responses.

The child's initial reality is then distorted by his or her parents' needs and pretenses. Growing up out of sync with reality, the child quickly becomes insecure themselves, developing basic anxiety. To deal with this anxiety, the growing child's own imagination goes to work, creating an idealized self-image:

Each person builds up his personal idealized image from the materials of his own special experiences, his earlier fantasies, his particular needs, and also his given faculties. If it were not for the personal character of the image, he would not attain a feeling of identity and unity. He idealizes, to begin with, his particular "solution" of his basic conflict: compliance becomes goodness, love, saintliness; aggressiveness becomes strength, leadership, heroism, omnipotence; aloofness becomes wisdom, self-sufficiency, independence. What—according to his particular solution—appear as shortcomings or flaws are always dimmed out or retouched.

Once one identifies with the idealized image, a number of effects follow. One will make claims on others and on life based on the prestige one feels entitled to because of the idealized image. One will impose a rigorous set of standards on oneself in order to attempt to actually measure up to what the idealized image is. One will cultivate pride, and with that will come the vulnerabilities associated with pride that lacks a foundation of real esteem. Finally, one will hate and despise oneself for all one's factual limitations, which keep getting in the way and threatening to pop the bubble. Vicious circles operate to strengthen all of these factors.

Eventually, as one grows to adulthood, one particular "solution" to all the inner conflicts and vulnerabilities will solidify. One will be expansive and will display symptoms of narcissism, perfectionism, or vindictiveness. Or one will be self-effacing, and be compulsively compliant and display symptoms of neediness or codependence. Or one will be resigned, and display schizoid tendencies.

In Horney's view, milder anxiety disorders and full-blown personality disorders all fall under her basic scheme of neurosis as variances in the degree of severity and in the individual dynamics.

The opposite of neurosis is a condition Horney calls self-realization, which is when an individual responds to the world with the full depth of his or her spontaneous feelings rather than just anxiety-driven compulsion, resulting in the person growing to actualize his or her inborn potentialities, in a process Horney compares with an acorn growing into a tree.

Psychosis

Psychosis (from the Greek øõ÷Þ "psyche", for mind/soul, and -ùóéò "-osis", for abnormal condition or derangement) refers to an abnormal condition of the mind, and is a generic psychiatric term for a mental state often described as involving a "loss of contact with reality". People suffering from psychosis are described as psychotic. Psychosis is the term given to the more severe forms of psychiatric disorder, during which hallucinations and/or delusions, violence and impaired insight may occur.

The term "psychosis" is very broad and can mean anything from relatively normal aberrant experiences through to the complex and catatonic expressions of schizophrenia and bipolar type 1 disorder. Moreover a wide variety of central nervous system diseases, from both external substances and internal physiologic illness, can produce symptoms of psychosis. This led many professionals to say that psychosis is not specific enough as a diagnostic term. Despite this, the term "psychosis" is generally given to noticeable deficits in normal behaviour (negative signs) and more commonly to diverse types of hallucinations or delusional beliefs (e.g. grandiosity, delusions of persecution). Someone exhibiting very obvious signs may be described as "acutely psychotic", whereas one exhibiting very subtle signs could be classified in the category of an "attenuated psychotic risk syndrome".

An excess in dopaminergic signalling is hypothesized to be linked to the positive symptoms of psychosis, especially those of schizophrenia; however, this hypothesis has not been definitively supported. The dopaminergic mechanism is thought to involve the aberrant salience of environmental stimuli. Many antipsychotic drugs accordingly target the dopamine system; however, meta-analyses of placebo-controlled trials of these drugs show either no significant difference in effects between drug and placebo, or a very small effect size, suggesting that the pathophysiology of psychosis is much more complex than an overactive dopamine system.

People experiencing psychosis may exhibit some personality changes and thought disorder. Depending on its severity, this may be accompanied by unusual or bizarre behaviour, as well as difficulty with social interaction and impairment in carrying out daily life activities.

Signs and Symptoms

People with psychosis may have one or more of the following: hallucinations, delusions, catatonia, or a thought disorder, as described below. Impairments in social cognition also occur.

Hallucinations

A hallucination is defined as sensory perception in the absence of external stimuli. Hallucinations are different from illusions, or perceptual distortions, which are the misperception of external stimuli. Hallucinations may occur in any of the five senses and take on almost any form, which may include simple sensations (such as lights, colours, tastes, and smells) to experiences such as seeing and interacting with fully formed animals and people, hearing voices, and having complex tactile sensations.

Auditory hallucinations, particularly experiences of hearing voices, are a common and often prominent feature of psychosis. Hallucinated voices may talk about, or to, the person, and may involve several speakers with distinct personas. Auditory hallucinations tend to be particularly distressing when they are derogatory, commanding or preoccupying. However, the experience of hearing voices need not always be a negative one. One research study has shown that the majority of people who hear voices are not in need of psychiatric help. The Hearing Voices Movement has subsequently been created to support voice hearers, regardless of whether they are considered to have a mental illness or not.

Delusions

Psychosis may involve delusional beliefs, some of which are paranoid in nature. Put simply, delusions are false beliefs which a person holds on to, without adequate evidence. It may be difficult to change the belief even with evidence to the contrary. Common themes of delusions are persecutory (person believes that others are out to harm him/her), grandiose (person believing that he or she has special powers or skills) etc. Depressed persons may have delusions consistent with their low mood e.g., delusions that they have sinned, or have contracted serious illness etc. Karl Jaspers has classified psychotic delusions into primary and secondary types. Primary delusions are defined as arising suddenly and not being comprehensible in terms of normal mental processes, whereas secondary delusions may be understood as being influenced by the person's background or current situation (e.g., ethnicity; religious, superstitious, or political beliefs).

Catatonia

Catatonia describes a profoundly agitated state in which the experience of reality is generally considered to be impaired. There are two primary manifestations of catatonic behaviour. The classic presentation is a person who does not move or interact with the world in any way while awake. This type of catatonia presents with waxy flexibility. Waxy flexibility is when someone physically moves part of a catatonic person's body and the person stays in the position even if it is bizarre and otherwise nonfunctional (such as moving a person's arm straight up in the air and the arm stays there).

The other type of catatonia is more of an outward presentation of the profoundly agitated state described above. It involves excessive and purposeless motor behaviour as well as extreme mental preoccupation which prevents intact experience of reality. An example would be someone walking very fast in circles to the exclusion of anything else with a level of mental preoccupation (meaning not focused on anything relevant to the situation) that was not typical of the person prior to the symptom onset. In both types of catatonia there is generally no reaction to anything that happens outside of them. It is important to distinguish catatonic agitation from severe bipolar mania, although someone could have both.

Thought Disorder

Thought disorder describes an underlying disturbance to conscious thought and is classified largely by its effects on speech and writing. Affected persons show loosening of associations, that is, a disconnection and disorganization of the semantic content of speech and writing. In the severe form speech becomes incomprehensible and it is known as "word salad".

Psychiatric Disorders

From a diagnostic standpoint, organic disorders were those held to be caused by physical illness affecting the brain (that is, psychiatric disorders secondary to other conditions), while functional disorders were considered to be disorders of the functioning of the mind in the absence of physical disorders (that is, primary psychological or psychiatric disorders). The materialistic view of the mind–body problem holds that mental disorders arise from physical processes; in this view, the distinction between brain and mind, and therefore between organic and functional disease, is an artificial one. Subtle physical abnormalities have been found in illnesses traditionally considered functional, such as schizophrenia. The DSM-IV-TR avoids the functional/organic distinction, and instead lists traditional psychotic illnesses, psychosis due to general medical conditions, and substance-induced psychosis.

Primary psychiatric causes of psychosis include the following:

- schizophrenia and schizophreniform disorder
- affective (mood) disorders, including severe depression, and severe depression or mania in bipolar disorder (manic depression). People experiencing a psychotic episode in the context of depression may experience persecutory or self-blaming delusions or hallucinations, while people experiencing a psychotic episode in the context of mania may form grandiose delusions.
- schizoaffective disorder, involving symptoms of both schizophrenia and mood disorders
- brief psychotic disorder, or acute/transient psychotic disorder
- delusional disorder (persistent delusional disorder)
- chronic hallucinatory psychosis

Psychotic symptoms may also be seen in

- schizotypal disorder
- certain personality disorders at times of stress (including paranoid personality disorder, schizoid personality disorder, and borderline personality disorder)
- major depressive disorder in its severe form although it is possible and more likely to have severe depression without psychosis
- bipolar disorder in severe mania and/or severe depression although it is possible to have severe mania and/or severe depression without psychosis as well, in fact that is more commonly the case
- post-traumatic stress disorder
- induced delusional disorder
- Sometimes in obsessive-compulsive disorder

Stress is known to contribute to and trigger psychotic states. A history of psychologically traumatic events, and the recent experience of a stressful event, can both contribute to the development of psychosis. Short-lived psychosis triggered by stress is known as brief reactive psychosis, and patients may spontaneously recover normal functioning within two weeks. In some rare cases, individuals may remain in a state of full-blown psychosis for many years, or perhaps have attenuated psychotic symptoms (such as low intensity hallucinations) present at most times.

Normal States

Brief hallucinations are not uncommon in those without any psychiatric disease. Causes or triggers include

- falling asleep and waking: hypnagogic and hypnopompic hallucinations, which are entirely normal
- bereavement, in which hallucinations of a deceased loved one are common
- severe sleep deprivation
- sensory deprivation and sensory impairment
- caffeine intoxication
- extremely stressful event

Subtypes

Subtypes of psychosis include:

- Menstrual psychosis, including circa-mensual (approximately monthly) periodicity, in rhythm with the menstrual cycle.
- Postpartum psychosis, occurring recently after childbirth
- Monothematic delusions
- Myxedematous psychosis
- Occupational psychosis
- Stimulant psychosis
- Tardive psychosis
- Shared psychosis
- Cycloid psychosis

Cycloid Psychosis

Cycloid psychosis is psychosis that progresses from normal to full-blown usually within a few hours, not related to drug intake or brain injury. In addition, diagnostic criteria include at least four of the following symptoms:

- Confusion
- Mood-incongruent delusions

- Hallucinations
- Pan-anxiety, a severe anxiety not bound to particular situations or circumstances
- Happiness or ecstasy of high degree
- Motility disturbances of akinetic or hyperkinetic type
- Concern with death
- Mood swings to some degree, but less than what is needed for diagnosis of an affective disorders

Cycloid psychosis occurs in people of generally 15–50 years of age.

Medical Conditions

A very large number of medical conditions can cause psychosis, sometimes called secondary psychosis. Examples include:

- disorders causing delirium (toxic psychosis), in which consciousness is disturbed
- neurodevelopmental disorders and chromosomal abnormalities, including velocardiofacial syndrome
- neurodegenerative disorders, such as Alzheimer's disease, dementia with Lewy bodies, and Parkinson's disease
- focal neurological disease, such as stroke, brain tumors, multiple sclerosis, and some forms of epilepsy
- malignancy (typically via masses in the brain, paraneoplastic syndromes, or drugs used to treat cancer)
- infectious and postinfectious syndromes, including infections causing delirium, viral encephalitis, HIV, malaria, Lyme disease, syphilis
- endocrine disease, such as hypothyroidism, hyperthyroidism, adrenal failure, Cushing's syndrome, hypoparathyroidism and hyperparathyroidism; sex hormones also affect psychotic symptoms and sometimes childbirth can provoke psychosis, termed puerperal psychosis
- inborn errors of metabolism, such as porphyria and metachromatic leukodystrophy
- nutritional deficiency, such as vitamin B_{12} deficiency
- other acquired metabolic disorders, including electrolyte disturbances such as hypocalcemia, hypernatremia, hyponatremia, hypokalemia, hypomagnesemia, hypermagnesemia,

hypercalcemia, and hypophosphatemia, but also hypoglycemia, hypoxia, and failure of the liver or kidneys

- autoimmune and related disorders, such as systemic lupus erythematosus (lupus, SLE), sarcoidosis, Hashimoto's encephalopathy, and anti-NMDA-receptor encephalitis
- poisoning, by therapeutic drugs, recreational drugs, and a range of plants, fungi, metals, organic compounds, and a few animal toxins
- some sleep disorders, including hallucinations in narcolepsy (in which REM sleep intrudes into wakefulness)

Psychosis can even be caused by familiar ailments such as flu or mumps.

Psychoactive Drugs

Various psychoactive substances (both legal and illegal) have been implicated in causing, exacerbating, and/or precipitating psychotic states and/or disorders in users. This may be upon intoxication, for a more prolonged period after use, or upon withdrawal. Individuals who have a substance induced psychosis tend to have a greater awareness of their psychosis and tend to have higher levels of suicidal thinking compared to individuals who have a primary psychotic illness. Drugs that can induce psychotic symptoms include cannabis, cocaine, amphetamines, cathinones, psychedelic drugs (such as LSD and psilocybin), ê-opioid receptor agonists (such as enadoline and salvinorin A) and NMDA receptor antagonists (such as phencyclidine and ketamine).

Alcohol

Approximately 3 percent of people who are suffering from alcoholism experience psychosis during acute intoxication or withdrawal. Alcohol related psychosis may manifest itself through a kindling mechanism. The mechanism of alcohol-related psychosis is due to the long-term effects of alcohol resulting in distortions to neuronal membranes, gene expression, as well as thiamin deficiency. It is possible in some cases that alcohol abuse via a kindling mechanism can cause the development of a chronic substance induced psychotic disorder, i.e. schizophrenia. The effects of an alcohol-related psychosis include an increased risk of depression and suicide as well as causing psychosocial impairments.

Cannabis

The more often cannabis is abused the more likely a person is to develop a psychotic illness, with frequent use being correlated with twice the risk of psychosis and schizophrenia. While cannabis use is accepted as a contributory cause of schizophrenia by many, it remains controversial. Some studies indicate that the effects of the two active compounds in cannabis, Tetrahydrocannabinol (THC) and Cannabidiol (CBD), are separable with respect to psychosis. While THC by itself tends to induce psychotic symptoms, CBD tends to reduce them, particularly in people who already exhibit these symptoms. Cannabis use has increased dramatically over the past few decades whereas the rate of psychosis has not increased. Together, these findings suggest that cannabis only hastens the onset of psychosis in those who would otherwise become psychotic at a later date.

Methamphetamine

Methamphetamine induces a psychosis in 26-46 percent of heavy users. Some of these people develop a long-lasting psychosis that can persist for longer than 6 months. Those who have had a short-lived psychosis from methamphetamine can have a relapse of the methamphetamine psychosis years later after a stress event such as severe insomnia or a period of heavy alcohol abuse despite not relapsing back to methamphetamine. Individuals who have long history of methamphetamine abuse and who have experienced psychosis in the past from methamphetamine abuse are highly likely to rapidly relapse back into a methamphetamine psychosis within a week or so of going back onto methamphetamine. Violence is common during a methamphetamine psychosis.

Medication

Administration, or sometimes withdrawal, of a large number of medications may provoke psychotic symptoms. Drugs that can induce psychosis experimentally and/or in a significant proportion of patients include amphetamine and other sympathomimetics, dopamine agonists, ketamine, corticosteroids (often with mood changes in addition), and some anticonvulsants such as vigabatrin.

Pathophysiology

The first brain image of an individual with psychosis was completed as far back as 1935 using a technique called pneumoencephalography (a painful and now obsolete procedure where cerebrospinal fluid is drained from around the brain and replaced with air to allow the structure of the brain to show up more clearly on an X-ray picture).

The purpose of the brain is to collect information from the body (pain, hunger, etc.), and from the outside world, interpret it to a coherent world view, and produce a meaningful response. The information from the senses enter the brain in the primary sensory areas. They process the information and send it to the secondary areas where the information is interpreted. Spontaneous activity in the primary sensory areas may produce hallucinations which are misinterpreted by the secondary areas as information from the real world.

For example, a PET or fMRI scan of a person who claims to be hearing voices may show activation in the primary auditory cortex, or parts of the brain involved in the perception and understanding of speech.

Tertiary brain cortex collects the interpretations from the secondary cortexes and creates a coherent world view of it. A study investigating structural changes in the brains of people with psychosis showed there was significant grey matter reduction in the right medial temporal, lateral temporal, and inferior frontal gyrus, and in the cingulate cortex bilaterally of people before and after they became psychotic. Findings such as these have led to debate about whether psychosis itself causes excitotoxic brain damage and whether potentially damaging changes to the brain are related to the length of psychotic episode. Recent research has suggested that this is not the case although further investigation is still ongoing.

Studies with sensory deprivation have shown that the brain is dependent on signals from the outer world to function properly. If the spontaneous activity in the brain is not counterbalanced with information from the senses, loss from reality and psychosis may occur after some hours. A similar phenomenon is paranoia in the elderly when poor eyesight, hearing and memory causes the person to be abnormally suspicious of the environment.

On the other hand, loss from reality may also occur if the spontaneous cortical activity is increased so that it is no longer counterbalanced with information from the senses. The 5-HT2A receptor seems to be important for this, since psychedelic drugs which activate them produce hallucinations.

However, the main feature of psychosis is not hallucinations, but the inability to distinguish between internal and external stimuli. Close relatives to psychotic patients may hear voices, but since they are aware that they are unreal they can ignore them, so that the hallucinations do not affect their reality perception. Hence they are not considered to be psychotic.

Psychosis has been traditionally linked to the neurotransmitter dopamine. In particular, the dopamine hypothesis of psychosis has been influential and states that psychosis results from an overactivity of dopamine function in the brain, particularly in the mesolimbic pathway. The two major sources of evidence given to support this theory are that dopamine receptor D2 blocking drugs (i.e., antipsychotics) tend to reduce the intensity of psychotic symptoms, and that drugs which boost dopamine activity (such as amphetamines and cocaine) can trigger psychosis in some people. However, increasing evidence in recent times has pointed to a possible dysfunction of the excitory neurotransmitter glutamate, in particular, with the activity of the NMDA receptor.

This theory is reinforced by the fact that dissociative NMDA receptor antagonists such as ketamine, PCP and dextromethorphan (at large overdoses) induce a psychotic state more readily than dopaminergic stimulants, even at "normal" recreational doses. The symptoms of dissociative intoxication are also considered to mirror the symptoms of schizophrenia, including negative psychotic symptoms, more closely than amphetamine psychosis. Dissociative induced psychosis happens on a more reliable and predictable basis than amphetamine psychosis, which usually only occurs in cases of overdose, prolonged use or with sleep deprivation, which can independently produce psychosis. New antipsychotic drugs which act on glutamate and its receptors are currently undergoing clinical trials.

The connection between dopamine and psychosis is generally believed to be complex. While dopamine receptor D2 suppresses adenylate cyclase activity, the D1 receptor increases it. If D2-blocking drugs are administered the blocked dopamine spills over to the D1 receptors. The increased adenylate cyclase activity affects genetic expression in the nerve cell, a process which takes time. Hence antipsychotic drugs take a week or two to reduce the symptoms of psychosis. Moreover, newer and equally effective antipsychotic drugs actually block slightly less dopamine in the brain than older drugs whilst also blocking 5-HT2A receptors, suggesting the 'dopamine hypothesis' may be oversimplified. Soyka and colleagues found no evidence of dopaminergic dysfunction in people with alcohol-induced psychosis and Zoldan et al. reported moderately successful use of ondansetron, a 5-HT_3 receptor antagonist, in the treatment of levodopa psychosis in Parkinson's disease patients.

Psychiatrist David Healy has criticised pharmaceutical companies for promoting simplified biological theories of mental illness that seem to imply the primacy of pharmaceutical treatments while ignoring social and developmental factors which are known to be important influences in the aetiology of psychosis.

Some theories regard many psychotic symptoms to be a problem with the perception of ownership of internally generated thoughts and experiences. For example, the hallucination of hearing voices may arise from internally generated speech that is mislabelled by the psychotic person as coming from an external source.

It has been suggested that persons with bipolar disorder may have increased activity of the left hemisphere compared to the right hemisphere of the brain, while persons with schizophrenia have increased activity in the right hemisphere.

Increased level of right hemisphere activation has also been found in people who have high levels of paranormal beliefs and in people who report mystical experiences. It also seems to be the case that people who are more creative are also more likely to show a similar pattern of brain activation. Some researchers have been quick to point out that this in no way suggests that paranormal, mystical or creative experiences are in any way by themselves a symptom of mental illness, as it is still not clear what makes some such experiences beneficial and others distressing.

Neurobiology

In otherwise normal individuals, exogenous ligands can produce psychotic symptoms. NMDA receptor antagonists, such as ketamine, can produce a similar psychosis to that experienced in schizophrenia.

Prolonged or high dose use of psychostimulants can alter normal functioning to be similar to the manic phase of bipolar disorder. NMDA antagonists replicate some of the so-called "negative" symptoms like thought disorder in subanesthetic doses (doses insufficient to induce anesthesia), and catatonia in high doses. Psychostimulants, especially in one already prone to psychotic thinking, can cause some "positive" symptoms, such as delusional beliefs, particularly those persecutory in nature.

Diagnosis

Diagnosing the presence and/or extent of psychosis may be distinguished from diagnosing the cause of psychosis.

The presence of psychosis is typically diagnosed by clinical interview, incorporating mental state examination. Its extent may be established by formal rating scales. The Brief Psychiatric Rating Scale (BPRS) assesses the level of 18 symptom constructs of psychosis such as hostility, suspicion, hallucination, and grandiosity. It is based on the clinician's interview with the patient and observations of the patient's behaviour over the previous 2–3 days. The patient's family can also provide the behaviour report. During the initial assessment and the follow-up, both positive and negative symptoms of psychosis can be assessed using the 30 item Positive and Negative Symptom Scale (PANSS).

Establishing the cause of psychosis requires clinical examination, and sometimes special investigations, to diagnose or exclude secondary causes of psychosis; if these are excluded, a primary psychiatric diagnosis can be established.

Prevention

The evidence for the effectiveness of early interventions to prevent psychosis appeared inconclusive. Whilst early intervention in those with a psychotic episode might improve short term outcomes, little benefit was seen from these measures after five years. However more recently there has been some evidence that cognitive behavioural therapy (CBT) may reduce the risk of becoming psychotic in those at high risk.

Treatment

The treatment of psychosis depends on the specific diagnosis (such as schizophrenia, bipolar disorder or substance intoxication). The first line treatment for many psychotic disorders is antipsychotic medication (oral or intramuscular injection), and sometimes hospitalization is needed. However, there are significant problems associated with this class of drugs. There is evidence that they can cause brain damage including prefrontal cortex atrophy, long-lasting parkinsonian symtoms (tardive dyskinesia), and personality change. Nancy Andreasen has argued for an association between antipsychotic drugs and smaller grey matter volumes independent of illness severity. Furthermore, antipsychotic drugs can themselves induce psychotic symptoms if they are administered for a long time and then discontinued.

There is growing evidence that cognitive behaviour therapy, acceptance and commitment therapy and family therapy can be effective in managing psychotic symptoms. When other treatments for psychosis are ineffective, electroconvulsive therapy or ECT (also known as shock treatment) is sometimes applied to relieve the underlying symptoms of psychosis due to depression. There is also increasing research suggesting that animal-assisted therapy can contribute to the improvement in general well-being of people with schizophrenia.

Early Intervention

Early intervention in psychosis is on the observation that identifying and treating someone in the early stages of a psychosis can improve their longer term outcome. This approach advocates the use of an intensive multi-disciplinary approach during what is known as the critical period, where intervention is the most effective, and prevents the long term morbidity associated with chronic psychotic illness.

History

The word psychosis was introduced to the psychiatric literature in 1841 by Karl Friedrich Canstatt in his work Handbuch der Medizinischen Klinik. He used it as a shorthand for 'psychic neurosis'. At that time neurosis meant any disease of the nervous system, and Canstatt was thus referring to what was thought to be a psychological manifestation of brain disease. Ernst von Feuchtersleben is also widely credited as introducing the term in 1845, as an alternative to insanity and mania.

The term stems from the Greek psychosis, "a giving soul or life to, animating, quickening" and that from psyche, "soul" and the suffix -osis, in this case "abnormal condition".

The word was also used to distinguish disorders which were thought to be disorders of the mind, as opposed to "neurosis", which was thought to be a disorder of the nervous system. The psychoses thus became the modern equivalent of the old notion of madness, and hence there was much debate on whether there was only one (unitary) or many forms of the new disease. One type of broad usage would later be narrowed down by Koch in 1891 to the 'psychopathic inferiorities' - later renamed abnormal personalities by Schneider.

The division of the major psychoses into manic depressive illness (now called bipolar disorder) and dementia praecox (now called schizophrenia) was made by Emil Kraepelin, who attempted to create a synthesis of the various mental disorders identified by 19th century psychiatrists, by grouping diseases together based on classification of common symptoms. Kraepelin used the term 'manic depressive insanity' to describe the whole spectrum of mood disorders, in a far wider sense than it is usually used today.

In Kraepelin's classification this would include 'unipolar' clinical depression, as well as bipolar disorder and other mood disorders such as cyclothymia. These are characterised by problems with mood control and the psychotic episodes appear associated with disturbances in mood, and patients will often have periods of normal functioning between psychotic episodes even without medication. Schizophrenia is characterized by psychotic episodes which appear to be unrelated to disturbances in mood, and most non-medicated patients will show signs of disturbance between psychotic episodes.

During the 1960s and 1970s, psychosis was of particular interest to counterculture critics of mainstream psychiatric practice, who argued that it may simply be another way of constructing reality and is not necessarily a sign of illness. For example, R. D. Laing argued that psychosis is a symbolic way of expressing concerns in situations where such views may be unwelcome or uncomfortable to the recipients. He went on to say that psychosis could be also seen as a transcendental experience with healing and spiritual aspects.

Arthur J. Deikman suggested use of the term "mystical psychosis" to characterize first-person accounts of psychotic experiences that are similar to reports of mystical experiences. Thomas Szasz focused on the social implications of labelling people as psychotics, a label he argues unjustly medicalises different views of reality so such unorthodox people can be controlled by society. Psychoanalysis has a detailed account of psychosis which differs markedly from that of psychiatry. Freud and Lacan outlined their perspective on the structure of psychosis in a number of works.

Since the 1970s, the introduction of a recovery approach to mental health, which has been driven mainly by people who have experienced psychosis (or whatever name is used to describe their experiences), has led to a greater awareness that mental illness is not a lifelong disability, and that there is an expectation that recovery is possible, and probable with effective support.

Psychiatric conditions associated with psychotic spectrum symptoms may be possible explanations for revelatory driven experiences and activities such as those of Abraham, Moses, Jesus and Saint Paul.

Psychotherapy

Psychotherapy is a general term referring to therapeutic interaction or treatment contracted between a trained professional and a client, patient, family, couple, or group. The problems addressed are psychological in nature and can vary in terms of their causes, influences, triggers, and potential resolutions. Accurate assessment of these and other variables is dependent on the practitioner's capability and can change or evolve as the practitioner acquires greater experience, knowledge, and insight.

Psychotherapy includes interactive processes between a person or group and a qualified mental health professional (psychiatrist, psychologist, clinical social worker, licensed counsellor, or other trained practitioner). Its purpose is the exploration of thoughts, feelings and behaviour for the purpose of problem solving or achieving higher levels of functioning. Psychotherapy aims to increase the individual's sense of his/her own well-being. Psychotherapists employ a range of techniques based on experiential relationship building, dialogue, communication and behaviour change that are designed to improve the mental health of a client or patient, or to improve group relationships (such as in a family).

Psychotherapy may also be performed by practitioners with a number of different qualifications, including psychiatry, clinical psychology, counselling psychology, clinical or psychiatric social work, mental health counselling, marriage and family therapy, rehabilitation counselling, school counselling, hypnotherapy, play therapy, music therapy, art therapy, drama therapy, dance/movement therapy, occupational therapy, psychiatric nursing, psychoanalysis and those from other psychotherapies. It may be legally regulated, voluntarily regulated or unregulated, depending on the jurisdiction. Requirements of these professions vary, but often require graduate school and supervised clinical experience. Psychotherapy in Europe is increasingly being seen as an independent profession, rather than being restricted to being practiced only by psychologists and psychiatrists as is stipulated in some countries.

Regulation

Continental Europe: In Germany, the Psychotherapy Act (PsychThG, 1998) restricts the practice of psychotherapy for adults to the professions of psychology who have completed a five-year course. Children may receive such therapy from social pedagogues and social workers who have completed a five-year postgraduate course. For physicians they must complete a residency in psychotherapeutic medicine till 2003. A training in psychotherapy is also part of residency in psychiatry and psychosomatic medicine the title of those professionals is consultant for psychiatry and psychotherapy and consultant for psychosomatic medicine and psychotherapy. All consultant physicans are able to specialize themselves in psychotherapy for there province e.g. in psychotherapy for oncology in a five-year course.

In Italy, the Ossicini Act (no. 56/1989, art. 3) restricts the practice of psychotherapy to graduates in psychology or medicine who have completed a four-year postgraduate course in psychotherapy at a training school recognised by the state;

French legislation restricts use of the title "psychotherapist" to professionals on the National Register of Psychotherapists; the inscription on this register requires a training in clinical psychopathology and a period of internship which is only open to physicians or titulars of a master's degree in psychology or psychoanalysis.

Sweden has a similar restriction on the title "psychotherapist", which may only be used by professionals who have gone through a post-graduate training in psychotherapy and then applied for a licence, issued by the National Board of Health and Welfare.

Austria and Switzerland (2011) have laws that recognize multidifunctional-disciplinary approaches.

United Kingdom

In the United Kingdom, psychotherapy is voluntarily regulated. National registers for psychotherapists and counsellors are maintained by three main umbrella bodies:

1. the United Kingdom Council for Psychotherapy (UKCP)
2. the British Association for Counselling and Psychotherapy (BACP)
3. the British Psychoanalytic Council (BPC - formerly the British Confederation of Psychotherapists).

There are many smaller professional bodies and associations such as the Association of Child Psychotherapists (ACP) and the British Association of Psychotherapists (BAP).

Following a 2007 United Kingdom Government White Paper, "Trust Assurance and Safety – The Regulation of Health Professionals in the 21st Century" the Health Professions Council (HPC) consulted on potential statutory regulation of psychotherapists and counsellors. The HPC is an official state regulator that regulates some 15 professions at present. Research by academics at King's College London subsequently studied the effects of increasing regulation of psychotherapists and counsellors, compared with the effects of statutory regulation of medical doctors. The research found significant unintended effects of statutory regulation, especially defensive practice, and concluded that mandatory professional regulation was a more effective way of regulating the practices of psychotherapists and counsellors.

Government policy subsequently moved away from statutory regulation, and the Professional Standards Authority for Health and Social Care (PSA) launched an Accredited Voluntary Registers scheme.

Hong Kong

In Hong Kong, there is no statutory regulation of psychologist profession in providing psychotherapy at present. Hong Kong Association of Doctors in Clinical Psychology (HKADCP) is the only professional association established in 2011 purely by a group of doctorate clinical psychologists who are endeavoured to build the community of clinical psychologists with professional standard for better serving the needs of the society. The HKADCP's Register of Clinical Psychologists is an official register implemented and maintained by Hong Kong Association of Doctors in Clinical Psychology (HKADCP), in accordance with stipulations contained in the By-Laws of the Association.

Etymology

Psychotherapy is an English word of Greek origin, deriving from Ancient Greek psyche (meaning "breath; spirit; soul") and therapia ("healing; medical treatment").

According to the Oxford English Dictionary, psychotherapy first meant "hypnotherapy" instead of "psychotherapy". The original meaning, "the treatment of disease by 'psychic' [i.e., hypnotic] methods", was first recorded in 1853 as "Psychotherapeia, or the remedial influence of mind". The modern meaning, "the treatment of disorders of the mind or personality by psychological or psychophysiological methods", was first used in 1892 by Frederik van Eeden translating "Suggestive Psycho-therapy" for his French "Psychothérapie Suggestive". Van Eeden credited borrowing this term from Daniel Hack Tuke and noted, "Psycho-therapy ... had the misfortune to be taken in tow by hypnotism."

The psychiatrist Jerome Frank defined psychotherapy as the relief of distress or disability in one person by another, using an approach based on a particular theory or paradigm, and a requirement that the agent performing the therapy has had some form of training in delivering this. It is these latter two points which distinguish psychotherapy from other forms of counselling or caregiving. Psychologist Hans J. Eysenck in explaining the relationship between psychotherapy, behaviour therapy and behaviour modification defines it in its broadest sense as "the use of psychological therories and methods in the treatment of psychiatric disorders." He goes on to state that psychotherapy "has a narrower meaning, namely the use of interpretative (mostly Freudian) methods of therapy."

Forms

Most forms of psychotherapy use spoken conversation. Some also use various other forms of communication such as the written word, artwork, drama, narrative story or music. Psychotherapy with children and their parents often involves play, dramatization (i.e. role-play), and drawing, with a co-constructed narrative from these non-verbal and displaced modes of interacting. Psychotherapy occurs within a structured encounter between a trained therapist and client(s). Purposeful, theoretically based psychotherapy began in the 19th century with psychoanalysis; since then, scores of other approaches have been developed and continue to be created.

Therapy is generally used in response to a variety of specific or non-specific manifestations of clinically diagnosable and/or existential crises. Treatment of everyday problems is more often referred to as counselling (a distinction originally adopted by Carl Rogers). However, the term counselling is sometimes used interchangeably with "psychotherapy".

While some psychotherapeutic interventions are designed to treat the patient using the medical model, many psychotherapeutic approaches do not adhere to the symptom-based model of "illness/cure". Some practitioners, such as humanistic therapists, see themselves more in a facilitative/helper role. As sensitive and deeply personal topics are often discussed during psychotherapy, therapists are expected, and usually legally bound, to respect client or patient confidentiality. The critical importance of confidentiality is enshrined in the regulatory psychotherapeutic organizations' codes of ethical practice.

Systems

There are several main broad systems of psychotherapy:

- Psychoanalytic - This was the first practice to be called a psychotherapy. It encourages the verbalization of all the patient's thoughts, including free associations, fantasies, and dreams, from which the analyst formulates the nature of the unconscious conflicts which are causing the patient's symptoms and character problems.

- Behaviour therapy/applied behaviour analysis - Focuses on changing maladaptive patterns of behaviour to improve emotional responses, cognitions, and interactions with others.
- Cognitive behavioural - Generally seeks to identify maladaptive cognition, appraisal, beliefs and reactions with the aim of influencing destructive negative emotions and problematic dysfunctional behaviours.
- Psychodynamic - A form of depth psychology, whose primary focus is to reveal the unconscious content of a client's psyche in an effort to alleviate psychic tension. Although its roots are in psychoanalysis, psychodynamic therapy tends to be briefer and less intensive than traditional psychoanalysis.
- Existential - Based on the existential belief that human beings are alone in the world. This isolation leads to feelings of meaninglessness, which can be overcome only by creating one's own values and meanings. Existential therapy is philosophically associated with phenomenology.
- Humanistic - Emerged in reaction to both behaviourism and psychoanalysis and is therefore known as the Third Force in the development of psychology. It is explicitly concerned with the human context of the development of the individual with an emphasis on subjective meaning, a rejection of determinism, and a concern for positive growth rather than pathology. It posits an inherent human capacity to maximize potential, 'the self-actualizing tendency'. The task of Humanistic therapy is to create a relational environment where this tendency might flourish. Humanistic psychology is philosophically rooted in existentialism.
- Brief - "Brief therapy" is an umbrella term for a variety of approaches to psychotherapy. It differs from other schools of therapy in that it emphasizes (1) a focus on a specific problem and (2) direct intervention. It is solution-based rather than problem-oriented. It is less concerned with how a problem arose than with the current factors sustaining it and preventing change.
- Systemic - Seeks to address people not at an individual level, as is often the focus of other forms of therapy, but as people in relationship, dealing with the interactions of groups, their

patterns and dynamics (includes family therapy & marriage counselling). Community psychology is a type of systemic psychology.

- Transpersonal - Addresses the client in the context of a spiritual understanding of consciousness.
- Body Psychotherapy - Addresses problems of the mind as being closely correlated with bodily phenomena, including a person's sexuality, musculature, breathing habits, physiology etc. This therapy may involve massage and other body exercises as well as talking.

There are hundreds of psychotherapeutic approaches or schools of thought. By 1980 there were more than 250; by 1996 there were more than 450. The development of new and hybrid approaches continues around the wide variety of theoretical backgrounds. Many practitioners use several approaches in their work and alter their approach based on client need.

History

In an informal sense, psychotherapy can be said to have been practiced through the ages, as individuals received psychological counsel and reassurance from others.

According to Colin Feltham, "The Stoics were one of the main Hellenistic schools of philosophy and therapy, along with the Sceptics and Epicureans (Nussbaum, 1994). Philosophers and physicians from these schools practised psychotherapy among the Greeks and Romans from about the late 4th century BC to the 4th century AD." Indeed, Stoic philosophy was explicitly cited by the founders of cognitive therapy and rational-emotive behaviour therapy as the principal precursor and inspiration for their own approaches.

Psychoanalysis was perhaps the first specific school of psychotherapy, developed by Sigmund Freud and others through the early 20th century. Trained as a neurologist, Freud began focusing on problems that appeared to have no discernible organic basis, and theorized that they had psychological causes originating in childhood experiences and the unconscious mind. Techniques such as dream interpretation, free association, transference and analysis of the id, ego and superego were developed. Many theorists, including Anna Freud, Alfred Adler, Carl Jung, Karen Horney, Otto Rank, Erik Erikson, Melanie Klein, and Heinz Kohut, built upon Freud's fundamental ideas and often developed their own systems of psychotherapy. These were all later categorized as psychodynamic, meaning anything that involved the psyche's conscious/unconscious influence on external relationships and the self. Sessions tended to number into the hundreds over several years.

Behaviourism developed in the 1920s, and behaviour modification as a therapy became popularized in the 1950s and 1960s. Notable contributors were Joseph Wolpe in South Africa, M.B. Shipiro and Hans Eysenck in Britain, and John B. Watson and B.F. Skinner in the United States. Behavioural therapy approaches relied on principles of operant conditioning, classical conditioning and social learning theory to bring about therapeutic change in observable symptoms. The approach became commonly used for phobias, as well as other disorders.

Some therapeutic approaches developed out of the European school of existential philosophy. Concerned mainly with the individual's ability to develop and preserve a sense of meaning and purpose throughout life, major contributors to the field in the US (e.g., Irvin Yalom, Rollo May) and Europe (Viktor Frankl, Ludwig Binswanger, Medard Boss, R.D.Laing, Emmy van Deurzen) and later in the 1960s and 1970s both in the United Kingdom and in Canada, Eugene Heimler attempted to create therapies sensitive to common 'life crises' springing from the essential bleakness of human self-awareness, previously accessible only through the complex writings of existential philosophers (e.g., Søren Kierkegaard, Jean-Paul Sartre, Gabriel Marcel, Martin Heidegger, Friedrich Nietzsche). The uniqueness of the patient-therapist relationship thus also forms a vehicle for therapeutic enquiry. A related body of thought in psychotherapy started in the 1950s with Carl Rogers. Based on existentialism and the works of Abraham Maslow and his hierarchy of human needs, Rogers brought person-centred psychotherapy into mainstream focus. The primary requirement of Rogers is that the client should be in receipt of three core 'conditions' from his counsellor or therapist: unconditional positive regard, also sometimes described as 'prizing' the person or valuing the humanity of an individual, congruence [authenticity/genuineness/transparency], and empathic understanding. The aim in using the 'core conditions' is to facilitate therapeutic change within a non-directive relationship conducive to enhancing the client's psychological well being. This type of interaction enables the client to fully experience and express himself. Others developed the approach, like Fritz and Laura Perls in the creation of Gestalt therapy, as well as Marshall Rosenberg, founder of Nonviolent Communication, and Eric Berne, founder of Transactional Analysis. Later these fields of psychotherapy would become what is known as humanistic psychotherapy today. Self-help groups and books became widespread.

During the 1950s, Albert Ellis originated Rational Emotive Behaviour Therapy (REBT). A few years later, psychiatrist Aaron T. Beck developed a form of psychotherapy known as cognitive therapy. Both of these generally included relatively short, structured and present-focused therapy aimed at identifying and changing a person's beliefs, appraisals and reaction-patterns, by contrast with the more long-lasting insight-based approach of psychodynamic or humanistic therapies. Cognitive and behavioural therapy approaches were combined and grouped under the heading and umbrella-term Cognitive behavioural therapy (CBT) in the 1970s. Many approaches within CBT are oriented towards active/directive collaborative empiricism and mapping, assessing and modifying clients core beliefs and dysfunctional schemas. These approaches gained widespread acceptance as a primary treatment for numerous disorders. A "third wave" of cognitive and behavioural therapies developed, including Acceptance and Commitment Therapy and Dialectical behaviour therapy, which expanded the concepts to other disorders and/or added novel components and mindfulness exercises. Counselling methods developed, including solution-focused therapy and systemic coaching. During the 1960s and 1970s Eugene Heimler, after training in the new discipline of psychiatric social work, developed Heimler method of Human Social Functioning, a methodology based on the principle that frustration is the potential to human flourishing. Positive psychotherapy (PPT) (since 1968) is the name of the method of the psychotherapeutic modality developed by Nossrat Peseschkian and co-workers. Prof. Peseschkian, MD, (1933–2010) was a specialist in neurology, psychiatry, psychotherapy and psychotherapeutic medicine. Positive psychotherapy is a method in the field of humanistic and psychodynamic psychotherapy and is based on a positive image of man, which correlates with a salutogenetic, resource-oriented, humanistic and conflict-centred approach.

Postmodern psychotherapies such as Narrative Therapy and Coherence Therapy did not impose definitions of mental health and illness, but rather saw the goal of therapy as something constructed by the client and therapist in a social context. Systems Therapy also developed, which focuses on family and group dynamics—and Transpersonal psychology, which focuses on the spiritual facet of human experience. Other important orientations developed in the last three decades include Feminist therapy, Brief therapy, Somatic Psychology,

Expressive therapy, applied Positive psychology and the Human Givens approach which is building on the best of what has gone before. A survey of over 2,500 US therapists in 2006 revealed the most utilized models of therapy and the ten most influential therapists of the previous quarter-century.

General Description

Psychotherapy can be seen as an interpersonal invitation offered by (often trained and regulated) psychotherapists to aid clients in reaching their full potential or to cope better with problems of life. Psychotherapists usually receive remuneration in some form in return for their time and skills. This is one way in which the relationship can be distinguished from an altruistic offer of assistance.

Psychotherapists and counsellors are often required to create a therapeutic environment referred to as the frame, which is characterized by a free yet secure climate that enables the client to open up. The degree to which client feels related to the therapist may well depend on the methods and approaches used by the therapist or counsellor.

Psychotherapy often includes techniques to increase awareness and the capacity for self-observation, change behaviour and cognition, and develop insight and empathy. Desired results may be to enable other choices of thought, feeling or action, and to increase the sense of well-being and to better manage subjective discomfort or distress. Perception of reality is hopefully improved. Grieving might be enhanced producing less long term depression. Psychotherapy can improve medication response where such medication is also needed. Psychotherapy can be provided on a one-to-one basis, in group therapy, conjointly with couples and with entire families. It can occur face to face (individual), over the telephone, or, much less commonly, the Internet. Its time frame may be a matter of weeks or many years. Therapy may address specific forms of diagnosable mental illness, or everyday problems in managing or maintaining interpersonal relationships or meeting personal goals. Treatment in families with children can favourably influence a childs development, lasting for life and into future generations. Better parenting may be an indirect result of therapy or purposefully learned as parenting techniques. Divorces can be prevented, or made far less traumatic. Treatment of everyday problems is more often referred to as counselling (a distinction originally adopted by Carl Rogers) but the term is sometimes used interchangeably with "psychotherapy". Therapeutic skills can be used in mental health consultation to business and public agencies to improve efficiency and assist with coworkers or clients.

Psychotherapists use a range of techniques to influence or persuade the client to adapt or change in the direction the client has chosen. These can be based on clear thinking about their options; experiential relationship building; dialogue, communication and adoption of behaviour change strategies. Each is designed to improve the mental health of a client or patient, or to improve group relationships (as in a family). Most forms of psychotherapy use only spoken conversation, though some also use other forms of communication such as the written word, artwork, drama, narrative story, or therapeutic touch. Psychotherapy occurs within a structured encounter between a trained therapist and client(s). Because sensitive topics are often discussed during psychotherapy, therapists are expected, and usually legally bound, to respect client or patient confidentiality.

Psychotherapists are often trained, certified, and licensed, with a range of different certifications and licensing requirements depending on the jurisdiction. Psychotherapy may be undertaken by clinical psychologists, counselling psychologists, rehabilitation counsellors, social workers, marriage-family therapists, adult and child psychiatrists and expressive therapists, trained nurses, psychiatrists, psychoanalysts, mental health counsellors, school counsellors, or professionals of other mental health disciplines.

Psychiatrists have medical qualifications and may also administer prescription medication. The primary training of a psychiatrist uses the ' Bio-Psycho-Social' model, medical training in practical psychology and applied psychotherapy. Psychiatric training begins in medical school, first in the doctor patient relationship with ill people, and later in psychiatric residency for specialists. The focus is usually eclectic but includes biological, cultural, and social aspects. They are advanced in understanding patients from the inception of medical training. Today there are two doctoral degrees in psychology, the PsyD and PhD. Training for these degrees overlap, but the PsyD is more clinical and the Phd stresses research. Both degrees have clinical education components. Clinical Social Workers have specialized training in clinical casework. They hold a masters in social work which entails two years of clinical internships, and a period of at least three years in the US of post-masters experience in psychotherapy. Marriage-family therapists have specific training and experience working with relationships and family issues. A licensed professional counsellor (LPC) generally has special training in career, mental health, school, or rehabilitation counselling to include evaluation and assessments as well as psychotherapy. Many of the wide variety of training programmes are multiprofessional, that is, psychiatrists, psychologists, mental health nurses, and social workers may be found in the same training group. All these degrees commonly work together as a team, especially in institutional settings. All those doing specialized psychotherapeutic work, in most countries, require a programme of continuing education after the basic degree, or involve multiple certifications attached to one specific degree, and 'board certification' in psychiatry. Speciality exams are used to confirm competence or board exams with psychiatrists .

Medical and non-medical Models

A distinction can also be made between those psychotherapies that employ a medical model and those that employ a humanistic model. In the medical model the client is seen as unwell and the therapist employs their skill to help the client back to health. The extensive use of the DSM-IV, the diagnostic and statistical manual of mental disorders in the United States, is an example of a medically exclusive model.

The humanistic model of non medical in contrast strives to depathologise the human condition. The therapist attempts to create a relational environment conducive to experiential learning and help build the client's confidence in their own natural process resulting in a deeper understanding of themselves. An example would be gestalt therapy.

Some psychodynamic practitioners distinguish between more uncovering and more supportive psychotherapy. Uncovering psychotherapy emphasizes facilitating the client's insight into the roots of their difficulties. The best-known example of an uncovering psychotherapy is classical psychoanalysis. Supportive psychotherapy by contrast stresses strengthening the client's defences and often providing encouragement and advice. Depending on the client's personality, a more supportive or more uncovering approach may be optimal. Most psychotherapists use a combination of uncovering and supportive approaches.

Specific Schools and Approaches

In practices of experienced psychotherapists, the therapy is typically not of one pure type, but draws aspects from a number of perspectives and schools.

Psychoanalysis

Psychoanalysis was developed in the late 19th century by Sigmund Freud. His therapy explores the dynamic workings of a mind understood to consist of three parts: the hedonistic id (German: das Es, "the it"), the rational ego (das Ich, "the I"), and the moral superego (das Überich, "the above-I"). Because the majority of these dynamics are said to occur outside people's awareness, Freudian psychoanalysis seeks to probe the unconscious by way of various techniques, including dream interpretation and free association. Freud maintained that the condition of the unconscious mind is profoundly influenced by childhood experiences. So, in addition to dealing with the defense mechanisms used by an overburdened ego, his therapy addresses fixations and other issues by probing deeply into clients' youth.

Other psychodynamic theories and techniques have been developed and used by psychotherapists, psychologists, psychiatrists, personal growth facilitators, occupational therapists and social workers. For example, object relations theory is a psychodynamic theory that has been widely applied to general psychotherapy and to psychiatry by such authors as N. Gregory Hamilton and Glen O. Gabbard. Techniques for group therapy have also been developed. While behaviour is often a target of the work, many approaches value working with feelings and thoughts. This is especially true of the psychodynamic schools of psychotherapy, which today include Jungian therapy and Psychodrama as well as the psychoanalytic schools and object relations theory.

Theories

The predominant psychoanalytic theories can be organised into several theoretical "schools." Although these theoretical "schools" differ, most of them continue to emphasise the strong influence of unconscious elements affecting people's mental lives. There has also been considerable work done on consolidating elements of conflicting theory (cf. the work of Theodore Dorpat, B. Killingmo, and S. Akhtar). As in all fields of healthcare, there are some persistent conflicts regarding specific causes of some syndromes, and disputes regarding the best treatment techniques. In the 21st century, psychoanalytic ideas are embedded in Western culture, especially in fields such as childcare, education, literary criticism, cultural studies, and mental health, particularly psychotherapy. Though there is a mainstream of evolved analytic ideas, there are groups who follow the precepts of one or more of the later theoreticians. Psychoanalytic ideas also play roles in some types of literary analysis such as Archetypal literary criticism.

Topographic Theory

Topographic theory was named and first described by Freud in The Interpretation of Dreams (1900). The theory hypothesises that the mental apparatus can be divided into the systems Conscious, Pre-conscious and Unconscious. These systems are not anatomical structures of the brain but, rather, mental processes. Although Freud retained this theory throughout his life he largely replaced it with the Structural theory. The Topographic theory remains as one of the metapsychological points of view for describing how the mind functions in classical psychoanalytic theory.

Structural Theory

Structural theory divides the psyche into the id, the ego, and the super-ego. The id is present at birth as the repository of basic instincts, which Freud called "Triebe" ("drives"): unorganised and unconscious, it operates merely on the 'pleasure principle', without realism or foresight. The ego develops slowly and gradually, being concerned with mediating between the urgings of the id and the realities of the external world; it thus operates on the 'reality principle'. The super-ego is held to be the part of the ego in which self-observation, self-criticism and other reflective and judgemental faculties develop. The ego and the super-ego are both partly conscious and partly unconscious.

Ego Psychology

Ego psychology was initially suggested by Freud in Inhibitions, Symptoms and Anxiety (1926). The theory was refined by Hartmann, Loewenstein, and Kris in a series of papers and books from 1939 through the late 1960s. Leo Bellak was a later contributor. This series of constructs, paralleling some of the later developments of cognitive theory, includes the notions of autonomous ego functions: mental functions not dependent, at least in origin, on intrapsychic conflict. Such functions include: sensory perception, motor control, symbolic thought, logical thought, speech, abstraction, integration (synthesis), orientation, concentration, judgement about danger, reality testing, adaptive ability, executive decision-making, hygiene, and self-preservation. Freud noted that inhibition is one method that the mind may utilize to interfere with any of these functions in order to avoid painful emotions. Hartmann (1950s) pointed out that there may be delays or deficits in such functions.

Frosch (1964) described differences in those people who demonstrated damage to their relationship to reality, but who seemed able to test it. Deficits in the capacity to organize thought are sometimes referred to as blocking or loose associations (Bleuler), and are characteristic of the schizophrenias. Deficits in abstraction ability and self-preservation also suggest psychosis in adults. Deficits in orientation and sensorium are often indicative of a medical illness affecting the brain (and therefore, autonomous ego functions). Deficits in certain ego functions are routinely found in severely sexually or physically abused children, where powerful effects generated throughout childhood seem to have eroded some functional development.

According to ego psychology, ego strengths, later described by Kernberg (1975), include the capacities to control oral, sexual, and destructive impulses; to tolerate painful effects without falling apart; and to prevent the eruption into consciousness of bizarre symbolic fantasy. Synthetic functions, in contrast to autonomous functions, arise from the development of the ego and serve the purpose of managing conflictual processes. Defences are synthetic functions that protect the conscious mind from awareness of forbidden impulses and thoughts. One purpose of ego psychology has been to emphasize that some mental functions can be considered to be basic, rather than derivatives of wishes, affects, or defences. However, autonomous ego functions can be secondarily affected because of unconscious conflict. For example, a patient may have an hysterical amnesia (memory being an autonomous function) because of intrapsychic conflict (wishing not to remember because it is too painful).

Taken together, the above theories present a group of metapsychological assumptions. Therefore, the inclusive group of the different classical theories provides a cross-sectional view of human mentation. There are six "points of view", five described by Freud and a sixth added by Hartmann. Unconscious processes can therefore be evaluated from each of these six points of view. The "points of view" are: 1. Topographic 2. Dynamic (the theory of conflict) 3. Economic (the theory of energy flow) 4. Structural 5. Genetic (propositions concerning origin and development of psychological functions) and 6. Adaptational (psychological phenomena as it relates to the external world).

Modern Conflict Theory

A variation of ego psychology, termed "modern conflict theory", is more broadly an update and revision of structural theory (Freud, 1923, 1926); it does away with some of structural theory's more arcane features, such as where repressed thoughts are stored. Modern conflict theory centres around how emotional symptoms and character traits are complex solutions to mental conflict. It dispenses with the concepts of a fixed id, ego and superego, and instead posits conscious and unconscious conflict among wishes (dependent, controlling, sexual, and aggressive), guilt and shame, emotions (especially anxiety and depressive affect), and defensive operations that shut off from consciousness some aspect of the others. Moreover, healthy functioning (adaptive) is also determined, to a great extent, by resolutions of conflict.

A major objective of modern conflict-theory psychoanalysis is to change the balance of conflict in a patient by making aspects of the less adaptive solutions (also called "compromise formations") conscious so that they can be rethought, and more adaptive solutions found. Current theoreticians following Brenner's many suggestions include Sandor Abend, MD (Abend, Porder, & Willick, (1983), Borderline Patients: Clinical Perspectives), Jacob Arlow (Arlow and Brenner (1964), Psychoanalytic Concepts and the Structural Theory), and Jerome Blackman (2003), 101 Defences: How the Mind Shields Itself).

Object Relations Theory

Object relations theory attempts to explain the ups and downs of human relationships through a study of how internal representations of the self and others are organised. The clinical symptoms that suggest object relations problems (typically developmental delays throughout life) include disturbances in an individual's capacity to feel warmth, empathy, trust, sense of security, identity stability, consistent emotional closeness, and stability in relationships with significant others. (It is not suggested that one should trust everyone, for example.) Concepts regarding internal representations (also sometimes termed, "introjects," "self and object representations," or "internalizations of self and other") although often attributed to Melanie Klein, were actually first mentioned by Sigmund Freud in his early concepts of drive theory (Three Essays on the Theory of Sexuality, 1905). Freud's 1917 paper "Mourning and Melancholia", for example, hypothesized that unresolved grief was caused by the survivor's internalized image of the deceased becoming fused with that of the survivor, and then the survivor shifting unacceptable anger towards the deceased onto the now complex self-image.

Vamik Volkan, in "Linking Objects and Linking Phenomena", expanded on Freud's thoughts on this, describing the syndromes of "Established pathological mourning" vs. "reactive depression" based on similar dynamics. Melanie Klein's hypotheses regarding internalizations during the first year of life, leading to paranoid and depressive positions, were later challenged by René Spitz (e.g., The First Year of Life, 1965), who divided the first year of life into a coenesthetic phase of the first six months, and then a diacritic phase for the second six months. Margaret Mahler (Mahler, Fine, and Bergman, "The Psychological Birth of the Human Infant", 1975) and her group, first in New York, then in Philadelphia, described distinct phases and subphases of child development leading to "separation-individuation" during the first three years of life, stressing the importance of constancy of parental figures, in the face of the child's destructive aggression, to the child's internalizations, stability of affect management, and ability to develop healthy autonomy.

Later developers of the theory of self and object constancy as it affects adult psychiatric problems such as psychosis and borderline states have been John Frosch, Otto Kernberg, Salman Akhtar and Sheldon Bach. Peter Blos described (in a book called On Adolescence, 1960) how similar separation-individuation struggles occur during adolescence, of course with a different outcome from the first three years of life: the teen usually, eventually, leaves the parents' house (this varies with the culture). During adolescence, Erik Erikson (1950–1960s) described the "identity crisis," that involves identity-diffusion anxiety. In order for an adult to be able to experience "Warm-ETHICS" (warmth, empathy, trust, holding environment (Winnicott), identity, closeness, and stability) in relationships, the teenager must resolve the problems with identity and redevelop self and object constancy.

Self Psychology

Self psychology emphasizes the development of a stable and integrated sense of self through empathic contacts with other humans, primary significant others conceived of as "selfobjects." Selfobjects meet the developing self's needs for mirroring, idealization, and twinship, and thereby strengthen the developing self. The process of treatment proceeds through "transmuting internalizations" in which the patient gradually internalizes the selfobject functions provided by the therapist. Self psychology was proposed originally by Heinz Kohut, and has been further developed by Arnold Goldberg, Frank Lachmann, Paul and Anna Ornstein, Marian Tolpin, and others.

Jacques Lacan and Lacanian Psychoanalysis

Lacanian psychoanalysis, which integrates psychoanalysis with structural linguistics and Hegelian philosophy, is especially popular in France and parts of Latin America. Lacanian psychoanalysis is a departure from the traditional British and American psychoanalysis, which is predominantly Ego psychology. Jacques Lacan frequently used the phrase "retourner à Freud" ("return to Freud") in his seminars and writings, as he claimed that his theories were an extension of Freud's own, contrary to those of Anna Freud, the Ego Psychology, object relations and "self" theories and also claims the necessity of reading Freud's complete works, not only a part of them. Lacan's concepts concern the "mirror stage", the "Real", the "Imaginary" and the "Symbolic", and the claim that "the unconscious is structured as a language".

Though a major influence on psychoanalysis in France and parts of Latin America, Lacan and his ideas have taken longer to be translated into English and he has thus had a lesser impact on psychoanalysis and psychotherapy in the English-speaking world. In the UK and the US, his ideas are most widely used to analyze texts in literary theory. Due to his increasingly critical stance towards the deviation from Freud's thought, often singling out particular texts and readings from his colleagues, Lacan was excluded from acting as a training analyst in the International Psychoanalytic Association, thus leading him to create his own School in order to maintain an institutional structure for the many candidates who desired to continue their analysis with him

Interpersonal Psychoanalysis

Interpersonal psychoanalysis accents the nuances of interpersonal interactions, particularly how individuals protect themselves from anxiety by establishing collusive interactions with others, and the relevance of actual experiences with other persons developmentally (e.g. family and peers) as well as in the present. This is contrasted with the primacy of intrapsychic forces, as in classical psychoanalysis. Interpersonal theory was first introduced by Harry Stack Sullivan, MD, and developed further by Frieda Fromm-Reichmann, Clara Thompson, Erich Fromm, and others who contributed to the founding of the William Alanson White Institute and Interpersonal Psychoanalysis in general.

Culturalist Psychoanalysts

Some psychoanalysts have been labelled culturalist, because of the prominence they attributed culture in the genesis of behaviour. Among others, Erich Fromm, Karen Horney, Harry Stack Sullivan, have been called culturalist psychoanalysts. They were famously in conflict with orthodox psychoanalysts.

Adaptive Paradigm of Psychoanalysis and Psychotherapy

The "adaptive paradigm of psychotherapy" develops out of the work of Robert Langs. The adaptive paradigm interprets psychic conflict primarily in terms of conscious and unconscious adaptation to reality. Langs' recent work in some measure returns to the earlier Freud, in that Langs prefers a modified version of the topographic model of the mind (conscious, preconscious, and unconscious) over the structural model (id, ego, and super-ego), including the former's emphasis on trauma (though Langs looks to death-related traumas rather than sexual traumas). At the same time, Langs' model of the mind differs from Freud's in that it understands the mind in terms of evolutionary biological principles.

6

Relational Psychoanalysis

Relational psychoanalysis combines interpersonal psychoanalysis with object-relations theory and with inter-subjective theory as critical for mental health, was introduced by Stephen Mitchell. Relational psychoanalysis stresses how the individual's personality is shaped by both real and imagined relationships with others, and how these relationship patterns are re-enacted in the interactions between analyst and patient. In New York, key proponents of relational psychoanalysis include Lew Aron, Jessica Benjamin, and Adrienne Harris. Fonagy and Target, in London, have propounded their view of the necessity of helping certain detached, isolated patients, develop the capacity for "mentalization" associated with thinking about relationships and themselves. Arietta Slade, Susan Coates, and Daniel Schechter in New York have additionally contributed to the application of relational psychoanalysis to treatment of the adult patient-as-parent, the clinical study of mentalization in parent-infant relationships, and the intergenerational transmission of attachment and trauma.

Interpersonal-relational Psychoanalysis

The term interpersonal-relational psychoanalysis is often used as a professional identification. Psychoanalysts under this broader umbrella debate about what precisely are the differences between the two schools, without any current clear consensus.

Intersubjective Psychoanalysis

The term "intersubjectivity" was introduced in psychoanalysis by George E. Atwood and Robert Stolorow (1984). Intersubjective approaches emphasize how both personality development and the therapeutic process are influenced by the interrelationship between the patient's subjective perspective and that of others. The authors of the interpersonal-relational and intersubjective approaches: Otto Rank, Heinz Kohut, Stephen A. Mitchell, Jessica Benjamin, Bernard Brandchaft, J. Fosshage, Donna M.Orange, Arnold "Arnie" Mindell, Thomas Ogden, Owen Renik, Irwin Z. Hoffman, Harold Searles, Colwyn Trewarthen, Edgar A. Levenson, Jay R. Greenberg, Edward R. Ritvo, Beatrice Beebe, Frank M. Lachmann, Herbert Rosenfeld and Daniel Stern.

Modern Psychoanalysis

"Modern psychoanalysis" is a term coined by Hyman Spotnitz and his colleagues to describe a body of theoretical and clinical approaches that aim to extend Freud's theories so as to make them applicable to the full spectrum of emotional disorders and broaden the potential for treatment to pathologies thought to be untreatable by classical methods. Interventions based on this approach are primarily intended to provide an emotional-maturational communication to the patient, rather than to promote intellectual insight. These interventions, beyond insight directed aims, are used to resolve resistances that are presented in the clinical setting. This school of psychoanalysis has fostered training opportunities for students in the United States and from countries worldwide. Its journal Modern Psychoanalysis has been published since 1976.

Psychopathology (Mental Disturbances)

Adult Patients

The various psychoses involve deficits in the autonomous ego functions of integration (organization) of thought, in abstraction ability, in relationship to reality and in reality testing. In depressions with psychotic features, the self-preservation function may also be damaged (sometimes by overwhelming depressive affect). Because of the integrative deficits (often causing what general psychiatrists call "loose associations," "blocking," "flight of ideas," "verbigeration," and "thought withdrawal"), the development of self and object representations is also impaired. Clinically, therefore, psychotic individuals manifest limitations in warmth, empathy, trust, identity, closeness and/or stability in relationships (due to problems with self-object fusion anxiety) as well.

In patients whose autonomous ego functions are more intact, but who still show problems with object relations, the diagnosis often falls into the category known as "borderline." Borderline patients also show deficits, often in controlling impulses, affects, or fantasies – but their ability to test reality remains more or less intact. Adults who do not experience guilt and shame, and who indulge in criminal behaviour, are usually diagnosed as psychopaths, or, using DSM-IV-TR, antisocial personality disorder.

Panic, phobias, conversions, obsessions, compulsions and depressions (analysts call these "neurotic symptoms") are not usually caused by deficits in functions. Instead, they are caused by intrapsychic conflicts. The conflicts are generally among sexual and hostile-aggressive wishes, guilt and shame, and reality factors. The conflicts may be conscious or unconscious, but create anxiety, depressive affect, and anger. Finally, the various elements are managed by defensive operations – essentially shut-off brain mechanisms that make people unaware of that element of conflict. "Repression" is the term given to the mechanism that shuts thoughts out of consciousness. "Isolation of affect" is the term used for the mechanism that shuts sensations out of consciousness. Neurotic symptoms may occur with or without deficits in ego functions, object relations, and ego strengths. Therefore, it is not uncommon to encounter obsessive-compulsive schizophrenics, panic patients who also suffer with borderline personality disorder, etc.

This section above is partial to ego psychoanalytic theory "autonomous ego functions." As the "autonomous ego functions" theory is only a theory, it may yet be proven incorrect.

Childhood Origins

Freudian theories believe that adult problems can be traced to unresolved conflicts from certain phases of childhood and adolescence, caused by fantasy, stemming from their own drives. Freud, based on the data gathered from his patients early in his career, suspected that neurotic disturbances occurred when children were sexually abused in childhood (the so-called seduction theory). Later, Freud came to believe that, although child abuse occurs, neurotic symptoms were not associated with this. He believed that neurotic people often had unconscious conflicts that involved incestuous fantasies deriving from different stages of development. He found the stage from about three to six years of age (preschool years, today called the "first genital stage") to be filled with fantasies of having romantic relationships with both parents. Arguments were quickly generated in early 20th-century Vienna about whether adult seduction of children, i.e. child sexual abuse, was the basis of neurotic illness. There still is no complete agreement, although nowadays professionals recognize the negative effects of child sexual abuse on mental health.

Many psychoanalysts who work with children have studied the actual effects of child abuse, which include ego and object relations deficits and severe neurotic conflicts. Much research has been done on these types of trauma in childhood, and the adult sequelae of those. In studying the childhood factors that start neurotic symptom development, Freud found a constellation of factors that, for literary reasons, he termed the Oedipus complex (based on the play by Sophocles, Oedipus Rex, where the protagonist unwittingly kills his father Laius and marries his mother Jocasta). The validity of the Oedipus complex is now widely disputed and rejected. The shorthand term, "oedipal" — later explicated by Joseph Sandler in "On the Concept Superego" (1960) and modified by Charles Brenner in "The Mind in Conflict" (1982) — refers to the powerful attachments that children make to their parents in the preschool years. These attachments involve fantasies of sexual relationships with either (or both) parent, and, therefore, competitive fantasies towards either (or both) parents. Humberto Nagera (1975) has been particularly helpful in clarifying many of the complexities of the child through these years.

"Positive" and "negative" oedipal conflicts have been attached to the heterosexual and homosexual aspects, respectively. Both seem to occur in development of most children. Eventually, the developing child's concessions to reality (that they will neither marry one parent nor eliminate the other) lead to identifications with parental values. These identifications generally create a new set of mental operations regarding values and guilt, subsumed under the term "superego." Besides superego development, children "resolve" their preschool oedipal conflicts through channeling wishes into something their parents approve of ("sublimation") and the development, during the school-age years ("latency") of age-appropriate obsessive-compulsive defensive maneuvers (rules, repetitive games).

Treatment

Using the various analytic and psychological techniques to assess mental problems, some believe that there are particular constellations of problems that are especially suited for analytic treatment whereas other problems might respond better to medicines and other interpersonal interventions. To be treated with psychoanalysis, whatever the presenting problem, the person requesting help must demonstrate a desire to start an analysis. The person wishing to start an analysis must have some capacity for speech and communication. As well, they need to be able to have or develop trust and insight within the psychoanalytic session. Potential patients must undergo a preliminary stage of treatment to assess their amenability to psychoanalysis at that time, and also to enable the analyst to form a working psychological model which the analyst will use to direct the treatment. Psychoanalysts mainly work with neurosis and hysteria in particular; however, adapted forms of psychoanalysis are used in working with schizophrenia and other forms of psychosis or mental disorder. Finally, if a prospective patient is severely suicidal a longer preliminary stage may be employed, sometimes with sessions which have a twenty minute break in the middle. There are numerous modifications in technique under the heading of psychoanalysis due to the individualistic nature of personality in both analyst and patient.

The most common problems treatable with psychoanalysis include: phobias, conversions, compulsions, obsessions, anxiety, attacks, depressions, sexual dysfunctions, a wide variety of relationship problems (such as dating and marital strife), and a wide variety of character problems (for example, painful shyness, meanness, obnoxiousness, workaholism, hyperseductiveness, hyperemotionality, hyperfastidiousness). The fact that many of such patients also demonstrate deficits above makes diagnosis and treatment selection difficult.

Analytical organizations such as the International Psychoanalytic Association, The American Psychoanalytic Association, and the European Federation for Psychoanalytic Psychotherapy, have established procedures and models for the indication and practice of psychoanalytical therapy for trainees in analysis. The match between the analyst and the patient can be viewed as another contributing factor for the indication and contraindication for psychoanalytic treatment. The analyst decides whether the patient is suitable for psychoanalysis. This decision made by the analyst, besides made on the usual indications and pathology, is also based to a certain degree by the "fit" between analyst and patient. A person's suitability for analysis at any particular time is based on their desire to know something about where their illness has come from. Someone who is not suitable for analysis expresses no desire to know more about the root causes of their illness. An evaluation may include one or more other analysts' independent opinions and will include discussion of the patient's financial situation and insurances.

Techniques

The basic method of psychoanalysis is interpretation of the patient's unconscious conflicts that are interfering with current-day functioning – conflicts that are causing painful symptoms such as phobias, anxiety, depression, and compulsions. Strachey (1936) stressed that figuring out ways the patient distorted perceptions about the analyst led to understanding what may have been forgotten. In particular, unconscious hostile feelings towards the analyst could be found in symbolic, negative reactions to what Robert Langs later called the "frame" of the therapy – the setup that included times of the sessions, payment of fees, and necessity of talking. In patients who made mistakes, forgot, or showed other peculiarities regarding time, fees, and talking, the analyst can usually find various unconscious "resistances" to the flow of thoughts (sometimes called free association).

When the patient reclines on a couch with the analyst out of view, the patient tends to remember more, experiences more resistance and transference, and is able to reorganize thoughts after the development of insight – through the interpretive work of the analyst. Although fantasy life can be understood through the examination of dreams, masturbation fantasies (cf. Marcus, I. and Francis, J. (1975), Masturbation from Infancy to Senescence) are also important. The analyst is interested in how the patient reacts to and avoids such fantasies (cf. Paul Gray (1994), The Ego and the Analysis of Defense). Various memories of early life are generally distorted – Freud called them "screen memories" – and in any case, very early experiences (before age two) – cannot be remembered.

Variations in Technique

There is what is known among psychoanalysts as "classical technique," although Freud throughout his writings deviated from this considerably, depending on the problems of any given patient. Classical technique was summarized by Allan Compton, MD, as comprising instructions (telling the patient to try to say what's on their mind, including interferences); exploration (asking questions); and clarification (rephrasing and summarizing what the patient has been describing). As well, the analyst can also use confrontation to bringing an aspect of functioning, usually a defense, to the patient's attention. The analyst then uses a variety of interpretation methods, such as dynamic interpretation (explaining how being too nice guards against guilt, e.g. – defense vs. affect); genetic interpretation (explaining how a past event is influencing the present); resistance interpretation (showing the patient how they are avoiding their problems); transference interpretation (showing the patient ways old conflicts arise in current relationships, including that with the analyst); or dream interpretation (obtaining the patient's thoughts about their dreams and connecting this with their current problems). Analysts can also use reconstruction to estimate what may have happened in the past that created some current issue.

These techniques are primarily based on conflict theory. As object relations theory evolved, supplemented by the work of Bowlby, Ainsworth, and Beebe, techniques with patients who had more severe problems with basic trust (Erikson, 1950) and a history of maternal deprivation led to new techniques with adults. These have sometimes been called interpersonal, intersubjective (cf. Stolorow), relational, or corrective object relations techniques. These techniques include expressing an empathic attunement to the patient or warmth; exposing a bit of the analyst's personal life or attitudes to the patient; allowing the patient autonomy in the form of disagreement with the analyst (cf. I.H. Paul, Letters to Simon.); and explaining the motivations of others which the patient misperceives. Ego psychological concepts of deficit in functioning led to refinements in supportive therapy. These techniques are particularly applicable to psychotic and near-psychotic (cf., Eric Marcus, "Psychosis and Near-psychosis") patients. These supportive therapy techniques include discussions of reality; encouragement to stay alive (including hospitalization); psychotropic medicines to relieve overwhelming depressive affect or overwhelming fantasies (hallucinations and delusions); and advice about the meanings of things (to counter abstraction failures).

The notion of the "silent analyst" has been criticized. Actually, the analyst listens using Arlow's approach as set out in "The Genesis of Interpretation"), using active intervention to interpret resistances, defences creating pathology, and fantasies. Silence is not a technique of psychoanalysis. "Analytic Neutrality" is a concept that does not mean the analyst is silent. It refers to the analyst's position of not taking sides in the internal struggles of the patient. For example, if a patient feels guilty, the analyst might explore what the patient has been doing or thinking that causes the guilt, but not reassure the patient not to feel guilty. The analyst might also explore the identifications with parents and others that led to the guilt.

Interpersonal-Relational psychoanalysts emphasize the notion that it is impossible to be neutral. Sullivan introduced the term "participant-observer" to indicate the analyst inevitably interacts with the analysand, and suggested the detailed enquiry as an alternative to interpretation. The detailed enquiry involves noting where the analysand is leaving out important elements of an account and noting when the story is obfuscated, and asking careful questions to open up the dialogue.

Group Therapy and Play Therapy

Although single-client sessions remain the norm, psychoanalytic theory has been used to develop other types of psychological treatment. Psychoanalytic group therapy was pioneered by Trigant Burrow, Joseph Pratt, Paul F. Schilder, Samuel R. Slavson, Harry Stack Sullivan, and Wolfe. Child-centred counselling for parents was instituted early in analytic history by Freud, and was later further developed by Irwin Marcus, Edith Schulhofer, and Gilbert Kliman. Psychoanalytically based couples therapy has been promulgated and explicated by Fred Sander, MD. Techniques and tools developed in the first decade of the 21st century have made psychoanalysis available to patients who were not treatable by earlier techniques. This meant that the analytic situation was modified so that it would be more suitable and more likely to be helpful for these patients. M.N. Eagle (2007) believes that psychoanalysis cannot be a self-contained discipline but instead must be open to influence from and integration with findings and theory from other disciplines.

Psychoanalytic constructs have been adapted for use with children with treatments such as play therapy, art therapy, and storytelling. Throughout her career, from the 1920s through the 1970s, Anna Freud adapted psychoanalysis for children through play. This is still used today for children, especially those who are preadolescent. Using toys and games, children are able to demonstrate, symbolically, their fears, fantasies, and defences; although not identical, this technique, in children, is analogous to the aim of free association in adults. Psychoanalytic play therapy allows the child and analyst to understand children's conflicts, particularly defences such as disobedience and withdrawal, that have been guarding against various unpleasant feelings and hostile wishes. In art therapy, the counsellor may have a child draw a portrait and then tell a story about the portrait. The counsellor watches for recurring themes—regardless of whether it is with art or toys.

Cultural Variations

Psychoanalysis can be adapted to different cultures, as long as the therapist or counsellor understands the client's culture. For example,

Tori and Blimes found that defense mechanisms were valid in a normative sample of 2,624 Thais. The use of certain defense mechanisms was related to cultural values. For example Thais value calmness and collectiveness (because of Buddhist beliefs), so they were low on regressive emotionality. Psychoanalysis also applies because Freud used techniques that allowed him to get the subjective perceptions of his patients. He takes an objective approach by not facing his clients during his talk therapy sessions. He met with his patients wherever they were, such as when he used free association — where clients would say whatever came to mind without self-censorship. His treatments had little to no structure for most cultures, especially Asian cultures. Therefore, it is more likely that Freudian constructs will be used in structured therapy (Thompson, et al., 2004). In addition, Corey postulates that it will be necessary for a therapist to help clients develop a cultural identity as well as an ego identity.

Cost and Length of Treatment

The cost to the patient of psychoanalytic treatment ranges widely from place to place and between practitioners. Low-fee analysis is often available in a psychoanalytic training clinic and graduate schools. Otherwise, the fee set by each analyst varies with the analyst's training and experience. Since, in most locations in the United States, unlike in Ontario and Germany, classical analysis (which usually requires sessions three to five times per week) is not covered by health insurance, many analysts may negotiate their fees with patients whom they feel they can help, but who have financial difficulties. The modifications of analysis, which include dynamic therapy, brief therapies, and certain types of group therapy (cf. Slavson, S. R., A Textbook in Analytic Group Therapy), are carried out on a less frequent basis – usually once, twice, or three times a week – and usually the patient sits facing the therapist.

Many studies have also been done on briefer "dynamic" treatments; these are more expedient to measure, and shed light on the therapeutic process to some extent. Brief Relational Therapy (BRT), Brief Psychodynamic Therapy (BPT), and Time-Limited Dynamic Therapy (TLDP) limit treatment to 20–30 sessions. On average, classical analysis may last 5.7 years, but for phobias and depressions uncomplicated by ego deficits or object relations deficits, analysis may run for a shorter period of time. Longer analyses are indicated for those with more serious disturbances in object relations, more symptoms, and more ingrained character pathology (such as obnoxiousness, severe passivity, or heinous procrastination).

Training and Research

Psychoanalytic training in the United States, in most locations, involves personal analytic treatment for the trainee, conducted confidentially, with no report to the Education Committee of the Analytic Training Institute; approximately 600 hours of class instruction, with a standard curriculum, over a four-year period. Classes are often a few hours per week, or for a full day or two every other weekend during the academic year; this varies with the institute; and supervision once per week, with a senior analyst, on each analytic treatment case the trainee has. The minimum number of cases varies between institutes, often two to four cases. Male and female cases are required. Supervision must go on for at least a few years on one or more cases. Supervision is done in the supervisor's office, where the trainee presents material from the analytic work that week, examines the unconscious conflicts with the supervisor, and learns, discusses, and is advised about technique.

Many psychoanalytic training centres in the United States have been accredited by special committees of the American Psychoanalytic Association or the International Psychoanalytical Association. Because of theoretical differences, other independent institutes arose, usually founded by psychologists, who until 1987 were not permitted access to psychoanalytic training institutes of the American Psychoanalytic Association. Currently there are between 75 and 100 independent institutes in the United States. As well, other institutes are affiliated to other organizations such as the American Academy of Psychoanalysis and Dynamic Psychiatry, and the National Association for the Advancement of Psychoanalysis. At most psychoanalytic institutes in the United States, qualifications for entry include a terminal degree in a mental health field, such as Ph.D., Psy.D., M.S.W., or M.D. A few institutes restrict applicants to those already holding an M.D. or Ph.D., and most institutes in Southern California confer a Ph.D. or Psy.D. in psychoanalysis upon graduation, which involves completion of the necessary requirements for the state boards that confer that doctoral degree.The first training institute in America to educate non-medical psychoanalysts was The National Psychological Association for Psychoanalysis., (1978) in New York City. It was founded by the analyst Theodor Reik.

Some psychoanalytic training has been set up as a post-doctoral fellowship in university settings, such as at Duke University, Yale University, New York University, Adelphi University, and Columbia University. Other psychoanalytic institutes may not be directly associated with universities, but the faculty at those institutes usually hold contemporaneous faculty positions with psychology Ph.D. programmes and/or with medical school psychiatry residency programmes.

The International Psychoanalytical Association (IPA) is the world's primary accrediting and regulatory body for psychoanalysis. Their mission is to assure the continued vigour and development of psychoanalysis for the benefit of psychoanalytic patients. It works in partnership with its 70 constituent organizations in 33 countries to support 11,500 members. In the US, there are 77 psychoanalytical organizations, institutes associations in the United States, which are spread across the states of America. The American Psychoanalytic Association (APSaA) has 38 affiliated societies, which have 10 or more active members who practice in a given geographical area. The aims of the APSaA and other psychoanalytical organizations are: provide ongoing educational opportunities for its members, stimulate the development and research of psychoanalysis, provide training and organize conferences. There are eight affiliated study groups in the USA (two of them are in Latin America). A study group is the first level of integration of a psychoanalytical body within the International Psychoanalytic Association (IPA), followed by a provisional society and finally a member society.

The Division of Psychoanalysis (39) of the American Psychological Association (APA) was established in the early 1980s by several psychologists. Until the establishment of the Division of Psychoanalysis, psychologists who had trained in independent institutes had no national organization. The Division of Psychoanalysis now has approximately 4,000 members and approximately 30 local chapters in the United States. The Division of Psychoanalysis holds two annual meetings or conferences and offers continuing education in theory, research and clinical technique, as do their affiliated local chapters. The European Psychoanalytical Federation (EPF) is the organization which consolidates all European psychoanalytic societies. This organization is affiliated with the IPA. In 2002 there were approximately 3,900 individual members in 22 countries, speaking 18 different languages. There are also 25 psychoanalytic societies.

The American Association of Psychoanalysis in Clinical Social Work (AAPCSW) was established by Crayton Rowe in 1980 as a division of the Federation of Clinical Societies of Social Work and became an independent entity in 1990. Until 2007 is was known as the National Membership Committee on Psychoanalysis. The organization was originally founded because although social workers represented the larger number of people who were training to be psychoanalysts, they were underrepresented as supervisors and teachers at the institutes they attended. AAPCSW now has over 1000 members and has over 20 chapters. It holds a bi-annual national conference and numerous annual local conferences.

Experiences of psychoanalysts and psychoanalytic psychotherapists and research into infant and child development have led to new insights. Theories have been further developed and the results of empirical research are now more integrated in the psychoanalytic theory.

Psychoanalysis in Britain

The London Psychoanalytical Society was founded by Ernest Jones on 30 October 1913. With the expansion of psychoanalysis in the United Kingdom the Society was renamed the British Psychoanalytical Society in 1919. Soon after, the Institute of Psychoanalysis was established to administer the Society's activities. These include: the training of psychoanalysts, the development of the theory and practice of psychoanalysis, the provision of treatment through The London Clinic of Psychoanalysis, the publication of books in The New Library of Psychoanalysis and Psychoanalytic Ideas. The Institute of Psychoanalysis also publishes The International Journal of Psychoanalysis, maintains a library, furthers research, and holds public lectures. The society has a Code of Ethics and an Ethical Committee. The society, the institute and the clinic are all located at Byron House.

The society is a component of the International Psychoanalytical Association, a body with members on all five continents that safeguards professional and ethical practice. The society is a member of the British Psychoanalytic Council (BPC); the BPC publishes a register of British psychoanalysts and psychoanalytical psychotherapists. All members of the British Psychoanalytical Society are required to undertake continuing professional development.

Gestalt Therapy

Gestalt Therapy is a major overhaul of psychoanalysis. In its early development, its founders, Frederick and Laura Perls, called it "concentration therapy". By the time Gestalt Therapy, Excitement and Growth in the Human Personality (Perls, Hefferline, and Goodman) was written (1951), the approach became known as "Gestalt Therapy".

Gestalt Therapy stands on top of essentially four load-bearing theoretical walls: phenomenological method, dialogical relationship, field-theoretical strategies, and experimental freedom. Some have considered it an existential phenomenology while others have described it as a phenomenological behaviourism. Gestalt Therapy is a humanistic, holistic, and experiential approach that does not rely on talking alone; instead it facilitates awareness in the various contexts of life by moving from talking about relatively remote situations to action and direct current experience.

Phenomenological Method

The goal of a phenomenological exploration is awareness. This exploration works systematically to reduce the effects of bias through repeated observations and enquiry.

The phenomenological method comprises three steps: (1) the rule of epoché, (2) the rule of description, and (3) the rule of horizontalization. Applying the rule of epoché one sets aside one's initial biases and prejudices in order to suspend expectations and assumptions. Applying the rule of description, one occupies oneself with describing instead of explaining. Applying the rule of horizontalization one treats each item of description as having equal value or significance.

The rule of epoché sets aside any initial theories with regard to what is presented in the meeting between therapist and client. The rule of description implies immediate and specific observations, abstaining from interpretations or explanations, especially those formed from the application of a clinical theory superimposed over the circumstances of experience. The rule of horizontalization avoids any hierarchical assignment of importance such that the data of experience become prioritized and categorized as they are received. A Gestalt therapist utilizing the phenomenological method might say something like, "I notice a slight tension at the corners of your mouth when I say that, and I see you shifting on the couch and folding your arms across your chest ... and now I see you rolling your eyes back". Of course, the therapist may make a clinically relevant evaluation, but when applying the phenomenological method, temporarily suspends the need to express it.

Dialogical Relationship

To create the conditions under which a dialogic moment might occur, the therapist attends to his or her own presence, creates the space for the client to enter in and become present as well (called inclusion), and commits him or herself to the dialogic process, surrendering to what takes place, as opposed to attempting to control it. With presence, the therapist judiciously "shows up" as a whole and authentic person, instead of assuming a role, false self or persona. The word 'judicious' used above refers to the therapist's taking into account the specific strengths, weaknesses and values . The only 'good' client is a 'live' client, so driving a client away by injudicious exposure of intolerable [to this client] experience of the therapist is obviously counter-productive. For example for an atheistic therapist to tell a devout client that religion is myth would not be useful, especially in the early stages of the relationship. To practice inclusion is to accept however the client chooses to be present, whether in a defensive and obnoxious stance or a superficially cooperative one. To practice inclusion is to support the presence of the client, including his or her resistance, not as a gimmick but in full realization that this is how the client is actually present and is the best this client can do at this time. Finally, the Gestalt therapist is committed to the process, trusts in that process, and does not attempt to save him or herself from it (Brownell, in press, 2009, 2008)).

Field-theoretical Strategies

"The field" can be considered in two ways. There are ontological dimensions and there are phenomenological dimensions to one's field. The phenomenological dimensions are all those physical and environmental contexts in which we live and move. They might be the office in which one works, the house in which one lives, the city and country of which one is a citizen, and so forth. The ontological field is the objective reality that supports our physical existence. The ontological dimensions are all mental and physical dynamics that contribute to a person's sense of self, one's subjective experience—not merely elements of the environmental context. These might be the memory of an uncle's inappropriate affection, one's colour blindness, one's sense of the social matrix in operation at the office in which one works, and so forth. The way that Gestalt therapists choose to work with field dynamics makes what they do strategic. Gestalt therapy focuses upon character structure; according to Gestalt theory, the character structure is dynamic rather than fixed in nature. To become aware of one's character structure, the focus is upon the phenomenological dimensions in the context of the ontological dimensions.

Experimental Freedom

Gestalt therapy is distinct because it moves towards action, away from mere talk therapy, and for this reason is considered an experiential approach. Through experiments, the therapist supports the client's direct experience of something new, instead of merely talking about the possibility of something new. Indeed, the entire therapeutic relationship may be considered experimental, because at one level it is a corrective, relational experience for many clients, and it is a "safe emergency" that is free to turn out however it will. An experiment can also be conceived as a teaching method that creates an experience in which a client might learn something as part of their growth. Examples might include: (1) Rather than talking about the client's critical parent, a Gestalt therapist might ask the client to imagine the parent is present, or that the therapist is the parent, and talk to that parent directly; (2) If a client is struggling with how to be assertive, a Gestalt therapist could either (a) have the client say some assertive things to the therapist or members of a therapy group, or (b) give a talk about how one should never be assertive; (3) A Gestalt therapist might notice something about the non-verbal behaviour or tone of voice of the client; then the therapist might have the client exaggerate the non-verbal behaviour and pay attention to that experience; (4) A Gestalt therapist might work with the breathing or posture of the client, and direct awareness to changes that might happen when the client talks about different content. With all these experiments the Gestalt therapist is working with process rather than content, the How rather than the What.

Noteworthy Issues

Self

In field theory, self is a phenomenological concept, existing in comparison with other. Without the other there is no self, and how one experiences the other is inseparable from how one experience herself. The continuity of selfhood (functioning personality) is something that is achieved in relationship, rather than something inherently "inside" the person. This can have its advantages and disadvantages. At one end of the spectrum, one may not have enough self-continuity to be able to make meaningful relationships, or to have a workable sense of who she is. In the middle, her personality is a loose set of ways of being that work for her, including commitments to relationships, work, culture and outlook, always open to change where she needs to adapt to new circumstances or just want to try something new. At the other end, her personality is a rigid defensive denial of the new and spontaneous. She acts in stereotyped ways, and either induces other people to act in particular and fixed ways towards her, or she redefines their actions to fit with fixed stereotypes.

In Gestalt therapy, the process is not about the self of the client being helped or healed by the fixed self of the therapist, rather it is an exploration of the co-creation of self and other in the here-and-now of the therapy. There is no assumption that the client will act in all other circumstances as he or she does in the therapy situation. However, the areas that cause problems will be either the lack of self-definition leading to chaotic or psychotic behaviour, or the rigid self-definition in some area of functioning that denies spontaneity and makes dealing with particular situations impossible. Both of these conditions show up very clearly in the therapy, and can be worked with in the relationship with the therapist.

The experience of the therapist is also very much part of the therapy. Since we co-create our self-other experiences, the way a therapist experiences being with a client is significant information about how the client experiences themselves. The proviso here is that a therapist is not operating from their own fixed responses. This is why Gestalt therapists are required to undertake significant therapy of their own during training.

From the perspective of this theory of self, neurosis can be seen as fixed predictability - a fixed Gestalt - and the process of therapy can be seen as facilitating the client to become unpredictable - more responsive to what is in the client's present environment, rather than responding in a stuck way to past introjects or other learning. If the therapist has expectations of how the client should end up, this defeats the aim of therapy.

Change

In what has now become a "classic" of Gestalt therapy literature, Arnold Beisser described Gestalt's paradoxical theory of change. The paradox is that the more one attempts to be who one is not, the more one remains the same. Conversely, when people identify with their current experience, the conditions of wholeness and growth support change. Put another way, change comes about as a result of "full acceptance of what is, rather than a striving to be different".

The Empty Chair Technique

Empty chair technique or chairwork is typically used in Gestalt therapy to explore patients' relationships with themselves, with aspects of their personality, their concepts, ideas, feelings etc., or other people in their lives. The technique involves the client addressing the empty chair as if another person, or aspects of their personality, or a certain feeling etc. was in it. They may also move between chairs and act out two or more sides of a discussion, typically involving the patient and persons significant to them. A form of role-playing, the technique focuses on exploration of self and is utilized by therapists to help patients self-adjust. Gestalt techniques were originally a form of psychotherapy, but are now often used in counselling, for instance, by encouraging clients to act out their feelings helping them prepare for a new job.

Historical Development

Fritz Perls was a German-Jewish psychoanalyst who fled Europe with his wife Laura Perls to South Africa in order to escape Nazi oppression in 1933. After World War II the couple emigrated to New York City, which had become a centre of intellectual, artistic and political experimentation by the late 1940s and early 1950s.

Early Influences

Perls grew up on the bohemian scene in Berlin, participated in Expressionism and Dadaism, and experienced the turning of the artistic avant-garde towards the revolutionary left. Deployment to the front line, the trauma of war, anti-Semitism, intimidation, escape, and the Holocaust are further key sources of biographical influence.

Perls served in the German Army during World War I, and was wounded in the conflict. After the war he was educated as a medical doctor. He became an assistant to Kurt Goldstein, who worked with brain injured soldiers. Perls went through a psychoanalysis with Wilhelm Reich and became a psychiatrist. Perls assisted Goldstein at Frankfurt University where he met his wife Lore (Laura) Posner, who had earned a doctorate in Gestalt psychology. They fled Nazi Germany in 1933 and settled in South Africa. Perls established a psychoanalytic training institute and joined the South African armed forces, serving as a military psychiatrist. During these years in South Africa Perls was influenced by Jan Smuts and his ideas about "holism".

In 1936 Fritz Perls attended a psychoanalyst's conference in Marienbad, Czechoslovakia, where he presented a paper on oral resistances, mainly based on Laura Perls' notes on breastfeeding their children. Perls' paper was turned down. Perls did present his paper in 1936, but it met with "deep disapproval". Perls wrote his first book, Ego, Hunger and Aggression (1942, 1947), in South Africa, based in part on the rejected paper. It was later re-published in the United

States. Laura Perls wrote two chapters of this book, but she was not given adequate recognition for her work.

The Seminal Book

Perls' seminal work was Gestalt Therapy: Excitement and Growth in the Human Personality, published in 1951, co-authored by Fritz Perls, Paul Goodman, and Ralph Hefferline (a university psychology professor, and sometime patient of Fritz Perls). Most of the Part II of the book was written by Paul Goodman from Perls' notes, and it contains the core of Gestalt theory. This part was supposed to go first. However, the publishers decided that Part I, written by Hefferline, fit into the nascent self-help ethos of the day, and they made it an introduction to the theory. Isadore From, a leading early theorist of Gestalt therapy, taught Goodman's Part II for an entire year to his students, going through it phrase by phrase.

First Instances of Gestalt Therapy

Fritz and Laura founded the first Gestalt Institute in 1952, running it out of their Manhattan apartment. Isadore From became a patient, first of Fritz, and then Laura. Fritz soon made From a trainer, and also gave him some patients. From lived in New York until his death, at age 75, in 1993. He was known worldwide for his philosophical and intellectually rigorous take on Gestalt therapy. Acknowledged as a supremely gifted clinician, he was indisposed to writing, so what remains of his work is merely transcripts of interviews.

Of great importance to understanding the development of gestalt therapy is the early training which took place in experiential groups in the Perls' apartment, led by both Fritz and Laura before Fritz left for the West Coast, and after by Laura alone. These 'trainings' were unstructured with little didactic input from the leaders, although many of the principles were discussed in the monthly meetings of the institute, as well as at local bars after the sessions. Many notable gestalt therapists emerged from these crucibles in addition to Isidore From, e.g., Richard Kitzler, Dan Bloom, Bud Feder, Carl Hodges, Ruth Ronall, etc. In these sessions both Fritz and Laura used some variation of the 'hot seat' method in which the leader essentially works with one individual in front of an audience, with little or no attention to group dynamics. In reaction to this omission emerged a more interactive approach in which gestalt therapy principles were blended with group dynamics. Notably in 1980 the book 'Beyond the Hot Seat', edited by Feder and Ronall, was published, with contributions from members of both the NY and Cleveland Institutes, as well as others.

Fritz left Laura and New York in 1960, then briefly lived in Miami, and ended up in California. Jim Simkin was a psychotherapist who became a client of Perls in New York, and then a co-therapist with Perls in Los Angeles. Simkin was responsible for Perls coming to California, where Perls began a psychotherapy practice. Ultimately, the life of a peripatetic trainer and workshop leader was a better suited to Fritz's personality. So, starting in 1963, Simkin and Perls co-led some of the early Gestalt workshops and training groups at Esalen Institute, in Big Sur, California, where Perls eventually settled and built a home. Jim Simkin then purchased property next to Esalen. Simkin started his own training centre, which he ran until his death in 1984. Simkin refined his precise version of Gestalt therapy, training psychologists, psychiatrists, counsellors and social workers within a very rigorous residential training model.

The Schism

In the 1960s Perls became infamous among the professional elite for his public workshops at Esalen Institute. Isadore From referred to some of Fritz' brief workshops as "hit-and-run" therapy, because of Perls' alleged emphasis on showmanship with little or no follow-through. But Perls never considered these workshops to be complete therapy. Rather, he felt he was giving demonstrations of key points for a largely professional audience. Unfortunately, some films and tapes of his work were all that most graduate students were exposed to, along with the misperception that this was the entirety of Perls' work.

When Fritz Perls left New York for California, there began to be a split with those who saw Gestalt therapy as a therapeutic approach similar to psychoanalysis. This view was represented by Isadore From, who practiced and taught mainly in New York, as well as by the members of the Cleveland Institute, which was co-founded by From. An entirely different approach was taken, primarily in California, by those who saw Gestalt therapy not just as a therapeutic modality, but as a way of life. The East Coast, New York-Cleveland axis was often appalled by the notion of Gestalt therapy leaving the consulting room and becoming a way-of-life on the West Coast in the 1960s. An alternate view of this split saw Perls in his last years continuing to develop his a-theoretical and phenomenological methodology, while others, inspired by From, were inclined to theoretical rigor which verged on replacing experience with ideas.

The split continues between what has been called "East Coast Gestalt" and "West Coast Gestalt", at least from an Amerocentric point of view. While the communitarian form of Gestalt continues to flourish, Gestalt therapy was largely replaced in the United States by Cognitive Behavioural Therapy, and many Gestalt therapists in the U.S. drifted towards organizational management and coaching. At the same time, contemporary Gestalt Practice (to a large extent based upon Gestalt therapy theory and practice) was developed by Dick Price, the co-founder of Esalen Institute. Price was one of Perls' students at Esalen.

Post-Perls

In 1969 Fritz Perls left the United States to start a Gestalt community at Lake Cowichan on Vancouver Island, Canada. He died almost a year later, on 14 March 1970, in Chicago. One member of the Gestalt community was Barry Stevens. Her book about that phase of her life, Don' t Push the River, became very popular. She developed her own form of Gestalt therapy body work, which is essentially a concentration on the awareness of body processes.

The Polsters

Erving and Miriam Polster started a training centre in La Jolla, California, which also became very well known, as did their book, Gestalt Therapy Integrated, in the 1970s.

The Polsters played an influential role in advancing the concept of contact boundary phenomena. The standard contact boundary resistances in Gestalt theory were confluence, introjection, projection and retroflection. A disturbance described by Miriam and Erving Polster was "deflection", which referred to a means of avoiding contact. Instances of boundary phenomena can have pathological or non-pathological aspects. For example, it is appropriate for an infant and mother to merge, or become "confluent", but inappropriate for a client and therapist. If the latter become confluent, there can be no growth, because there is no boundary at which one can contact the other. The client will not be able to learn anything new because the therapist essentially becomes an extension of the client.

Influences upon Gestalt Therapy

Some Examples

There were a variety of psychological and philosophical influences upon the development of Gestalt therapy; not the least of which were the social forces at the time and place of its inception. Gestalt therapy is an approach that is holistic (including mind, body and culture). It is present-centred and related to existential therapy in its emphasis on personal responsibility for action, and on the value of "I-thou" relationship in therapy. In fact, Perls considered calling Gestalt therapy existential-phenomenological therapy. "The I and thou in the Here and Now" was a semi-humorous shorthand mantra for Gestalt therapy referring to the substantial influence of the work of Martin Buber on Perls and Gestalt. Buber's work was focused on the "I-thou, here and now" concept following his postponing a response to a client's request for help, following which the client committed suicide. Following that incident, Buber committed to the "I-Thou here and now" concept as of primary importance and focus in the therapeutic relationship. This concept became figural in much of Gestalt theory and practice.

Both Fritz and Laura Perls were students and admirers of the neuropsychiatrist Kurt Goldstein. Gestalt therapy was based in part on Goldstein's concept called "Organismic theory". Goldstein viewed a person in terms of a holistic and unified experience. He encouraged a "big picture" perspective, taking into account the whole context of a person's experience. The word Gestalt means whole, or configuration. Laura Perls, in an interview, denotes the "Organismic theory" as the base of Gestalt therapy.

There were additional influences on Gestalt therapy from existentialism, particularly the I-thou relationship as it applies to therapy, and the notion of personal choice and responsibility.

The late 1950s–1960s movement towards personal growth and the human potential movement in California fed into, and was itself influenced by Gestalt therapy. In this process Gestalt therapy somehow became a "coherent Gestalt", which is the Gestalt psychology term for a perceptual unit that holds together and forms a unified whole.

Psychoanalysis

Fritz Perls trained as a neurologist at major medical institutions and as a Freudian psychoanalyst in Berlin and Vienna, the most important international centres of the discipline in his day. He worked as a training analyst for several years with the official recognition of the International Psychoanalytic Association (IPA) and must be considered an experienced clinician. Gestalt therapy was influenced by psychoanalysis. It was part of a continuum moving from the early work of Freud, to the later Freudian ego analysis, to Wilhelm Reich and his character analysis and notion of character armor, with attention to nonverbal behaviour This was consonant with Laura Perls' background in dance and movement therapy. To this was added the insights of academic Gestalt psychology, including perception, Gestalt formation and the tendency of organisms to complete an incomplete Gestalt, and to form "wholes" in experience.

Central to Fritz and Laura Perls' modifications of psychoanalysis was the concept of "dental or oral aggression". In Ego, Hunger and Aggression (1947), Fritz Perls' first book, to which Laura Perls contributed (ultimately without recognition), Perls suggested that when the infant develops teeth, he or she has the capacity to chew, to break apart food, and by analogy to experience, to taste, accept, reject or assimilate. This was opposed to Freud's notion that only introjection takes place in early experience. Thus Perls made "assimilation", as opposed to "introjection", a focal theme in his work, and the prime means by which growth occurs in therapy.

In contrast to the psychoanalytic stance, in which the "patient" introjects the (presumably more healthy) interpretations of the analyst, in Gestalt therapy the client must "taste" his or her experience, and either accept or reject it, but not introject or "swallow whole". Hence, the emphasis is on avoiding interpretation, and instead encouraging discovery. This is the key point in the divergance of Gestalt therapy from traditional psychoanalysis — growth occurs through gradual assimilation of experience in a natural way, rather than by accepting the interpretations of the analyst; thus, the therapist should not interpret, but lead the client to discover for himself or herself.

The Gestalt therapist contrives experiments that lead the client to greater awareness and fuller experience of his or her possibilities. Experiments can be focussed on undoing projections or retroflections. The therapist can work to help the client with closure of unfinished Gestalts ("unfinished business" such as unexpressed emotions towards somebody in the client's life). There are many kinds of experiments that might be therapeutic. But the essence of the work is that it is experiential rather than interpretive, and in this way Gestalt therapy distinguishes itself from psychoanalysis.

7

Positive Psychotherapy

Positive psychotherapy (PPT) (since 1968) is the name of the method of the psychotherapeutic modality developed by Nossrat Peseschkian and co-workers. Prof. Peseschkian, MD, (1933–2010) was a specialist in neurology, psychiatry, psychotherapy and psychotherapeutic medicine. Positive psychotherapy is a method in the field of humanistic and psychodynamic psychotherapy and is based on a positive image of man, which correlates with a salutogenetic, resource-oriented, humanistic and conflict-centred approach. It is accredited by several institutions (e.g. State Medical Chamber of Hessen, Germany, European Association for Psychotherapy EAP; World Council for Psychotherapy WCP, International Federation of Psychotherapy IFP and other statutory institutions).

Main Principles

The three main principles of positive psychotherapy address the positive, content-wise and strategic approach (Principle of Hope – Principle of Balance - Principle of Consultation).

The Principle of Hope implies that one does not try to immediately eliminate a disturbance but to first understand it in a broader context and to respond to its positive aspects. The word "positive" (lat. positum) means "the actual", "the given", "really" – the aim of positive psychotherapists is to help their patients to clear the view on the disturbance and recognize their meaning (basic-capabilities and actual-capabilities). Accordingly the disorder will be reinterpreted.

Some examples:

- Sleep disturbance is the ability to be watchful and get by with little sleep

- Depression is the ability to react with deepest emotionality to conflicts
- Schizophrenia is the ability to live in two worlds or to resort to living in a fantasy world
- Anorexia nervosa is the ability to get along with few meals and identify with the hunger of the world

Through this positive view a change of standpoint becomes possible, not only for the patient, but also for his environment. Hence, illnesses have a symbolic function which has to be recognized by both therapist and patient. The patient learns that the symptoms and complaints of the illness are signals to bring his or her four qualities of life into new balance.

Principle of Balance: Conflict Dynamics and Conflict Contents. The four qualities of life. Primary and Secondary capacities. Despite social and cultural differences and the uniqueness of every human being, it can be observed that during the management of their problems that all humans refer to typical forms of coping. Thomas Kornbichler explains: "Nossrat Peseschkian formulated with the Balance Model of Positive Psychotherapy (an innovative contemporary approach to dynamic psychotherapy) a vivid model of coping with conflicts in different cultures." According to the balance model, the four areas of life are: 1. body/sense – psychosomatic; 2. achievement/activities - stress factors; 3. contact/environment – depression; 4. fantasy/future/world view/meaning of life - fears and phobia.

If we get into conflict by stress or micro-trauma, we can express our conflict-situation in four typical forms of the conflict-solution:

- body-oriented modes
- achievement-oriented modes
- relationship-oriented modes
- fantasy-oriented modes

Though these four ranges are inherent in all humans, in the western hemisphere the emphasis is more often on the areas of body/ senses and profession/achievement in contrast to the eastern hemisphere where the areas are contact, fantasy and future (cross-cultural aspect of positive psychotherapy). Lack of contact and imagination are some of the causes of many psychosomatic diseases. Everybody develops his or her own preferences on how to cope with conflicts that occur. Through a one-sided mode to the conflict solution, the other modes are getting eclipsed. This one-sidedness in the four qualities of life leads to eight typical modes of conflict reaction, depending on an active or passive type of coping:

- Overcompensation in body-cult (narcissistic over-valuation of the body)
- Decompensation in somatic illness (somatisation, addictive behaviours, risk factors: overweight etc.)
- Overcompensation in activity and achievement
- Decompensation in achievement- and concentration-problems
- Overcompensation in sociality
- Decompensation in loneliness
- Overcompensation in megalomania, delusions, etc.
- Decompensation in senselessness, existential fears.

The conflict contents (e.g. punctuality, orderliness, politeness, trust, time, patience) are described in terms of primary and secondary capacities, based on the basic capacities of loving and knowing. This can be seen as a content-wise differentiation of Freud's classical model of the instances.

Principle of Consultation: Five-stages of therapy and self-help. The five stages of positive psychotherapy represent a concept in which therapy and self-help are closely interrelated. The patient and the family are getting informed together about the illness and the individual solution to it.

- 1st Step: Observation; distancing (perception: the capacity to express desire and problems)
- 2nd Step: Taking inventory (cognitive capacities: events in the last 5 to 10 years)
- 3rd Step: Situational encouragement (self-help and resource-activation of the patient: the ability to use past successes in conflict solution)
- 4th Step: Verbalization (communicative capacities: the ability to express outstanding conflicts and problems in the four qualities of life)

Help to Change Standpoint: Instead of insistently turning over old and well-known problems, the resources of the patient are mobilized by wisdoms, stories, parables, allegories for the emotional and mental relocation according to the wisdom: "You can stand on your position, but you should not sit on it". With cross-cultural examples and stories, prejudices and resentments are abolished. Stories can be seen as a decisive approach to a change of awareness which in turn is the premise for a change in, for example, political, economic, medical and environmental behaviour.

Image of man: Positive psychotherapy places the individual development of a person into the context of globalization. It is argued that for the first time in the history of mankind, a global, interconnected society is emerging whose characteristic feature is its cultural diversity. The process of globalization – not only on a political level but primarily on a mental level – does not take place without challenges. From this emerges the challenge to also adapt the methodological approach to the situation today. A shift from a monocultural and monocausal consideration to a multicultural and multicausal one is required.

These kind of experiences and considerations led Nossrat Peseschkian to conceiving man – especially in psychotherapy – not only as an isolated individual, but also to take into account his interpersonal relationships as well, and – in accordance with his own development – his "cross-cultural" situation, which, after all, makes up what he essentially is ("If you work alone, you can only add, if you work together with others, you can multiply.")

The idea of man in positive psychotherapy can be compared to the one in humanistic psychology. In contrast to the determinism of physical and emotional drives in classical psychoanalysis or the view of a "human machine" of the classical behaviourism, in positive psychotherapy the person is seen as basically good and healthy. He or she has a lot of capacities which are created like seeds but need to be developed by education and self-education. This in turn can be compared to the salutogenetic approach of Antonovsky.

Group Psychotherapy

The therapeutic use of groups in modern clinical practice can be traced to the early 20th century, when the American chest physician Pratt, working in Boston, described forming 'classes' of 15 to 20 patients with tuberculosis who had been rejected for sanatorium treatment. The term group therapy, however, was first used around 1920 by Jacob L. Moreno, whose main contribution was the development of psychodrama, in which groups were used as both cast and audience for the exploration of individual problems by reenactment under the direction of the leader. The more analytic and exploratory use of groups in both hospital and out-patient settings was pioneered by a few European psychoanalysts who emigrated to the USA, such as Paul Schilder, who treated severely neurotic and mildly psychotic out-patients in small groups at Bellevue Hospital, New York. The power of groups was most influentially demonstrated in Britain during the Second World War, when several psychoanalysts and psychiatrists proved the value of group methods for officer selection in the War Office Selection Boards. A chance to run an Army psychiatric unit on group lines was then given to several of these pioneers, notably Wilfred Bion and Rickman, followed by S. H. Foulkes, Main, and Bridger. The Northfield Hospital in Birmingham gave its name to what came to be called the two 'Northfield Experiments', which provided the impetus for the development since the war of both social therapy, that is, the therapeutic community movement, and the use of small groups for the treatment of neurotic and personality disorders. Today group therapy is used in clinical settings and in private practice settings. The Psychotherapeutic Institute Bergerhausen (Director: Prof. Dr. Hans-Werner Gessmann) in Germany is using group-psychotherapy since 1973. It has been shown to be as or more effective than individual therapy.

Therapeutic Principles

Yalom's therapeutic factors (originally termed curative factors but renamed therapeutic factors .in the 5th edition of 'The Theory and Practice of Group Psychotherapy').

Universality

The recognition of shared experiences and feelings among group members and that these may be widespread or universal human concerns, serves to remove a group member's sense of isolation, validate their experiences, and raise self-esteem

Altruism: The group is a place where members can help each other, and the experience of being able to give something to another person can lift the member's self esteem and help develop more adaptive coping styles and interpersonal skills.

Instillation of Hope: In a mixed group that has members at various stages of development or recovery, a member can be inspired and encouraged by another member who has overcome the problems with which they are still struggling.

Imparting Information: While this is not strictly speaking a psychotherapeutic process, members often report that it has been very helpful to learn factual information from other members in the group. For example, about their treatment or about access to services.

Corrective Recapitulation of the Primary Family Experience: Members often unconsciously identify the group therapist and other group members with their own parents and siblings in a process that is a form of transference specific to group psychotherapy. The therapist's interpretations can help group members gain understanding of the impact of childhood experiences on their personality, and they may learn to avoid unconsciously repeating unhelpful past interactive patterns in present-day relationships.

Development of Socializing Techniques: The group setting provides a safe and supportive environment for members to take risks by extending their repertoire of interpersonal behaviour and improving their social skills

Imitative Behaviour: One way in which group members can develop social skills is through a modelling process, observing and imitating the therapist and other group members. For example, sharing personal feelings, showing concern, and supporting others.

Cohesiveness: It has been suggested that this is the primary therapeutic factor from which all others flow. Humans are herd animals with an instinctive need to belong to groups, and personal development can only take place in an interpersonal context. A cohesive group is one in which all members feel a sense of belonging, acceptance, and validation.

Existential Factors: Learning that one has to take responsibility for one's own life and the consequences of one's decisions.

Catharsis: Catharsis is the experience of relief from emotional distress through the free and uninhibited expression of emotion. When members tell their story to a supportive audience, they can obtain relief from chronic feelings of shame and guilt.

Interpersonal Learning: Group members achieve a greater level of self-awareness through the process of interacting with others in the group, who give feedback on the member's behaviour and impact on others.

Self-understanding: This factor overlaps with interpersonal learning but refers to the achievement of greater levels of insight into the genesis of one's problems and the unconscious motivations that underlie one's behaviour.

Settings

Group therapy can form part of the therapeutic milieu of a psychiatric in-patient unit or ambulatory psychiatric Partial hospitalization (also known as Day Hospital treatment). In addition to classical "talking" therapy, group therapy in an institutional setting can also include group-based expressive therapies such as drama therapy, psychodrama, art therapy, and non-verbal types of therapy such as music therapy and dance/movement therapy. Group psychotherapy is a key component of Milieu Therapy in a Therapeutic Community. The total environment or milieu is regarded as the medium of therapy, all interactions and activities regarded as potentially therapeutic and are subject to exploration and interpretation, and are explored in daily or weekly community meetings. However, interactions between the culture of group psychotherapeutic settings and the more managerial norms of external authorities may create 'organizational turbulence' which can critically undermine a group's ability to maintain a safe yet challenging 'formative space'. Academics at the University of Oxford studied the inter-organizational dynamics of a national democratic therapeutic community over a period of four years; they found external steering by authorities eroded the community's therapeutic model, produced a crisis, and led to an intractable conflict which resulted in the community's closure.

A form of group therapy has been reported to be effective in psychotic adolescents and recovering addicts. Projective psychotherapy uses an outside text such as a novel or motion picture to provide a "stable delusion" for the former cohort and a safe focus for repressed and suppressed emotions or thoughts in the latter. Patient groups read a novel or collectively view a film. They then participate collectively in the discussion of plot, character motivation and author motivation. In the case of films, sound track, cinematography and background are also discussed and processed. Under the guidance of the therapist, defense mechanisms are bypassed by the use of signifiers and semiotic processes. The focus remains on the text rather than on personal issues. It was popularized in the science fiction novel, Red Orc's Rage.

Group therapy is now often utilized in private practice settings.

Group-analysis has become widespread in Europe, and especially the United Kingdom, where it has become the most common form of group psychotherapy. Interest from Australia, the Soviet Union and the African continent is also growing.

Research on Effectiveness

There is clear evidence for the effectiveness of group psychotherapy for depression: a meta-analysis of 48 studies showed an overall effect size of 1.03, which is clinically highly significant. Similarly, a meta-analysis of five studies of group psychotherapy for adult sexual abuse survivors showed moderate to strong effect sizes, and there is also good evidence for effectiveness with chronic traumatic stress in war veterans. There is less robust evidence of good outcomes for patients with borderline personality disorder, with some studies showing only small to moderate effect sizes. The authors comment that these poor outcomes might reflect a need for additional support for some patients, in addition to the group therapy. This is borne out by the impressive results obtained using Mentalization based treatment, a model that combines dynamic group psychotherapy with individual psychotherapy and case management. Most outcome research is carried out using time-limited therapy with diagnostically homogenous groups. However, long-term intensive interactional group psychotherapy assumes diverse and diagnostically heterogeneous group membership, and an open-ended time scale for therapy. Good outcomes have also been demonstrated for this form of group therapy. Group Therapy has been shown to be as or more effective than individual therapy for higher functioning adults (Gardenswartz, 2009, Los Angeles, CA). Clinical cases has shown that the combination of both individual and group therapy is most beneficial for such clients. (the "multiplicative" effect).

Cognitive Behavioural Therapy

Cognitive behavioural therapy refers to a range of techniques which focus on the construction and re-construction of people's cognitions, emotions and behaviours. Generally in CBT, the therapist, through a wide array of modalities, helps clients assess, recognize and deal with problematic and dysfunctional ways of thinking, emoting and behaving.

Description

Mainstream cognitive behavioural therapy assumes that changing maladaptive thinking leads to change in affect and behaviour, but recent variants emphasize changes in one's relationship to maladaptive thinking rather than changes in thinking itself. Therapists or computer-based programmes use CBT techniques to help individuals challenge their patterns and beliefs and replace "errors in thinking such as overgeneralizing, magnifying negatives, minimizing positives and catastrophizing" with "more realistic and effective thoughts, thus decreasing emotional distress and self-defeating behaviour" or to take a more open, mindful, and aware posture towards them so as to diminish their impact. Mainstream CBT helps individuals replace "maladaptive... coping skills, cognitions, emotions and behaviours with more adaptive ones", by challenging an individual's way of thinking and the way that he/she reacts to certain habits or behaviours, but there is still controversy about the degree to which these traditional cognitive elements account for the effects seen with CBT over and above the earlier behavioural elements such as exposure and skills training.

Modern forms of CBT include a number of diverse but related techniques such as exposure therapy, stress inoculation training, cognitive processing therapy, cognitive therapy, relaxation training, dialectical behaviour therapy, and acceptance and commitment therapy.

CBT has six phases:

1. Assessment or psychological assessment;
2. Reconceptualization;
3. Skills acquisition;
4. Skills consolidation and application training;
5. Generalization and maintenance;
6. Post-treatment assessment follow-up.

The reconceptualization phase makes up much of the "cognitive" portion of CBT. A summary of modern CBT approaches is given by Hofmann.

There are different protocols for delivering cognitive behavioural therapy, with important similarities among them. Use of the term CBT may refer to different interventions, including "self-instructions (e.g. distraction, imagery, motivational self-talk), relaxation and/or biofeedback, development of adaptive coping strategies (e.g. minimizing negative or self-defeating thoughts), changing maladaptive beliefs about pain, and goal setting". Treatment is sometimes manualized, with brief, direct, and time-limited treatments for individual psychological disorders that are specific technique-driven. CBT is used in both individual and group settings, and the techniques are often adapted for self-help applications. Some clinicians and researchers are cognitively oriented (e.g. cognitive restructuring), while others are more behaviourally oriented (e.g. in vivo exposure therapy). Interventions such as imaginal exposure therapy combine both approaches.

Specific Applications

CBT has been applied in both clinical and non-clinical environments to treat disorders such as personality conditions and behavioural problems. A systematic review of CBT in depression and anxiety disorders concluded that "CBT delivered in primary care, especially including computer- or Internet-based self-help programmes, is potentially more effective than usual care and could be delivered effectively by primary care therapists."

Emerging evidence suggests a possible role for CBT in the treatment of attention deficit hyperactivity disorder (ADHD); hypochondriasis; coping with the impact of multiple sclerosis; sleep disturbances related to aging; dysmenorrhea; and bipolar disorder, but more study is needed and results should be interpreted with caution. CBT has been studied as an aid in the treatment of anxiety associated with stuttering. Initial studies have shown CBT to be effective in reducing social anxiety in adults who stutter, but not in reducing stuttering frequency.

Martinez-Devesa et al (2010) found no evidence that CBT is effective for tinnitus, although there appears to be an effect on management of associated depression and quality of life in this condition. Turner et al (2007) found no convincing evidence that CBT training helps foster care providers manage difficult behaviours in the youth under their care, and Smedslund et al (2007) found that it was not helpful in treating men who abuse their intimate partners.

In the case of metastatic breast cancer, Edwards et al (2008) maintained that the current body of evidence is not sufficient to rule out the possibility that psychological interventions may cause harm to women with this advanced neoplasm.

In adults, CBT has been shown to have a role in the treatment plans for anxiety disorders; depression; eating disorders; chronic low back pain; personality disorders; psychosis; schizophrenia; substance use disorders; in the adjustment, depression, and anxiety associated with fibromyalgia; and with post-spinal cord injuries. There is some evidence that CBT is superior in the long-term to benzodiazepines and the nonbenzodiazepines in the treatment and management of insomnia.

In children or adolescents, CBT is an effective part of treatment plans for anxiety disorders; body dysmorphic disorder; depression and suicidality; eating disorders and obesity; obsessive–compulsive disorder; and posttraumatic stress disorder; as well as tic disorders, trichotillomania, and other repetitive behaviour disorders.

In the United Kingdom, the National Institute for Health and Clinical Excellence (NICE) recommends CBT in the treatment plans for a number of mental health difficulties, including posttraumatic stress disorder, obsessive–compulsive disorder (OCD), bulimia nervosa, and clinical depression.

Anxiety Disorders

CBT has been shown to be effective in the treatment of all anxiety disorders.

A basic concept in some CBT treatments used in anxiety disorders is in vivo exposure, a term describing a technique where the patient is gradually exposed to the actual, feared stimulus. The treatment is based on the theory that the fear response has been classically conditioned, and that avoidance of it negatively reinforces and maintains the fear. This "two-factor" model is often credited to O. Hobart Mowrer. Through exposure to the stimulus, this harmful conditioning can be "unlearned" (referred to as extinction and habituation).

Schizophrenia, Psychosis and Mood Disorders

Cognitive behavioural therapy has been shown as an effective treatment for clinical depression. The American Psychiatric Association Practice Guidelines (April 2000) indicated that, among psychotherapeutic approaches, cognitive behavioural therapy and interpersonal psychotherapy had the best-documented efficacy for treatment of major depressive disorder. One etiological theory of depression is Aaron T. Beck's cognitive theory of depression. His theory states that depressed people think the way they do because their thinking is biased towards negative interpretations. According to this theory, depressed people acquire a negative schema of the world in childhood and adolescence as an effect of stressful life events, and the negative schema is activated later in life when the person encounters similar situations.

Beck also described a negative cognitive triad, made up of the negative schemata and cognitive biases of the person, theorizing that depressed individuals make negative evaluations of themselves, the world, and the future. Depressed people, according to this theory, have views such as, "I never do a good job", "It is impossible to have a good day", and "things will never get better." A negative schema helps give rise to the cognitive bias, and the cognitive bias helps fuel the negative schema. This is the negative triad. Beck further proposed that depressed people often have the following cognitive biases: arbitrary inference, selective abstraction, over-generalization, magnification, and minimization. These cognitive biases are quick to make negative, generalized, and personal inferences of the self, thus fuelling the negative schema.

In long-term psychoses, CBT is used to complement medication and is adapted to meet individual needs. Interventions particularly related to these conditions include exploring reality testing, changing delusions and hallucinations, examining factors which precipitate relapse, and managing relapses. Several meta-analyses have shown CBT to be effective in schizophrenia, and the American Psychiatric Association includes CBT in its schizophrenia guideline as an evidence-based treatment. There is also some (limited) evidence of effectiveness for CBT in bipolar disorder and severe depression.

A 2010 meta-analysis found that no trial employing both blinding and psychological placebo has shown CBT to be effective in either schizophrenia or bipolar disorder, and that the effect size of CBT was small in major depressive disorder. They also found a lack of evidence to conclude that CBT was effective in preventing relapses in bipolar disorder. Evidence that severe depression is mitigated by CBT is also lacking, with anti-depressant medications still viewed as significantly more effective than CBT, although success with CBT for depression was observed beginning in the 1990s.

According to Cox, Abramson, Devine, and Hollon (2012), cognitive behavioural therapy can also be used to reduce prejudice towards others. This other-directed prejudice can cause depression in the "others," or in the self when a person becomes part of a group he or she previously had prejudice towards (i.e. deprejudice). "Devine and colleagues (2012) developed a successful Prejudice Perpetrator intervention with many conceptual parallels to CBT. Like CBT, their intervention taught Sources to be aware of their automative thoughts and to intentionally deploy a variety of cognitive techniques against automatic stereotyping."

Chronic Fatigue Syndrome

CBT has been shown to be moderately effective for treating chronic fatigue syndrome.

Cognitive Behavioural Therapy with Older Adults

CBT is used to help people of all ages, but the therapy should be adjusted based on the age of the patient with whom the therapist is dealing. Older individuals in particular have certain characteristics that need to be acknowledged and the therapy altered to account for these differences thanks to age. Some of the challenges to CBT because of age include the following:

The Cohort Effect: The times that each generation lives through partially shape its thought processes as well as values, so a 70-year-old may react to the therapy very differently from a 30-year-old, because of the different culture in which they were brought up. A tie-in to this effect is that each generation has to interact with one another, and the differing values clashing with one another may make the therapy more difficult.

Established Role: By the time one reaches old age, the person has a definitive idea of her or his role in life and is invested in that role. This social role can dominate who the person thinks he or she is and may make it difficult to adapt to the changes required in CBT.

Mentality Towards Aging: If the older individual sees aging itself as a negative this can exacerbate whatever malady the therapy is trying to help (depression and anxiety for example). Negative stereotypes and prejudice against the elderly cause depression as the stereotypes become self-relevant.

Processing Speed Decreases: As we age, we take longer to learn new information, and as a result may take more time to learn and retain the cognitive therapy. Therefore, therapists should slow down the pacing of the therapy and use any tools both written and verbal that will improve the retention of the cognitive behavioural therapy.

Methods of Access

Therapist

A typical CBT programme would consist of face-to-face sessions between patient and therapist, made up of 6-18 sessions of around an hour each with a gap of a 1–3 weeks between sessions. This initial programme might be followed by some booster sessions, for instance after one month and three months. CBT has also been found to be effective if patient and therapist type in real time to each other over computer links.

Cognitive behavioural therapy is most closely allied with the scientist–practitioner model in which clinical practice and research is informed by a scientific perspective, clear operationalization of the problem, and an emphasis on measurement, including measuring changes in cognition and behaviour and in the attainment of goals. These are often met through "homework" assignments in which the patient and the therapist work together to craft an assignment to complete before the next session. The completion of these assignments – which can be as simple as a person suffering from depression attending some kind of social event – indicates a dedication to treatment compliance and a desire to change. The therapists can then logically gauge the next step of treatment based on how thoroughly the patient completes the assignment. Effective cognitive behavioural therapy is dependent on a therapeutic alliance between the healthcare practitioner and the person seeking assistance. Unlike many other forms of psychotherapy, the patient is very involved in CBT. For example, an anxious patient may be asked to talk to a stranger as a homework assignment, but if that is too difficult, he or she can work out an easier assignment first. The therapist needs to be flexible and willing to listen to the patient rather than acting as an authority figure.

Computerized CBT

Computerized Cognitive Behavioural Therapy (CCBT) has been described by NICE as a "generic term for delivering CBT via an interactive computer interface delivered by a personal computer, internet, or interactive voice response system", instead of face-to-face with a human therapist. CCBT has potential to improve access to evidence-based therapies, and to overcome the prohibitive costs and lack of availability sometimes associated with retaining a human therapist.

CCBT completion rates and treatment efficacy have been found in some studies to be higher when use of CCBT is prescribed and supported, than when use is in a self-help form without medical professional involvement.

In February 2006 NICE recommended that CCBT be made available for use within the NHS across England and Wales for patients presenting with mild-to-moderate depression, rather than immediately opting for antidepressant medication, and CCBT is made available by some health systems. The 2009 NICE guideline recognized that there are likely to be a number of computerized CBT products that are useful to patients, but removed endorsement of any specific product.

A relatively new avenue of research is the combination of artificial intelligence and CCBT. It has been proposed to use modern technology to create CCBT that simulates face-to-face therapy. This might be achieved in cognitive behaviour therapy for a specific disorders using the comprehensive domain knowledge of CBT. One area where this has been attempted, is the specific domain area of social anxiety in those who stutter.

Reading Self-help Materials

Enabling patients to read self-help CBT guides has been shown to be effective by some studies. However one study found a negative effect in patients who tended to ruminate, and another meta-analysis found that the benefit was only significant when the self-help was guided (e.g. by a medical professional).

Group Educational Course

Patient participation in group courses has been shown to be effective.

Evaluation of Effectiveness

In adults, CBT has been shown to have effectiveness and a role in the treatment plans for anxiety disorders, depression, eating disorders, chronic low back pain, personality disorders, psychosis, schizophrenia, substance use disorders, in the adjustment, depression, and anxiety associated with fibromyalgia, and with post-spinal cord injuries. Evidence has shown CBT is effective in helping treat schizophrenia, and it is now offered in most treatment guidelines.

In children or adolescents, CBT is an effective part of treatment plans for anxiety disorders, body dysmorphic disorder, depression and suicidality, eating disorders and obesity, obsessive–compulsive disorder, and posttraumatic stress disorder, as well as tic disorders, trichotillomania, and other repetitive behaviour disorders.

Cochrane reviews have found no evidence that CBT is effective for tinnitus, although there appears to be an effect on management of associated depression and quality of life in this condition. Other recent Cochrane Reviews found no convincing evidence that CBT training helps foster care providers manage difficult behaviours in the youth under their care, nor was it helpful in treating men who abuse their intimate partners.

According to a 2004 review by INSERM of three methods, cognitive behavioural therapy was either "proven" or "presumed" to be an effective therapy on several specific mental disorders. According to the study, CBT was effective at treating schizophrenia, depression, bipolar disorder, panic disorder, post-traumatic stress, anxiety disorders, bulimia, anorexia, personality disorders and alcohol dependency.

Some meta-analyses find CBT more effective than psychodynamic therapy and equal to other therapies in treating anxiety and depression. However, psychodynamic therapy may provide better long-term outcomes.

Computerized CBT (CCBT) has been proven to be effective by randomized controlled and other trials in treating depression and anxiety disorders, as well as insomnia. Some research has found similar effectiveness to an intervention of informational websites and weekly telephone calls. CCBT was found to be equally effective as face-to-face CBT in adolescent anxiety and insomnia.

Criticism of CBT sometimes focuses on implementations (such as the UK IAPT) which may result initially in low quality therapy being offered by poorly trained practitioners. However evidence supports the effectiveness of CBT for anxiety and depression.

Mounting evidence suggests that the addition of hypnotherapy as an adjunct to CBT improves treatment efficacy for a variety of clinical issues.

Hypnotherapy

Hypnotherapy is therapy that is undertaken with a subject in hypnosis. Hypnotherapy is often applied in order to modify a subject's behaviour, emotional content, and attitudes, as well as a wide range of conditions including dysfunctional habits, anxiety, stress-related illness, pain management, and personal development.

Traditional Hypnotherapy

The form of hypnotherapy practiced by most Victorian hypnotists, including James Braid and Hippolyte Bernheim, mainly employed direct suggestion of symptom removal, with some use of therapeutic relaxation and occasionally aversion to alcohol, drugs, etc.

Hypnoanalysis

In 1895 Sigmund Freud and Joseph Breuer published a seminal clinical text entitled Studies in Hysteria (1895) which promoted a new approach to psychotherapy.

Ericksonian Hypnotherapy

In the 1950s, Milton H. Erickson developed a radically different approach to hypnotism, which has subsequently become known as "Ericksonian hypnotherapy" or "Neo-Ericksonian hypnotherapy." Erickson made use of an informal conversational approach with many clients and complex language patterns, and therapeutic strategies. This divergence from tradition led some of his colleagues, including Andre Weitzenhoffer, to dispute whether Erickson was right to label his approach "hypnosis" at all.

The founders of Neurolinguistic Programming (NLP), a methodology similar in some regards to hypnotism, claimed that they had modelled the work of Erickson extensively and assimilated it into their approach. Weitzenhoffer disputed whether NLP bears any genuine resemblance to Erickson's work.

Cognitive/behavioural Hypnotherapy

Cognitive behavioural hypnotherapy (CBH) is an integrated psychological therapy employing clinical hypnosis and cognitive behavioural therapy (CBT). The use of CBT in conjunction with hypnotherapy may result in greater treatment effectiveness. A meta-analysis of eight different researches revealed "a 70% greater improvement" for patients undergoing an integrated treatment to those using CBT only.

In 1974, Theodore Barber and his colleagues published an influential review of the research which argued, following the earlier social psychology of Theodore R. Sarbin, that hypnotism was better understood not as a "special state" but as the result of normal psychological variables, such as active imagination, expectation, appropriate attitudes, and motivation. Barber introduced the term "cognitive-behavioural" to describe the nonstate theory of hypnotism, and discussed its application to behaviour therapy.

The growing application of cognitive and behavioural psychological theories and concepts to the explanation of hypnosis paved the way for a closer integration of hypnotherapy with various cognitive and behavioural therapies. However, many cognitive and behavioural therapies were themselves originally influenced by older hypnotherapy techniques, e.g., the systematic desensitisation of Joseph Wolpe, the cardinal technique of early behaviour therapy, was originally called "hypnotic desensitisation" and derived from the Medical Hypnotism (1948) of Lewis Wolberg.

Behaviour Therapy

Behaviour therapy focuses on modifying overt behaviour and helping clients to achieve goals. This approach is built on the principles of learning theory including operant and respondent conditioning, which makes up the area of applied behaviour analysis or behaviour modification. This approach includes acceptance and commitment therapy, functional analytic psychotherapy, and dialectical behaviour therapy. Sometimes it is integrated with cognitive therapy to make cognitive behaviour therapy. By nature, behavioural therapies are empirical (data-driven), contextual (focused on the environment and context), functional (interested in the effect or consequence a behaviour ultimately has), probabilistic (viewing behaviour as statistically predictable), monistic (rejecting mind-body dualism and treating the person as a unit), and relational (analyzing bidirectional interactions).

Scientific Basis

The behavioural approach to therapy assumes that behaviour that is associated with psychological problems develops through the same processes of learning that affects the development of other behaviours. Therefore behaviourists see personality problems in the way that personality was developed. They do not look at behaviour disorders as something a person has but that it reflects how learning has influenced certain people to behave in a certain way in certain situations. Understanding how the process of learning takes place comes from research that has been done on operant and classical conditioning.

Behaviour therapy is based upon the principles of classical conditioning developed by Ivan Pavlov and operant conditioning developed by B.F. Skinner. Classical conditioning happens when a neutral stimulus comes right before another stimulus that triggers a reflexive response. The idea is that if the neutral stimulus and whatever other stimulus that triggers a response is paired together often enough that the neutral stimulus will produce the reflexive response. Operant conditioning has to do with rewards and punishments and how they can either strengthen or weaken certain behaviours. There has been a good deal of confusion on how these two conditionings differ and whether the various techniques of behaviour therapy have any common scientific base. Contingency management programmes are a direct product of research from operant conditioning. These programmes have been highly successful with those suffering from panic disorders, anxiety disorders, and phobias.

Systematic desensitisation and exposure and response prevention both evolved from respondent conditioning and have also received considerable research.

Behaviour avoidance test (BAT) is a behavioural procedure in which the therapist measures how long the client can tolerate an anxiety-inducing stimulus. The BAT falls under the exposure-based methods of Behaviour Therapy. Exposure-based methods of behavioural therapy are well suited to the treatment of phobias, which include intense and unreasonable fears (e.g., of spiders, blood, public speaking). The therapist needs some type of behavioural assessment to record the continuing progress of a client undergoing an exposure-based treatment for phobia. The simplest possible assessment approach for this is the BAT. The BAT approach is predicted on the reasonable assumption that the client's fear is the main determinant of behaviour in the testing situation. BAT can be conducted visual, virtually, or physically, depending on the clients' maladaptive behaviour. Its application is not limited to phobias, it is applied to various disorders such as Post-Traumatic Stress Disorder (PTSD) and Obsessive-Compulsive Disorder (OCD).

Assessment

Behaviour therapists complete a functional analysis or a functional assessment that looks at four important areas: stimulus, organism, response and consequences. The stimulus is the condition or environmental trigger that causes behaviour. An organism involves the internal responses of a person, like physiological responses, emotions and cognition. A response is the behaviour that a person exhibits and the consequences are the result of the behaviour. These four things are incorporated into an assessment done by the behaviour therapist.

Most behaviour therapists use objective assessment methods like structured interviews, objective psychological tests or different behavioural rating forms. These types of assessments are used so that the behaviour therapist can determine exactly what a client's problem may be and establish a baseline for any maladaptive responses that the client may have. By having this baseline, as therapy continues this same measure can be used to check a client's progress, which can help determine if the therapy is working. Behaviour therapists do not typically ask the why questions but tend to be more focused on the how, when, where and what questions. Traditional tests like the Rorschach inkblot test or personality tests like the MMPI(Minnesota Multiphasic Personality Inventory) are traditionally used for behavioural assessment because they are based on the personality trait theory where it assumes that a persons answer to these methods can predict behaviour. Behaviour assessment is more focused on the observations of a persons behaviour in their natural environment.

Behavioural Assessment specifically attempts to find out what the environmental and self-imposed variables are. These variables are the things that are allowing a person to maintain their maladaptive feelings, thoughts and behaviours. In a behavioural assessment "person variables" are also considered. These "person variables" come from a person's social learning history and they effect the way in which the environment affects that person's behaviour. An example of a person variable would be behavioural competence. Behavioural competence looks at whether a person has the appropriate skills and behaviours that are necessary when performing a specific response to a certain situation or stimuli.

When making a behavioural assessment the behaviour therapist wants to answer two questions: (1) what are the different factors(environmental or psychological) that are maintaining the maladaptive behaviour and (2) what type of behaviour therapy or technique that can help the individual improve most effectively. The first question involves looking at all aspects of a person, which can be summed up by the acronym BASIC ID. This acronym stands for behaviour, affective responses, sensory reactions, imagery, cognitive processes, interpersonal relationships and drug use.

Clinical Applications

Behaviour therapy based its core interventions on functional analysis. Just a few of the many problems that behaviour therapy have functionally analysed include intimacy in couples relationships, forgiveness in couples, chronic pain, stress-related behaviour problems of being an adult child of an alcoholic, anorexia, chronic distress, substance abuse, depression, anxiety, insomnia and obesity.

Functional analysis has even been applied to problems that therapists commonly encounter like client resistance, partially engaged clients and involuntary clients. Applications to these problems have left clinicans with considerable tools for enhancing therapeutic effectiveness. One way to enhance therapeutic effectiveness is to use positive reinforcement or operant conditioning. Although behaviour therapy is based on the general learning model, it can be applied in a lot of different treatment packages that can be specifically developed to deal with problematic behaviours. Some of the more well known types of treatments are: Relaxation training, systematic desensitization, virtual reality exposure, exposure and response prevention techniques, social skills training, modelling, behavioural rehearsal and homework, and aversion therapy and punishment.

Relaxation training involves clients learning to lower arousal to reduce their stress by tensing and releasing certain muscle groups throughout their body. Systematic desensitization is a treatment in which the client slowly substitutes a new learned response for a maladaptive response by moving up a hierarchy of situations involving fear. Systematic desensitization is based in part on counter conditioning. Counter conditioning is learning new ways to change one response for another and in the case of desensitization it is substituting that maladaptive behaviour for a more relaxing behaviour. Exposure and response prevention techniques is also known as flooding and response prevention. Flooding and response prevention is the general technique in which you expose an individual to anxiety-provoking stimuli while keeping them from having any avoidance responses or keeping them from freaking out.

Virtual reality therapy provides realistic, computer-based simulations of troublesome situations. The modelling process involves a person being subjected to watching other individuals who demonstrate behaviour that is considered adaptive and that should be adopted by the client. This exposure involves not only the cues of the "model person" as well as the situations of a certain behaviour that way the relationship can be seen between the appropriateness of a certain behaviour and situation in which that behaviour occurs is demonstrated. With the behavioural rehearsal and homework treatment a client gets a desired behaviour during a therapy session and then they practice and record that behaviour between their sessions. Aversion therapy and punishment is a technique in which an aversive (painful or unpleasant) stimulus is used to decrease unwanted behaviours from occurring. It is concerned with two procedures: 1) the procedures are used to decrease the likelihood of the frequency of a certain behaviour and 2) procedures that will reduce the attractiveness of certain behaviours and the stimuli that elicit them. The punishment side of aversion therapy is when an aversive stimulus is presented at the same time that a negative stimulus and then they are stopped at the same time when a positive stimulus or response is presented. Examples of the type of negative stimulus or punishment that can be used is shock therapy treatments, aversive drug treatments as well as response cost contingent punishment which involves taking away a reward.

Applied behaviour analysis is using behavioural methods to modify certain behaviours that are seen as being important socially or personally. There are four main characteristics of applied behaviour analysis. First behaviour analysis is focused mainly on overt behaviours in an applied setting. Treatments are developed as a way to alter the relationship between those overt behaviours and their consequences.

Another characteristic of applied behaviour analysis is how it(behaviour analysis) goes about evaluating treatment effects. The individual subject is where the focus of study is on, the investigation is centred on the one individual being treated. A third characteristic is that it focuses on what the environment does to cause significant behaviour changes. Finally the last characteristic of applied behaviour analysis is the use of those techniques that stem from operant and classical conditioning such as providing reinforcement, punishment, stimulus control and any other learning principles that may apply.

Social skills training teaches clients skills to access reinforcers and lessen life punishment. Operant conditioning procedures in meta-analysis had the largest effect size for training social skills, followed by modelling, coaching, and social cognitive techniques in that order. Social skills training has some empirical support particularly for schizophrenia. However, with schizophrenia, behavioural programmes have generally lost favour.

Some other techniques that have been used in behaviour therapy are contingency contracting, response costs, token economies, biofeedback, and using shaping and grading task assignments.

Shaping and graded task assignments are used when behaviour that needs to be learned is complex. The complex behaviours that need to be learned are broken down into simpler steps where the person can achieve small things gradually building up to the more complex behaviour. Each step approximates the eventual goal and helps the person to expand their activities in a gradual way. This behaviour is used when a person feels that something in their lives can not be changed and life's tasks appear to be overwhelming.

Another technique of behaviour therapy involves holding a client or patient accountable of their behaviours in an effort to change them. This is called a contingency contract, which is a formal written contract between two or more people that defines the specific expected behaviours that you wish to change and the rewards and punishments that go along with that behaviour. In order for a contingency contract to be official it needs to have five elements. First it must state what each person will get if they successfully complete the desired behaviour. Secondly those people involved have to monitor the behaviours. Third, if the desired behaviour is not being performed in the way that was agreed upon in the contract the punishments that were defined in the contract must be done. Fourth if the persons involved are complying with the contract they must receive bonuses. The last element involves documenting the compliance and noncompliance while using this treatment in order to give the persons involved consistent feedback about the target behaviour and the provision of reinforcers.

Token economies is a behaviour therapy technique where clients are reinforced with tokens that are considered a type of currency that can be used to purchase desired rewards, like being able to watch television or getting a snack that they want when they perform designated behaviours. Token economies are mainly used in institutional and therapeutic settings. In order for a token economy to be effective their must be consistency in administering the programme by the entire staff. Procedures must be clearly defined so that there is no confusion among the clients. Instead of looking for ways to punish the patients or to deny them of rewards, the staff has to reinforce the positive behaviours so that the clients will increase the occurrence of the desired behaviour. Over time the tokens need to be replaced with less tangible rewards such as compliments so that the client will be prepared when they leave the institution and wont expect to get something every time they perform a desired behaviour.

Closely related to token economies is a technique called response costs. This technique can either be used with or without token economies. Response costs is the punishment side of token economies where there is a loss of a reward or privilege after someone performs an undesirable behaviour. Like token economies this technique is used mainly in institutional and therapeutic settings.

Considerable policy implications have been inspired by behavioural views of various forms of psychopathology. One form of behaviour therapy, (habit reversal training) has been found to be highly effective for treating tics.

Third Generation

Of particular interest in behaviour therapy today are the areas often referred to as Third-Generation Behaviour Therapy. This movement has been called clinical behaviour analysis because it represents a movement away from cognitivism and back towards radical behaviourism and other forms of behaviourism, in particular functional analysis and behavioural models of verbal behaviour. This area includes Acceptance and Commitment Therapy (ACT), Cognitive Behavioural Analysis System of Psychotherapy (CBASP) (McCullough, 2000), behavioural activation (BA), Kohlenberg & Tsai's Functional Analytic Psychotherapy, integrative behavioural couples therapy and dialectical behavioural therapy. These approaches are squarely within the applied behaviour analysis tradition of behaviour therapy.

ACT is probably the most well-researched of all the third-generation behaviour therapy models. It is based on Relational Frame Theory. Other authors object to the term "third generation" or "third wave" and incorporate many of the "third wave" therapeutic techniques under the general umbrella term of modern cognitive behavioural therapies.

Functional Analytic Psychotherapy is based on a functional analysis of the therapeutic relationship. It places a greater emphasis on the therapeutic context and returns to the use of in-session reinforcement. In general, 40 years of research supports the idea that in-session reinforcement of behaviour can lead to behavioural change.

Behavioural activation emerged from a component analysis of cognitive behaviour therapy. This research found no additive effect for the cognitive component. Behavioural activation is based on a matching model of reinforcement. A recent review of the research, supports the notion that the use of behavioural activation is clinically important for the treatment of depression.

Integrative behavioural couples therapy developed from dissatisfaction with traditional behavioural couples therapy. Integrative behavioural couples therapy looks to Skinner (1966) for the difference between contingency-shaped and rule-governed behaviour. It couples this analysis with a thorough functional assessment of the couple's relationship. Recent efforts have used radical behavioural concepts to interpret a number of clinical phenomena including forgiveness.

Organizations

Many organisations exist for behaviour therapists around the world. The World Association for Behaviour Analysis offers a certification in behaviour therapy . In the United States, the American Psychological Association's Division 25 is the division for behaviour analysis. The Association for Contextual Behaviour Therapy is another professional organisation. ACBS is home to many clinicians with specific interest in third generation behaviour therapy. The Association for Behavioural and Cognitive Therapies (formerly the Association for the Advancement of Behaviour Therapy) is for those with a more cognitive orientation. Internationally, most behaviour therapists find a core intellectual home in the International Association for Behaviour Analysis (ABAI).

Treatment of Mental Disorders

Many have argued that behaviour therapy is at least as effective as drug treatment for depression, ADHD, and OCD. Although, two large studies done by the Faculty of Health Sciences at Simon Fraser University indicates that both behaviour therapy and cognitive-behavioural therapy(CBT) are equally effective for OCD. CBT has been proven to perform slightly better at treating co-occurring depression.

Considerable policy implications have been inspired by behavioural views of various forms of psychopathology. One form of behaviour therapy (habit reversal training) has been found to be highly effective for treating tics.

There has been a development towards combining techniques to treat psychiatric disorders. Cognitive interventions are used to enhance the effects of more established behavioural interventions based on operant and classical conditioning. An increased effort has also been placed to address the interpersonal context of behaviour.

Behaviour therapy can be applied to a number of mental disorders and in many cases is more effective for specific disorders as compared to others. Behaviour therapy techniques can be used to deal with any phobias that a person may have. Desensitization has also been applied to other issues such as dealing with anger, if a person has trouble sleeping and certain speech disorders. Desensitization does not occur over night, there is a process of treatment. Desensitization is done on a hierarchy and happens over a number of sessions. The hierarchy goes from situations that make a person less anxious or nervous up to things that are considered to be extreme for the patient.

Modelling has been used in dealing with fears and phobias. Modelling has been used in the treatment of fear of snakes as well as a fear of water.

Aversive therapy techniques have been used to treat sexual deviations as well as alcoholism.

Exposure and prevention procedure techniques can be used to treat people who have anxiety problems as well as any fears or phobias. These procedures have also been used to help people dealing with any anger issues as well as pathological grievers (people who have distressing thoughts about a deceased person).

Virtual reality therapy deals with fear of heights, fear of flying, and a variety of other anxiety disorders. VRT has also been applied to help people with substance abuse problems reduce their responsiveness to certain cues that trigger their need to use drugs.

Shaping and graded task assignments has been used in dealing with suicide and depressed or inhibited individuals. This is used when a patient feel hopeless and they have no way of changing their lives. This hopelessness involves how the person reacts and responds to someone else and certain situations and their perceived powerlessness to change that situation that adds to the hopelessness. For a person with suicidal ideation, it is important to start with small steps. Because that person may perceive everything as being a big step, the smaller you start the easier it will be for the person to master each step. This technique has also been applied to people dealing with agoraphobia, or fear of being in public places or doing something embarrassing.

Contingency contracting is used to treat any behavioural problems that an individual may have. It has been used to deal with behaviour problems in delinquents and when dealing with on task behaviours in students.

Token economies are used in controlled environments and are found mostly in psychiatric hospitals. They can be used to help patients with different mental illnesses but it doesn't focus on the treatment of the mental illness but instead on the behavioural aspects of a patient. The response cost technique has been used to address a variety of behaviours such as smoking, overeating,stuttering, and psychotic talk.

Treatment Outcomes

Systematic desensitization has been shown to successfully treat phobias about heights, driving, insects as well as any anxiety that a person may have. Anxiety can include social anxiety, anxiety about public speaking as well as test anxiety. It has been shown that the use of systematic desensitization is an effective technique that can be applied to a number of problems that a person may have.

When using modelling procedures this technique is often compared to another behavioural therapy technique. When compared to desensitization, the modelling technique does appear to be less effective. However it is clear that the greater the interaction between the patient and the subject he is modelling the greater the effectiveness of the treatment.

Aversive treatment of sexual deviations according to the empirical literature has generally seen a reasonable degree of success and this includes follow up periods.

While undergoing exposure therapy a person usually needs five sessions to see if the treatment is working. After five sessions exposure treatment is seen to benefit the patient and help with their problems. However even after five sessions it is recommended that the patient or client should still continue treatment.

Virtual Reality treatment has shown to be effective for a fear of heights. It has also been shown to help with the treatment of a variety of anxiety disorders. Virtual reality therapy can be very costly so therapists are still awaiting results of controlled trials for VR treatment to see which applications show the best results.

For those with suicidal ideation treatment depends on how severe the person's depression and feeling of hopelessness is. If these things are severe the person's response to completing small steps will not be of importance to them because they don't consider it to be a big deal. Generally those who aren't severely depressed or fearful, this technique has been successful because the completion of simpler activities build up their confidences and allows them to continue on to more complex situations.

Contingency contracts have been seen to be effective in changing any undesired behaviours of individuals. It has been seen to be effective in treating behaviour problems in delinquents regardless of the specific characteristics of the contract.

Token economies have been shown to be effective when treating patients in psychiatric wards who had chronic schizophrenia. The results showed that the contingent tokens were controlling the behaviour of the patients.

Response costs has been shown to work in suppressing a variety of behaviours such as smoking, overeating or stuttering with a diverse group of clinical populations ranging from sociopaths to school children. These behaviours that have been suppressed using this technique often do not recover when the punishment contingency is withdrawn. Also undesirable side effects that are usually seen with punishment are not typically found when using the response cost technique.

Characteristics

By nature, behavioural therapies are empirical (data-driven), contextual (focused on the environment and context), functional (interested in the effect or consequence a behaviour ultimately has), probabilistic (viewing behaviour as statistically predictable), monistic (rejecting mind–body dualism and treating the person as a unit), and relational (analysing bidirectional interactions).

Behavioural therapy develops, adds and provides behavioural intervention strategies and programmes for clients, and training to people who care to facilitate successful lives in the communities.

Body-oriented Psychotherapy

Body-oriented psychotherapy or Body Psychotherapy is also known as Somatic Psychology, especially in the USA. There are many very different body-oriented or somatic psychotherapeutic approaches. They generally focus on the link between the mind and the body and try to access deeper levels of the psyche through greater awareness of the physical body and the emotions which gave rise to the various body-oriented based psychotherapeutic approaches, such as Reichian (Wilhelm Reich) Character-Analytic Vegetotherapy and Orgonomy; neo-Reichian Alexander Lowen's Bioenergetic analysis; Peter Levine's Somatic Experiencing; Jack Rosenberg's Integrative body psychotherapy; Ron Kurtz's Hakomi psychotherapy; Pat Ogden's sensorimotor psychotherapy; David Boadella's Biosynthesis psychotherapy; Gerda Boyesen's Biodynamic psychotherapy; etc. These body-oriented psychotherapies are not to be confused with alternative medicine body-work or body-therapies that seek primarily to improve physical health through direct work (touch and manipulation) on the body because, despite the fact that bodywork techniques (for example Alexander Technique, Rolfing, and the Feldenkrais Method) can also affect the emotions, these techniques are not designed to work on psychological issues, neither are their practitioners so trained.

Expressive Therapy

Expressive therapy is a form of therapy that utilizes artistic expression as its core means of treating clients. Expressive therapists use the different disciplines of the creative arts as therapeutic interventions. This includes the modalities dance therapy, drama therapy, art therapy, music therapy, writing therapy, among others. Expressive therapists believe that often the most effective way of treating a client is through the expression of imagination in a creative work and integrating and processing what issues are raised in the act.

Types

Expressive therapy is an umbrella term. Some common types of expressive therapy include:

- art therapy
- dance therapy, also known as dance/movement therapy
- drama therapy
- psychodrama
- music therapy
- writing therapy, a term which may encompass journaling, poetry therapy, and bibliotherapy
- horticultural therapy

Horticultural therapy is often not listed with other expressive therapies; it is not universally considered a form of expressive therapy or creative arts therapy.

All expressive therapists share the belief that through creative expression and the tapping of the imagination, a person can examine the body, feelings, emotions and his or her thought process. However, expressive arts therapy is its own therapeutic discipline, an inter-modal discipline where the therapist and client move freely between drawing, dancing, music, drama, and poetry. Although often separated by the form of creative art, some expressive therapists consider themselves intermodal, using expression in general, rather than a specific discipline to treat clients, altering their approach based on the clients' needs, or through using multiple forms of expression with the same client to aid with deeper exploration.

Expressive arts therapy is the practice of using imagery, storytelling, dance, music, drama, poetry, movement, horticulture, dreamwork, and visual arts together, in an integrated way, to foster human growth, development, and healing. It is about reclaiming our innate capacity as human beings for creative expression of our individual and collective human experience in artistic form. Expressive arts therapy is also about experiencing the natural capacity of creative expression and creative community for healing.

Interpersonal Psychotherapy

Interpersonal psychotherapy (IPT) is a time-limited psychotherapy that focuses on the interpersonal context and on building interpersonal skills. IPT is based on the belief that interpersonal factors may contribute heavily to psychological problems. It is commonly distinguished from other forms of therapy in its emphasis on interpersonal processes rather than intrapsychic processes. IPT aims to change a person's interpersonal behaviour by fostering adaptation to current interpersonal roles and situations.

Narrative Therapy

Narrative therapy gives attention to each person's "dominant story" by means of therapeutic conversations, which also may involve exploring unhelpful ideas and how they came to prominence. Possible social and cultural influences may be explored if the client deems it helpful.

Integrative Psychotherapy

Integrative psychotherapy is an attempt to combine ideas and strategies from more than one theoretical approach. These approaches include mixing core beliefs and combining proven techniques. Forms of integrative psychotherapy include multimodal therapy, the transtheoretical model, cyclical psychodynamics, systematic treatment selection, cognitive analytic therapy, Internal Family Systems Model, multitheoretical psychotherapy and conceptual interaction. In practice, most experienced psychotherapists develop their own integrative approach over time.

Human Givens Therapy

The human givens approach was developed in the 1990s by an Irish and British psychotherapist, Joe Griffin and Ivan Tyrrell. Rather than focusing on symptomatology, the human givens approach works within the framework of emotional needs, such as those for security, autonomy and social connection, which decades of health and social psychology research have shown to be essential for physical and mental health. It is a brief, solution-focused approach which aims to help people identify needs not met, or inadequately or inappropriately met, and to address these using psychoeducation and therapeutic techniques such as cognitive restructuring, cognitive reframing and imaginal exposure – all methods endorsed by the standard-setting National Institute for Health and Clinical Excellence (NICE).

Adaptations for Children

Counselling and psychotherapy must be adapted to meet the developmental needs of children. Many counselling preparation programmes include courses in human development. Since children often do not have the ability to articulate thoughts and feelings, counsellors will use a variety of media such as crayons, paint, clay, puppets, bibliocounseling (books), toys, board games, et cetera. The use of play therapy is often rooted in psychodynamic theory, but other approaches such as Solution Focused Brief Counselling may also employ the use of play in counselling. In many cases the counsellor may prefer to work with the care taker of the child, especially if the child is younger than age four. Yet, by doing so, the counsellor risks the perpetuation of maladaptive interactive patterns and the adverse effects on development that have already been affected on the child's end of the relationship. Therefore, contemporary thinking on working with this young age group has leaned towards working with parent and child simultaneously within the interaction, as well as individually as needed.

Confidentiality

Confidentiality is an integral part of the therapeutic relationship and psychotherapy in general. It includes protecting specific groups of people, like children, while treating private information in a manner that is in line with a professional ethics code.

Criticisms and Questions Regarding Effectiveness

Within the psychotherapeutic community there has been some discussion of empirically based psychotherapy, e.g.

Virtually no comparisons of different psychotherapies with long follow-up times have been done. The Helsinki Psychotherapy Study is a randomized clinical trial, in which patients were monitored for 10 years after the onset of short-term (6 months) psychodynamic or solution-focused, or long-term (3 years) psychodynamic study treatments. The effectiveness, suitability and sufficiency of the therapies were compared also with that of psychoanalysis (5 years), within a quasi-experimental design. The assessments were completed at the baseline and 14 times thereafter during the follow-up. The results of the 3- and 5-year follow-up indicate that the length of therapy is important when predicting the outcome of therapy. Patients in the two short-term therapies improved faster, but in the long run long-term psychotherapy and psychoanalysis gave greater benefits. Several patient and therapist factors appear to predict suitability for different psychotherapies. Follow-up evaluations of this study will continue up to 2014.

There is considerable controversy about which form of psychotherapy is most effective, and more specifically, which types of therapy are optimal for treating which sorts of problems. Furthermore, it is controversial whether the form of therapy or the presence of factors common to many psychotherapies best separates effective therapy from ineffective therapy. Common factors theory asserts it is precisely the factors common to the most psychotherapies that make any psychotherapy successful: this is the quality of the therapeutic relationship.

The dropout level is quite high; one meta-analysis of 125 studies concluded that the mean dropout rate was 46.86%. The high level of dropout has raised some criticism about the relevance and efficacy of psychotherapy. There are different drop out rates depending on how drop-out is defined. Another large meta-analysis reports drop-oute rates not larger than 20 to 25%.

Psychotherapy outcome research—in which the effectiveness of psychotherapy is measured by questionnaires given to patients before, during, and after treatment—has had difficulty distinguishing between the success or failure of the different approaches to therapy. Those who stay with their therapist for longer periods are more likely to report positively on what develops into a longer-term relationship. This suggests that some "treatment" may be open-ended with concerns associated with ongoing financial costs.

As early as 1952, in one of the earliest studies of psychotherapy treatment, Hans Eysenck reported that two thirds of therapy patients improved significantly or recovered on their own within two years, whether or not they received psychotherapy.

For Children

Psychotherapy can be adapted in ways that are accessible and developmentally appropriate for children. It is generally held to be one part of an effective strategy for some purposes and not for others. These are four purposes that are generally considered inappropriate or pointless reasons for placing a child in psychotherapy:

- to determine why a child originally began misbehaving,
- to improve the child's self-esteem,
- to make up for inconsistent parenting, and
- to make the child capable of coping with a parent's drug addiction, interpersonal relationships, or other serious dysfunction.

In addition to therapy for the child, or even instead of it, children may benefit if their parents speak to a therapist, take parenting classes, attend grief counselling, or take other actions to resolve stressful situations that affect the child.

Bibliography

Arlow, Brenner: *Psychoanalytic Concepts and the Structural Theory*, International Universities Press, NY, 1964.

Barrows, H.: *Practice-Based Learning: Problem-Based Learning Applied to Medical Education*, Springfield, IL: Southern Illinois University School of Medicine, 1994.

Beloff, J.: *Psychological Sciences. A Review of Modern Psychology.* London: Crosby Lockwood Staples, 1973.

Bridges, E., Hallenger, P.: *Problem-based Learning for Educational Administrators*, Oregon, ERIC Clearinghouse on Educational Management, 1992.

Cohen, Stanley: *Visions of Social Control: Crime, Punishment, and Classification*, Polity Press, 1985.

Dicken, P. : *Wheels of Change, the Automobile Industry*, London, 2007.

Dubey, K.C. : *Experimental and Developmental Psychology*, Omega Pub, Delhi, 2009.

Ellis, A.: *Humanistic Psychology, The Rational-emotive Approach,* Julian Press, New York, 1973.

Eysenck, H. J.: *Personality, Genetics, and Behaviour,* Praeger, New York, 1982.

Eysenck, Hans: *Psychoticism as a Dimension of Personality*, Pergamon, Elsevier Science Inc, Amsterdam, 1997.

Fenichel, O.: *The psychoanalytic Theory of Neurosis,* Norton, New York, 1945.

Flavell, J. H. *Cognitive Development. Engle*wood Cliffs, N.J.: Prentice-Hall, 1977.

Gijselaers, W.H.: *Bringing Problem-Based Learning to Higher Education: Theory and Practice,* San Francisco, Jossey-Bass Publishers, 1996.

Grace, G. : *School Leadership: Beyond Educational Development*, London, Falmer, 1995.

Hallenger, P.: *Problem-based Learning for Educational Administrators*, Oregon, ERIC Clearinghouse on Educational Management, 1992.

Hoy, W.K. : *Instructional Leadership: A Learning-centered Guide*, Boston, Allyn & Bacon/Longman, 2003.

James. W. *The Principles of Psychology*. New York: Henry Holt & Co., 1896.

Kelly, C. A.: *Applied Psychology and Personality,* New York: Wiley, 1969.

Lee, Jeong-kyu : *Historic Factors Influencing Korean Higher Education,* Seoul, Jimoondang, 2000.

Miller, N.E.: *Personality and Psychotherapy. An analysis in terms of learning, thinking, and culture.* New York: McGraw-Hill, 1950.

Millican, J. : *Adult Literacy, A Handbook for Development Education,* Oxford, Oxfam, 1995.

Neisser, U.: *Cognitive Osychology,* Appleton-Century-Crafts, New York, 1967.

Polk, K., & Schafer, W.: *Schools and Delinquency*, Prentice-Hall, Englewood Cliffs, NJ, 1972.

Pratt, C.C.: *The Logic of Modern Psychology*. New York: MacMillan, 1948.

Ridley, T.: *Cool School: An Alternative Secondary School Experience,* Toronto, Ontario: Institute for Studies in Education, 1977.

Simkins, T. : *Non-formal Education and Development*, Manchester, Manchester University, 1977.

Smith, M.K. : *Local Education, Community, Conversation, Action,* Buckingham, Open University Press, 1994.

Stenhouse, L. : *Authority, Education and Emancipation,* London, Heinemann, 1983.

Watson, J.B.: *Psychology from the Standpoint of a Behaviourist,* Lippincott, Philadelphia, PA, 1919.

Wheeler, H.: *Beyond the Punitive Society*, San Francisco: Freeman, 1973.

Index

A

Ancient Civilizations, 149.
Applications in Teaching, 30.
Applying Psychology, 1.
Artificial Intelligence, 108, 121, 122, 314.

B

Become More Productive, 4.
Biology of Personality, 107.

C

Career Counselling, 94, 95.
Causal Factors, 141, 143.
Classification, 130, 131, 132, 149, 158, 178, 207, 211, 239, 259, 266.
Clinical Applications, 123.
Clinical Psychology, 4, 5, 13, 15, 17, 76, 80, 122, 123, 124, 125, 126, 127, 128, 129, 130, 145, 199, 266.
Conducting Research, 86.
Counselling Psychology, 5, 15, 87, 88, 93.
Criticisms and Controversies, 17.
Cultural Variations, 286.

D

Differential Psychology, 107, 108.

E

Effects of Disease, 83.
Eighteenth Century, 149.
Employment Outlook, 38.
Expressive Therapies, 307, 328.

G

General Description, 269.
Get Motivated, 1.
Group Psychotherapy, 306, 307, 308.

H

Health Psychology, 4, 62, 76, 77, 78, 80, 81, 82, 83, 84, 86, 87, 126.
Hong Kong, 129, 263.
Human Intelligence, 108, 112.
Hypotheses in Training, 63.

I

Individual Differences, 20, 23, 31, 33, 34, 41, 99, 100, 103, 109.

J

Job Performance, 40, 41, 43, 49, 50, 51, 52, 55, 58, 111, 114.

L

Latent Inhibition, 119.
Laws and Policies, 154.
Leadership Skills, 1.
Learning and Training, 63.

M

Main Schools, 9.
Managing Pain, 85.
Managing Training, 73.
Measuring Personality, 104.
Moral Judgement, 189, 190.
Multiple Intelligences, 20, 114.

O

Occupational Psychology, 64, 74, 75, 76, 79, 81.
Occupational Therapy, 228, 261.
Organizational Culture, 45, 48, 58.
Organizational Resources, 46, 48.
Other Offending, 187.
Other Perspectives, 12.
Outcome Measurement, 89.

P

Preventing Illness, 83.
Productive Behaviour, 50, 53, 56.
Professional Ethics, 13, 330.
Psychodynamic, 5, 8, 9, 122, 228, 265, 267, 268, 271, 272, 308, 323.
Psychology of Mental, 219.

Q

Quantitative Methods, 27.

R

Relational Psychoanalysis, 279.
Response to Intervention, 162.
Risk Assessment, 144, 185, 191, 199, 201.
Risk Factors, 83, 141, 143, 144, 185, 198, 202, 203, 227, 305.

S

School Psychology, 127.
Signs and Sympt[illegible] 230, 244, 248. [illegible]35, 207,
Sportsmanship, 53.

T

Task Design, 46, 47, 48.
Teaching and Communication, 84.
Team Composition, 46.
Team Goals, 46, 48, 49.
Team Rewards, 46.
Therapeutic Principles, 305.
Training and Supervision, 92.
Treatment, 4, 6, 7, 14, 15, 16, 17, 20, 28, 54, 77, 78, 80, 82, 84, 85, 86, 90, 101, 105, 107, 122, 123, 124, 126, 131, 140, 145, 146, 149, 153, 154, 155, 162, 167, 172, 177, 178, 185, 193, 198, 199, 200, 201, 202, 204, 208, 209, 210, 222, 223, 224, 225, 226, 227, 229, 256, 258, 260, 263, 264, 268, 272, 276, 279, 280, 282, 283, 286, 287, 288, 290, 304, 305, 307, 308, 309, 310, 311, 312, 313, 314, 315, 316, 317, 318, 320, 321, 322, 324, 325, 326, 329, 331, 332.
Triarchic Model, 175, 177, 187, 188, 192, 193, 195.
Twentieth Century, 149.

U

United Kingdom, 81, 86, 129, 155, 170, 180, 200, 223, 242, 243, 263, 264, 268, 291, 309, 312.

❑❑❑